RESILIENCE, ADAPTIVE PEACEBUILDING AND TRANSITIONAL JUSTICE

Processes of post-war reconstruction, peacebuilding and reconciliation are partly about fostering stability and adaptive capacity across different social systems. Nevertheless, these processes have seldom been expressly discussed within a resilience framework. Similarly, although the goals of transitional justice – among them (re)establishing the rule of law, delivering justice and aiding reconciliation – implicitly encompass a resilience element, transitional justice has not been explicitly theorised as a process for building resilience in communities and societies that have suffered large-scale violence and human rights violations. The chapters in this unique volume theoretically and empirically explore the concept of resilience in diverse societies that have experienced mass violence and human rights abuses. They analyse the extent to which transitional justice processes have – and can – contribute to resilience and how, in so doing, they can foster adaptive peacebuilding. This book is available as Open Access.

Janine Natalya Clark is Professor of Gender, Transitional Justice and International Criminal Law at the University of Birmingham. She has written three research monographs and her work has been published in a wide variety of journals. She is currently leading a European Research Council-funded research project about resilience and survivors of conflict-related sexual violence.

Michael Ungar is a family therapist and Professor of Social Work at Dalhousie University where he holds the Canada Research Chair in Child, Family and Community Resilience. He has published over 200 peer-reviewed articles and 17 books on the subject of resilience for parents, researchers and mental health professionals.

Resilience, Adaptive Peacebuilding and Transitional Justice

HOW SOCIETIES RECOVER AFTER COLLECTIVE VIOLENCE

Edited by

JANINE NATALYA CLARK

University of Birmingham

MICHAEL UNGAR

Dalhousie University, Nova Scotia

CAMBRIDGE
UNIVERSITY PRESS

Shaftesbury Road, Cambridge CB2 8EA, United Kingdom

One Liberty Plaza, 20th Floor, New York, NY 10006, USA

477 Williamstown Road, Port Melbourne, VIC 3207, Australia

314–321, 3rd Floor, Plot 3, Splendor Forum, Jasola District Centre, New Delhi – 110025, India

103 Penang Road, #05–06/07, Visioncrest Commercial, Singapore 238467

Cambridge University Press is part of Cambridge University Press & Assessment,
a department of the University of Cambridge.

We share the University's mission to contribute to society through the pursuit of
education, learning and research at the highest international levels of excellence.

www.cambridge.org
Information on this title: www.cambridge.org/9781108826358

DOI: 10.1017/9781108919500

First published 2021
First paperback edition 2023

A catalogue record for this publication is available from the British Library

Library of Congress Cataloging-in-Publication data
NAMES: Clark, Janine N. (Janine Natalya), editor. | Ungar, Michael, 1963– editor.
TITLE: Resilience, adaptive peacebuilding and transitional justice : how societies recover after
collective violence / edited by Janine Natalya Clark, University of Birmingham, Michael
Ungar, Dalhousie University, Nova Scotia.
DESCRIPTION:Cambridge,United Kingdom ;New York,NY : CambridgeUniversity Press, 2021.
| Includes index.
IDENTIFIERS: LCCN 2021028139 (print) | LCCN 2021028140 (ebook) | ISBN 9781108843621
(hardback) | ISBN 9781108826358 (paperback) | ISBN 9781108919500 (ebook)
SUBJECTS: LCSH: Atrocities – Psychological aspects. | Ethnic conflict – Psychological aspects. |
Resilience (Personality trait) – Social aspects. | Victims of violent crime – Psychology. |
Transitional justice. | Peace-building. | BISAC: LAW / General
CLASSIFICATION: LCC HM1116 .R475 2021 (print) | LCC HM1116 (ebook) | DDC 155.2/32–dc23
LC record available at https://lccn.loc.gov/2021028139
LC ebook record available at https://lccn.loc.gov/2021028140

ISBN   978-1-108-84362-1   Hardback
ISBN   978-1-108-82635-8   Paperback

In memory of all the victims of the COVID-19 global pandemic

Contents

List of Figures   *page* ix

List of Contributors   x

Acknowledgements   xvi

List of Abbreviations   xvii

Introduction: Resilience, Adaptive Peacebuilding
and Transitional Justice   1
Janine Natalya Clark and Michael Ungar

PART I   CONCEPTS AND RELATIONSHIPS   21

1 Mapping the Resilience Field: A Systemic Approach   23
Michael Ungar

2 Conceptualising Resilience in the Context of Transitional
Justice   46
Wendy Lambourne

PART II   EMPIRICAL CASE STUDIES   71

3 A Systemic Analysis of Resilience and Transitional Justice
Impact in a Central Bosnian Village   73
Janine Natalya Clark

4 Transitional Justice as Interruption: Adaptive Peacebuilding
and Resilience in Rwanda   95
Jennie E. Burnet

5 Resilience, Adaptive Peacebuilding and Transitional Justice in Post-Conflict Uganda: The Participatory Potential of Survivors' Groups 119
Philipp Schulz and Fred Ngomokwe

6 The *Birangonas* (War Heroines) in Bangladesh: Generative Resilience of Sexual Violence in Conflict through Graphic Ethnography 143
Nayanika Mookherjee

7 Resilience in Post-Khmer Rouge Cambodia: Systemic Dimensions and the Limited Contributions of Transitional Justice 164
Timothy Williams

8 The Personal and Socio-Economic Dynamics of Resilience and Transitional Justice in Colombia 187
Sanne Weber

9 Redressing Injustice, Reframing Resilience: Mayan Women's Persistence and Protagonism as Resistance 210
M. Brinton Lykes, Alison Crosby and Sara Beatriz Alvarez Medrano

10 Transitional or Transformative Justice? Decolonial Enactments of Adaptation and Resilience Within Palestinian Communities 234
Devin G. Atallah and Hana R. Masud

11 Fitting the Pieces Together: Implications for Resilience, Adaptive Peacebuilding and Transitional Justice 257
Cedric de Coning

Index 276

Figures

1.1	An ecological and multi-systemic model of resilience	*page* 24
3.1	Ahmići memorial to the 116 men, women and children who were killed on 16 April 1993	76
3.2	Ahmići today	80
4.1	Destroyed house	98
4.2	Kibuye church genocide memorial	100
5.1	Signpost of Acholi War Debt Claimants' Association in Gulu town	128
5.2	Meeting of survivor group of formerly abducted women in Awach sub-county, northern Uganda	134
6.1	Generative resilience – Nanu/Rehana's story	153
6.2	Generative resilience – rehabilitation and the women's movement in Bangladesh	156
7.1	Memorial to those killed after being incarcerated at the S-21 security centre, one of the ECCC reparation projects	179
7.2	Pka Sla Krom Angkar dance performance	180
8.1	The need for clean drinking water	194
8.2	The asbestos houses in the FARC reincorporation zone	197
9.1	Mayan women visualise embodied suffering and resilience	225
9.2	Mayan women represent life and growth and the integrality of humans and land	226
10.1	Image of an orange tree that I (Hana) planted as a child in my home	240
10.2	Israeli wall enclosing a community in the West Bank	242

Contributors

SARA BEATRIZ ALVAREZ MEDRANO, Maya K'iche', spiritual guide, social therapist, strives for the recovery and valuing of the Mayan cosmovision. She is the coordinator of the Women's Rights Unit of the Centre for Legal Action in Human Rights (CALDH), one of Guatemala's most important human rights non-governmental organisations (NGOs). For over two decades, together with other Mayan women, she has designed and facilitated training and healing processes to strengthen the leadership of Mayan women in their struggle to defend their human rights and achieve historical justice. Since 2000, she has been a political associate of the Kaqla Mayan Women's Group, which works to heal historical, transgenerational traumas, including racialised and gendered violence, through participatory workshops that draw on diverse healing practices from the Mayan cosmovision, both ancestral and contemporary. She received an MA in Clinical Psychology and Mental Health from the Universidad del Valle de Guatemala in 2017.

DEVIN G. ATALLAH, PHD, is Assistant Professor of Psychology, Racial/Cultural Focus, in the Psychology Department at the University of Massachusetts, Boston. He engages decolonising narrative and community-based participatory approaches in his critical inquiry. As an activist, scholar, practitioner and healer, Dr Atallah focuses on understanding, amplifying and directly contributing to intergenerational resilience, resistance, healing, justice and decolonisation/decoloniality. He aims to honour and anchor his work in local and/or Indigenous knowledges of communities in struggle and contesting racism and settler colonialism, primarily through his long-term partnerships with communities in Palestine, communities of colour in Boston and Mapuche people in Chile.

JENNIE E. BURNET, PHD, is Associate Professor of Anthropology at Georgia State University. Her research explores the social, cultural and psychological aspects of war, genocide and mass violence, and the micro-level impact of large-scale social change in the context of conflict. Dr Burnet has been studying Rwanda, the 1994 genocide of Tutsis and its aftermath, and women in politics for more than twenty years. Her research has appeared in *Politics & Gender, African Affairs, African Studies Review* and the *Women's Studies International Forum.* Dr Burnet's award-winning book, *Genocide Lives in Us: Women, Memory and Silence in Rwanda*, was published in 2012 by the University of Wisconsin Press. She is currently writing a book, *To Save Heaven and Earth: Rescue during the Rwandan Genocide*, which examines how and why some Rwandans risked their lives to save Tutsi and others targeted in the genocide.

JANINE NATALYA CLARK, PHD, is Professor of Gender, Transitional Justice and International Criminal Law at the University of Birmingham. She has particular interests in conflict-related sexual violence, transitional justice, resilience and post-conflict reconciliation. She has been conducting research in Bosnia-Herzegovina for more than ten years. Her current research – a comparative study of resilience focused on victims/survivors of conflict-related sexual violence in Bosnia-Herzegovina, Colombia and Uganda – is being funded by the European Research Council through a five-year Consolidator Grant (2017–2022). Professor Clark has three research monographs and her interdisciplinary work has been published in a wide variety of journals, including the *International Journal of Transitional Justice*, the *Journal of International Criminal Justice, Theoretical Criminology, Sociology, Memory Studies* and *International Studies Review.*

ALISON CROSBY, PHD, is Associate Professor in the School of Gender, Sexuality and Women's Studies at York University in Toronto. She was director of the Centre for Feminist Research at York from 2014 to 2019. Her research projects and publications use an anti-racist, transnational feminist lens and participatory methodologies to explore protagonists' multifaceted struggles to redress and memorialise harm in the aftermath of racialised gendered violence, with a particular focus on Guatemala. She is the author, with M. Brinton Lykes, of *Beyond Repair? Mayan Women's Protagonism in the Aftermath of Genocidal Harm* (Rutgers University Press, 2019), published in Spanish as *Más Allá de la Reparación: Protagonismo de Mujeres Mayas en las Secuelas del Daño Genocida* (Cholsamaj, 2019). She currently directs the project Remembering and Memorializing Violence: Transnational Feminist Dialogues, https://memorializingviolence.com/, which is funded by the Social Sciences and Humanities Research Council of Canada (SSHRC).

CEDRIC DE CONING, PHD, is Research Professor with the Norwegian Institute of International Affairs (NUPI) and Senior Advisor for the African Centre for the Constructive Resolution of Disputes (ACCORD). His research covers African, Global South and United Nations peace and security issues. He holds a PhD in Applied Ethics from the Department of Philosophy at the University of Stellenbosch in South Africa. He has a special interest in the application of complexity theory to Peace and Conflict Studies, and in this context he has introduced Adaptive Peacebuilding as a new analytical, normative and operational approach to guide international interventions. He has served in a number of advisory capacities for the African Union and United Nations (UN), including the UN Secretary-General's Advisory Board for the Peacebuilding Fund. He tweets at @CedricdeConing.

WENDY LAMBOURNE, PHD, is Chair of the Department of Peace and Conflict Studies at the University of Sydney. Her interdisciplinary research on trauma healing, transitional justice, reconciliation and peacebuilding after genocide and other mass violence has a regional focus on sub-Saharan Africa and the Asia/Pacific. The results of her field research, conducted over the past twenty-three years in Rwanda, Burundi, Sierra Leone, Cambodia and Timor Leste, have been published extensively. They include articles in *Human Rights Review*, the *Journal of Peacebuilding and Development* and the *International Journal of Transitional Justice*, and book chapters in *Knowledge for Peacebuilding and Transitional Justice: Epistemic Communities and the Politics of Knowledge* (Edward Elgar, 2021), *The Palgrave Handbook of Ethnicity* (Springer Nature, 2019), *Advocating Transitional Justice in Africa: The Role of Civil Society* (Springer, 2018), *Restorative Justice in Transitional Settings* (Routledge, 2016) and *Breaking Intergenerational Cycles of Repetition: A Global Dialogue on Historical Trauma and Memory* (Barbara Budrich, 2016).

M. BRINTON LYKES, PHD, is Professor of Community-Cultural Psychology and Co-Director of the Centre for Human Rights and International Justice at Boston College. Her anti-racist feminist activist scholarship focuses on (1) rethreading life in the wake of racialised and gendered violence during armed conflict and in post-genocide transitions, and (2) migration and post-deportation human rights violations and resistance. She has published extensively in refereed journals and edited volumes; she has co-edited four books and co-authored four others, and is also co-editor-in-chief of the *International Journal of Transitional Justice*. She is the recipient of the Ignacio Martín-Baró Lifetime Peace Practitioner Award, the American Psychological Association's International Humanitarian Award, the

Florence L. Denmark and Mary E. Reuder Award for Outstanding International Contributions to the Psychology of Women and Gender and the Seymour B. Sarason Award for Community Research and Action. She is a board member on several NGOs, including Women's Rights International, Impunity Watch and Grassroots International.

HANA R. MASUD, PHD, is a postdoctoral research fellow in Dr Atallah's Research Team at the University of Massachusetts, Boston. Dr Masud is also currently chair of Decolonial Racial Justice in Praxis, an initiative of Psychologists for Social Responsibility. Dr Masud received her doctorate in Community Psychology from the National Louis University in Chicago. Her research focuses on the coloniality of mental health services and its impact on re-colonising local resistance. In her work, she aims to build collaborative partnerships with mental health workers and marginalised communities in shared efforts to transform conditions of inequity towards wellness and justice in Palestine.

NAYANIKA MOOKHERJEE, PHD, is Professor of Political Anthropology at Durham University. Her research involves ethnographic exploration of public memories of violent pasts and aesthetic practices of reparative futures. Based on her award-winning book *The Spectral Wound: Sexual Violence, Public Memories and the Bangladesh War of 1971*, in 2019 she co-authored (with visual artist Najmunnahar Keya) a survivor-led guideline, graphic novel and animation film *Birangona and Ethical Testimonies of Sexual Violence during Conflict*. This received the 2019 Praxis Award from the Association of Professional Anthropologists. Professor Mookherjee has had fellowships with the Economic and Social Research Council, the Wenner-Gren Foundation for Anthropological Research, the British Academy, the Leverhulme Trust and the Rockefeller Foundation at Bellagio. She has published extensively and her work has appeared in a variety of journals, including the *Journal of Royal Anthropological Institute*, the *Journal of Historical Sociology* and the *Journal of Material Culture*. She is working on a manuscript entitled *Arts of Irreconciliation* and continuing research on transnational adoption.

FRED NGOMOKWE works with the Refugee Law Project (RLP) at the School of Law at Makerere University in Uganda as a transitional justice practitioner and office coordinator of the organisation's Gulu office. For the past decade he has worked closely with victims and survivors of the war in northern Uganda. He is also the focal point person for human rights defenders in Acholiland, northern Uganda.

PHILIPP SCHULZ, PHD, is a postdoctoral researcher at the Institute for Intercultural and International Studies (InIIS) at the University of Bremen. His work focuses on gender and sexualities in (post-)conflict settings, with a particular focus on wartime sexual violence. His book *Male Survivors of Wartime Sexual Violence: Perspectives from Northern Uganda* (2021) is published with the University of California Press, and his research has appeared in *International Affairs*, the *International Feminist Journal of Politics* and *Security Dialogue*.

MICHAEL UNGAR, PHD, is the Canada Research Chair (Tier 1) in Child, Family and Community Resilience at Dalhousie University, where he founded and directs the Resilience Research Centre. He has designed multi-site longitudinal research and evaluation projects in collaboration with organisations including the Human Development and Education Branch of the World Bank, NATO, the Red Cross and national public health agencies. With more than $10,000,000 in funded research, Professor Ungar's research projects span more than a dozen low-, middle- and high-income countries, with many focused on the resilience of marginalised youth and their communities. He is one of the most well-known scholars on human resilience in the world and has published more than 200 peer-reviewed articles and book chapters on the topic. He is the author of sixteen books for mental health professionals, researchers and lay audiences.

SANNE WEBER, PHD, is a Leverhulme research fellow in the International Development Department at the University of Birmingham. Her research explores how conflict affects gender relations. She uses ethnographic, participatory and creative research methods to understand whether and how transitional justice mechanisms are capable of transforming gendered and other structural inequalities. She has worked primarily in Latin America, particularly in Colombia and Guatemala. Her current project examines the gendered and socio-economic dynamics of the reintegration of ex-combatants. In the past, she has worked as a researcher and team coordinator on gender programmes for human rights and development organisations in Guatemala. She has published in journals such as the *International Journal of Transitional Justice*, the *Journal of Refugee Studies* and the *International Feminist Journal of Politics*.

TIMOTHY WILLIAMS, PHD, is a junior professor of insecurity and social order at the Bundeswehr University Munich. He was previously a postdoctoral fellow at the Centre for Conflict Studies at the University of Marburg, where he also completed his PhD. His research deals with violence, focusing on its dynamics, particularly at the micro level, as well as its consequences for post-conflict societies and the politics of memory. He has conducted extensive field research in Cambodia, as well as in Armenia and Rwanda, and he was awarded the Emerging Scholar Prize of the International Association of Genocide Scholars in 2017. Timothy is the co-editor of a volume on perpetrators (with Susanne Buckley-Zistel, Routledge, 2018) and the author of *The Complexity of Evil: Perpetration and Genocide* (Rutgers University Press, 2020).

Acknowledgements

The idea for this book developed out of a five-year (2017–2022) research project, funded by the European Research Council under grant number 724518 and led by Janine Natalya Clark, about resilience and victims/survivors of conflict-related sexual violence. As the research project progressed, so too did an intellectual curiosity about the possibility of developing an edited volume that would widen the focus beyond conflict-related sexual violence and bring together eminent scholars from diverse disciplines to explore the concept of resilience in the context of societies that have experienced mass violence and human rights abuses. Michael Ungar, as a member of the project's International Advisory Board and a global authority on resilience, was a natural choice as co-editor.

We thank all of the book's contributors – a mixture of academics and practitioners – for their work and commitment to keeping the book on schedule in the very difficult and challenging circumstances of a global pandemic. We also sincerely thank our editors at Cambridge University Press, Finola O'Sullivan and Marianne Nield, for all their support. Thank you also to two anonymous reviewers for their very helpful comments on the book proposal. Finally, we are very grateful to Igor Pekelny, a research associate at the Resilience Research Centre – part of Dalhousie University in Canada – for his work in formatting the chapters.

Abbreviations

AAR	Agreement on Accountability and Reconciliation
ABiH	Army of Bosnia-Herzegovina
AL	Awami League
ANUC	National Association of Peasant Users
AWDCA	Acholi War Debt Claimants' Association
BiH	Bosnia-Herzegovina
BLM	Black Lives Matter
CALDH	Centre for Legal Action in Human Rights
CAVR	Commission for Reception, Truth and Reconciliation
CEH	Historical Clarification Commission
CHRIJ	Center for Human Rights and International Justice
CHW	Community Health Worker
CNRP	Cambodian National Rescue Party
CPP	Cambodian People's Party
DDR	Disarmament, Demobilisation and Reintegration
ECCC	Extraordinary Chambers in the Courts of Cambodia
ELN	National Liberation Army
FAPs	formerly abducted persons
FARC	Revolutionary Armed Forces of Colombia
FGDs	focus group discussions
HDZ	Croatian Democratic Union
HVO	Croatian Defence Council
ICC	International Criminal Court
ICD	International Crimes Division
ICTJ	International Center for Transitional Justice
ICTR	International Criminal Tribunal for Rwanda
ICTY	International Criminal Tribunal for the former Yugoslavia
IDPs	internally displaced persons

IDRC	International Development Research Centre
JEP	Special Jurisdiction for Peace
JLOS	Justice Law and Order Sector
JRP	Justice and Reconciliation Project
LANGO	Law on Associations and Non-governmental Organizations
LRA	Lord's Resistance Army
MMIWG2S	missing and murdered Indigenous women and girls, trans and Two-Spirit people
NGO	non-governmental organisations
OECD	Organisation for Economic Co-operation and Development
OSCE	Organization for Security and Co-operation in Europe
PDETs	Development Programmes with a Territorial Focus
PNR	National Reparations Programme
PRDP	Peace and Recovery Development Plan
PTSD	post-traumatic stress disorder
RAF	Rwandan Armed Forces
RLP	Refugee Law Project
RPF	Rwandan Patriotic Front
RRC	Resilience Research Collaborative
SCRA	Society of Community Research and Action
SCSL	Special Court for Sierra Leone
SSHRC	Social Sciences and Humanities Research Council of Canada
THARS	Trauma Healing and Reconciliation Services
TJWG	Transitional Justice Working Group
TPO	Transcultural Psychological Organization
TRC	Truth and Reconciliation Commission
UK	United Kingdom
UN	United Nations
UNAMG	National Union of Guatemala Women
UNFAO	United Nations Food and Agriculture Organization
UNICEF	United Nations Children's Fund
UNPROFOR	United Nations Protection Force
UNTAC	United Nations Transitional Authority in Cambodia
US	United States
Victims' Law	Victims and Land Restitution Law
VRS	Army of Republika Srpska
VSLA	Village Savings and Loan Associations
WAN	Women's Advocacy Network

Introduction

Resilience, Adaptive Peacebuilding and Transitional Justice

Janine Natalya Clark and Michael Ungar

Since the idea for this book first took shape, the world has fundamentally changed. The shocks and stressors of the COVID-19 pandemic have affected all aspects of life and powerfully overturned the 'normality' that once was. As Walsh (2020: 899) notes:

> [M]any families are experiencing an ongoing, pervasive sense of loss: the tragic deaths and threatened loss of loved ones; the loss of physical contact with family members and social networks; the loss of jobs, financial security, and livelihoods; the loss of pre-crisis ways of life and threatened loss of hopes and dreams for the future; and the loss of a sense of normalcy in shattered assumptions about our lives and connections with the world around us.

The pandemic has inevitably triggered a wealth of new research, particularly within the fields of medicine, epidemiology and vaccine studies. Due to the immense challenges posed by this coronavirus, and its multi-systemic effects, some scholars have also examined it through a resilience lens (see, e.g., Chen and Bonanno, 2020; Labrague and De los Santos, 2020; Legido-Quigley et al., 2020; Shanahan et al., 2020). Indeed, Barzilay et al. (2020) argue that '[t]he rapid spread of COVID-19 creates a unique opportunity to evaluate resilience in the face of a single global adversity'. The pandemic and some of the research surrounding it have thus added to an already extremely rich and vast body of scholarship addressing and exploring the theme of resilience.

Referring to the concept's 'effortless ability to move across the natural, social and psychological sciences', Duffield (2012: 480) underlines that resilience is 'multidisciplinary in a radical sense of the term, while also enjoying epic scalability'. In short, '[i]t can be invoked at the level of organisms and individual psychology, is found in natural habitats and social institutions, and forms a vital property of the built environment' (Duffield, 2012: 480). This diversity is well captured by Xu and Kajikawa (2017), whose citation network analysis shows ten overlapping domains of resilience scholarship, with clusters of papers appearing in fields as different as marine science and psychiatry. While the most popular discourse on resilience remains in the psychological sciences, the concept of adaptation under adversity is finding relevance in many other disciplines as well. The COVID-19 pandemic is making resilience research even more relevant, especially emerging science which is showing that the robustness of one system can dramatically affect the capacity of co-occurring systems to survive and thrive (Brown, 2016). Just as individual lifestyles and biology make us more or less susceptible to the virus, our trust in institutions like public health and accommodations by our workplaces are also having a dramatic effect on our ability to weather the changes we have all experienced.

RESILIENCE, VIOLENCE AND CONFLICT

Notwithstanding the aforementioned 'effortless ability' of the resilience concept to move across and between different fields and disciplines, it is striking that resilience has received only limited attention in the context of communities and societies that have experienced conflict, violence and large-scale human rights abuses. Concepts such as reconciliation and reconstruction are given far more prominence. Some scholars, however, have discussed the resilience of particular groups in war situations. These include children (Betancourt and Khan, 2008; Fernando and Ferrari, 2011; Halevi et al., 2016; Masten and Narayan, 2012), former prisoners of war (Freeman et al., 2006; Gold et al., 2000; Jones and Wessely, 2010) and war veterans (Elliott et al., 2017 Portnoy et al., 2018; Vogt and Tanner, 2007). More broadly, others have underlined the resilience of entire populations dealing with a multitude of conflict- and violence-related stressors. Focusing on Islamic State violence against the Yezidi minority in northern Iraq, for example, Isakhan and Shahab (2020: 18) underscore that '[i]n returning to their traditional homelands and reconstructing their heritage sites, the Yezidi people have demonstrated remarkable resistance and resilience'. Focused on the Syrian war that began in 2011, and particularly on the city of Homs which was under siege for three years from 2012, Azzouz (2019: 108) argues that 'despite mass destruction and monumental displacement, citizens in conflict zones such as this have shown extraordinary levels of resilience and have created mechanisms and strategies to carry on with their everyday lives'.

While such research is important, two particular points should be underlined. The first is that the use of adjectives like 'remarkable' and 'extraordinary' is problematic because these words convey the idea that those who demonstrate resilience are somehow exceptional. Not only does this sit uneasily with the argument that 'resilience is common' (Bonanno, 2004: 26; see also Barber, 2013: 463; Masten, 2014), but it also feeds the normative criticism that resilience discourse places an unfair burden on individuals (Ungar, 2011). Howell and Voronka (2012: 4), for example, maintain that 'getting citizens to be resilient in the face of challenges is not only cheap (in that it diverts patients out of public health care systems, in favour of self-help and positive thinking), it is also about aspiring to create a resilient citizenry, able to cope with uncertainty'.

The second, broader issue is that, because discussions about resilience in the context of conflict and violence often have a strong individual focus, this necessarily decontextualises the very meaning of resilience – and thus detracts from the wider social ecologies that have a crucial role to play in fostering and sustaining resilience. Discussing two Pakistani women who were raped, Haeri (2007: 299) underlines: 'The cases of Rahila and Veena highlight multiple sources within their immediate community environment that assisted each woman to empower herself, to engage with families and friends, to seek solace from religion and politics, and to pursue an individually meaningful course of action to overcome unspeakable brutality.' The crucial point is that, in societies overcoming the shocks and stressors of violence, an individual-centred resilience discourse can deflect from the vital importance of building and fostering systems that need to function optimally for people to experience psychosocial growth under adversity. Contrary to neoliberal critiques, resilience is not about encouraging 'people to individually respond to collective instabilities and uncertainties' (Garrett, 2016: 1920; see also Brassett and Vaughan-Williams, 2015; Chandler, 2013; Joseph, 2013), but, rather, about developing and strengthening vital protective factors and resources within individuals' social ecologies (Ungar, 2011).

This unique edited volume is the first to explore the concept of resilience across a range of different societies that have experienced – and in some cases are continuing to experience – mass violence linked to war and conflict (and related structural violence). The eight case study chapters – Bosnia-Herzegovina, Rwanda, Uganda, Bangladesh, Cambodia, Columbia, Guatemala and Palestine – provide rich conceptual and empirical analyses of resilience, what it 'looks' like and how it is expressed. They include stories of individual resilience, but ultimately they tell a bigger story about resilience, systems and the multi-systemic legacies of mass violence. Three central strands run through the book, weaving together the different chapters. These are its conceptualisation of resilience as a multi-systemic concept, its emphasis on transitional justice and its discussions of how transitional justice processes might contribute to adaptive peacebuilding.

RESILIENCE AS A MULTI-SYSTEMIC CONCEPT

While the most persistent definition of resilience comes from earlier studies of psychological invulnerability (Anthony, 1987) (with some of those studies originating in contexts of war – see, for example, Cohler, 1991), the past two decades have seen a transformation in how the term is used. No longer understood as an attribute of an individual, human resilience is now studied as a dynamic process in which individuals and their environments interact to optimise human potential (Ungar, 2018).

This change from person-centric definitions of resilience focused on individual capacities towards more complex social-ecological (and processual) definitions has taken scholars decades to validate. Resilience can now be defined as 'the capacity of both individuals and their environments to interact in ways that optimize developmental processes' (Ungar, 2013: 256). This definition informs a new agenda for research, and one that is attentive to the promotive and protective mechanisms that support positive change at multiple systemic levels. For example, Mahdiani et al. (2020) have shown that even in communities undergoing massive social disruption, as is occurring for communities dependent upon the oil and gas extraction and processing industries, sustainability is a reflection of each community's capacity to anticipate change and build the institutional responses that facilitate individual coping amid changes to economic conditions tied to the price of oil. It is studies like this that are driving greater interdisciplinarity in the field of resilience scholarship (a trend that is abundantly evident in this volume) and providing clues to the following questions: (1) How does the resilience of one system at one scale (e.g. biological, psychological, social, political, economic, environmental) influence the resilience of other systems? (2) Are there similarities and differences in the processes, mechanisms and patterns associated with resilience across systems and at different scales? (3) How can a multi-systemic understanding of resilience inform changes to policy and practice that will improve the well-being of humans, societies and ecosystems?

Reflecting this understanding of resilience, our first aim, then, is to show that exploring resilience, and more specifically some of the multi-level resources and protective factors that help to buffer the impact of violent and traumatic shocks and stressors, can offer new insights into societies that have experienced mass violence and the types of help and support that they might need. Awareness of the diversity of forms that resilience can take in these societies, and of how individuals and communities – in interaction with their wider social ecologies – utilise and develop their own resilience resources is, in turn, an important part of moving away from template approaches to 'building peace'.

TRANSITIONAL JUSTICE

The second strand of focus on resilience is to explore its links to transitional justice, which the United Nations (UN) (2010) has defined as 'the full range of processes and mechanisms associated with a society's attempt to come to terms with a legacy of large-scale past abuses, in order to ensure accountability, serve justice and achieve reconciliation'. To date, the ever-expanding field of transitional justice has largely overlooked the concept of resilience. However, some scholars have started to address this gap, particularly drawing attention to various inter-connections and linkages between transitional justice and resilience.

Kastner (2020: 372), for example, points out that '[b]oth transitional justice and resilience are concepts that are employed in the context of seemingly intractable problems that are encountered and that need to be dealt with, managed or adapted to'. Wiebelhaus-Brahm (2017: 142), for his part, underlines that '[i]ntentionally or not, transitional justice is one policy intervention that likely affects the resilience of human societies'. Most obviously, the atrocities and human rights violations that create a need for transitional justice interventions constitute major shocks and stressors across entire social systems. Addressing the legacies of these crimes and abuses, transitional justice processes necessarily affect – as part of their own legacies – the long-term impact of the past and how individuals, communities and societies deal with it. In this way, transitional justice can potentially promote resilience. It may do so, for example, by 'enhancing the effectiveness and legitimacy of international rules and procedures, thereby (re)building connections between authorities and the masses' (Wiebelhaus-Brahm, 2017: 154). Through institutional reforms and the re-establishment of the rule of law, transitional justice can also contribute to providing 'the kinds of public goods that enhance resilience' (Wiebelhaus-Brahm, 2017: 154).

Conversely, transitional justice processes might also have the opposite effect. Resilience is quintessentially a relational concept. According to Luthar (2006: 780), '[r]esilience rests, fundamentally, on relationships'; Hayward (2013) maintains that 'human resilience is best understood as the interrelationships among the individuals and their community, environment, and social institutions'; and Hartling (2008: 53) underlines that *'resilience is all about relationships*' (emphasis in the original). Transitional justice processes can thus potentially undermine resilience when they polarise communities and contribute to entrenching ethnic and social divides. On this point, Leebaw (2008: 96–97) notes that '[b]ecause truth commissions and criminal tribunals investigate extremely divisive and violent histories, they have often been viewed as obstacles to reconciliation and charged with "opening old wounds", generating political instability and interfering with forward-looking political change'.

Furthermore, transitional justice processes have traditionally given little attention to socio-economic and structural injustices, including those related to colonialism (see, e.g., Balint et al., 2014; Maddison and Shepherd, 2014; Mullen, 2015). If transitional justice overlooks these injustices, it thereby also neglects the importance of 'resilient infrastructures so that considerations of social justice can be addressed more adequately' (Doorn et al., 2019: 119). In this regard, Kastner (2020: 374) suggests that resilience thinking can actually pose risks for transitional justice; the latter typically 'does not seek to or allow the individuals and communities most immediately concerned by the violence in question to challenge the factors that enabled and perpetuated the violence in the first place'. Taking a different view, however, Duthie (2017: 12) maintains that '[n]otions such as development, resilience, and transformation are useful in thinking about the extent to which transitional justice processes are affected by and can at the same time address root causes and contribute to broad change'. He also accentuates what he calls 'the bi-directional relationship between contexts of social and economic structures and transitional justice' (Duthie, 2017: 24).

Part of what makes this book highly novel is its in-depth analysis of the relationship between resilience and transitional justice. Going beyond the question of whether and how transitional justice processes might contribute to or undermine resilience, it surveys some of the ways that these processes shape and affect resilience – across multiple systemic levels – in practice. For example, a rights-based approach to community empowerment in a post-colonial world, like that explored by Atallah et al. (2019) in Chile and Palestine, forces us to consider the need for significant changes to social relations and government structures if populations that have experienced historical oppression are to recover and transform. Anything less multi-systemic runs the risk of blaming populations that have been starved of resources for their challenges, while doing little to resource them sufficiently to succeed in contexts of structural disadvantage.

For these reasons, there are important synergies and a number of discordances – largely unexplored to date – between resilience and key transitional justice goals, including peace and reconciliation. Certain types of resilience, for example, can work against reconciliation. Discussing the issue of political reconciliation between Indigenous peoples and settler nations, Whyte (2018: 287) asserts that 'For at least some Indigenous persons, it's not unreasonable at all to see settler attempts at reconciliation, from apologies to truth and reconciliation commissions, as new forms of the same old system that portrays indigenous peoples as parasites who clamour for aid and special accommodations from benevolent hosts'. He further argues that '[t]he maintenance of this illusion is itself the operation of a parasitic system – a very resilient parasitic system' (Whyte, 2018: 287). The broader point in this regard is that 'undesirable states, systems or institutions [can] also be highly resilient – and resilient systems can be highly unequal with the benefits from such resilience unevenly distributed' (Walsh-Dilley and Wolford, 2015: 174). In this case, as with all scholarly investigations of resilience, one has to ask if the resilience of one system comes with a trade-off – the vulnerability of another co-occurring system (Folke, 2006).

To take a more positive example, Ungar (2013: 258) argues that the more that environments 'make available and accessible the resources that promote well-being', the more likely individuals are 'to engage in processes associated with positive development such as forming secure attachments, experiencing self-esteem, engaging in expressions of personal agency, and meaningful employment'. In other words, if people are not worrying about basic life necessities such as food, housing and medical care, they can potentially invest more – including emotionally – in transitional justice processes. As Millar (2011: 529) discusses in the context of Sierra Leone's Truth and Reconciliation Commission (TRC), 'the very nature of the deprivation the average resident of Makeni [the town in which he conducted fieldwork] experiences on a day-to-day basis limits the applicability of such mechanisms of justice at any given time. Life is experienced as flowing and ongoing, and so are infringements upon rights'.

In focusing on the relationship between resilience and transitional justice, our starting premise for this volume is that '[r]esilience arguably offers a fresh perspective on transitional justice' (Kastner, 2020: 369). In their research on Colombia, for example, Nussio et al. (2015: 354) found that 'differences between victims and nonvictims are small when it comes to attitudes toward several aspects of transitional justice, like punishment of perpetrators, truth seeking, historical memory and reparations'. They accordingly underline the need for further research examining 'to what extent the development of an institutional framework and budget addressing the needs of victims in itself provides an incentive for the differentiation of victims and the development of a victim-centered agenda by hundreds of fledgling victims' organizations, beyond actual differences in political preferences and opinions between victims and other groups' (Nussio et al., 2015: 354). The bigger issue is that adding a resilience lens underscores the importance of focusing not just on direct victims (or 'non-victims') of violence and human rights abuses, but also on their wider social ecologies.

This, in turn, is directly linked to the book's second core aim. It seeks to demonstrate that thinking about resilience as a multi-systemic concept (see Ungar, 2021) opens a space for developing new ways of theorising and operationalising transitional justice that are more responsive to the wider social ecologies that link individuals and communities to their environments – and to the broader systems within which transitional justice work takes place (Clark, 2020a, 2020b). The chapters explore whether transitional justice processes – including criminal trials, TRCs and reparations – have shaped resilience in various societies that have experienced mass violence. Windle (2011: 165) argues that, in order to be most effective, interventions should address the 'dynamic interplay' across different system levels, rather than focus only on developing individual strengths. This book explores the 'dynamic interplay' of different transitional justice processes within complex social systems. More broadly, the chapters reflect on some of the ways that transitional justice might potentially contribute to resilience. Central to this particular discussion is the book's third key strand.

ADAPTIVE PEACEBUILDING

de Coning (2018: 301) reflects that '[t]he era of liberal idealism and interventionism is on the ebb and in its place we are witnessing a pragmatic turn in peacebuilding'. As one illustration, the UN has embraced a 'new sustaining peace concept' – as part of its 'Sustaining Peace' agenda (see UN, n.d.) – according to which the role of the organisation is 'to assist countries to sustain their own peace processes by strengthening the resilience of local social institutions, and by investing in social cohesion' (de Coning, 2018: 301).[1] de

[1] In Resolution 70/262, for example, the UN General Assembly (2016: para. 3) – in its review of UN 'peacebuilding architecture' – reaffirmed, inter alia, 'the importance of national ownership and leadership in peacebuilding, whereby the responsibility for sustaining peace is broadly shared by the Government and all other national stakeholders'. It also underlined 'the importance, in this regard, of inclusivity in order to ensure that the needs of all segments of society are taken into account' (UN General Assembly, 2016: para. 3). The UN Security Council (2016) echoed these points in its Resolution 2282. In 2018, in a report pursuant to these two Resolutions, the UN Secretary-General emphasised: 'My aim is to forge a common vision and common systems and capacities across the United Nations to consistently and adequately

Coning (2018: 304–305) proposes adaptive peacebuilding specifically as one approach to operationalise this sustaining peace concept.

As he defines adaptive peacebuilding, there are three key concepts that inform it – namely complexity, resilience and local ownership. Complexity theory is quintessentially about complex systems and, when applied to peacebuilding, it underscores the fact that peacebuilding is a multi-systemic endeavour that both engages and extends across myriad systems. These complex systems naturally adjust to shocks and stressors: 'In complex systems, the elements react to stimuli in non-linear ways and this enables the system to adapt and evolve, so that it can find new ways to pursue its goals and reach its objectives' (de Coning, 2016: 173). Enhancing these adaptations is a crucial part of fostering sustainable peace. Fundamentally, 'Peacebuilding in the sustaining peace context is about stimulating those processes in a society that enable self-organization and that will lead to strengthening the resilience of the social institutions that manage internal and external stressors and shocks' (de Coning, 2018: 307).

Local ownership and inclusivity are crucial in this regard. Complexity theory makes it clear that there are no simple or clear-cut solutions to complex problems, and, hence, '[o]ne should, therefore, not attempt to solve such problems with determined-design methodologies aimed at definitively diagnosing a problem and prescribing a solution' (de Coning, 2018: 313). Rather, an adaptive peacebuilding approach entails working closely with affected communities on the ground 'to collaboratively develop self-awareness of the causes and drivers of conflict in the system' and, thus, 'to ultimately support the emergence of local resilient social institutions that can self-manage future tensions' (de Coning, 2018: 313).

The book's third principal aim is to further develop the idea of adaptive peacebuilding, both conceptually and empirically. The chapters in this volume analyse whether and how transitional justice processes themselves can contribute to adaptive peacebuilding in the sense of helping to foster adaptive capacity and resilience across complex systems that have experienced the shocks and stressors of war, conflict and large-scale violence. de Coning (2016: 177) underlines that 'Whenever we attempt to change something in a complex system, the system responds to our intervention in a number of ways'. In other words, transitional justice processes affect entire systems, and an important way of thinking about these multi-systemic effects is precisely to look at whether these processes can help societies 'to develop the resilience

---

support Member States in their endeavour to sustain peace and build resilient and prosperous nations in line with their commitments to leave no one behind' (UN, 2018: para. 4).

and robustness they need to cope with and adapt to change' (de Coning, 2018: 316).

By linking resilience and adaptive peacebuilding, this volume helps to show that multi-systemic resilience can be operationalised in the everyday practices of how individuals and their communities interact and 'rebuild' their lives. Methodologically, this volume is innovative as scholars develop the tools to investigate change across systems that occur at the same time or sequentially. In the field of transitional justice, this means paying as much attention to cultural traditions and attitudinal shifts (individual psychological systems) as to people's familial and community relationships and the structures and institutions tasked with delivering 'justice' (Betancourt, 2008). The chapters throughout this volume are, therefore, illustrative of both the complexity of these interacting systems and the detailed research required to critically examine resilience in relation to individuals and societies that have experienced the shocks and stressors of conflict and large-scale violence.

CONTENT SUMMARY

The book is divided into two parts. The first part, *Concepts and Relationships*, lays the conceptual foundations, sets out the book's approach to resilience and discusses the linkages between the three core strands of resilience, transitional justice and adaptive peacebuilding. The chapter by Michael Ungar explores broadly the concept of multi-systemic resilience and its relevance to the field of transitional justice. The concept of resilience is best understood as a process whereby individual capital and social capital interact in ways that create optimal outcomes in stressed environments. As a process, Ungar explains that resilience can look very different in different contexts, with any single system (including systems that promote social justice, human rights and enforce laws) showing patterns of persistence, resistance, recovery, adaptation or transformation depending on the resources each system has available to support change. Ungar's chapter explores these processes and how they affect systems simultaneously at multiple levels. This understanding of resilience as a multi-systemic concept can help to explain how systems affected by transitional justice (both judicial and non-judicial) respond to stressors, in turn shaping individual, community and institutional responses. Ungar uses brief case examples to show how resilience changes depending on a population's exposure to extreme forms of potentially traumatising events, such as war, forced migration, genocide and chronic economic disruption. In doing so, his chapter positions resilience as a concept that can be integrated into the field of transitional justice.

Wendy Lambourne's chapter shows what this integration might look like, setting the stage for an integration of concepts and a bridge between different areas of research. She explores how resilience thinking can contribute to the transformative potential of transitional justice processes, and how these processes can foster and deepen our understanding of both resilience and adaptive peacebuilding. The chapter examines how key transitional justice processes – namely criminal trials, truth commissions and reparations – can aid societal resilience, supporting resilient social structures, which, in turn, can improve individual capacities to cope in the aftermath of social shocks and violence. The chapter also discusses how building resilient communities is a logical consequence of more inclusive facilitated justice and participation (core processes of both resilience and transitional justice), along with healing and reconciliation. As a challenge to conventional understandings of transitional justice and its politico-legal, state-based, backward-looking framework, Lambourne argues that resilience thinking supports a greater focus on psychosocial, community-based, forward-looking approaches to transitional justice, consistent with the transformative turn in the field.

The second part of the book, *Empirical Case Studies*, examines resilience, transitional justice and adaptive peacebuilding through the lens of eight different country studies. In varied and unique ways, all of the chapters address the following four questions:

1. What does resilience, conceptualised systemically and ecologically, look like in societies that have experienced mass atrocities and collective violence?
2. What are the multi-systemic factors and processes that have helped individuals and communities to rebuild and positively adapt to shocks and stressors?
3. What role, if any, have different transitional justice processes played – directly or indirectly – in fostering resilience in these societies?
4. How can transitional justice work aid adaptive peacebuilding?

Janine Natalya Clark's chapter focuses on Bosnia-Herzegovina (BiH), and more specifically on the ethnically mixed village of Ahmići. On 16 April 1993, a massacre in the village – at the height of the Bosnian war – resulted in the deaths of 116 Bosniaks. Drawing on fieldwork conducted in July 2019, Clark explores how individuals in Ahmići frequently demonstrate everyday resilience, despite suffering huge losses. However, she maintains that Ahmići cannot be accurately described as a resilient community – the sum of its parts – because it has not dealt with what happened in 1993 *as a community*. A major reason for this is that multiple systemic factors – including the persistence of ethnic divisions in BiH and the related demands of 'enmeshed cohesion' (Winton, 2008) – have not allowed the community to come together as one and to rebuild crucial social connections. Exploring the work of the International Criminal Tribunal for the former Yugoslavia (ICTY), she shows that its trials further entrenched ethnic divisions in Ahmići; and, in this way, they undermined the function of both the community and, systems of justice as potential resilience resources. Ultimately, her chapter calls for a social-ecological reframing of transitional justice that gives greater attention to the complex systems that necessarily shape what transitional justice processes can achieve on the ground; and, in this regard, she explores a crucial nexus between transitional justice and adaptive peacebuilding.

Jennie E. Burnet's chapter is the first of two African case study chapters. Focused on the 1994 Rwandan genocide and its aftermath, Burnet strongly emphasises the tensions between resilience models of recovery, adaptive peacebuilding and transitional justice. On one hand, ordinary Rwandans and civil society leaders have adapted to the trauma and shocks of the Rwandan genocide by drawing on cultural resources, including religious beliefs and social customs. According to her, 'These ad hoc processes of getting by, which emerged in the wake of the genocide, can be understood as forms of resilience and adaptive peacebuilding where people adapt to new circumstances out of necessity rather than through formal state or NGO intervention'. On the other hand, some national peacebuilding and reconciliation efforts in Rwanda have undermined and worked against adaptive peacebuilding efforts at the grassroots level. In this way, political processes that have created the appearance of stability and resilience have, in fact, sown the seeds for future instability and new divides. These same political factors have also permeated transitional justice work in Rwanda, including the Gacaca courts. If, in the long term, these courts ultimately increased stability (and, by extension, resilience), they did so by further consolidating and reinforcing the political dominance of the Rwandan Patriotic Front (RPF). In other words, 'resilience' in Rwanda has come at a significant political cost, marginalising the local ownership dimension of adaptive peacebuilding.

Uganda is the book's second African case study. The chapter authors, Philipp Schulz and Fred Ngomokwe, focus on survivors' groups as 'an under-utilised element of transitional justice and peacebuilding at the local level'. Drawing on their fieldwork in northern Uganda, and exploring some of the many ways that survivors' groups offer support, Schulz and Ngomokwe argue that these groups facilitate 'a local ecology of resilience'. They do so, inter alia, by creating a space for survivors to support each other, to share their experiences and deal with them in locally owned ways and, by extension, to (re-)gain a sense of communality and social belonging. Particularly in the case of male survivors of conflict-related sexual violence, moreover, these groups can enable survivors to renegotiate their gender identities and to develop new understandings of masculinity. In this way, the chapter links survivors' groups with adaptive peacebuilding. It is significant in this regard that the formation of these groups reflects the absence of effective measures at the state level to address individuals' experiences of suffering and harm. This, in turn, highlights an interesting contrast to Rwanda, where heavy state intervention has undermined adaptive peacebuilding. Schulz and Ngomokwe further demonstrate that adaptive peacebuilding within survivors' groups has wider social-ecological implications, carrying over into survivors' relations with their families and communities. The chapter thus strongly accentuates the relational and communal dimensions of resilience.

Nayanika Mookherjee's chapter addresses the use of sexual violence during the war in Bangladesh in 1971. Six days after the war ended, the new government publicly designated women who had suffered sexual violence as '*birangonas*' or war heroines. This is not, however, the dominant image that has prevailed. Discussing the Bangladesh War Crimes Tribunal, as the main example of (belated) transitional justice in the country, Mookherjee argues that its work represents an attempt 'to keep the wounds of 1971 open'. In this way, the Tribunal contributes to a 'resilient' multi-systemic process that upholds the 'horrific figure of the *birangona*'. Mookherjee powerfully challenges this image – captured in 'That *birangona* hair photograph' by Naibuddin Ahmed. Drawing on ethnographic research, she rejects a narrow framing of conflict-related sexual violence that elevates concepts such as silence, shame, honour and stigma. Rather, she tells a more complex story – of generative resilience, of the different ways that *birangonas* (and their families) have dealt with the violence of rape, of how these women refused government attempts to 'marry them off'. Ultimately, she demonstrates that systemic factors such as patriarchy need not restrict expressions of resilience. Rather, they create new possibilities for how resilience might be articulated and framed. Generative resilience by itself, however, attests to a broader set of systemic failures that fundamentally undermine adaptive peacebuilding. Mookherjee thus cautions against an overemphasis on resilience when past injustices have not been resolved.

The book's second Asian case study chapter focuses on post-Khmer Rouge Cambodia. Timothy Williams examines resilience from two angles. First, he explores how intersecting political, legal and economic systems 'limit resilience and access to potential resources that could, in theory, support resilience'. However, he also emphasises that particular systemic dynamics can help to foster resilience. He uses the example of patronage networks, which essentially provide individuals with a route to access the resources they need. Second, Williams discusses whether and how transitional justice processes in Cambodia have contributed to resilience, focusing on the work of the country's main transitional justice mechanism – the Extraordinary Chambers in the Courts of Cambodia (ECCC). He argues that, while the ECCC has made some small contributions to resilience, including through establishing individual criminal responsibility for Khmer Rouge crimes, overall its work has done little to foster resilience. One of the key reasons, he suggests, is the heavy politicisation of the tribunal, underscoring the broader point that transitional justice necessarily takes place within a political context. According to Williams, what the example of Cambodia ultimately demonstrates is the very limited scope for transitional justice to contribute to adaptive peacebuilding when political elites essentially use and co-opt transitional justice processes for their own ends.

In the first South American case study chapter, Sanne Weber looks at Colombia and incorporates her fieldwork with former internally displaced persons (IDPs) and former guerrillas from the Revolutionary Armed Forces of Colombia (FARC). She explores how her research participants in both groups had found their own ways of dealing with the adversities and challenges they faced, including through making jokes. The salient theme in her chapter, however, is social resilience, as outlined in Ungar's chapter. Social resilience, she argues, 'enables individuals and communities to navigate and negotiate access to the resources they need, such as land and financial support'. She particularly emphasises organisation and collective struggle as examples of social resilience. While there has been significant transitional justice work in Colombia, which remains ongoing, Weber maintains that this has not contributed to social resilience. Indeed, it has had the opposite effect. She thus underscores the need – which picks up on points made by Jennie Burnet and by Philipp Schulz and Fred Ngomokwe – for transitional justice to 'promote the capacity of survivors to organise themselves – as communities or groups of survivors – to protect and promote their own well-being'. She asserts that transitional justice has a role to play in fostering resilience and furthering adaptive peacebuilding by enabling and empowering communities to direct their own reconstruction processes, and by helping to revive and strengthen previous practices of active citizenship.

M. Brinton Lykes, Alison Crosby and Sara Beatriz Alvarez Medrano are the authors of the Guatemala case study. Their chapter discusses the resilience of Mayan women protagonists as they have engaged in transitional justice processes and organised in defence of their rights. It uses the protagonists' own understanding of resilience as 'resistance, persistence, permanence, strength and determination', and underlines that Indigenous resilience is quintessentially multi-systemic and relational, 'rooted in an integral, collective relationship of land-body-territory'. In this way, it demonstrates that the Mayan cosmovision disrupts Western dualisms – of nature and culture, human and nonhuman, knowing and being – which are linked to ongoing colonial violence. The authors underscore that transitional justice processes can potentially only contribute to resilience in Guatemala if they recognise historical injustices done to Mayan people and – consistent with adaptive peacebuilding – support locally owned processes aimed at repairing multi-systemic legacies of colonial harms, including harms done to bodies, land and people's cosmovision. This is a powerful example of what a social-ecological approach to transitional justice might look like. Mayan protagonists' ongoing demands for 'justice' that respects and acknowledges their own integrated plurivision are themselves important expressions of resilience. Lykes, Crosby and Alvarez also accentuate the imperative for transitional justice processes to create a space for what the Indigenous scholar Eve Tuck (2009) has termed 'desire-based frameworks' – as opposed to 'damage-based narratives' – that foreground agency and resilience.

Devin Atallah and Hana Masud's chapter is the final case study and addresses the complexities of resilience and transformative justice in Palestine. Their chapter shows that, in conditions marked by structural violence resulting from the legacies of colonisation, transformative justice is a far better option for social resilience than transitional efforts to adapt people to their circumstances. For Atallah and Masud, transformative justice offers an opportunity for collective re-envisioning that is grounded in Indigenous knowledges and social practices that emerge from below, rather than being imposed from above. This iterative transformative process, which is congruent with a multi-systemic conceptualisation of resilience, requires change across different systems (from the psychological to the political) at the same time. The chapter uses (counter-)stories to show what this resilience and transformative justice look like and the complexity that such work entails. Through deeply personal narratives, the authors share memories of their villages, their lands and their loved ones who were lost to annexation and incarceration. From these experiences, they draw out three decolonial enactments related to resilience, embodying themes of self-determination, radical coalitions and the everyday acts of love that move people forward under conditions of extreme oppression.

In the final chapter, Cedric de Coning reflects on how the chapters in this edited volume enrich, conceptually and empirically, the concepts of resilience and adaptive peacebuilding, and what they tell us about the complex ways that resilience manifests in different transitional and post-conflict contexts. Exploring three common themes (self-organisation, unintended consequences and process), one of the key points that he underlines – linked to the complexity dimension of adaptive peacebuilding – is that transitional justice interventions take place within highly complex systems, meaning that unintended or undesired consequences are a very real possibility. This lends support to the case for a social-ecological reframing of transitional justice advocated in Clark's chapter on BiH. de Coning also underscores that resilience can manifest very unevenly in post-conflict and transitioning societies, potentially entrenching deeper structural injustices; and as Burnet and Williams discuss in their chapters on Rwanda and Cambodia, respectively, 'resilient' systems can impede or restrict individual and community expressions of resilience. de Coning accordingly accentuates that resilience is not something that is inherently good or positive for the sorts of societies examined in this volume. Yet, what he also emphasises is that the use of a resilience lens offers new ways of thinking about transitional justice. The link with adaptive peacebuilding is not only about doing transitional justice in ways that support local ownership of the process but also about enhancing how complex systems respond and adapt to stressors.

REFERENCES

Anthony, E. J. (1987). Risk, vulnerability, and resilience: An overview. In E. J. Anthony and B. J. Cohler (eds.), *The Invulnerable Child*. New York: Guilford Press, pp. 3–48.

Atallah, D. G., Bacigalupe, G. and Repetto, P. (2019). Centering at the margins: Critical community resilience praxis. *Journal of Humanistic Psychology*, https://doi.org/10.1177%2F0022167818825305

Azzouz, A. (2019). A tale of a Syrian city at war: Destruction, resilience and memory in Homs. *City* 23(1), 107–122.

Balint, J., Evans, J. and Mcmillan, N. (2014). Rethinking transitional justice, redressing indigenous harm: A new conceptual approach. *International Journal of Transitional Justice*, 8(2), 194–216.

Barber, B. K. (2013). Annual research review: The experience of youth with political conflict – Challenging notions of resilience and encouraging research refinement. *Journal of Child Psychology and Psychiatry*, 54(4), 461–473.

Barzilay, R., Moore, T. M., Greenberg, G. M., DiDomenico, G. E., Brown, L. A., White, L. K., Gur, R. C. and Gur, R. E. (2020). Resilience, COVID-19-related stress, anxiety and depression during the pandemic in a large population enriched for healthcare providers. *Translational Psychiatry*, 10(291).

Betancourt, T. S. (2008). Child soldiers: Reintegration, pathways to recovery and reflections from the field. *Journal of Developmental and Behavioral Pediatrics*, 29 (2), 138–41.

Betancourt, T. S. and Khan, K. T. (2008). The mental health of children affected by armed conflict: Protective processes and pathways to resilience. *International Review of Psychiatry*, 20(3), 317–328.

Bonanno, G. A. (2004). Loss, trauma and human resilience: Have we underestimated the human capacity to thrive after extremely aversive events? *American Psychologist*, 59(1), 20–28.

Brassett, J. and Vaughan-Williams, N. (2015). Security and the performative politics of resilience: Critical infrastructure protection and humanitarian emergency preparedness. *Security Dialogue*, 46 (1), 32–50.

Brown, K. (2016). *Resilience, Development and Global Change*. New York: Routledge.

Chandler, D. (2013). International statebuilding and the ideology of resilience. *Politics*, 33(4), 276–286.

Chen, S. and Bonanno, G. A. (2020). Psychological adjustment during the global outbreak of COVID-19: A resilience perspective. *Psychological Trauma: Theory, Research, Practice and Policy*, 12(S1), S51–S54.

Clark, J. N. (2020a). Beyond 'bouncing': Resilience as an expansion-contraction dynamic within a holonic frame. *International Studies Review*, https://doi.org/10 .1093/isr/viaa048

Clark, J. N. (2020b). Re-thinking memory and transitional justice: A novel application of ecological memory. *Memory Studies*, https://doi.org/10.1177%2F1750698020959813

Cohler, B. (1991). The life story and the study of resiliency and response to adversity. *Journal of Narrative and Life History*, 1(2–3), 169–200.

de Coning, C. (2016). From peacebuilding to sustaining peace: Implications of complexity for resilience and sustainability. *Resilience*, 4(3), 166–181.

de Coning, C. (2018). Adaptive peacebuilding. *International Affairs*, 94(2), 301–317.

Doorn, N., Gardoni, P. and Murphy, C. (2019). A multidisciplinary definition and evaluation of resilience: The role of social justice in defining resilience. *Sustainable and Resilient Infrastructure*, 4(3), 112–123.

Duffield, M. (2012). Challenging environments: Danger, resilience and the aid industry. *Security Dialogue*, 43(5), 475–492.

Duthie, R. (2017). Introduction. In Duthie, R. and Seils, P. (eds.), *Justice Mosaics: How Context Shapes Transitional Justice in Fractured Societies*. New York: International Center for Transitional Justice, pp. 8–38.

Elliott, T. R., Hsiao, Y. Y., Kimbrel, N. A., Meyer, E., DeBeer, B. B., Gulliver, S. B. Kwok, O. M. and Morissette, S. M. (2017). Resilience and traumatic brain injury among Iraq/Afghanistan war veterans· Differential patterns of adjustment and quality of life. *Journal of Clinical Psychology*, 73(9), 1160–1178.

Fernando, C. and Ferrari, M. (2011). Spirituality and resilience in children of war in Sri Lanka. *Journal of Spirituality in Mental Health*, 13(1), 52–77.

Folke, C. (2006). Resilience: The emergence of a perspective for social–ecological systems analyses. *Global Environmental Change*, 16(3), 253–267.

Freeman, T., Kimbrell, T., Booe, L., Myers, M., Cardwell, D., Lindquist, D. M., Hart, J. and Komoroski, R. A. (2006). Evidence of resilience: Neuroimaging in former prisoners of war. *Psychiatry Research: Neuroimaging*, 146(1), 59–64.

Garrett, P. M. (2016). Questioning tales of 'ordinary magic': 'Resilience' and neo-liberal reasoning. *British Journal of Social Work*, 46, 1909–1925.

Gold, P. B., Engdahl, B. E., Eberly, R. E., Blake, R. J., Page, W. F. and Frueh, B. C. (2000). Trauma exposure, resilience, social support and PTSD construct validity among former prisoners of war. *Social Psychiatry and Psychiatric Epidemiology*, 35, 36–42.

Haeri, S. (2007). Resilience and post-traumatic recovery in cultural and political context. *Journal of Aggression, Maltreatment and Trauma*, 14(1–2), 287–304.

Halevi, G., Djalovski, A., Vengrober, A. and Feldman, R. (2016). Risk and resilience trajectories in war-exposed children across the first decade of life. *The Journal of Child Psychology and Psychiatry*, 57(10), 1183–1193.

Hartling, L. M. (2008). Strengthening resilience in a risky world: It's all about relationships. *Women and Therapy*, 31(2–4), 51–70.

Hayward, B. M. (2013). Rethinking resilience: Reflections on the earthquakes in Christchurch, New Zealand, 2010 and 2011. *Ecology and Society*, 18(4), 37.

Howell, A. and Voronka, J. (2012). Introduction: The politics of resilience and recovery in mental health care. *Studies in Social Justice*, 6(1), 1–7.

Isakhan, B. and Shahab, S. (2020). The Islamic state's destruction of Yezidi heritage: Responses, resilience and reconstruction after genocide. *Journal of Social Archaeology*, 20(1), 3–25.

Jones, E. and Wessely, S. (2010). British prisoners-of-war: From resilience to psychological vulnerability: Reality or perception. *20th Century British History*, 21 (2), 163–183.

Joseph, J. (2013). Resilience as embedded neoliberalism: A governmentality approach. *Resilience*, 1(1), 38–52.

Kastner, P. (2020). A resilience approach to transitional justice? *Journal of Intervention and Statebuilding*, 14(3), 368–388.

Labrague, L. J. and De los Santos, J. A. A. (2020). COVID-19 anxiety among front-line nurses: Predictive role of organizational support, personal resilience and social support. *Journal of Nursing Management*, 28(7), 1653–1661.

Leebaw, B. A. (2008). The irreconcilable goals of transitional justice. *Human Rights Quarterly*, 30(1), 95–118.

Legido-Quigley, H., Asgari, N., Teo, Y. Y., Leung, G. M., Oshitani, H., Fekuda, K., Cook, A. R., Hsu, L. Y., Shibuya, K. and Heymann, D. (2020). Are high-performing health systems resilient against the COVID-19 pandemic? *The Lancet*, 395(10227), 848–850.

Luthar, S. S. (2006). Resilience in development: A synthesis of research across five decades. In D. J. Cohen and D. Cicchetti (eds.), *Developmental Psychopathology: Risk, Disorder and Adaptation*. Hoboken, NJ: John Wiley & Sons, pp. 739–795.

Maddison, S. and Shepherd, L. J. (2014). Peacebuilding and the postcolonial politics of transitional justice. *Peacebuilding*, 2(3), 253–269.

Mahdiani, H., Höltge, J., Theron, L. and Ungar, M. (2020). Resilience in times of economic boom and bust: A narrative study of a rural population dependent upon the oil and gas industry. *Journal of Adult Development*, https://doi.org/10.1007/s10804-020-09363-z

Masten, A. S. (2014). *Ordinary Magic. Resilience in Development*. New York: Guilford Press.

Masten, A. S. and Narayan, A. J. (2012). Child development in the context of disaster, war and terrorism: Pathways of risk and resilience. *Annual Review of Psychology*, 63, 227–257.

Millar, G. (2011). Local evaluations of justice through truth telling in Sierra Leone: Postwar needs and transitional justice. *Human Rights Review*, 12, 515–535.

Mullen, M. (2015). Reassessing the focus of transitional justice: The need to move structural and cultural violence to the centre. *Cambridge Review of International Affairs*, 28(3), 462–479.

Nussio, E., Rettberg, A. and Ugarriza, J. E. (2015). Victims, nonvictims and their opinions on transitional justice: Findings from the Colombian case. *International Journal of Transitional Justice*, 9(2), 336–354.

Portnoy, G. A., Relyea, M. R., Decker, S., Shamaskin-Garroway, A, Driscoll, M., Brandt, C. A. and Haskell, S. G. (2018). Understanding gender differences in resilience among veterans: Trauma history and social ecology. *Journal of Traumatic Stress*, 31(6), 845–855.

Shanahan, L., Steinhoff, A., Bechtiger, L., Murray, A. L., Nivette, A., Hepp, U., Ribeaud, D. and Eisner, M. (2020). Emotional distress in young adults during the COVID-19 pandemic: Evidence of risk and resilience from a longitudinal cohort study. *Psychological Medicine*, https://doi.org/10.1017/S003329172000241X

Tuck, E. (2009). Suspending damage: A letter to communities. *Harvard Educational Review*, 79(3), 409–428.

Ungar, M. (2011). The social ecology of resilience. Addressing contextual and cultural ambiguity of a nascent construct. *American Journal of Orthopsychiatry*, 81(1), 1–17.

Ungar, M. (2013). Resilience, trauma, context and culture. *Trauma, Violence and Abuse*, 14(3), 255–266.

Ungar, M. (2018). Systemic resilience: Principles and processes for a science of change in contexts of adversity. *Ecology and Society*, 23(4), 34.

Ungar, M. (2021). *Multisystemic Resilience: Adaptation and Transformation in Contexts of Change*. New York: Oxford University Press.

United Nations. (2010). Guidance note of the Secretary-General: United Nations approach to transitional justice. www.un.org/ruleoflaw/files/TJ_Guidance_Note_March_2010FINAL.pdf (accessed 9 September 2020).

United Nations (2018). Peacebuilding and sustaining peace: Report of the Secretary-General. https://undocs.org/a/72/707 (accessed 14 September 2020).

United Nations (n.d.). Sustaining peace. www.un.org/peacebuilding/tags/sustaining-peace (accessed 11 May 2020).

United Nations General Assembly. (2016). Resolution adopted by the General Assembly on 27 April 2016 – 70/262. Review of the United Nations peacebuilding architecture. www.un.org/en/development/desa/population/migration/generalassembly/docs/globalcompact/A_RES_70_262.pdf (accessed 11 May 2020).

United Nations Security Council. (2016). Resolution 2282 (2016). https://undocs.org/S/RES/2282(2016) (accessed 13 May 2020).

Vogt, D. S. and Tanner, L. R. (2007). Risk and resilience factors for posttraumatic stress symptomology in Gulf War I veterans. *Journal of Traumatic Stress*, 20(1), 27–38.

Walsh, F. (2020). Loss and resilience in the time of COVID-19: Meaning making, hope and transcendence. *Family Process*, 59(3), 898–911.

Walsh-Dilley, M. and Wolford, W. (2015). (Un)Defining resilience: Subjective understandings of 'resilience' from the field. *Resilience*, 3(3), 173–182.

Whyte, K. P. (2018). On resilient parasitisms, or why I'm sceptical of indigenous/settler reconciliation. *Journal of Global Ethics*, 14(2), 277–289.

Wiebelhaus-Brahm, E. (2017). After shocks: Exploring the relationships between transitional justice and resilience in post-conflict societies. In: R. Duthie and P. Seils (eds.), *Justice Mosaics: How Context Shapes Transitional Justice in Fractured Societies*. New York: International Center for Transitional Justice, pp. 140–165.

Windle, G. (2011). What is resilience? A review and concept analysis. *Reviews in Clinical Gerontology*, 21, 152–169.

Winton, M. A. (2008). Dimensions of genocide: The circumplex model meets violentization theory. *Qualitative Report*, 13(4), 605–629.

Xu, L. and Kajikawa, Y. (2017). An integrated framework for resilience research: A systematic review based on citation network analysis. *Sustainability Science*, 13 (1), 235–254.

PART I

CONCEPTS AND RELATIONSHIPS

Mapping the Resilience Field: A Systemic Approach

Michael Ungar

INTRODUCTION

When referring to biological, psychological, social and institutional aspects of people's lives, the term 'resilience' is best used to describe processes whereby individuals interact with their environments in ways that facilitate positive psychological, physical and social development. While earlier definitions emphasised individual traits and the invulnerability of individuals who coped well with adversity (Anthony and Cohler, 1987), more contextualised research has challenged the neoliberal bias of these earlier studies (Sanders et al., 2015). When resilience was described as a trait, even if those traits were malleable, the implication was that individuals had the responsibility to develop the qualities necessary for optimal development, whether physical, psychological or social (like attachments). Resilience as a process, however, shifts the focus from individual responsibility for change to the interactions between individuals and their environments (Birgden, 2015; Ungar, 2015). The environment, whether referring to legal institutions, community services or the availability of intimate bonds and other antecedents of mental health (e.g., a sense of coherence [Antonovsky, 1996; Mittelmark et al., 2017]), combines to provide individuals with the internal and external resources necessary to cope with exceptional and uncommon stressors. For this reason, when resilience is understood as a process involving multiple systems, the responsibility for optimal functioning (whether psychological well-being or peace and security) under stress is shared across many different systems and at different scales (Ungar, 2018).

It is this understanding of resilience that informs a deeper analysis of how systems, including those concerned with governance, education, health, human rights and law, influence the ability of populations to survive and thrive in contexts where there has been exposure to extreme forms of marginalisation (e.g., racism, homophobia, poverty) or social disruption (e.g., civil war, genocide). Stabilising and improving these systems is an important and necessary part of transitional justice work and related security-oriented practices like adaptive peacebuilding (de Coning, 2018; see also Chapter 11). This is especially the case when systems at the individual, family, community, national and international levels are involved at the same time in the provision of resources that people need to overcome histories of violence. Put simply, resilience, like transitional justice, requires the engagement of many different systems to create the individual and social capital necessary to cope well with adversity.

Figure 1.1 illustrates the nested relationships between these systems, with a subsystem of elements (the Xs) forming their own system comprised of the many resources required to sustain the well-being of both the individual and the individual's community. To think about resilience at a single level, like a change in cognition or the exercise of human rights, misattributes change to the qualities of one system and risks making any change that does occur unsustainable. When multiple systems at multiple scales change at the same time, the work they do together produces a more enduring pattern of change and transformation. In practice, this means that efforts to promote transitional justice, like the interventions discussed throughout this volume, will produce the most sustainable resilience across a population when they address the

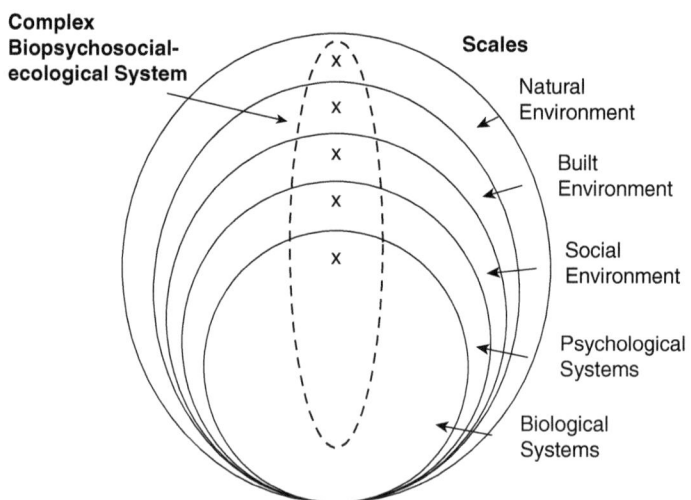

FIGURE 1.1 An ecological and multi-systemic model of resilience (Ungar and Theron, 2020)

systemic dimensions of war crimes and human rights abuses – and engage with different systems that give people access to new resources.

This discussion of commonalities between resilience and transitional justice addresses a gap in both fields, with far too little of the resilience literature paying attention to structural and judicial processes that create the conditions for people to recover from mass violence (see, e.g., Chapter 9). Likewise, transitional justice literature has rarely discussed the impact of transitional justice mechanisms – including criminal trials, truth and reconciliation commissions (TRCs) or reparations – on the resilience of a community, or the need to think ecologically about the many systems that interact (or conflict) when transitional justice processes are utilised. For example, criminal trials to address war crimes may become extremely divisive for communities, disrupting social cohesion or even traumatising some victims, even as they appear to re-establish order with regard to governance and the rule of law (Clark, 2014; see also Chapter 3, this volume). The science of resilience helps to explain these dynamic feedback loops in which one system's resilience can trigger another's success or undermine the ability of co-occurring systems to function at all.

Fortunately, in recent years, a more multidisciplinary body of research on resilience has grown to include studies of biological human systems like the microbiome (Rea et al., 2016), human-environment systems like epigenetics (Bush and Boyce, 2016), workplaces (Crane, 2017) and the natural ecologies with which humans interact – such as coral reefs, forests and wetlands (Adger et al., 2013). Governance and legal systems shape the context for each of these interactions, from influencing the availability of food people need to maintain health to regulating the development of farmland in nature preserves. The relationship between these systems and resilience nevertheless remains underexplored. Key processes within these broader governance and legal architectures, for example – including the promotion of human rights, peacebuilding and the restoration of rule of law – are seldom discussed through a resilience lens.

An emerging body of work on therapeutic jurisprudence (Wexler, 2008; Winick, 2009), however, is starting to address this shortcoming, by studying the impact on individual well-being of formal legal institutions, criminal trials and TRCs (Doak, 2011), and looking at whether new initiatives like drug courts and restorative justice improve the desistance of offenders (Birgden et al., 2015). Nevertheless, more research is needed to account for what occurs at multiple systemic levels when victims of crime seek justice. For example, we know little about the impact of transitional justice processes on victims' mental health during and after these processes, or about how these processes affect the functioning and sustainability of other human systems like community cohesion or extended family dynamics. Fundamentally, we know little about how transitional justice and peacebuilding processes more generally can transform psychological and social systems.

It also remains the case that there is little cross-fertilisation of ideas across the fields of resilience, law, transitional justice and human rights. This is part of a wider problem; network citation analyses show that there is little transdisciplinary exchange across domains of resilience research (Xu and Kajikawa, 2017). This may explain why the connection between the resilience of one system and the resilience of co-occurring systems at different scales has yet to be well explained. Further compounding the problem is the fact that definitional ambiguity exists in all fields of resilience research, although this is an issue now being addressed on many fronts (see, e.g., Southwick et al., 2014).

The present volume addresses these various challenges. In this chapter, I will introduce the concept of resilience as a multi-systemic set of processes, an idea that is common to all the chapters that follow. I will then briefly show how these processes are relevant to governance, legal systems and transitional justice. The chapter will also discuss several concepts that must be accounted for when detailing the resilience of any system. These concepts include equifinality, multifinality and differential impact. Though this volume is focused on the systems involved in transitional justice and their resilience-enabling processes, potential or actual, this chapter will look more broadly at different resilience enablers in order to show that initiatives to tackle impunity, deliver justice and foster social healing and reconciliation are consistent with the principles that govern the resilience of all human systems.

A MULTI-SYSTEMIC UNDERSTANDING OF RESILIENCE

In *Rwanda after Genocide*, Caroline Williamson Sinalo (2018) describes her narrative analysis of victims' accounts of the genocide that unfolded during the early 1990s. Sinalo takes a controversial approach to the subject, first by arguing that there were many dysfunctional systems to blame for the atrocities, from the practices of past colonial governments to Rwandan norms regarding masculinity and warriorhood. She also, however, asserts that one can find examples of personal and social growth (also known as post-traumatic growth [Tedeschi and Calhoun, 2004]) among survivors of the genocide – growth that is mirrored at the level of community governance, social cohesion and legal processes that have come into place since 1994.

To see this growth, one must challenge Eurocentric discourses that view trauma as the result of exposure to single episodes of an atypical stressor.

According to Craps (2013), trauma is more an everyday and insidious phenomenon than an unusual event. This is especially true for those who are marginalised, whether living in economically developed countries as minorities or in low- and middle-income countries, many of these with long and violent histories of colonisation (Atallah et al., 2019). In both contexts, poverty, racism and the intersectionality of multiple forms of oppression make trauma quotidian because of institutionalised forms of exclusion and dysfunction (e.g., corruption). In such a case, resilience can resist the effects of coloniality and reinforce models of Indigenous well-being (Sinalo, 2018).

This perspective of why atrocities occur and where responsibility lies for social repair positions resilience in a collective discourse of shared causality and complex systems. Addressing past or present human rights abuses cannot be accomplished by any one system alone. Multiple social and institutional factors must be involved, which, in turn, affect and are affected by individual responses to trauma and the continuity of those changes across time and even generations. Resilience-enablers (van Breda and Theron, 2018) occur at multiple levels, refuting the idea that individuals bounce back from adversity, or bounce forward to new patterns of coping on their own. There is, of course, more to this critique than a simple vilification of neoliberalism. As Hall and Lamont (2013) argue, a heightened sense of personal responsibility inherent in neoliberalism may have harmed many, but it has also opened opportunities for wealth generation on a scale never before seen in human history.

A better critique would be to understand how neoliberalism has blinded us to the locus of control of systems that must cope with extraordinary circumstances. Individual capacity to look after one's self will only be effective when risks are relatively few. The rugged individualism promoted by US President Herbert Hoover in the late 1920s was shown to be wrong only a year later when recovery from the Great Depression required government intervention. In this sense, it was changes to governance and law which triggered an economic turnaround, even if these changes were opposed on ideological grounds by those who most benefitted from the previous regime. Social resilience, then, is 'the capacity of groups of people bound together in an organization, class, racial group, community or nation to sustain and advance their well-being in the face of challenges to it' (Hall and Lamont, 2013: 2).

This shift to the social is the step we need to understand resilience across systems, though it runs the risk of making the same error that many psychologists have made – which is to focus on one level and exclude others. For example, we now know that badly traumatised people who have experienced social marginalisation or exposure to domestic violence may be genetically altered by these experiences or become neurologically susceptible if future stress occurs. Excessive burden on biological, psychological and social systems at the same time (what has been termed 'allostatic load' [Hobfoll, 2011]) compromises our ability to function socially and participate in community processes, including good governance and possibly legal proceedings. Though these connections across systems are still more conjecture than fact, a case can be built through a review of the biological, psychological and social systems literature that risk and resilience at any one system level will compromise or be advantageous to other systems at other levels. For these reasons, just as the psychological scientist needs to understand the social environment, those studying the influence of legal systems and other institutions need to appreciate the biological and psychological factors that inhibit healthy responses to social processes that are in the perceived best interest of individuals.

The experience of Rwandans before, during and after the genocide demonstrates patterns of resilience as a process occurring simultaneously at multiple levels (see also Chapter 4). Changes to a distal factor, like national policies on race, have influenced proximal systems, like peer relationships and even intransigent psychological systems related to an individual's co-construction of personal identity. If these interrelated systems are to demonstrate resilience, whether that is recovery to a stable prior state or transformation to a new status quo, there needs to be some understanding of the mechanisms by which a change that makes one system function optimally improves the functioning of other systems as well. This may explain why Sinalo (2018) found that Rwandan men, post-genocide, tended to report a far greater sense of collective responsibility and move away from warriorship, while women shifted from thinking about themselves as 'we' (symbolising communion) and more as 'I' (symbolising greater agency and a focus on personal identity).

Of course, these ideological shifts came at a terrible price: the mass destruction and mutilation of lives. From the point of view of the study of resilience, however, such transformations suggest that processes of change look very different in different contexts. Just as trauma has been plagued by a Eurocentric bias in how it is understood and treated by the institutions tasked with responding, so too is resilience theory biased by Eurocentric notions of a shortlist of factors that promote well-being under stress that are popular in psychology. It is far better to imagine many different patterns to resilience across many different systems, from identity and gender relations to government structures, cultural practices and conflict resolution (including those that are part of transitional justice).

It is now recognised that, within different disciplines, there are generalisable principles that govern processes of resilience (for a review, see Biggs et al., 2012; Ungar, 2018). Among the most important are that resilience occurs in contexts of adversity where exposure to atypical stressors occurs and is a process that is influenced by how well people and resources interact. For this reason, I define resilience as the process through which individuals and groups navigate their way to the many different resources they need to sustain themselves and thrive, as well as the processes that systems use to negotiate for the resources that are most meaningful (Ungar, 2011). The dual concepts of navigation and negotiation that are at the core of this social–ecological description of resilience underline the need to think about the individual's environment and culture just as much as individual strengths and traits. To navigate does not mean individual motivation or personal agency; it implicates systems at other levels to provide the resources to individuals to support optimal functioning. Likewise, these resources must be those that the individual is able to negotiate for, so that they are provided in ways that match the individual's belief systems or physical needs. The process is more circular than linear, with systems influencing what the individual values and needs, while individuals place demands on systems to provide novel resources as values change. In other words, individuals are not wholly autonomous in deciding which resources they need or how these resources will be provided.

For example, in research currently underway with two communities dependent upon the oil and gas industry as their major employer, my colleagues and I are documenting competing discourses concerning the resilience of these communities (Mahdiani et al., 2020). On the one hand, community leaders and vested government interests insist on the persistence of the oil and gas industry, maintaining that it should be supported through taxation policies that preserve the industry as it is, including abolishing requirements for more fuel-efficient cars and building pipelines to get more products to market. These individuals argue fervently that they and their livelihoods are being treated unfairly and that any changes to the economic viability of their communities should be resisted. For them, their jobs and way of life are a matter of human rights.

On the other hand, there are those who perceive a rapidly approaching turn towards a zero-carbon economy and a need to dramatically decrease the production of petrochemical products. This group argues that the resilience of oil- and gas-dependent communities lies in their ability to quickly diversify their economy away from oil and gas extraction and production. For this group, the end to oil and gas production is an issue of environmental justice, though they are willing to compensate communities being affected by these changes with financial help during the transitional period. A compromise ideology supports a transformation but believes a slower period of change is required. Instituting a carbon tax, building pipelines and investing in cleaner technologies to extract and use oil and gas could give these communities the resources and time they need to adapt to a changing economy that is a response to climate change. All three processes are ways of dealing with an environmental crisis, but each reflects different patterns of navigation and negotiation for the resources that these communities value during periods of economic downturn and different definitions of what they perceive as just.

While this example is about economics and politics, it is also illustrative of how communities make themselves more resilient by changing multiple systems at once. Among those being displaced by the downturn in the oil and gas industry, there are feelings that their right to employment is being sacrificed by federal government policies and special interest groups that see these workers as expendable. These socio-economic changes also threaten individual mental health, as well as the social cohesion of the community itself. Seeking justice in the form of human rights and economic self-determination, however, has meant mostly resisting change, rather than establishing new institutional supports or arguing for compensation for retraining, relocation or economic diversification (all possible strategies for resilience).

On the other side of the debate, those who support the downturn see the closing of the industry as a means to achieve environmental justice. Viewed in this way, the factors that predict resilience will depend on which systems we want to sustain and which outcomes are preferred and by whom. As the case examples throughout this volume show, communities experiencing and engaging with transitional justice are heterogeneous, and myriad views on what constitutes 'justice' necessarily exist. Finding ways to build individual and social capital that different stakeholders experience as just, and therefore as a source of resilience, is a major challenge and one that requires local communities to have a say over the processes that they engage in.

The notion of resilience as a process is often misunderstood, particularly when researchers describe individuals, communities and governments as 'resilient'. The preferred description is that these systems 'show resilience', meaning that they are in a process whereby they are able to take advantage of opportunities to improve their functioning. The issue is more than semantic. At the core of this ontological debate is the need to focus on what systems do to function better rather than their intrinsic qualities. Intrinsic qualities may never be realised if oppressive forces are beyond the capacity of the individual to change, with the result that resilience is reserved for the exceptional few who overcome the barriers around them. These processes, however, need not always be externally focused. As treatises on the resilience of the human spirit attest (see, e.g., Beah, 2007; Westover, 2018; Wiesel, 1956), reflective processes or belief in a special connection with one's culture, God or ancestors have the power to carry us through periods of darkness. Even these responses to social injustice, however, should not be described as static traits of individuals. These are characteristics that are dormant until activated through processes that make them meaningful to the individual. In other words, resilience is always a process of realising the potential of systems.

The process of resilience is not, however, uniform. There are at least five patterns well documented in the literature (Ungar, 2018), and each pattern is influenced by the qualities of the system under stress, human and social capital and by the economic and environmental resources available. These patterns of resilience include persistence, resistance, recovery, adaptation and transformation. A review of these patterns shows remarkable synergy between processes associated with resilience and the intent of processes and practices related to transitional justice, as other chapters in this volume demonstrate.

Persistence A system shows persistence despite exposure to atypical stress when it maintains its functioning as a consequence of other systems sheltering the vulnerable system from harm. The system may appear to be resting or stable, but the effect is an illusion caused by its isolation or protection against outside threats that mitigate the need for reorganisation. Examples include traditional societies that are protected from outsiders like Brazil's Kawahiva. Their precarious resilience and fragile experience of environmental justice are evident in the persistence of their culture and traditional lifestyle, but that persistence is a reflection of the efficacy of institutionalised laws imposed on outsiders through government processes at a scale quite separate from the community itself. Though these efforts have largely come too late and without sufficient enforcement to ensure the safety of the Kawahiva, their experience shows that resilience depends on external forces far more than individual qualities when populations face a threat like genocide or the destruction of the natural environment upon which they depend. To some extent, the same patterns are found among Amish peoples in North America, where tolerance by the cultural majority has been institutionalised so that the Amish can maintain their traditional way of life with minimal compliance with external rules (e.g., they still pay income tax, and children must still receive an education at least until the eighth grade). As these examples illustrate, legal systems can make it more or less feasible for communities to persist with behaviours that are viewed as non-normative by cultural outsiders.

Resistance Resistance refers to a process whereby an individual, community or institution is under threat but is not sufficiently protected by outsiders to maintain its functioning. In this case, the system that is threatened must mobilise resources on its own to actively resist encroachment and maintain its right to be unique. Resistance is often a reflection of a lack of formal legal protection or of the need to adapt systems that are supposed to support human rights to account for differences. Indigenous peoples in countries like Canada and Australia, who have suffered past (and, arguably, ongoing) genocidal practices perpetrated against them, have lacked the social or legal protections to experience resilience (Atallah et al., 2018). Instead, patterns of resistance have emerged where groups have become political in their efforts to secure their rights. Only recently have changes at the local level been reflected in changes at regional, national and international levels, with documents such as the United Nations Declaration on the Rights of Indigenous Peoples encouraging the protections and access to resources required for Indigenous communities to experience resilience. Where resistance occurs as a strategy for resilience, there are usually competing discourses regarding what is and is not a success, with different interests defining preferred outcomes. The process of resistance has the added advantage, however, of mobilising new resources when a system is under threat – resources that may create stronger systems as a consequence (e.g., a return to a community's traditional cultural practices). Resistance may also change other contingent systems such as national bureaucracies or policing services. For example, institutionalised forms of racism against Indigenous peoples are still extremely prevalent but are being challenged to ensure better services and respect for human rights (Blackstock, 2016). In such cases, transitional justice initiatives like TRCs or honouring victims through memorials and reparations programmes can validate efforts to resist further threats to a population's well-being.

Recovery The concept of recovery is ontologically problematic as systems never 'bounce back' (Zolli, 2012) to their previous state but instead are changed by the experience of dealing with stress. Usually, this return to functioning reflects some nuanced change to the system's behavioural regime, making it possible for the system to learn from past challenges and integrate what is learned. If a system returns to its previous role and appears to be doing the same thing it did before, it may even look recovered if small adaptations and transformations have occurred (see below). By way of illustration, recovery efforts after Hurricane Katrina on the southern coast of the United States seemed to signal a return by communities, like New Orleans, to previous levels of economic functioning and the resettlement of people to areas that were flooded. A closer look, however, shows changes to how new homes are being built (Cutter et al., 2014) and changes to practices during disasters to address racial inequalities experienced by minorities, though these changes have yet to be widely adopted (Gotham and Campanella, 2013).

Adaptation When systems experience a stressor and are changed as a consequence, adaptation occurs. Where recovery returns a system to a former regime of behaviour, adaptation produces a novel set of processes designed to deal with the stressor now and into the future. The focal system changes so that it can survive. This adaptation, however, is not simply change at one systemic level. Typically, adaptation requires changes at multiple levels for the adaptation to be sustainable. For example, when urban planners allow (or encourage) the gentrification of inner-city communities, the results are often disastrous for the residents who were already living there. Adaptation may mean preserving these communities during a period of rapid change by building subsidised housing or ensuring services for those who are displaced. These adaptations are seldom satisfactory to the individuals displaced, though they work better at decreasing the largely negative impact on displaced residents when multiple levels of government, social services and community organisations work together to develop solutions to maintain the continuity of a community. In an example like this, persistence was likely never an option (there was no benign government looking out for the community) as the economic pressures on the community and rising housing costs would be beyond the capacity of any single level of government to prevent. Nor was resistance likely sufficient to oppose redevelopment. Recovery is nonsensical as it is unreasonable to expect a community with widespread poverty to return to that state after gentrification has started, even if the community seeks to preserve its unique identity. Adaptation, then, implies a 'messy set of inter-actions occurring simultaneously across multiple systems at multiple scales' (Ungar, 2018: 34) and may be the best choice when there are few other available options. It can also implicate informal and formal justice systems through forms of remediation or protection of rights (e.g., the right to return to the community once new housing is built), though the process of adaptation seldom challenges the fundamental legal principles which cause people to experience injustice and exclusion.

Transformation When human systems are exposed to stressors beyond their capacity to cope, transformation in how a system maintains itself is an ideal solution that implicates multiple systems in the development of new and sustainable regimes of behaviour that alter both individuals and their environments. Although one of the expressed aims of transitional justice and its many different forms is to seed such social transformation, the case examples in this volume highlight the multiple challenges that this entails across different systems. Transitional justice does contribute to processes leading to peace and reconciliation, which can result in structural changes to society at large. However, more often the changes that occur are modest in scale. Individual experiences – for example, of testifying in court – may increase individual resilience, but it remains unclear if they are catalysts for larger social transformations. Instead, the pathways to these transformations seem less direct, with small incremental changes in individual cognitions, social inter-actions and experiences of justice accumulating over time. Such adaptations leave the environment around the individual or system unchanged and the likelihood of another catastrophic challenge occurring in the future. Transformation, meanwhile, seeks change to the surrounding systems to avoid future exposure to stress. At the macro level, legislative systems play an obvious role in creating transformations that make other systems more resilient.

For example, the Clean Air Act Amendments of 1990 in the United States changed regulations for coal-fired power-generating stations that helped to protect lakes across North America from the impact of acid rain. Advocates for these imperilled ecosystems sought fundamental transformation in how power plants operated to prevent further devastation. A similar pattern of transform-ation can be seen in the dismantling of Apartheid in South Africa (though many of the problems that were synonymous with Apartheid continue today) and the relatively peaceful change of government that resulted. In each example, there is evidence of multiple human, institutional and even natural systems being transformed in response to changes at different systemic levels. To the extent that transitional justice processes contribute to these changes, the more likely they are to foster long-term resilience of multiple personal, social and environmental systems.

DYNAMIC RESILIENCE: EQUIFINALITY, MULTIFINALITY AND DIFFERENTIAL IMPACT

Each of the five processes of resilience that were described above produce a number of different outcomes depending on the population affected and the environment that surrounds them. In general, however, the benefits of resili-ence are not shared equally, with different systems benefitting more or less from the change process. A number of concepts appear in the resilience literature to explain these different patterns and outcomes, among them equifinality, multifinality and differential impact. All three concepts are also relevant to the many forms of transitional justice.

Equifinality refers to various means to achieve a single desirable end. Studies of resilience tend to focus on equifinality and define a limited number of outcomes as positive aspects of change and development. When context is controlled, and homogeneity among actors and environments assumed, then the link between risk exposure, protective process and desired outcome is easier to describe. This simplified model, however, can suffer from the myopia that accompanies de-contextualisation, especially when cultural minorities and populations from low- and middle-income countries are the focus of the work. In the case of establishing peace post-conflict, or environmental justice for a community affected by rising sea levels due to climate change, the end goal may appear obvious (peaceful co-existence; a built environment that is sustainable), though the pathways to achieve these ends can still be many.

The various goals associated with transitional justice, for example, have an extensive desirability yet can look very different in different contexts, as this volume shows. As an illustration, one could debate the advantages and disadvantages of centralised power and authoritarianism in contexts where there has been a breakdown of social order and no history of democratic institutions. In such cases, an effective government may look very different during a period of transformation, while becoming dysfunctional and making a country vulnerable to future violence when it becomes institutionalised as a totalitarian regime (e.g., an elected president becomes president for life). It is common in studies of resilience to see a common set of outcomes defined for specific systems, with multiple strategies to achieve that end.

In contrast, multifinality is typical of systems that are adaptive and complex, especially when their resilience is being studied across cultures and contexts where there has been very little previous research. In these cases, there may be multiple desirable outcomes that are negotiated between local and state actors. Resilience-promoting processes may not be obvious to cultural outsiders whose Eurocentricity (or other social location) privileges one set of behaviours over another. To illustrate, women's and men's gender-normative behaviour can be responsive to changing economic and social conditions, making family systems more resilient. In the Philippines, for example, many women have found employment overseas as domestic workers, leaving their male partners to look after children and assume more household duties, tasks not typically taken on by men (these patterns can be disrupted when a grandmother is available to assume the role of primary caregiver for the children; see Parreñas, 2000). Similarly, in Senegal, the large number of men who have migrated to Europe for work has resulted in women assuming men's work despite the stigma of doing so (Searcey, 2019). In both examples, the assumption of non-traditional gender roles makes families and communities more resilient, but each context shapes which pattern of behaviour is preferred.

As these examples show, there are many similarities between the concept of multifinality as applied to resilience and de Coning's (2018) description of adaptive peacebuilding – a central concept that runs throughout this book (see also Chapter 11, this volume). de Coning challenges the idea that there is one right outcome from peacebuilding, and indeed honours multiple cultural traditions as potentially positive sources of inspiration for ways to recreate social cohesion and stability after a period of violence. As de Coning (2018: 304) writes, adaptive peacebuilding:

> [R]ejects the liberal peace theory of change – namely, that an external peacebuilding intervention can set in motion and control a causal sequence of events that will result in a sustainable peace outcome. In its place, it argues that the role of the UN is to assist countries to sustain their own peace processes by strengthening the resilience of local social institutions, and by investing in social cohesion.

The concept of multifinality simply describes this pattern of sensitivity to context and flexible outcomes as common to many different systems when they operate in complex environments. To understand resilience, however, one must also account for the nature of both those doing the navigation and negotiation and the environment in which it occurs. In the field of human biology, an emerging concept of differential susceptibility has shown that depending on one's genes or other traits, interventions will have a different impact on individual change (Belsky and van Ijzendoorn, 2015). Susceptibility implies individual responsibility for change with personal qualities determining which environmental trigger is most useful for personal success. Differential impact switches the focus to the quality of the environmental trigger, something which is far more malleable than individual qualities like one's genome (Ungar, 2017). When examining the differential impact of an intervention, social policy or legal system, one asks, 'Which population, at what level of risk, is likely to most benefit from this support?' The question challenges us to consider how different kinds of support produce resilience in highly stressed environments and how each is tailored to the needs of populations with specific profiles.

When interventions underperform or fail to produce desired changes in behaviour, the responsibility for the lack of success is attributed to the intervention, not the individual. The concept of differential impact, then, opens possibilities for understanding why some interventions may work better in some contexts and cultures than others (Birgden et al., 2015). It is the dynamic fit between interventions and individuals that is critical. Because the model is adaptive, it is not uncommon to see the same intervention having a positive effect with one population and a deleterious effect with another, or a small impact with one and a very large impact with another. Designing interventions to promote resilience of any system requires that attention is paid not only to the end goal but also to the quality of the interactions between those needing help and those providing it.

MAKING JUSTICE SYSTEMS RESILIENT

The advantage of transitional justice and its many variations is that it has the potential to offer formal legal systems the means to adapt to changing demands by those using them, especially in contexts where legislated systems have largely failed to maintain peace and need to recover and show resilience. Ruhl et al. (2021) describe formal legal systems as themselves needing this resilience if they are to be sustainable. That sustainability and effective functioning means that both formal and informal systems of accountability, whether from the courts or community talking circles, can also influence the resilience of other co-occurring systems. Ruhl et al. (2021: 510) write: 'Resilience in legal systems is, thus, often used to facilitate normative social purposes fulfilled through other social systems.' For Ruhl et al. (2021: 511), legal systems are complex, meaning that they have many interrelated parts which together form 'a large network of components with no central control and simple rules of operation giving rise to complex collective behavior, sophisticated information processing, and adaptation via learning or evolution'.

This complexity, which is also a fundamental dimension of adaptive peacebuilding (see de Coning, Chapter 11), means that legal systems are able to respond to, or look different in, different contexts. Transitional justice processes can help them to become more responsive by broadening the definition of what constitutes a legal system to include the many ways that societies support economic and human rights, land rights and environmental justice. This means, for example, integrating cultural and/or Indigenous practices where appropriate, or using combinations of formal codified legal institutions like courts and legislation, community justice forums, collaborative law practices and other means to achieve transitional justice. These practices require many and varied systems to co-exist, though which system is needed and when will depend on the conditions in which they operate and on competing discourses of justice expressed by those whose rights have been transgressed.

These tensions are obvious in contexts like fly-in courts in the Canadian Arctic, which serve the needs of mostly Indigenous communities. In that context, the judiciary uses both formal and community-based legal mechanisms to maintain the social cohesion of communities and facilitate the reintegration of offenders. While these efforts are noteworthy, they are also controversial with some perceiving the sentencing of offenders (e.g., perpetrators of domestic violence) as too lenient to act as a deterrent (Rudin, 2018).

Despite these difficulties, systems that promote transitional justice or the enforcement of laws and still show resilience when strained are typically those that are adaptive (Murray et al., 2019), are moving away from an exclusive focus on the individual's responsibility for a problem and are becoming more adept at interpreting crime in ways that account for the social contexts of offenders and their past experiences of trauma (drug courts are a well-studied example; Latimer et al., 2006). Thus, we are seeing a move away from the neoliberalism that characterised earlier resilience research. The earliest efforts to study resilience documented the exceptional few who did better than expected, and implied that their success could be reproduced if better understood. This initial work, however, was badly flawed, mostly because of its decontextualisation. It failed to account for different amounts of privilege and barriers to optimal human development, including access to justice. Many marginalised communities rejected resilience as a consequence, seeing it as an excuse for blaming victims of oppression who did not manage to 'beat the odds'.

Fortunately, a shift has occurred in how resilience is understood, a conceptualisation that is much closer to the way peacebuilding is now undertaken. Where we once imagined peace as an end state, a trait of a community that was no longer at war, peace and justice are now understood as processes that are a 'more open-ended or goal-free approach towards peacebuilding, where the focus is on the means or process, and the end-state is open to context-specific interpretations of peace' (de Coning, 2018: 301). It is this embrace of many good means to many good ends that makes resilience and efforts like transitional justice a good match.

Though all of this makes the resilience of legal systems and systems associated with transitional justice and peacebuilding seem unpredictable, these systems tend to reflect five principles when operating well. According to Ruhl et al. (2021: 517), these include the following:

1. *They are reliable.* When one component fails, a justice system can still maintain its resilience and function properly despite an unanticipated (or anticipated) stressor. This, in turn, means that subsystems (such as individuals seeking compensation) maintain their belief (a system of cognitions and socially constructed values) in the institutions that govern and regulate their lives.

2. *They are efficient.* They are not overly burdened by swollen bureaucracies that make seeking justice interminable or excessively expensive. They appear accessible to the individuals needing to use formal and informal legal systems, and they promise expedient resolution of conflict. A justice system like this will encourage compliance and be more sustainable if people do not feel the need to turn to vigilantism or other

forms of extra-judicial actions as when farmers arm themselves to protect their property from thieves.

3. *They are scalable.* As problems tend to affect multiple systems at multiple levels, a justice system that shows resilience will engage in processes across jurisdictions so that local processes that may appear less formal but instil a sense of fair treatment are not subsequently overturned by a court or other legislative body. For example, if a local restorative justice process resolves a criminal matter but the individual charged still faces sanctions beyond the community, the advantages of a resilient justice system at the local level quickly diminish.

4. *They are modular.* Justice systems show the most adaptability when there are multiple systems that can step in to resolve an issue should one system fail. In the case of environmental justice, where state governments in the United States have been lowering pollution standards to remain competitive for investment and jobs, it has taken the federal government to establish laws that are in the best interest of the country as a whole. The reverse is also true; when the federal government abdicates its responsibility to tackle challenges like climate change, it is state governments that have stepped in to press forward with legislation in areas like tailpipe emission standards (Vogel, 2018).

5. *They evolve.* Justice systems show resilience when they change as social contexts and natural environments put pressure on human systems. While not all justice systems need to evolve (national constitutions are meant to resist the vagaries of changing governments), laws and legal practices need to be malleable to respond to the exigencies of emerging crises, whether that is the mass migration of undocumented refugees or the need for adaptive peacebuilding efforts at a local or national level. Justice systems are most resilient when they embrace this tension between their ability to change and their need for stability over time.

Together, these five principles reflect much of what we know about resilience-promoting processes and the way justice systems like transitional justice or adaptive peacebuilding support adaptation and transformation when individuals and communities are placed under stress.

THE NEED FOR A BETTER UNDERSTANDING OF JUSTICE SYSTEMS AND RESILIENCE

Unfortunately, there has been limited research on resilience that is sufficiently complex to capture the interactions between systems at different scales. In practice, this means that we may study individual trauma and coping strategies but not investigate whether the quality or quantity of trauma confounds the efficacy of a transitional justice initiative, or for that matter whether cultural norms and indigeneity influence the reliability of formal legal systems in contexts of extreme poverty. Where such questions do arise, protective mechanisms tend to be studied at a single scale, while risk factors like coloniality are homogenised and controlled as a simple variable that is thought to affect everyone equally. The emerging science of resilience is changing this. It is showing the need to think about complex, interacting systems and how to best account for the relationship between risk exposure, protective processes (resilience) and outcomes across multiple systems at once.

In practice, this means understanding why communities might or might not work together to preserve a natural resource given past histories of collective trauma, gender norms, economic conditions, trust in government (and each other), identity and confidence in legal systems. The following brief case examples illustrate the need for multiple systems to show resilience if new regimes of peace and security are to result. The first example shows what can happen when there are no available means for economic or social justice, while the second example illustrates what happens when residents in a community under stress are treated more fairly and in ways that support both social and environmental justice.

Embalenhle The South African township of Embalenhle is within sight of one of the world's largest petrochemical processing plants operated by the state-owned corporation SASOL. With over 100,000 inhabitants, many of them economic migrants, Embalenhle is a chaotic mix of permanent homes, government-built shelters and informal tin-roofed shacks crisscrossed by a river choked with rubbish. The streets are dangerous, the schools woefully underfunded and in bad repair. SASOL, through a programme of corporate social responsibility, funds initiatives like libraries, sports centres and even public infrastructure like roads and sidewalks. Unfortunately, the level of mismanagement at the local and national government levels and people's general frustration with their social and economic marginalisation have resulted in frequent outbreaks of violence by residents, targeting municipal offices, the local mall and even the rubbish trucks that were meant to pick up the refuse (but were inefficient at the task).

In this environment, children make educational decisions that focus on securing work at the plant, choosing science courses whenever possible. Beyond the structural challenges, the local population deals with violence in the streets, high rates of substance abuse and the lack of family cohesion as one or both biological parents leave to find employment elsewhere. In this context, there is a general breakdown of social order, with elections fraught with violence and a general malaise when it comes to believing that institutional actors will make things better. Corruption creates daily hassles, with even sitting an entrance exam to a local college requiring a bribe. The police are perceived as exploitive and a threat.

Though South Africa is a society that holds collectivist values, young people have adopted a more competitive attitude when interacting with others beyond their families. In this context where fair treatment is perceived as unattainable, there are few opportunities for resilience to occur, or for formal and informal justice systems to be perceived as trustworthy and supportive. Psychological trauma, threats to physical health (including pollution), inadequacies of the educational system and a lack of government or legal institutions that function optimally have left the population largely unable to move forward. The few individuals that do succeed do so as a consequence of exceptional talent or personality traits, rather than institutional supports available equally to all. At this time, there are very few ways for community members to experience economic justice or respect for their human rights within or beyond the institutions regulating their lives.

Ruhengeri This is a community adjacent to the Volcanoes National Park in Rwanda and part of a three-nation protected area that is home to the endangered mountain gorilla. At risk of extinction a decade ago, the population of gorillas has more than doubled to more than 1,000 animals. Both human encroachment on habitat and poaching have been stopped, in large part by strict enforcement of laws and a paramilitary force that protects the gorillas. All of this has been a deliberate plan to ensure communities closest to the park benefit from the efforts to protect the animals, reflecting a form of environmental justice in which those whose lands are being used benefit from their use. In the case of Ruhengeri, a percentage of the money paid by tourists to trek and view the gorillas is used for community development across the region. Locals are hired as guides and porters, rangers and security forces. There is also a growing network of hotels, as well as work for drivers and others involved in the tourism industry. While it is debatable whether this kind of development, which caters to the very wealthy from other countries, is beneficial to Rwanda, and whether it spurs sustainable growth, the government has proceeded with this approach. The result is some obvious economic benefits to the local population and an even bigger positive impact on the mountain gorilla's ecosystem.

To understand the resilience of a community like this, one needs a theory of change that accounts for what is occurring rather than one that describes static outcomes (Valters et al., 2016). As conditions have changed for people, and with recognition for their histories, culture and context, which include the recent experience of genocide, structural inequality, colonisation and lack of environmental justice, one sees that the right solution for resilience has to be carefully adapted and implemented (no such efforts for justice other than popular uprisings are in evidence in Embalenhle). Even though success is possible, there is a level of uncertainty as complex personal, social and institutional systems respond to pressing challenges like environmental and economic justice. This means that resilience, like processes of transitional justice, must be responsive to previous risk exposures and local exigencies, but it must also be driven by adherence to principles that make the model useable even if outcomes vary. Thus, one community's solution to poaching and environmental injustice post-conflict is unlikely to suit another if historical and economic conditions and incentives are different. As de Coning (2018) explains, there needs to be a shift from a focus on ends (and their replication) to means (and their nuanced adaptation to context).

CONCLUSION

The concept of resilience is gaining traction in the discourse surrounding concepts like justice and peacebuilding, though it is not yet widely understood. When applied, the term 'resilience' refers to the capacity of individuals to succeed because internal and external systems work together to help people achieve their potential. Resilience also includes the capacity of these systems (including systems of justice) to demonstrate robustness and cohesion with other systems to maintain themselves, despite social and economic disruptions or natural disasters. There are multiple processes that produce resilience, depending on the environment in which individuals, communities and institutions are struggling to cope. Whether a system persists, resists, recovers, adapts or transforms is a reflection of the resources available and the discourses that define success. Protective and promotive processes need not be focused on a single end, nor can we predict with certainty how a change in intervention, public policy or transitional justice process is going to affect all members of a community. Resilience is, however, a concept that describes complex series of interactions across multiple systems and at different scales. To the extent that transitional justice, peacebuilding and legal mechanisms are adaptive and flexible with regards to the goals that they seek to achieve, the more likely resilience is to be experienced by individuals and their communities.

REFERENCES

Adger, W. N., Barnett, J., Brown, K., Marshall, N. and O'Brien, K. (2013). Cultural dimensions of climate change impacts and adaptation. *Nature Climate Change*, 3 (2), 112–117.

Anthony, E. J. and Cohler, B. J. (1987). *The Invulnerable Child*. New York: The Guilford Press.

Antonovsky, A. (1996). The salutogenic model as a theory to guide health promotion. *Health Promotion International*, 11(1), 11–18.

Atallah, D. G., Bacigalupe, G. and Repetto, P. (2019). Centering at the margins: Critical community resilience praxis. *Journal of Humanistic Psychology*, https://doi .org/10.1177/0022167818825305

Atallah, D. G., Contreras Painemal, C., Albornoz, L., Salgado, F. and Pilquil Lizama, E. (2018). Engaging critical community resilience praxis: A qualitative study with Mapuche communities in Chile facing structural racism and disasters. *Journal of Community Psychology*, 46(5), 575–597.

Beah, I. (2007). *A Long Way Gone: Memoirs of a Boy Soldier*. Vancouver, BC: Douglas & MacIntyre.

Belsky, J. and van Ijzendoorn, M. H. (2015). What works for whom? Genetic moderation of intervention efficacy. *Development and Psychopathology*, 27(1), 1–6.

Biggs, R., Schlüter, M., Biggs, D., Bohensky, E. L., BurnSilver, S., Cundill, G., Dakos, V., Daw, T. M., Evans, L. S., Kotschy, K., Leitch, A. M., Meek, C., Quinlan, A., Raudsepp-Hearne, C., Robards, M. D., Schoon, M. L., Schultz, L. and West, P. C. (2012). Toward principles for enhancing the resilience of ecosystem services. *Annual Review of Environment and Resources*, 37, 421–448.

Birgden, A., Arrigo, B. and Ward, T. (2015). Maximizing desistance: Adding therapeutic jurisprudence and human rights to the mix. *Criminal Justice and Behavior*, 42(1), 19–31.

Blackstock, C. (2016). Toward the full and proper implementation of Jordan's principle: An elusive goal to date. *Paediatric Child Health*, 21(5), 245–246.

Bush, N. R. and Boyce, W. T. (2016). Differential sensitivity to context: Implications for developmental psychopathology. In D. Cicchetti (ed.), *Developmental Psychopathology*, 3rd ed., vol. 2. Hoboken, NJ: John Wiley, pp. 107–137.

Clark, J. N. (2014). *International Trials and Reconciliation: Assessing the Impact of the International Criminal Tribunal for the Former Yugoslavia*. Abingdon: Routledge.

de Coning, C. (2018). Adaptive peacebuilding. *International Affairs*, 94(2), 301–317.

Crane, M. F. (ed.) (2017). *Managing for Resilience: A Practical Guide for Employee Wellbeing and Organizational Performance*. London: Routledge.

Craps, S. (2013) *Postcolonial Witnessing: Trauma Out of Bounds*. London: Palgrave Macmillan.

Cutter, S. L., Emrich, C. T., Mitchell, J. T., Piegorsch, W. W., Smith, M. M. and Weber, L. (2014). *Hurricane Katrina and the Forgotten Coast of Mississippi*. Cambridge: Cambridge University Press.

Doak, J. (2011). The therapeutic dimension of transitional justice: Emotional repair and victim satisfaction in international trials and truth commissions. *International Criminal Law Review*, 11(2), 263–298.

Gotham, K. F. and Campanella, R. (2013). Constructions of resilience: Ethnoracial diversity, inequality and post-Katrina recovery, the case of New Orleans. *Social Sciences*, 2(4), 298–317.

Hall, P. A. and Lamont, M. (eds.) (2013). *Social Resilience in the Neo-Liberal Era.* New York: Cambridge University Press.

Hobfoll, S. (2011). Conservation of resources theory: Its implication for stress, health and resilience. In S. Folkman (ed.), *The Oxford Handbook of Stress, Health and Coping*. New York: Oxford University Press, pp. 127–147.

Latimer, J., Morton-Bourgon, K. and Chrétien, J. A. (2006). *A Meta-Analytic Examination of Drug Treatment Courts: Do they Reduce Recidivism?* Ottawa, ON: Research and Statistics Division, Department of Justice.

Mahdiani, H., Höltge, J., Theron, L. and Ungar, M. (2020). Resilience in times of economic boom and bust: A narrative study of a rural population dependent upon the oil and gas industry. *Journal of Adult Development*, https://doi.org/10.1007/s10804-020-09363-z

Mittelmark, M. B., Bull, T., Daniel, M. and Urke, H. (2017). Specific resistance resources in the salutogenic model of health. In M. B. Mittelmark, S. Sagy, M. Eriksson, G. F. Bauer, J. Pelikan, B. Lindström and G. A. Espnes (eds.), *The Handbook of Salutogenesis*. New York: Springer, pp. 71–76.

Murray, J., Webb, T. E. and Wheatley, S. (2019). *Complexity Theory and Law: Mapping an Emergent Jurisprudence*. Abingdon: Routledge.

Parreñas, R. S. (2000). Migrant Filipina domestic workers and the international division of reproductive labor. *Gender and Society*, 14(4), 560–580.

Rea, K., Dinan, T. G. and Cryan, J. F. (2016). The microbiome: A key regulator of stress and neuroinflammation. *Neurobiology of Stress*, 4(4), 23–33.

Rudin, J. (2018). *Aboriginal Peoples and the Criminal Justice System*. Toronto, ON: Emond Publishing.

Ruhl, J. B., Cosens, B. and Soininen, N. (2021). Resilience of legal systems: Towards adaptive governance. In M. Ungar (ed.), *Multisystemic Resilience: Adaptation and Transformation in Contexts of Change*. New York: Oxford University Press, pp. 509–529.

Sanders, J., Munford, R., Thimasarn-Anwar, T., Liebenberg, L. and Ungar, M. (2015). The role of positive youth development practices in building resilience and enhancing wellbeing for at-risk youth. *Child Abuse & Neglect*, 42, 40–53.

Searcey, D. (2019). Left behind by migrant husbands, women break the rules and go to work. *New York Times*. www.nytimes.com/2019/12/30/world/africa/migrants-women-work.html (accessed 3 February 2020).

Sinalo, C. W. (2018). *Rwanda after Genocide: Gender, Identity and Post-Traumatic Growth*. Cambridge: Cambridge University Press.

Southwick, S. M., Bonanno, G. A., Masten, A. S., Panter-Brick, C. and Yehuda, R. (2014). Resilience definitions, theory, and challenges: Interdisciplinary perspectives. *European Journal of Psychotraumatology*, 5(1), 1–14.

Tedeschi, R. G. and Calhoun, L. G. (2004). Posttraumatic growth: Conceptual foundations and empirical evidence. *Psychological Inquiry*, 15(1), 1–18.

Ungar, M. (2011). The social ecology of resilience: Addressing contextual and cultural ambiguity of a nascent construct. *American Journal of Orthopsychiatry*, 81(1), 1–17.

Ungar, M. (2015). Social ecological complexity and resilience processes. *Behavioral and Brain Sciences*, 38, 50–51.

Ungar, M. (2017). Which counts more? The differential impact of the environment or the differential susceptibility of the individual? *British Journal of Social Work*, 47(5), 1279–1289.

Ungar, M. (2018). Systemic resilience: Principles and processes for a science of change in contexts of adversity. *Ecology and Society*, 23(4), 34.

Ungar, M. and Theron, L. (2020). Resilience and mental health: How multisystemic processes contribute to positive outcomes. *The Lancet Psychiatry*, 7(5), 441–448.

Valters, C., Cummings, C. and Nixon, H. (2016). *Putting Learning at the Centre: Adaptive Development Programming in Practice*. London: Overseas Development Institute.

Van Breda, A. D. and Theron, L. C. (2018). A critical review of South African child and youth resilience studies, 2009–2017. *Child and Youth Services Review*, 91, 237–247.

Vogel, D. (2018). *California Greenin': How the Golden State Became an Environmental Leader*. Princeton, NJ: Princeton University Press.

Westover, T. (2018). *Educated*. Toronto, ON: HarperCollins.

Wexler, D. B. (2008). Two decades of therapeutic jurisprudence. *Touro Law Review*, 24, 17–30.

Wiesel, E. (1956). *Night*. New York: Hill & Wang.

Winick, B. J. (2009). Foreword: Therapeutic jurisprudence perspectives on dealing with victims of crime. *Nova Law Review*, 33, 535–544.

Xu, L. and Kajikawa, Y. (2017). An integrated framework for resilience research: A systematic review based on citation network analysis. *Sustainability Science*, 13 (1), 235–254.

Zolli, A. (2012). *Resilience: Why Things Bounce Back*. Toronto, ON: Simon & Schuster.

2

Conceptualising Resilience in the Context of Transitional Justice

Wendy Lambourne

This chapter reflects on the implications of resilience thinking for transitional justice as a transformative process that contributes to adaptive peacebuilding. Recognising that resilience is highly relevant to a number of core transitional justice goals, including the re-establishment of the rule of law, peace and reconciliation, it discusses how the concept creates a space for new thinking about transitional justice. In so doing, it explores the extent to which transitional justice processes affect and engage with multiple interacting systems in ways that can foster resilience and adaptive capacity across these systems and the relationships that underpin them.

The chapter examines how each of the primary state-based mechanisms of transitional justice – namely, criminal trials, truth commissions and reparations – might contribute to systemic societal resilience, notwithstanding their limitations, and discusses their potential for healing divisions and building relationships to support resilient social structures. It also considers how more community-driven facilitated justice processes, including traditional customary practices and psychosocial programmes, can expand the basis for building resilient communities and systems.

As part of this analysis, the chapter provides a critical appraisal of the overall approach to transitional justice that has dominated the field, considering transformative justice as an alternative perspective that challenges a politico-legal, state-based, backward-looking retributive framework. It argues that resilience thinking supports a greater focus on psychosocial, community-based, forward-looking restorative approaches to transitional justice, consistent with the transformative turn in the field (Gready and Robins, 2014; Lambourne, 2014a). This is demonstrated by exploring different understandings of justice, how they are pursued in the context of transitional justice and what they mean for building resilient societies after mass violence and human rights violations. The chapter concludes by reflecting on the potential for a transformative approach to transitional justice consistent with building resilience to support adaptive peacebuilding in practice.

UNDERSTANDING TRANSITIONAL JUSTICE AND TYPES OF JUSTICE

Transitional justice can be defined as a process intended to provide justice for mass human rights violations committed in the context of war or a past autocratic regime. The idea of 'transition' is key – from a past where human rights were violated with impunity to a future characterised by democracy and the rule of law, which, in turn, is assumed to lead to the protection of human rights (International Center for Transitional Justice, 2001). In the context of post-war transitions, the goals of transitional justice are more explicitly linked to peacebuilding, going beyond democracy and the rule of law to the pursuit of truth, reconciliation and institutional reform (United Nations [UN], 2004).

However, in some cases, transitional justice processes are also implemented in periods of non-transition, where justice is sought for ongoing mass human rights violations or where the regime that committed the violations in the past is still in place. Winter (2014), moreover, argues for a political theory of transitional justice that applies to the context of authorised wrongdoings by established democracies (such as those perpetrated against Japanese Americans during World War II). Transitional justice thinking has therefore been applied to situations of ongoing colonial and post-colonial oppression, including the treatment of Indigenous peoples by settler societies, such as in Canada where a Truth and Reconciliation Commission (TRC) on Indian residential schools was established in 2008 (Nagy, 2013; Niezen, 2013).

What transitional justice might look like thus varies across different settings. There might be a focus on retributive justice to punish those accused of committing mass atrocities as a means of ensuring non-repetition, as high-lighted by the example of the International Criminal Tribunal for the former Yugoslavia (ICTY). Alternatively, the main priority might be restorative justice and/or reconciliation, with the aim of healing individuals and rebuilding relationships and communities; the TRC set up in post-apartheid South Africa is just one example. Some transitional processes involve a combination of both retributive and restorative justice. In Sierra Leone, a Special Court and a TRC operated alongside each other; and in Rwanda, the traditional gacaca community justice process (see Chapter 4) that combined retributive and restorative justice aims was adapted to deal with the crimes of the genocide.

Reparative justice, another key approach to justice, seeks to repair the damage of the past through measures such as payment of compensation to victims or collective reparations in the form of projects to benefit the community. An example of reparative justice is the moral reparations pursued in the framework of the Extraordinary Chambers in the Courts of Cambodia (ECCC) in relation to human rights violations committed by the Khmer Rouge regime (see Chapter 7). Teitel (2000: 119) lists a number of measures that can be classified as contributing to what she calls reparatory justice, including reparations, damages, remedies, redress, restitution, compensation, rehabilitation and tribute.

With a more forward-oriented focus, distributive or socio-economic justice has been identified as important for building a future that goes beyond protecting civil and political rights and also addresses cultural, social and economic rights (Lambourne, 2014a; Mani, 2002). This is consistent with building a 'positive peace' that addresses the root causes of conflict and promotes a more politically and socio-economically just future, rather than simply a 'negative peace' that seeks to end the direct violence of war and mass atrocities (Galtung, 1969). Guatemala has been cited as an example where this approach was prioritised and where the pursuit of accountability for the crimes of former leaders existed alongside institutional and socio-economic provisions aimed at addressing the underlying causes of the conflict (Mani, 2002: 165).

The term 'historical justice' is used to encompass situations where the focus is not on transition per se, but rather on seeking redress for historical wrongs that are transmitted across generations through collective memory and memory practices. Examples include abuses committed in the context of colonisation and human rights violations against Indigenous peoples (Neumann and Thompson, 2015). Teitel (2000) uses historical justice as a term to frame the need for truth – a need that is often the primary driver for the creation of different types of historical commissions or truth commissions as defined and examined in theory and practice by Hayner (2011). The pursuit of the truth in the form of an account of historical wrongdoings is frequently combined with a restorative or reconciliatory focus in the form of a TRC as a particular form of truth commission (Hayner, 2011: 12). The aforementioned TRCs in South Africa and Canada are two such examples that focused on revealing the truth and promoting reconciliation for past wrongs. Additionally, the concept of historical justice goes beyond the idea of individual criminal justice to recognise the need for collective forms of accountability to match the collective nature of the crimes committed (Teitel, 2000: 75). This may take the form of political justice or rectificatory or corrective justice (Butt, 2015: 171).

TRANSITIONAL JUSTICE AND PEACEBUILDING

Notwithstanding the range of approaches to justice outlined above, transitional justice in practice has often been limited to a legal retributive approach, especially where practitioners follow the model of transitional justice promulgated by the UN (2004, 2010). Transitional justice, as part of a post-conflict peacebuilding agenda, has been pursued by the UN based on a 'one-size-fits-all' model of liberal democratic reforms and mechanisms designed to support individual accountability and the rule of law. The perception of a duty to prosecute in international law, as espoused by Orentlicher (1997, 2007), has manifested in a commitment to international criminal justice as the primary means of implementing transitional justice – what Drumbl (2002: 8) has described as the 'hegemonic imperative to implement criminal trials' and Sikkink (2011) later characterised as the 'justice cascade'.

Under international criminal law, criminal responsibility is assigned to individuals for particularly serious violations of human rights defined in international law as war crimes, crimes against humanity and genocide (sometimes grouped together as mass atrocity crimes). These international mass atrocity crimes can be prosecuted in international, hybrid (a mixture of international and national laws) or regional courts, or in national courts where states have enacted domestic legislation to criminalise such violations of human rights and the laws of war. They can also be prosecuted under the provisions of universal jurisdiction.

Following the precedent of the post-World War II trials at Nuremberg and in Tokyo, the two ad hoc international criminal tribunals for the former Yugoslavia and Rwanda, respectively, were created by the UN Security Council in the early 1990s, when the freedoms of the end of the Cold War enabled agreement to be reached on such measures intended to restore international peace and security. International prosecutions have been pursued as part of transitional justice in order to provide accountability for past atrocities, build peace and prevent future atrocities through combating impunity and promoting justice, reconciliation and the rule of law, at least in theory, if not in practice (UN, 2004).

The 'duty to prosecute' was derived from the 'right to justice', which former French jurist and human rights defender Louis Joinet determined was one of four 'Principles against Impunity' in his famous report to the UN Human Rights Commission (UN, 1997). These four principles – namely, the right to know, the right to justice, the right to reparation and guarantees of non-recurrence – were translated into the UN's four key pillars of transitional justice: prosecution initiatives, truth-seeking processes, reparation programmes and institutional reform (UN, 2010). In this politico-legal context, justice is assumed to mean legal justice in the form of prosecutions and punishment (i.e., retributive justice), which is intended to deter future war criminals and thus contribute to the fourth aforementioned principle of guarantees of non-recurrence. From this perspective, the future orientation of transitional justice is thus limited to rebuilding the rule of law and implementing institutional reform as a further means of ensuring non-repetition of past human rights violations.

However, while the 'right to justice' has been seen as paramount by the UN and other international actors, including the International Center for Transitional Justice (ICTJ), the 'right to know' through truth-seeking processes has also risen to prominence in the form of the truth commission (Hayner, 2011). The truth commission, like the criminal court or tribunal, is a mechanism representing a programmatic approach to transitional justice adopted by countries in order to deal with a history of past mass human rights violations, with or without the involvement of the international community. Originally associated with amnesties and the perpetuation of a culture of impunity, the early truth commissions of the 1990s were seen as representing a political compromise of revealing the truth in exchange for justice where 'political resistance to accountability was high' (Hayner, 2011: 91). A clear example of this is the case of El Salvador, where a blanket amnesty was passed into law following the release of the country's truth commission report in 1993 (Hayner, 2011: 102). In other cases, de facto blanket amnesties would result when no formal transitional justice was pursued, such as in post-civil war Angola and Mozambique (Olsen et al., 2010: 40).

The South African TRC, with its innovative approach of providing individual conditional amnesty rather than blanket amnesty (Hayner, 2011: 29), challenged this perception of compromise between justice and truth. Its emphasis on restorative justice as an alternative form of justice took a more forward-looking approach, aimed at rebuilding a new 'rainbow nation' by transforming the relationship between black and white South Africans through healing, forgiveness and reconciliation (Tutu, 1999: 51–52). The South African TRC also expanded notions of truth beyond victims' right to know the factual and forensic truth of what happened, to their own narrative truths and personal stories of what happened to them. By providing a public space for the expression of these personal/narrative truths, the South African TRC was seen as facilitating the creation of a shared social or dialogical truth that contributed to an experience of restorative or healing truth, thus expanding the 'right to know' from a historical concept to a future-oriented process of healing and reconciliation (Boraine, 2006).

As outlined by Hayner (2011), most truth commissions subsequently have called for prosecutions in their final report, and the use of amnesties has become less common, even though the political constraints on pursuing accountability have remained in such countries as Burundi and Sri Lanka, where truth commissions have been established but a culture of impunity prevails. In other cases, truth commissions have not precluded the pursuit of criminal prosecutions, as in post-civil war Sierra Leone (Ainley et al., 2015).

The 'right to reparation' has similarly undergone an evolution in transitional justice, from the original focus on seeking material compensation and payments to individuals through reparation programmes to a more pragmatic emphasis on the concept of moral or collective reparations, as illustrated by the example of the ECCC mentioned earlier. Laplante (2014) offers a justice continuum model of reparations, which starts at the narrowest end with reparative justice linked to the classical tradition of corrective justice through civil remedies or material compensation for specific harms or losses, as pursued in a number of cases including Chile and Morocco. Next in the continuum is restorative justice, involving the participation of victims as stakeholders and a focus on restoring their dignity and local ownership in the reparations process, as seen in many traditional customary practices, such as the *nahe biti* process incorporated into the East Timorese Commission for Reception, Truth and Reconciliation (CAVR) (Babo-Soares, 2004). This is followed by what Laplante (2014: 74) identifies as a civic justice approach, which moves beyond the micro-level reconciliation inherent in the restorative justice approach to a focus on the macro-level relationship 'between the government and the governed' and the potential for political transformation, as seen in the Peruvian reparations programme. Finally, at the broadest end of the spectrum, socio-economic justice, according to Laplante (2014: 77), provides the opportunity for reparations to 'remedy historical social and economic inequalities' and contribute to distributive justice that links directly to the goals of sustainable peacebuilding and transformative justice (Lambourne, 2009, 2014a), as discussed later in this chapter.

Despite developments in transitional justice focusing on broader understandings of truth, justice and reparations that are more consistent with building peace and reconciliation, they have remained secondary to the overriding imperative to pursue retributive justice and factual/forensic truth through criminal prosecutions as a means of fulfilling the 'right to justice' principle. There are, however, signs that this could be changing if transitional justice follows the same path as peacebuilding in its turn away from liberal democratic programmatic responses towards a more pragmatic approach associated with building local resilience to future crises (Chandler, 2017; de

Coning, 2016; Juncos and Joseph, 2020). As explained by de Coning (2016: 167), this new focus on pragmatic peacebuilding:

> ... is shifting the debate away from liberal top-down problem-solving approaches towards more pluralistic bottom-up, or hybrid, conflict management approaches that do not have the ambition to resolve conflict, but instead invest in the resilience of local social institutions to prevent, cope with and recover from conflict, i.e. to sustain peace.

This so-called pragmatic turn in peacebuilding can be related to the 'transformative turn' in transitional justice, in which scholars have proposed alternative approaches to justice that go beyond those promulgated by the UN's model of transitional justice with its emphasis on programmatic responses to support the four key pillars – prosecutions, truth, reparations and institutional reform. Accordingly, before moving to a discussion about the implications of different types of resilience thinking for transitional justice, the next section will first examine how notions of transformative justice have evolved to challenge the dominant politico-legal, prosecutorial approach to transitional justice.

THE TRANSFORMATIVE TURN IN TRANSITIONAL JUSTICE

Daly (2002) first proposed the idea of transformative justice as a means of recognising the transformative agenda inherent in transitional justice and supporting the social transformation necessary to meet the goals of reconciliation and deterrence. According to her:

> Simply changing the governors won't cure a problem that resides as well in the governed. ... This entails not just a transition, but rather a transformation. Transition suggests movement from one thing to another – from oppression to liberation, from oligarchy to democracy, from lawlessness to due process, from injustice to justice. Transformation, however, suggests that the thing that is moving from one place to another is itself changing as it proceeds through the transition; it can be thought of as radical change (Daly, 2002: 74).

As part of this transformative agenda, Daly (2002) proposed the need to consider other forms of response extending beyond retributive justice for individual harms to address different types of injustices – including collective economic or political injustices, as in South Africa. Lambourne (2009, 2014a) built on this idea of a transformative agenda to incorporate different types of justice in her model of transformative justice: legal (including both retributive and restorative) justice; socio-economic justice; political justice; and psychosocial justice and healing derived from truth, comprising both knowledge of what happened and acknowledgement that what happened was wrong.

Similar to Daly (2002: 92), Lambourne's model (2009, 2014a) was predicated on the need for a transformation that goes beyond the narrow confines of a transitional moment to a more pervasive transformation of society that would respond to the priorities of a particular cultural and conflict context, consistent with Ungar's (2008) emphasis on the critical role of cultural context in determining levels of resilience in at-risk populations. More specifically, Lambourne's model of transformative justice underlined that justice must be seen as more than transitional. It must set up structures, institutions and relationships to promote transformation and sustainability (Lambourne, 2009, 2014a).

Both Daly's (2002) and Lambourne's (2009) work also emphasises reconciliation as a process and outcome. For Lambourne (2009), this means paying attention to relational or psychosocial as well as structural transformation, consistent with Lederach's (1995, 1997) theories of conflict transformation and peacebuilding. In considering how justice can contribute to building inclusive political communities after war and other mass violence, Mani (2002: 15) identifies peacebuilding as a dynamic, social and associative process 'that rebuilds fractured relationships between people'. However, in the face of ongoing controversy about the definition of reconciliation and its relevance to macro-level peacebuilding and transitional justice, reconciliation as a concept has been marginalised in the UN model and in subsequent transitional justice practice (Lambourne, 2014b; UN, 2010). Despite being mentioned as a goal in the UN Secretary-General's 2004 report to the UN Security Council on the rule of law and transitional justice (UN, 2004), it is notably absent from the four key pillars subsequently outlined by the UN (2010). However, in reflecting on the pragmatic turn in peacebuilding towards a focus on sustaining peace, the UN (2015) mentions the role of reconciliation in local communities and maintains that 'efforts to sustain peace must build upon [local] institutions and the resilience and reconciliation processes of local communities, and not undermine them'. This perspective on sustaining peace in practice is thus consistent with the transformative turn in transitional justice advocated by both Daly (2002: 92) and Lambourne (2014a).

Gready and Robins (2014) and Evans (2016) have proposed a narrower conception of transformative justice, based on a human rights perspective that argues for a greater emphasis on socio-economic rights in addition to civil and political rights, but without considering the potential for relational or psychosocial transformation proposed by Lambourne (2014a), and without placing the same accent on reconciliation as both Daly (2002) and

Lambourne (2014a). Gready and Robins (2019: 33) situate their proposal for a transformative approach to transitional justice within a critique of the foundational limitations of transitional justice, linking it to liberal and neo-liberal conceptions of human rights. They cite two strands of globalisation underpinning this critique: the privileging of 'liberal paradigms of civil and political rights through an emphasis on elections, procedural democracy, constitutionalism and the rule of law, and various backward-looking truth and justice measures' along with 'market-driven, neoliberal economics' (Gready and Robins, 2019: 33).

McAuliffe (2017) underscores the potential of transformative justice for redressing the marginalisation of socio-economic issues as root causes of conflict (see also Evans, 2016). He explicitly links transformative justice to the local turn in peacebuilding and transitional justice, which he describes as promising in 'accordance with social needs, sustainability and transformation of social structures' (McAuliffe, 2017: 233). McAuliffe (2017: 246) cites examples of micro-level programmes developed independently of the state, such as *Fambul Tok* in Sierra Leone where a local and an international non-governmental organisation (NGO) collaborated to provide opportunities for village-level community healing and reconciliation following the civil war (Martin, 2020). *Fambul Tok* was later adapted to support local capacity-building in response to the failures of state institutions in responding to the Ebola crisis, focusing specifically on the importance of empowering local communities to self-organise as a means of sustaining peace (de Coning, 2016: 173). The example of *Fambul Tok* illustrates the potential for a transformative justice framework to address structural violence, thereby contributing to the building of community resilience – defined by Saul (2014: 8) as 'a community's capacity, hope and faith to withstand major trauma and loss, overcome adversity, and to prevail, usually with increased resources, competence and connectedness'.

Transformative justice theories thus criticise the emphasis on top-down, elite-driven policies and programmes implemented as part of transitional justice and focus more on the needs and priorities of the local affected communities (Evans, 2019). According to Gready and Robins (2014: 340), 'transformative justice entails a shift in focus from the legal to the social and political, and from the state and institutions to communities and everyday concerns'. Accordingly, and consistent with resilience thinking, 'transformative justice is not the result of a top-down imposition of external legal frameworks or institutional templates, but of a more bottom-up understanding and analysis of the lives and needs of populations' (Gready and Robins, 2014: 340).

Lambourne (2009, 2014a) developed her model of transformative justice inductively[1] by studying and listening to the voices of survivors of mass violence and atrocities who identified the types of justice that were important to them, and by observing micro-level peacebuilding and community practices that focus on healing and reconciliation (Lambourne and Niyonzima, 2016). The lived realities of affected communities suggest that transitional justice at the formal, elite level of tribunals and truth commissions is insufficient to meet their justice needs and interests (Lambourne, 2014a, 2014c). Local communities recognise the need to live together after mass violence and human rights violations and to focus therefore on pursuing programmes that build their socio-economic and psychosocial capacities. From a grassroots perspective, peace and reconciliation are no longer abstract concepts to be debated but essential means of survival, achieved through types of justice that build local resilience and do more to unite than to divide.

The local turn in transitional justice described here mirrors that in peacebuilding, with its focus on local participation and empowerment (Lambourne, 2014a; Robins, 2019). As such, it also invites the same criticisms regarding the lack of interrogation of the local – what it means and how it manifests in numerous guises which may or may not support a progressive agenda of equity, inclusiveness and participation at that local/community level. McAuliffe (2017: 283), for example, elaborates on the limits to the transformative potential of localised or bottom-up approaches to transitional justice and peacebuilding; 'peaceful individuals or peaceful communities do not automatically make peaceful societies or states'. According to him, the transformative process advocated by theorists such as Lambourne (2014a) and Evans (2016) does not in practice result in transformative outcomes because it ignores the realities of elite power over domestic politics. He argues that the inclusion of affected communities cannot in itself influence the policies and practices of elites and thus cannot transform socio-economic structures without a focus on what he calls the 'missing middle' and a process of vertical integration linking the local community with the state (McAuliffe, 2017: 280).

Robins (2019: 304) addresses this critique by suggesting that 'transformative participation demands an engagement of communities with institutions of the state and with national and international NGOs, that transforms the relationship from which it emerges'. This is another way of articulating the concept of relational transformation as advocated by Lambourne (2014a) in her model of

---

[1] Based on extensive fieldwork conducted over twenty years at different times in Burundi, Cambodia, East Timor, Rwanda, Sierra Leone and South Africa.

transformative justice – a process that transforms power relationships (see also Lambourne and Rodriguez Carreon, 2016: 90). While Waldorf (2012) has criticised transformative justice as being too all-encompassing and ambitious, Robins (2019) proposes a more transformative understanding of justice as emerging from social practice, rather than framed against an ideal of justice. 'This approach', he argues, 'perceives ideas of justice not as something circumscribed by legal instruments and a technocratic expert practice, but as emerging directly from action or struggle, created collectively and democratically in claimed spaces' (Robins, 2019: 302). Abe (2018) goes further, highlighting a more anarchical process at the local level that sees social recovery emerging from 'meaning-making' in accidental and ad hoc ways. The idea of 'planning for the unplanned' (Abe, 2018: 206) might sound paradoxical, yet is entirely consistent with resilience thinking and the notion of adapting to complexity and uncertainty (de Coning, 2018). Hoddy and Gready (2020: 3), meanwhile, situate transformative justice within a framework of critical social theory, systems thinking and complexity theory, claiming that:

> What is missing from this literature is the place of critical theorising in transformative practice, that is, where new knowledge is developed about the social systems where change is sought, and how these systems disempower and constrain, and how these features might be challenged.

Historical or intergenerational injustices also speak to the benefits of adding a transformative lens to ideas of transitional justice. Applying this lens to the legacies of colonialism and violations of Indigenous rights, for example, amplifies the intergenerational impacts of trauma and discrimination that affect the psychosocial well-being and socio-economic chances of subsequent generations. Maddison and Shepherd (2014) thus argue for an extension of the concept of transition, to enable proper accounting for colonial violence. In this way, they propose a post-colonial re-visioning of transitional justice that offers possibilities for deep social transformation at both the national and international levels.

The emergence of a transformative agenda for transitional justice has therefore turned a spotlight on local capacity building and systemic societal transformation, linked to the application of resilience thinking to transitional justice and peacebuilding. The psychosocial and relational aspects of transformative justice also speak to the potential contribution of a resilience-building approach to complement the more programmatic, institution-based agenda in transitional justice, albeit subject to potential critique if they focus only on supporting communities to adapt to crises – rather than taking steps to remove the sources and prevent such crises from recurring.

RESILIENCE THINKING, TRANSITIONAL JUSTICE
AND TRANSFORMATION

The emergence of resilience thinking reflects the shift from a programmatic liberal peacebuilding model to a more pragmatic or adaptive means of rebuilding the capacity of societies to respond to complexity and uncertainty (de Coning, 2018). In the field of transitional justice, scholars have just begun to grapple with the relevance and risks associated with different conceptualisations of resilience (Kastner, 2020; Wiebelhaus-Brahm, 2017). While resilience thinking may seem consistent with the transformative turn in transitional justice, it too has been criticised as prioritising localised bottom-up approaches that cannot succeed in the face of elite intransigence and continuing politico-legal and socio-economic structures of discrimination and oppression (Chandler, 2020).

Yet, at the same time, localised transformative processes can help build individual and community resilience to better deal with surrounding threats from elite actors and state-level institutions, which, through active oppression or neglect, undermine the well-being of local communities. In this sense, emerging understandings of resilience as a negotiated process which is sensitive to contextualised challenges have become increasingly relevant to adaptive peacebuilding efforts which are synonymous with new ways of doing transitional justice. As Kastner argues (2020: 383), a resilience approach to transitional justice 'shifts the focus from short-term objectives, such as obtaining a certain number of convictions before a criminal tribunal, to gradually (re)building relationships and social capital', consistent with models of transformative justice discussed in the previous section. As the chapters in this volume show, these efforts can begin at the level of individuals and communities who resist oppressive definitions of their experiences of injustice (see, for example, Nayanika Mookherjee's discussion of Bangladesh's *birangonas* or 'war heroines', Chapter 6), or they can be led by governments aiming to restore social and political stability.

At its simplest level, resilience is about the ability of systems – whether social, economic, political or environmental systems – to recover from crises (Ungar, 2021). Juncos and Joseph (2020: 294) cite the systemic approach of resilience thinking as an advantage over standard liberal peacebuilding as it 'goes beyond the project-driven and silo approaches of the past towards the transformation of entire systems or regimes'. As Ungar's explanation of a social-ecological definition of resilience in Chapter 1 shows, applying resilience thinking to the peacebuilding and transitional justice context raises the possibility that addressing the sources of resilience at multiple systemic levels is critical to both individual and societal recovery and transformation post-conflict.

There is a danger, however, with using resilience as a principle for societal reconstruction and justice. Just as the transformative turn in transitional justice has caused some to focus too much on local capacities to manage threats and adapt to complexity and change, a decontextualised, highly psychologised conception of personal resilience ignores power relations and fails to engage with the root causes of vulnerability (Kastner, 2020: 373). Adaptation, for example, can be seen as implying transformation at the micro level of individuals and local communities and a lack of focus on challenging the political and economic structures that contributed to the root causes of the violence, which is already something that is insufficiently addressed in transitional justice. Like transitional justice, resilience is better understood as a systemic process that implicates both individuals and the social and institutional structures that either oppress or liberate.

Ungar and Theron's (2020) ecological and multi-systemic model of resilience, referred to in the previous chapter, suggests new ways of thinking about transitional justice and its contribution to building democratic and peaceful futures – both incorporating yet also going beyond the turn to the local in peacebuilding and transitional justice. Transitional justice, although concerned with the past, must also focus on the future; while dealing with divisions from the past, it must build cooperative relationships for the future; while dealing with past crimes and root causes of violent conflict, it must heal wounds, redress harms, transform power relations and build new socio-economic and politico-legal structures that focus on attaining and protecting human rights in the future.

Therefore, the idea of resilience in relation to transitional justice is intimately connected with the liminal space of a transition towards peace and democracy. Resilience can be built through a willingness to take responsibility for the past, at the same time as reconciling with those who have committed atrocities. It involves embracing a future peaceful relationship between those defined as perpetrators and those defined as victims or survivors and committing to working together to build and maintain not only individual well-being, but also the social, political, legal, economic and environmental structures to support a sustainable peace with justice. This requires a reckoning with the past based on accountability and taking responsibility, combined with the willingness and strength – both individual and collective – to face, if not embrace, the possibility of a different future. In this sense, resilience, like peacebuilding and transitional justice, must attend to the transformation of multiple systems at once.

While this may be an argument in favour of integrating resilience thinking with approaches to transitional justice, Kastner (2020) offers a cautionary note. Resilience thinking can be in conflict with the transitional justice approach of dealing with the past in order to build a peaceful future. As he sees it, resilience is about breaking from the past, while transitional justice is explicitly concerned with such processes as establishing accountability, memorialising, repairing the damages and telling the truth about past experiences of human rights atrocities (Kastner, 2020: 369). Kastner (2020: 374) goes further, arguing that the traditional goals of transitional justice – 'revealing the truth, holding perpetrators accountable and trying to provide some sense of justice for the victims' – are 'made redundant in a resilience paradigm' that focuses only on the future rather than on addressing the past in order to build a better future. Furthermore, Kastner (2020: 374) maintains that 'resilient individuals and communities may never be able to address systemic factors or the responsibilities of external actors, which will largely remain beyond their scope of influence and "agential capacities"'.

Wiebelhaus-Brahm (2017: 159), meanwhile, retains a more optimistic perspective and concludes by arguing for a long-term commitment to the promotion of resilience and transitional justice as 'gradual, complex transformations' that are context-sensitive and understand existing capacities in order to respond with 'policy interventions that will address local needs'. By envisaging a long-term transformation, he is also tapping into the potential of a transformative justice approach that strives for structural transformation over and above individual and community resilience.

This potential is reflected in considerations of the relationship between resilience and peacebuilding. Pouligny (2014) proposes that we think of resilience as providing protective factors to counter-balance risk factors, as part of a dynamic process of experiencing and responding to violence at multiple systemic levels. As Pouligny (2014: 2) argues, 'violence transforms as much as it destroys. It creates new realities and forms of relationships'. Peacebuilding, seen as an intervention to support further transformation, thus plays a powerful role in the trajectory of post-violence relationships, as much as it does in transforming structures and institutions.

This broader societal resilience can be developed through giving attention to interventions that support the building of social cohesion and social capital, defined by Bourdieu as 'the aggregate of the actual or potential resources that are linked to the possession of a sustainable network of relationships' (cited in Saul, 2014: 10). The different dimensions of social capital are directly linked to protective factors that contribute to sustaining individual agency and empowerment in a context of strong and supportive inter-linkages horizontally within (bonding social capital) and between communities (bridging social capital), and vertically between individuals, communities and the state (linking social capital) (Bartolomei et al., 2013; Putnam, 2000). Relationships and social networks thus create the potential for social mobilisation, which, in turn, creates the possibility for social change, thus illustrating how individual and community resilience can contribute to building societal and state resilience.

Resilience is therefore more than a passive protective factor that enables individuals and communities to recover from stressful events such as mass violence. It also suggests an essential agentic quality that enables individuals and communities – and organisations – to adapt and evolve as necessary to maintain functionality beyond mere survival and to effect social change. This approach is reflected in Pouligny's (2014: 1) definition of societal resilience: 'the capacity of a group, community, or society at large to cope with stresses and disturbances as a result of social, political, and environmental change and adjust while still retaining essentially the same functions and feedbacks by the people'. She places emphasis on the resilience of a system based on its functions and capacities to perform, not on its stability.

According to Kastner (2020: 372), when resilience thinking is used in a more progressive way, it 'carries connotations of flexibility and reflexivity, capacity, agency and empowerment'; and, furthermore, it suggests that 'crises may even represent opportunities to implement innovative change'. At the same time, he points out that resilience thinking that focuses on 'flexibility, diversity and adaptive governance appears diametrically opposed to the currently dominant transitional justice paradigm' (Kastner, 2020: 382). Rather, it supports the local, participatory turn in transitional justice (McEvoy and McGregor, 2008; Shaw and Waldorf, 2010) that eschews a one-size-fits-all approach to imposing models of transitional justice and 'should be concerned with local understandings of justice and the transformative capacity of the individuals and communities primarily concerned' with a focus on 'facilitating, rather than producing, justice' (Kastner, 2020: 373). As Ungar explains in Chapter 1, resilience can describe a process of transformation that goes beyond recovery and adaptation, given that short-term survival strategies may be maladaptive and adaptation may not be consistent with long-term sustainability.

Civil society peacebuilding organisations have been leading the move towards a networked and transformative approach to resilience that is more applicable in the peacebuilding (and transitional justice) context and should serve to alleviate the risks associated with more traditional resilience thinking. The Geneva Peacebuilding Platform, for example, has focused on the network-driven, informal nature of peacebuilding, rather than the traditional system-based understanding of resilience inherited from other disciplines. The Platform suggests that 'the qualities that make up resilience ... involve dense patterns of trust networks, hybrid coalitions forged across a wide range of actors, shared narratives, common interests, multiple lines of communication, good leadership, and a commitment by local leaders to take risks for peace' (Geneva Peacebuilding Platform, 2013: 6). This is similar to a multi-systemic approach to resilience (Ungar and Theron, 2020).

The following section explores briefly the potential and limitations of different transitional justice mechanisms to build resilience. In so doing, it will take into account a number of key factors, as suggested by Pouligny's (2014: 3) proposed components of a resilient societal system: namely, psychosocial recovery, shared systems of meaning, solidarity among community members, community reintegration and trust, and broad and inclusive forms of governance.

TRANSITIONAL JUSTICE MECHANISMS AND RESILIENCE

Criminal trials

The organising and holding of criminal trials can contribute to building individual and community resilience, especially when those accused from a perpetrator group are found guilty and punished. For victims, the acknowledgement that they suffered wrongdoing and harm, and the experience of seeing the perpetrator/s held accountable and punished, can contribute to individual resilience. However, the criminal justice system is generally focused on individual accountability and deterrence rather than systemic transformation, making it incomplete as a resilience-building approach. As suggested by Kastner (2020: 381), criminal trials in themselves may undermine resilience if they reinforce divisions in society. Moreover, Wiebelhaus-Brahm (2017: 156) suggests that they may strengthen bonding social capital within one societal group, but without bridging social capital between social groups.

By focusing on individual responsibility rather than collective guilt, criminal trials can help a society to move towards a kind of reconciliation where individuals can rebuild as citizens and survivors, rather than as victims and perpetrators. However, this is only likely to work if it is the leaders who are prosecuted and found individually criminally liable, leaving those remaining to rebuild relationships and functioning political, legal and societal structures. If there are large numbers of perpetrators among the general population, as in Rwanda after the genocide, for example, where thousands of accused *génocidaires* were imprisoned, a retributive, individual criminal accountability approach will be more likely to undermine resilience as it serves only to stigmatise and further divide victims and perpetrators. The Rwandan government recognised this and, rather than continuing to focus only on retributive justice through the domestic courts, it instituted several measures to promote restorative justice and reconciliation in order to rebuild the country on a more sustainable and resilient basis.

Retributive justice through criminal trials can also further re-traumatise victims and witnesses when they are required to re-tell or re-live the traumatic events. Ungar (Chapter 1) argues that 'criminal trials to address war crimes may become extremely divisive for communities, disrupting social cohesion or even traumatising some victims, even as they appear to re-establish order with regard to governance and the rule of law'. Janine Natalya Clark also demonstrates this in her chapter on Bosnia-Herzegovina (Chapter 3). Criminal trials can therefore sometimes do more to undermine than to build individual and community resilience.

Furthermore, the imposition of criminal prosecutions can be criticised as encroaching on local agency and participation, thereby undermining resilience. International criminal justice can be viewed as part of the neo-liberal agenda that values individual accountability through state-driven, top-down processes, rather than bottom-up, communitarian approaches to locally meaningful justice and reconciliation processes. On the other hand, there can be long-term local benefits of criminal prosecutions, especially in the context of nationally located hybrid courts – like the Special Court for Sierra Leone (SCSL) and the ECCC (UN, 2004: para. 44). International involvement in these hybrid courts has sought to strengthen domestic legal systems and judicial capacity in order to leave a lasting legacy.

The capacity-building legacy of such courts, therefore, can potentially contribute to building resilience through promotion of the rule of law, but only if supported by systemic political transformation and associated institutional reform. Considering hybrid courts' interaction with other systems suggests that politico-legal transformation alone is unlikely to have an impact on long-term resilience without attention to psychosocial transformation through healing and reconciliation and a holistic approach to transitional justice, as discussed earlier in relation to some models of transformative justice.

Truth commissions

Truth commission goals of truth-seeking, truth-telling and truth recovery – sometimes but not always alongside reconciliation in a TRC – can be seen as a means of supporting individual and community resilience by building social cohesion and social capital. As argued by Wiebelhaus-Brahm (2017), truth commissions that explicitly promote reconciliation can promote resilience through building empathy to support relational transformation and bridging social capital, at the same time as reinforcing bonding capital. Furthermore, truth commissions have the potential to support political and social change, through the implementation of report recommendations that address root causes and the need for structural transformation via institutional reform to underpin state and societal resilience.

Applying the four types of truth defined by the South African TRC, enabling victims to tell their story about what happened to them can enable a truth commission to compile a historical account of multiple personal/narrative truths that can shed light on the factual/forensic truth. It can also contribute to the establishment of a social/dialogical shared truth, and, potentially, to a healing/restorative truth, depending on the context of the particular truth commission.

Clark (2020) has argued that giving victims more opportunity to control how they tell their stories as part of a transitional justice process can assist with narrative plasticity, and hence with adaptability and resilience. Narrative plasticity is more likely to develop in bottom-up, community-based processes than in the kinds of mechanisms set up by governments and the international community, such as criminal tribunals and truth commissions. This is especially true in criminal trials, for example, where victims are only allowed to appear as witnesses (although proceedings at the ECCC and the International Criminal Court offer victims a more expansive role) and to respond to questions intended to establish the guilt or innocence of the accused. Even in truth commissions, the structure determines the way in which victims are able to tell their story, thereby limiting the potential resilience-building impact.

Reparations

Reparations can contribute to individual, community and societal resilience if they facilitate socio-economic justice for individuals and communities in order to meet their basic needs and ability to recover and adapt to crises. However, this is rarely the case in practice, as both perpetrators and states alike have failed in their capacity to adequately compensate victims for past material and psychological harms. Reparations are more likely to be symbolic than sufficiently meaningful to effect real change in the socio-economic realities of survivors of mass violence. Moral and collective reparations may be seen as having a greater potential for building resilience, such as in the case of the ECCC's provision of moral reparations in the form of trauma recovery programmes that support psychosocial healing and transformation (Lambourne, 2014c; see also Chapter 7). Another example was Peru's collective reparations programme that included financing small development projects, in addition to commemorative events for victims and survivors (Garcia-Godos, 2017: 194–195).

As previously discussed, a number of scholars have argued for distributive and socio-economic justice to be included as part of a transformative approach to transitional justice, in order to address root causes such as poverty and relative deprivation and the potential for future violence. Such an approach would be consistent with a transformative approach to resilience that avoids returning to a status quo of exploitative power relations and structures that inhibit individual agency and empowerment.

Indigenous customary practices

Customary practices may afford greater legitimacy than top-down, externally driven transitional justice mechanisms. By drawing on the strengths and capacities of local communities, traditional or customary practices both reflect and help to foster resilience. On the other hand, the implementation of customary practices can potentially undermine resilience, by entrenching existing inequalities and 'reinforcing patriarchy and further empowering illegitimate, ineffective power structures at the local level' (Wiebelhaus-Brahm, 2017: 157). They are also unlikely to be able to affect state or societal structures and institutions responsible for past and/or ongoing human rights violations unless accompanied by initiatives to strengthen linking as well as bonding and bridging social capital.

Traditional practices often focus on healing, reconciliation, reintegration and restoration of the community, and thus can contribute to both individual and community resilience. For example, in the context of the CAVR in Timor-Leste, the grassroots reconciliation process of *nahe biti* involved the perpetrator and victim sitting together and reaching a voluntary acceptance of culpability and agreement on reconciliation acts such as reparation, community service or public apology. *Nahe biti* is usually finalised with a symbolic exchange of 'betel nut' ceremony, to show sincerity and commitment, and is traditionally seen as a bridge to achieve a much greater aim of harmony and peace in the society. The *nahe biti* process included as part of the CAVR can thus be seen as a means of promoting social cohesion, bonding and bridging social capital to potentially support individual – and especially community – resilience as part of transitional justice and peacebuilding.

Psychosocial healing and reconciliation

Community-based psychosocial programmes such as Healing of Memories and Alternatives to Violence workshops run by the local NGO Trauma Healing and Reconciliation Services (THARS) in Burundi add to transitional justice and peacebuilding by supporting recovery from trauma, promoting forgiveness and reconciliation, and building empathy and social capital (Lambourne and Niyonzima, 2016). Such programmes thus can directly contribute to building individual and community resilience by promoting individual and collective healing (Saul, 2014).

Rather than conceptualising trauma as a mental illness to be treated through counselling and psychotherapy, a psychosocial healing approach recognises the interconnections between the individual and their relational and structural environment. Community-based psychosocial programmes, such as those pursued by THARS in Burundi, can be seen as assisting the individual to recover from trauma through the stages proposed by Herman (1997): by providing safety, acknowledgement and an opportunity to reconnect with others through sharing stories and activities that help to build empathy, hope and a shared commitment to a peaceful future together. Such psychosocial healing and relational transformation at the interpersonal and community level can potentially build resilience and contribute to transformative justice (Lambourne, 2014a).

According to Herman (1997: 183), acknowledgement, remembrance and mourning can help to transform traumatic memory by enabling survivors to tell or reconstruct the story in a safe or protected relationship or therapeutic space. Trauma-healing workshops can provide a similar function, in addition to enabling acknowledgement and reconnection through the community group process, thereby addressing the social and relational dimensions of the traumatic experience through helping to rebuild trust and empathy (Herman, 1997; Lambourne and Niyonzima, 2016). Such programmes can also provide the opportunity for survivors (including both victims and perpetrators) to regain their agency through social, economic and political empowerment and social action (Herman, 1997: 207; Lambourne and Niyonzima, 2016). This step can further contribute to sustaining resilience in communities through the transformation of relationships and building of linking social capital with local and political leaders, with the aim of affecting socio-economic and political transformation. However, the potential impact of such bottom-up processes in Burundi has been severely limited by the elite political control of governance structures and lack of political commitment to societal transformation to support peacebuilding and transitional justice.

CONCLUSION

This chapter has raised questions about the adequacy of the politico-legal transitional justice framework for promoting resilience in societies recovering from mass atrocities and human rights violations. The strong focus of transitional justice on criminal legal accountability for perpetrators of mass human rights violations and on rebuilding the rule of law to support a democratic political transition reflects the technical, programmatic approach to peacebuilding criticised by scholars such as de Coning (2018). Such an approach is insufficient on its own to promote resilience and adaptive peacebuilding. This chapter argues that socio-economic and psychosocial transformation are critical components of a transformative and networked resilience approach to transitional justice that addresses root causes, responds to the past trauma of mass atrocities and ongoing trauma of relative and absolute poverty and deprivation, and (re)builds relationships in communities and throughout the political system.

The chapter has explored some of the potential opportunities and risks associated with resilience thinking in relation to transitional justice and its connection with adaptive peacebuilding. It has also sought to demonstrate that building resilience is more a function of how transitional justice is approached than the content of any transitional justice programme. In other words, process is more important than the type of mechanism employed. A transformative approach to transitional justice incorporates this emphasis on process, consistent with scholarship that has argued for the importance of participation, agency and empowerment at the local level.

Questions remain, however, about how best to facilitate local participation in transitional justice and peacebuilding processes in the context of new resilience thinking. For example, what happens when facilitation of endogenous, locally driven approaches to building peace and justice is prioritised over local participation in elite-driven, state-based mechanisms, such as criminal trials and truth commissions? Can ideas of local community and individual resilience transcend traditional resilience thinking, in order to develop into a networked and transformative approach to peacebuilding and transitional justice that seeks to do more than 'bounce back' from crises and instead attempts to influence structural politico-legal and socio-economic transformation? Finally, how does this connect in practice with de Coning's (2018: 305) concept of adaptive peacebuilding as an iterative, relational and transformative process 'informed by concepts of complexity, resilience and local ownership'?

REFERENCES

Abe, T. (2018). *Unintended Consequences in Transitional Justice: Social Recovery at the Local Level.* Boulder, CO: Lynne Rienner.

Ainley, K., Friedman, R. and Mahony, C. (eds.) (2015). *Evaluating Transitional Justice: Accountability and Peacebuilding in Post-Conflict Sierra Leone.* London: Palgrave Macmillan.

Babo-Soares, D. (2004). Nahe biti: The philosophy and process of grassroots reconciliation (and justice) in East Timor. *Asia Pacific Journal of Anthropology*, 5 (1), 15–33.

Bartolomei, L., Pittaway, E. and Ward, K. (2013). 'The Glue that Binds': The Social Capital Evaluation Tool.* Sydney: STARTTS and UNSW Centre for Refugee Research.

Boraine, A. (2006). Defining transitional justice: Tolerance in the search for justice and peace. In A. Boraine and S. Valentine (eds.), *Transitional Justice and Human Security.* Cape Town: International Center for Transitional Justice, pp. 22–37.

Burgess, P. (2006). A new approach to restorative justice: East Timor's community reconciliation process. In N. Roht-Arriaza and J. Mariexcurrena (eds.), *Transitional Justice in the Twenty-First Century: Beyond Truth versus Justice.* Cambridge: Cambridge University Press, pp. 176–205.

Butt, D. (2015). Historical justice in postcolonial contexts. In K. Neumann and J. Thompson (eds.), *Historical Justice and Memory.* Madison, WI: University of Wisconsin Press, pp. 166–184.

Chandler, D. (2017). The rise of resilience. In *Peacebuilding: The Twenty Years' Crisis, 1997–2017.* Cham, Switzerland: Palgrave Macmillan/Springer, pp. 165–187.

Chandler, D. (2020). Security through societal resilience: Contemporary challenges in the Anthropocene. *Contemporary Security Policy*, 41(2), 195–214.

Clark, J. (2020). Storytelling, resilience and transitional justice: Reversing narrative social bulimia. *Theoretical Criminology*, https://doi.org/10.1177/1362480620933230

Daly, E. (2002). Transformative justice: Charting a path to reconciliation. *International Legal Perspectives*, 12(1–2), 73–183.

de Coning, C. (2016). From peacebuilding to sustaining peace: Implications of complexity for resilience and sustainability. *Resilience*, 4(3), 166–181.

de Coning, C. (2018). Adaptive peacebuilding. *International Affairs*, 94(2), 301–317.

Drumbl, M. A. (2002). Restorative justice and collective responsibility: Lessons for and from the Rwandan genocide. *Contemporary Justice Review*, 5(1), 5–22.

Evans, M. (2016). Structural violence, socioeconomic rights, and transformative justice. *Journal of Human Rights*, 15(1), 1–20.

Evans, M. (ed.) (2019). *Transitional and Transformative Justice: Critical and International Perspectives.* New York: Routledge.

Galtung, J. (1969). Violence, peace, and peace research. *Journal of Peace Research*, 6 (3), 167–191.

Garcia-Godos, J. (2017). Reparations. In O. Simic (ed.), *An Introduction to Transitional Justice.* London/New York: Routledge, pp. 177–200.

Geneva Peacebuilding Platform (2013). *Making Sense of Resilience in Peacebuilding Contexts: Approaches, Applications, Implications.* Geneva: Geneva Peacebuilding Platform.

Gready, P. and Robins, S. (2014). From transitional to transformative justice: An agenda for practice. *International Journal of Transitional Justice*, 8(3), 339–361.

Gready, P. and Robins, S. (eds.) (2019). *From Transitional to Transformative Justice*. Cambridge: Cambridge University Press.

Hayner, P. B. (2011). *Unspeakable Truths: Transitional Justice and the Challenge of Truth Commissions*. New York/London: Routledge.

Herman, J. (1997). *Trauma and Recovery: The Aftermath of Violence – From Domestic Abuse to Political Terror*. New York: Basic Books.

Hoddy, E. T. and Gready, P. (2020). From agency to root causes: Addressing structural barriers to transformative justice in transitional and post-conflict settings. *Contemporary Social Science*, https://doi.org/10.1080/21582041.2020.1812706

International Center for Transitional Justice (2001). What is transitional justice? www.ictj.org/about/transitional-justice (accessed 28 October 2020).

Juncos, A. E. and Joseph, J. (2020). Resilient peace: Exploring the theory and practice of resilience in peacebuilding interventions. *Journal of Intervention and Statebuilding*, 14(3), 289–302.

Kastner, P. (2020). A resilience approach to transitional justice? *Journal of Intervention and Statebuilding*, 14(3), 368–388.

Lambourne, W. (2009). Transitional justice and peacebuilding. *International Journal of Transitional Justice*, 3(1), 28–48.

Lambourne, W. (2014a). Transformative justice, reconciliation and peacebuilding. In S. Buckley Zistel, T. Koloma Beck, C. Braun and F. Mieth (eds.), *Transitional Justice Theories*. New York: Routledge, pp. 19–39.

Lambourne, W. (2014b). What are the pillars of transitional justice? The United Nations and the justice cascade in Burundi. *Macquarie Law Journal*, 13, 41–60.

Lambourne, W. (2014c). Justice after genocide: Impunity and the Extraordinary Chambers in the Courts of Cambodia. *Genocide Studies and Prevention*, 8(2), Article 7.

Lambourne, W. and Niyonzima, D. (2016). Breaking cycles of trauma and violence: Psychosocial approaches to healing and reconciliation in Burundi. In P. Gobodo-Madikizela (ed.), *Breaking Intergenerational Cycles of Repetition: A Global Dialogue on Historical Trauma and Memory*. Opladen, Germany: Barbara Budrich Publishers, pp. 291–307.

Lambourne, W. and Rodriguez Carreon, V. (2016). Engendering transitional justice: A transformative approach to building peace and attaining human rights for women. *Human Rights Review*, 17(1), 71–93.

Laplante, L. J. (2014). The plural justice aims of reparations. In S. Buckley Zistel, T. Koloma Beck, C. Braun and F. Mieth (eds.), *Transitional Justice Theories*. New York: Routledge, pp. 66–84.

Lederach, J. P. (1995). *Preparing for Peace: Conflict Transformation Across Cultures*. Syracuse, NY: Syracuse University Press.

Lederach, J. P. (1997). *Building Peace: Sustainable Reconciliation in Divided Societies*. Washington, DC: United States Institute of Peace Press.

McAuliffe, P. (2017). *Transformative Transitional Justice and the Malleability of Post-Conflict States*. Cheltenham: Edward Elgar.

McEvoy, K. and McGregor, L. (eds.) (2008). *Transitional Justice from Below: Grassroots Activism and the Struggle for Change*. Oxford/Portland, OR: Hart Publishing.

Maddison, S. and Shepherd, L. J. (2014). Peacebuilding and the postcolonial politics of transitional justice. *Peacebuilding*, 2(3), 253–269.

Mani, R. (2002). *Beyond Retribution: Seeking Justice in the Shadows of War.* Cambridge: Polity Press.

Martin, L. M. (2020). Deconstructing the local in peacebuilding practice: Representations and realities of Fambul Tok in Sierra Leone. *Third World Quarterly*, https://doi.org/10.1080/01436597.2020.1825071

Nagy, R. L. (2013). The Scope and Bounds of Transitional Justice and the Canadian Truth and Reconciliation Commission. *International Journal of Transitional Justice*, 7(1), 52–73.

Neumann, K. and Thompson, J. (eds.) (2015). *Historical Justice and Memory.* Madison, WI: University of Wisconsin Press.

Niezen, R. (2013). *Truth and Indignation: Canada's Truth and Reconciliation Commission on Indian Residential Schools.* Toronto, ON: University of Toronto Press.

Office of the United Nations High Commissioner for Human Rights (2008). *Rule-of-Law Tools for Post-Conflict States: Maximizing the Legacy of Hybrid Courts.* New York/Geneva: United Nations.

Olsen, T. D., Payne, L. A. and Reiter, A. G. (2010). *Transitional Justice in Balance: Comparing Processes, Weighing Efficacy.* Washington, DC: United States Institute of Peace.

Orentlicher, D. F. (1997). Swapping Amnesty for Peace and the Duty to Prosecute Human Rights Crimes. *Journal of International and Comparative Law*, 3(2), 713–717.

Orentlicher, D. F. (2007). 'Settling Accounts' revisited: Reconciling global norms with local agency. *International Journal of Transitional Justice*, 1(1), 10–22.

Pouligny, B. (2014). *The Resilience Approach to Peacebuilding: A New Conceptual Framework.* Washington, DC: United States Institute of Peace.

Putnam, R. D. (2000). *Bowling Alone: The Collapse and Revival of American Community.* New York: Simon & Schuster.

Robins, S. (2019). Conclusion: Toward transformative justice. In P. Gready and S. Robins (eds.), *From Transitional to Transformative Justice.* Cambridge: Cambridge University Press.

Saul, J. (2014). *Collective Trauma, Collective Healing: Promoting Community Resilience in the Aftermath of Disaster.* New York/London: Routledge.

Shaw, R. and Waldorf, L. (eds.) (2010). *Localizing Transitional Justice: Interventions and Priorities After Mass Violence.* Stanford, CA: Stanford University Press.

Sikkink, K. (2011). *The Justice Cascade: How Human Rights Prosecutions are Changing World Politics.* New York/London: W. W. Norton.

Teitel, R. G. (2000). *Transitional Justice.* Oxford: Oxford University Press.

Tutu, D. (1999). *No Future Without Forgiveness.* London: Rider.

Ungar, M. (2008). Resilience across cultures. *British Journal of Social Work*, 38, 218–235.

Ungar, M. (2018). Systemic resilience: Principles and processes for a science of change in contexts of adversity. *Ecology and Society*, 23(4), 34–50.

Ungar, M. (ed.) (2021). *Multisystemic Resilience: Adaptation and Transformation in Contexts of Change.* New York: Oxford University Press.

Ungar, M. and Theron, L. (2020). Resilience and mental health: How multisystemic processes contribute to positive outcomes. *The Lancet Psychiatry*, 7(5), 441–448.

United Nations. (1997). Question of the Impunity of Perpetrators of Human Rights Violations (Civil and Political): Revised Final Report Prepared by Mr Joinet Pursuant to Sub-Commission Decision 1996/119.

United Nations. (2004). *Report of the Secretary-General, The Rule of Law and Transitional Justice in Conflict and Post-Conflict Societies*. New York: United Nations Security Council.

United Nations. (2010). *Guidance Note of the Secretary-General: United Nations Approach to Transitional Justice*. New York: United Nations.

United Nations. (2015). *Report of the High-level Independent Panel on Peace Operations on Uniting Our Strengths for Peace: Politics, Partnership and People*. General Assembly & Security Council. A/70/95–S/2015/446.

Waldorf, L. (2012). Anticipating the past: Transitional justice and socio-economic wrongs. *Social and Legal Studies*, 21(2), 171–186.

Wiebelhaus-Brahm, E. (2017). After shocks: Exploring the relationships between transitional justice and resilience in post-conflict societies. In R. Duthie and P. Seils (eds.), *Justice Mosaics: How Context Shapes Transitional Justice in Fractured Societies*. New York: International Center for Transitional Justice.

Winter, S. (2014). *Transitional Justice in Established Democracies: A Political Theory*. New York: Palgrave Macmillan.

PART II

EMPIRICAL CASE STUDIES

3

A Systemic Analysis of Resilience and Transitional Justice Impact in a Central Bosnian Village

Janine Natalya Clark

INTRODUCTION

Visitors to Bosnia-Herzegovina (BiH) often spend a few days in the capital city, Sarajevo, before travelling to Mostar in the south-west of the country, and from there across the border into Croatia. Few tourists head to Central Bosnia, despite its relative proximity to Sarajevo. An area rich in both history and natural resources, including the spectacular mountains of Vlašić and Kruščica, this part of BiH was the scene of fierce fighting between the Army of BiH (ABiH) and the Croatian Defence Council (HVO) during the 1992–1995 Bosnian war. In April 1993, the HVO launched an attack on the Lašva Valley, culminating in the massacre of more than 100 Bosniaks in the village of Ahmići. I visited Ahmići for the first time in July 2008 and since then I have returned many times. I confess that I have a deep attachment to the place. Each time that I am there, I find myself thinking about pre-war Ahmići and wishing that I had been able to experience – albeit as an outsider – the village life that Bosniaks and Croats (Bosnian Croats) alike speak about with great nostalgia. They used to visit each other's houses; jointly celebrate Christmas and Bajram (Eid); watch football matches together.

Today, although the village is peaceful, there is a distance between people and relationships have changed. The absence of a sense of community and the weakening of community ties constitute important resource deficits. Such deficits, moreover, exist alongside broader systemic and environmental stressors – including political rhetoric and segregated schooling – that have helped to keep the past alive. Drawing on my most recent fieldwork in Ahmići, carried out in July 2019, this chapter argues that, while some individuals have demonstrated resilience, despite suffering huge losses, overall the social ecologies in which they live offer few protective resources. This, in turn, has important implications for transitional justice, which is partly about social repair (Fletcher and Weinstein, 2002).

Several prosecutions took place at the International Criminal Tribunal for the former Yugoslavia (ICTY) in relation to the crimes committed in Ahmići. However, these trials had few positive effects and arguably contributed to further entrenching inter-ethnic divides; the supposed transformative impact of the 'truths' established within the ICTY's courtrooms critically neglected the wider ecologies that have shaped popular interpretations of and responses to those truths. The broader issue is that transitional justice, in both theory and practice, has significantly overlooked the concept of resilience, which is quintessentially about entire systems (see Chapter 1) – and about 'the inter-actions between an individual's environment, their social ecology, and an individual's assets' (Liebenberg and Moore, 2018: 3). This chapter outlines the case for a social-ecological reconceptualisation and reframing of transitional justice. Operationally linking this to adaptive peacebuilding (de Coning, 2018), it argues that transitional justice processes can potentially contribute to resilience – which overlaps with core transitional goals such as peace and reconciliation – by giving more attention to the social ecologies that necessarily shape processes of dealing with the past.

MASSACRE IN AHMIĆI, 16 APRIL 1993

According to the Organization for Security and Co-operation in Europe (OSCE, 2018: 7), 'The conflict in BiH ... resulted in an estimated 100,000 dead and 2.2 million displaced. The mixed Croat and Bosniak cantons of Zenica-Doboj, Central Bosnia and Herzegovina-Neretva were all areas of intense fighting, which resulted in the substantial displacement of one of the two ethnic groups'. At the start of the Bosnian war, the ABiH and HVO were allies against the Army of Republika Srpska (VRS). The military alliance between the two armies, however, gradually began to break down, and a Trial Chamber of the ICTY found 'compelling evidence to the effect that, starting in mid-1992, tensions and animosity between Croats and Muslims rapidly escalated' (Prosecutor v. Kupreškić et al., 2000: para. 125). The first major flare-up in Central Bosnia occurred in October 1992 (Prosecutor v. Kupreškić et al., 2000: para. 163). The Vance-Owen Peace Plan, in January 1993, further contributed to the deterioration in relations between the two sides. It proposed the establishment of ten largely autonomous provinces or cantons in BiH, each of which would have an ethnic majority. Bosnian Croats were to be the majority in three cantons, including canton 10 – Central Bosnia (Prosecutor v. Kordić and Čerkez, 2001: para. 559). According to the ICTY, 'In the minds of Croatian nationalists, and in particular of Mate Boban [the Bosnian Croat leader], this meant that Province 10 was Croatian' (Prosecutor v. Blaškić, 2000: para. 369; see also Hoare, 1997: 132).

From January 1993, relations between the ABiH and the HVO further deteriorated as the latter sought to establish its authority over the aforementioned cantons. After ABiH forces ignored an ultimatum to either surrender to the HVO or leave the cantons by 20 January, 'Croatian forces embarked on a series of actions intended to implement the "Croatisation" of the territories by force' (Prosecutor *v*. Blaškić, 2000: para. 372). The situation started to come to a head in mid-April 1993. The HVO had set a deadline of 15 April for the then Bosnian President, the late Alija Izetbegović, to sign an agreement that would place ABiH forces in the three cantons under HVO command. This deadline passed and, at 8 a.m. on the same day, ABiH forces abducted an HVO brigade commander and killed his four escorts. This was one of the 'provocations' from the side of the ABiH that Croats in Ahmići often refer to when discussing subsequent events. A Trial Chamber of the ICTY found 'direct evidence that the HVO planned an attack for the next day [16 April] at a series of meetings that afternoon and evening' (Prosecutor *v*. Kordić and Čerkez, 2001: para. 610).

At 5.30 a.m. on 16 April 1993, the HVO[1] launched a concerted attack on the village of Ahmići (and on several other towns and villages in the Lašva Valley). Only Bosniak homes were set alight (Prosecutor *v*. Bralo, 2005: para. 12). Some Bosniak villagers were shot and killed as they tried to escape. In total, 116 people were killed in Ahmići that day. More than twenty victims are still missing. Bosniaks started to return to Ahmići from the late 1990s onwards. Every year on 16 April, a memorial service takes place – starting in Stari Vitez where many of the victims are buried and ending at the *donja džamija* (lower mosque) (see Figure 3.1) – to remember and honour the dead.

In Ahmići, there are many examples of individual resilience, in the sense of 'positive adaptation within the context of significant adversity' (Luthar et al., 2000: 543). Resilience, however, is not only about individuals. As Ungar and Liebenberg (2011: 127) underline, 'resilience is the qualities of both the individual and the individual's environment that potentiate positive development'. In Ahmići, resource deficits and environmental stressors have critically hampered the community and community relations. These same deficits and stressors, which contributed to limiting the on-the-ground impact of the ICTY's work – both in Ahmići and in BiH more generally – ultimately underscore the need for a social-ecological reconceptualisation of transitional justice.

---

[1]   More specifically, the crime was committed by the 4th Military Police Battalion of the HVO and its anti-terrorist platoon, 'the Jokers' (Prosecutor *v*. Blaškić, 2004: para. 374).

FIGURE 3.1 Ahmići memorial to the 116 men, women and children who were killed on 16 April 1993. Photo by the author.

INDIVIDUAL RESILIENCE IN A DIVIDED COMMUNITY

My previous research in Ahmići, in 2008 and 2009, focused on inter-ethnic relations and reconciliation (Clark, 2012, 2014). More recently, in July 2019, I spent two weeks in the village. I wanted to explore how people had rebuilt their lives, what resources they had used to do so and the extent to which transitional justice processes – and specifically trials conducted at the ICTY – had contributed to fostering resilience, as manifested in the interactions between individuals and their environments (Berkes and Ross, 2013: 7). In total, I conducted ten semi-structured interviews with six men and four women. Seven interviewees were Bosniaks and three were Croats. In addition, a fourth local Croat (female) agreed to respond to questions via email, maintaining that she did not have time to participate in a face-to-face interview.

The relatively small number of interviews undertaken reflects the difficulties of doing research in this particular community. The place has an empty feel and there is no sense of bustling village life. Hence, there are few opportunities to interact with people. It is as if life in Ahmići today primarily takes place behind closed doors. Many people are also tired of telling their stories and dredging up painful memories from the past. The village receives large crowds on 16 April each year and continues to be the subject of media interest (see, e.g., Dajić, 2017). I relied primarily on a snowball sampling strategy, particularly for locating Croat participants. A local contact facilitated the interviews with Bosniak participants. Interviews typically lasted around forty-five minutes and were conducted in the interviewees' homes in the local languages (Bosnian, Croatian). It would have been impossible to write this chapter while anonymising the name of the village. However, any details that could help to identify the interviewees have been removed.

Regardless of their ethnicity, all interviewees expressed a deep sense of pain and hurt (Clark, 2020a). As one of them underlined, '[a]t the end of the day, we are all losers' (author interview, 9 July 2019). The Bosniak interviewees had lost several close family members in the attack on Ahmići. One of the Croat interviewees had lost family members in an ABiH attack on a nearby village. All interviewees, moreover, had lost the community that once existed, as well as neighbours and friends. More than twenty-five years on, the past thus remains raw. In the words of a survivor of the massacre who lost nine family members, '[t]ime goes by, the years pass by and the memories are fresh, the sadness is the same' (cited in Anadolija, 2019). Nevertheless, people have rebuilt their lives, and the interview data provided valuable insights into some of the ways that they have done so. Three particular points stand out in this regard.

The first is that the attack on Ahmići resulted in the loss and destruction of multiple resources. The victims lost their homes, their animals, their livelihoods, their way of life, their sense of belonging and security. When asked how he had dealt with everything that happened in Ahmići, for example, one interviewee stressed: 'You can't describe it.' He used to work hard and he had invested everything in his home; '[i]t was all destroyed in an instant'. What had most helped him to deal with everything that happened, he explained, was his desire to 'return to where I was born' (author interview, 8 July 2019). His land was charred and neglected, but it was still his '*dom*' (home) and a fundamental resource, highlighting the fact that – particularly in rural parts of BiH – people often have a deep attachment to land (see, e.g., Tuathail and O'Laughlin, 2009: 1052).

Another intangible resource that both this interviewee and several others indirectly spoke about was their desire to live – and what they frequently referred to as 'the fight for life'. Speaking only briefly about her own experiences on 16 April 1993, one interviewee stressed: 'You have to live. You carry inside you everything that you saw and survived, but you have to fight and to go forward' (author interview, 9 July 2019). The wish to live is an elemental resource that has similarly emerged prominently from other research on traumatic events. In his work with child survivors of the Holocaust, for example, Valent (1998: 520) found that many of them 'cited an inner surge or compulsion to live, a will to survive, as the most important factor in their survival. They used whatever capacities they had to do so'. In this way, he linked their resilience to 'the surge of life they manifested, a kind of sacred connection with a wider life force' (Valent, 1998: 522–523).

For some interviewees, this 'surge of life' was closely connected to their faith. One interviewee who lost several members of his family in the attack on Ahmići stressed that, whenever he closes his eyes, he can see all of them and the suffering they went through. However, he also underlined that '[y]our relationship with God and prayer bring you some solution and relief' (author interview, 11 July 2019). Faith had, in some cases, also contributed to meaning-making. One particular interviewee stood out in this regard. 'It is very difficult to come to terms with what happened in Ahmići', she reflected, 'but if you believe that something had to be, this helps you to deal with it' (author interview, 16 July 2019). According to Panter-Brick, 'What matters to individuals facing adversity is a sense of "meaning-making" and what matters to resilience is a sense of hope that life does indeed make sense, despite chaos, brutality, stress, worry, or despair' (Southwick et al., 2014). This particular interviewee had found a sense of meaning in her conviction that events in Ahmići were Allah's will, and this, in turn, had helped her to move forward.

The second point to underscore is that resilience is not simply about having access to what Ungar (2008: 221) has termed 'health-enhancing resources', but also about the clustering of those resources. In his work on Conservation of Resources Theory, for example, Hobfoll (2001: 349) argues that '[t]here is strong evidence that resources aggregate in resource caravans in both an immediate and a life-span sense'. Elaborating on the concept of 'resource caravans', he further explains that 'having one major resource is typically linked with having others, and likewise for their absence' (Hobfoll, 2001: 350). Illustrating this, one of the interviewees expressed a strong sense of contentment. She had many resources, through her own efforts, and in this regard her 'caravan' was full. Describing herself as a 'cheerful person', she spoke with great pride about her children and stressed the importance of making the most of life, underlining that she had overcome many adversities (author interview, 9 July 2019).

Another interviewee, in contrast, had various material resources yet his 'caravan' was somewhat empty. He led a solitary life and explained that he felt bored and frustrated as he saw no prospects for himself in BiH (author interview, 8 July 2019). Similarly, the interviewee who had stressed his desire to return to Ahmići and to his land was similarly dissatisfied with life. He had not worked for many years and repeatedly complained that no one had helped him and his wife, overlooking the fact that external donors had funded the reconstruction of the family's destroyed home (author interview, 8 July 2019). While his 'caravan' was relatively bare, he was not doing anything to change this and his entire demeanour exuded a sense of sadness and defeatism. The past had taken so much away from him and, although he had fulfilled his wish of returning to his land, he appeared to be observing life rather than actively living it.

The third point is that interviewees' answers revealed a critical absence of community in Ahmići, thus restricting what the community environment provides for resilience (Ungar, 2017: 1282). As Liebenberg and Moore (2018: 2) observe, '[i]t is now widely accepted that resilience is associated with individual capacities, relationships and the availability of community resources and opportunities'. When asked about resources within the community, one interviewee underscored the importance of land and agriculture (author interview, 11 July 2019). Illustrating this point, another interviewee had been out picking fruit and she was going to use them to make teas (author interview, 17 July 2019). Overall, however, interviewees significantly struggled with the question about community resources. Some interviewees talked about their pre-war resources. Some interviewees made vague references to the *mjesna zajednica* (local community association) as a body that can offer limited help. Yet, when asked to elaborate, they were unable to provide more details. Moreover, while some interviewees claimed that there is one *mjesna zajednica* for Ahmići, others maintained that Bosniaks and Croats each have their own *mjesna zajednica*. The fact that the interviewees gave such conflicting answers is an important indicator of a lack of community engagement.

What also emerged was a strong conviction on the part of some of the Bosniak interviewees that, as regards resources, there is unequal treatment. One interviewee, for example, complained that Bosniaks have to pay more for land than Croats and that the latter had blocked his attempts to purchase some land. He further insisted that Bosniaks have a second-class status within the municipality of Vitez (which encompasses Ahmići) (author interview, 8 July 2019).[2] Another interviewee maintained that, as a Bosniak, she has no rights and that the Croats have taken everything for themselves (author interview, 9 July 2019). While many such assertions were unsubstantiated and/or could not be verified, the common feeling among Bosniaks that they do not have the same rights and benefits as their Croat counterparts has undoubtedly contributed to further undermining a sense of community. Equating resilience with community processes, Comes et al. (2019:

---

[2] According to the pre-war 1991 census, 'Ahmići had about 500 inhabitants, of whom about 90 percent were Muslims, which meant 200 Muslim houses and fifteen or so Croat ones' (Prosecutor v. Blaškić, 2000: para. 384). Ahmići continues to be a primarily Bosniak village. Within the broader municipality of Vitez, Croats are the majority. According to the 2013 census, there were 14,350 Croats, 10,513 Bosniaks and 333 Serbs living in the municipality (Abramušić, 2016).

FIGURE 3.2 Ahmići today. Photo by the author.

126–127) argue that 'the ability to take part, benefit from and contribute to these processes becomes central if we are striving to ensure social justice'. In Ahmići, the perceived absence of social justice has undermined community processes that might contribute to bringing people together, including how the community deals with adversity and crises (Magis, 2010: 405).

Ahmići, in short, is a fragmented community where the overwhelming impression is that people simply get on with and live their own lives (see Figure 3.2). Some of them have demonstrated resilience in doing so, drawing on their own individual resources to move forward. However, Ahmići cannot be accurately described as a resilient community – the sum of its parts – because it has not dealt with what happened in 1993 *as a community*. A crucial reason for this is the existence of multiple systemic factors – which are central to the chapter's insistence on a social-ecological reframing of transitional justice – that have not allowed the community to come together as one and rebuild the social connections that are 'at the heart of resilient communities' (Ellis and Abdi, 2017: 290).

MULTI-SYSTEMIC HINDRANCES TO FOSTERING COMMUNITY RESILIENCE IN AHMIĆI

Brightly coloured Russian dolls can be purchased in BiH, particularly in tourist areas like Baščaršija in Sarajevo and the area around the Old Bridge (Stari Most) in Mostar. Stiles et al. invoke the analogy of Russian dolls to apply personal space boundary theory to traumatised adults in therapy. Likening the dolls to four different levels of personal space, they argue: 'The largest outer-most doll is the superficial public self. The next smaller doll is the thoughts and feelings perceived as "acceptable" to the client. The next smaller doll is the "deepest thoughts, feelings, secrets, and sins" of the client, and the inner-most doll is the "inner spirit"' (Stiles et al., 2009: 69). Extending the analogy, but in a different direction, I argue that Ahmići can be likened to a medium-sized doll. The smaller dolls inside it represent individual lives, but larger dolls – representing broader systemic influences – surround and encase it.

The massacre in Ahmići did not occur in a vacuum. It took place in the context of the Bosnian war, and both Bosniak and Croat nationalists subse-quently co-opted events to promote and support their particular and conflict-ing ethno-narratives. These political machinations and persistent attempts at ethnic outbidding (Zdeb, 2017) themselves take place within a broader consti-tutional system and structure where ethnicity is the central pivot. Fundamentally, 'The unique way in which Bosnia's Constitution has been realised allows ethnicity to become the most salient identification marker in political life' (Piersma, 2019: 937). The country's tripartite Presidency, the plethora of ethnic-based political parties and the fact that 'the confederal element of the Bosnian settlement transcends BiH's borders' (Bose, 2005: 327) – reaching into neighbouring Croatia and Serbia – powerfully highlight this. Involvement from these neighbouring states, moreover, also contributes to stoking nationalist flames.

In 2019, for example, the Bosniak member of the BiH presidency, Šefik Džaferović, criticised the then President of Croatia, Kolinda Grabar-Kitarović, for comments that she had made about Croats in BiH. During a speech in Mostar in November 2019, she told a large audience: 'Croats have two homes, the Republic of Croatia and Bosnia-Herzegovina, but we are one soul and one nation. Therefore I will not stop until Croats in BiH secure what belongs to you historically, politically and constitutionally; that is, total equality and the realisation of your rights as a constituent people'. She insisted that anyone who expects Croats to simply kneel down and disappear from BiH is deceived, and further offered a guarantee that she would not repeat her two predecessors' neglect of Croats in BiH (Radio Sarajevo, 2019; author's own translation). President Džaferović responded by accusing Grabar-Kitarović of being part of 'retrograde powers' that seek to create ethnic and territorial divides. Claiming that she had charged Bosniaks of wanting BiH for themselves, Džaferović underlined that Bosniaks had been victims of genocide and expelled from huge swathes of territory (Hina, 2019). The victim narratives that both Presidents promoted highlight the existence of meta hermeneutical/interpret-ative frameworks, fundamentally intersecting with political systems, that strongly shape popular discourse about the Bosnian war. It is within these systemic dynamics that everyday life in Ahmići takes place.

In their work with internally displaced people in Lebanon, Nuwayhid et al. (2011: 511) argue that one factor that helped to build resilience was 'a strong communal identity united around a common cause'. This common cause, in turn, 'provided the affected population with a sense of collective identity' (Nuwayhid et al., 2011: 511). Shiite communities particularly bore the brunt of Israeli military attacks (Telhami, 2007: 26), and 'shared destiny and the feeling of being collectively targeted strengthened the communal cohesiveness of the affected community' (Nuwayhid et al., 2011: 512). In Ahmići, no strong sense of communal identity exists, due to wider systemic influences that encourage division and the maintenance of 'us'/'them' boundaries. There is a critical absence of space for discussion and reflection about the pain and hurt that exist on both sides (Clark, 2020a) – or for the development of shared narratives. Bosniaks continue to grieve for their loved ones who perished on 16 April 1993. One interviewee underscored that '[t]here are a lot of tears and sadness that cannot be wiped away' (author interview, 11 July 2019). Croat interviewees, both in my most recent and previous research, have often expressed a sense of hurt that, as they see it, the suffering of their own people has been ignored (Clark, 2014: 80). Claiming that many 'untruths and lies have been told about Ahmići', one interviewee insisted that nobody talks about crimes committed in places such as Buhine Kuće.[3] Politics, he maintained, was the reason (author interview, 11 July 2019).

While there is a critical absence of community cohesion in Ahmići, another type of cohesion arguably exists. Olson's (2000) Circumplex Model of Marital and Family Systems, which emphasises cohesion as one of its three key elements (alongside flexibility and communication), identifies four different levels of cohesion – namely disengaged (very low), separated (low to moderate), connected (moderate to high) and enmeshed (very high). The model hypothesises that 'the central or balanced levels of cohesion (separated and connected) make for optimal family functioning. The extremes or unbalanced levels (disengaged or enmeshed) are generally seen as problematic for relationships over the long term' (Olson, 2000: 145). In a very different context, Winton's (2008) work utilises the model in relation to the crime of genocide, and specifically as a way of explaining different perpetrator group dynamics. 'Enmeshed cohesion', he argues, 'is demonstrated by a high level of emotional closeness within the perpetrator groups' (Winton, 2008: 607). The group is perceived as 'one big

---

[3] While it is the case that the deaths of Croats in the Lašva Valley have received less attention than the killing of Bosniaks in Ahmići, it is also important to stress that ABiH crimes in the area were not organised military attacks against a civilian population.

family', and high levels of loyalty are demanded. Deviations in this regard are punished. In contrast, emotional distance, low levels of loyalty and high levels of group member independence are characteristic of disengaged cohesion (Winton, 2008: 607). The concept of enmeshed cohesion is particularly pertinent to Ahmići and illustrates – at least in part – the feasibility of applying Olson's model to communities and societies as a whole.

In Ahmići, there are high levels of ethnic-based enmeshed cohesion in the sense of loyalty to a particular narrative, especially on the Croat side. In the hours after the massacre, the head of the British battalion within the United Nations Protection Force (UNPROFOR) in BiH, Colonel Bob Stewart, walked through charred shells of people's former homes. Coming across three HVO soldiers in a vehicle, he asked them who was responsible for the massacre. All of them denied any knowledge or involvement (SENSE Centre, 2019). This denial has persisted. Local Croats, for example, commonly distance themselves from the events of 16 April 1993. One interviewee repeatedly insisted that he would never have returned to Ahmići if he had known what was going to happen (author interview, 16 July 2019). Another interviewee had been in the HVO but maintained that, at the time of the attack, he was not in Ahmići and did not know what was happening (author interview, 11 July 2019). Some locals blame 'outsiders' or a few rogue elements (Clark, 2012: 245).[4] Furthermore, they often deflect attention from what happened in Ahmići by highlighting Croat suffering, in the same way that the conspicuous memorial cross, erected in the grounds of the local Catholic Church, only acknowledges Croat deaths in what it refers to as the 363-day Muslim siege of Vitez.

In April 2010, Ivo Josipović was the first Croatian President to visit Ahmići and he received a warm welcome. According to the then head of the Organisation of 16 April, the visit was 'first and foremost an expression of good will' that he believed would 'contribute to establishing true neighbourly relations in Ahmići' (Radio Sarajevo, 2010). The foundations for such relations, however, are necessarily highly unstable when they are linked to broader systems that contribute to fostering denial and the glorification of war criminals. In 2014, for example, the convicted war criminal Dario Kordić (discussed in the next section) landed at Zagreb airport following his release from prison. Bishop Vlado Košić was waiting to welcome him. Taking his hand, the Bishop declared that Kordić's patriotism should be a model to other Croats (Belak-Krile, 2019). Kordić's

---

[4]   In the Blaškić trial at the ICTY, the Trial Chamber noted that 'the idea that these crimes could have been committed by uncontrolled elements is impossible to reconcile with the scale and uniformity of the crimes committed on 16 April in the municipality of Vitez' (Prosecutor *v.* Blaškić, 2000: para. 467).

support from within the Catholic Church in Croatia – which often intervenes in politics (Vladisavljević, 2019) – has also provided him with several opportunities to speak in public. In April 2019, at the invitation of the Croatian priest Damir Stojić, Kordić delivered a lecture at a student dorm in Zagreb and spoke about how he had found God during his time in prison (Dnevnik, 2019).[5] He has not spoken publicly about what happened in Ahmići or expressed any remorse.[6]

If indicators of enmeshed cohesion include 'loyalty to the perpetrator group' and 'fear of negative sanctions for dissenting from the perpetrator view' (Winton and Unlu, 2008: 49), these indicators are present in Ahmići – among both Croats and Bosniaks. During my most recent and my previous research in the village, Croats always refrained from denouncing convicted war criminals (this will be discussed more in the next section), and, in some cases, they directly or indirectly expressed support for them. At the same time, however, there is little space or incentive for Bosniaks to dissent from a powerful metanarrative – exemplified by the persistent instrumentalisation of the 1995 Srebrenica genocide (Nielsen, 2013: 30) – that underlines Bosniak suffering and victimhood, and to acknowledge ABiH crimes against Croats in places such as Buhine Kuće and Križančevo Selo.[7] To cite Orentlicher (2018: 283), 'many Bosnians [regardless of ethnicity] feel strong community pressure *not* to condemn atrocities committed by their own ethnic group'.

The education system has further contributed to fostering enmeshed cohesion. Laketa (2019: 175) notes that '[s]egregated educational landscapes work forcefully to entrench fixed notions of identity so that any deviation from the norm becomes highly visible'. In BiH, the most striking example of segregation within the education system (or, more accurately, systems) is 'two schools under one roof', whereby young people from different ethnicities attend the same school in different shifts or use different parts of the building. There are fifty-six schools operating as 'two schools under one roof' in three particular cantons within the BiH Federation (OSCE, 2018: 6). Central Bosnia Canton, which encompasses Ahmići, has the largest number of divided schools (Piersma, 2019:

---

[5] A group of young activists briefly interrupted the lecture, calling Kordić a war criminal.

[6] During his appeal process at the ICTY, however, the Appeals Chamber noted that 'Kordić agrees that the killings in Ahmići on 16 April 1993 were "clearly crimes" and amounted to a massacre' (Prosecutor v. Kordić and Čerkez, 2004: para. 472).

[7] In February 2019, the State Court of BiH confirmed an indictment against eight former members of the ABiH in connection with events in Križančevo Selo in December 1993. Seven defendants have been charged with the criminal offence of War Crimes against Prisoners of War. The eighth defendant, Ibrahim Purić (the former commander of the 325th Mountain Brigade of the ABiH), is charged with War Crimes against Civilians. According to the indictment, at least twelve HVO soldiers were killed (after they had surrendered) in Križančevo Selo, as well as two civilians (State Court of BiH, 2019).

941).[8] In a 2018 report, the OSCE (2018: 4) stressed that what is common to all of these divided schools 'is that they segregate children, and through this segregation teach them that there are inherent differences between them'. In this way, divided schools not only impede reconciliation and long-term stability (Swimelar, 2013: 172). They also undermine resilience, and in particular the 'community capacity' that might be used to 'solve collective problems and improve or maintain the well-being of a given community' (Chaskin, 2008: 70).

In short, Ahmići is not a resilient community that has positively adapted to the shocks and stressors that occurred during the Bosnian war. Rather, it can be more accurately described as an ethnically based enmeshed community that responds to, and is constrained by, broader systemic influences. These influences have also reflected heavily on transitional justice work – and on the fact that it has had little impact on resilience.

TRANSITIONAL JUSTICE, THE ICTY AND RESILIENCE

In May 1993, as the war in BiH continued to rage, the UN Security Council used its Chapter VII powers (dealing with threats to international peace and security) to establish the ICTY, the first international war crimes tribunal since the post-World War II Nuremberg and Tokyo Tribunals. During the Tribunal's early years, several defendants stood trial for the crimes committed in Ahmići in April 1993. Two of the most important were Tihomir Blaškić and the aforementioned Dario Kordić, and their cases continue to provoke the most discussion in Ahmići today.

Blaškić was the HVO commander in Central Bosnia. A Trial Chamber of the ICTY assessed that he had ordered the attacks that gave rise to the crimes committed in Ahmići and other villages in the Lašva Valley (Prosecutor v. Blaškić, 2000: para. 437). It further found that '[i]n any event, it is clear that he never took any reasonable measure to prevent the crimes being committed or to punish those responsible for them' (Prosecutor v. Blaškić, 2000: para. 495). On the basis of Blaškić's individual criminal responsibility and superior criminal responsibility (reflecting his position as a commander), the Trial Chamber convicted him of crimes against humanity, violations of the laws or customs of war and grave breaches of the Geneva Conventions. It imposed a forty-five-year custodial sentence. The Appeals Chamber, however, admitted additional evidence and opined that the Trial Chamber had made a number of errors, including with respect to the constituent elements of command responsibility

---

[8] According to the OSCE (2018: 32), thirty-six schools (twenty central schools and sixteen branch schools) in eighteen locations in Central Bosnia Canton are divided.

(see, e.g., Prosecutor *v.* Blaškić, 2004: paras. 372–422). It accordingly reversed several of Blaškić's convictions and reduced his sentence to nine years' imprisonment. Just four days later, he was granted early release.

Kordić was the former president of the Croatian Democratic Union (HDZ) in BiH. In 2011, the ICTY convicted him of crimes against humanity, violations of the laws or customs of war and grave breaches of the Geneva Conventions and sentenced him to twenty-five years' imprisonment (upheld on appeal). The Appeals Chamber found that 'a reasonable trier of fact could have concluded beyond reasonable doubt that Kordić, as the responsible regional politician, planned, instigated and ordered the crimes which occurred in Ahmići on 16 April 1993' (Prosecutor *v.* Kordić and Čerkez, 2004: para. 700). In 2014, he was granted early release.

The cumulative effect of the trials that took place at the ICTY was to further entrench ethnic divisions in Ahmići (Clark, 2014: 63–63, 79–80), thereby undermining the function of both the community and systems of justice as potential resilience resources. The fundamental issue is that, for both Bosniaks and Croats alike, justice was not done. For many Bosniaks, the fault lies not only with the Tribunal itself (common complaints are that its sentences were too lenient) but also with their Croat neighbours. One interviewee reflected: 'The trials did not have any positive influence. For Croats, Kordić is a hero. He and Blaškić are viewed as national heroes.[9] So how is this useful or just?' (author interview, 8 July 2019). Another interviewee stressed that, while she is glad that at least some perpetrators have been held to account, it greatly bothered her when Croats celebrated the release of people like Kordić (author interview, 16 July 2019).

For Croat interviewees, however, the very fact that Blaškić and Kordić stood trial was itself an injustice. One interviewee lambasted the ICTY as 'a disastrous court that prosecutes innocent people'. While emphasising that he was not defending people like Kordić and Blaškić, he maintained that the Croats were completely surrounded in the Lašva Valley and that the ABiH made a huge mistake by not leaving a way out for them (author interview, 16 July 2019).[10] Another interviewee insisted that people like the Kupreškićs and Drago

---

9   The ICTY's Outreach Office, for example, noted that 'After the release of Tihomir Blaškić, one could hear a cacophony of celebratory voices in Croatia and areas of Bosnia largely populated by Bosnian Croats. These voices included much praise for Blaškić, a convicted war criminal who has served most of his sentence, but did not include the victims of crimes' (ICTY, 2004).

10   The ICTY Appeals Chamber found that there was a military justification for Blaškić to order the attack on Ahmići (Prosecutor *v.* Blaškić, 2004: para. 333). However, it also emphasised that 'in the context of this armed conflict which had been in the making for some time, involving both sides, the issue as to which side initiated the conflict is irrelevant for the purposes of determining the nature of its actions during the conflict. What concerns the International

Josipović[11] have no idea what happened in Ahmići and should have never gone on trial. Questioning why 'the real perpetrators' have not been prosecuted, although he failed to elaborate on who these individuals are, he stressed that many lives had been destroyed due to false testimony and lies (author interview, 11 July 2019). In a similar vein, a third interviewee opined that 'Unfortunately, many war criminals and commanders are free, and innocent people ... were found guilty'. She further argued that: 'Mothers, spouses, children did not get the truth from the Hague Tribunal. Justice did not win' (email correspondence with the author, 24 July 2019).

These examples underscore the fact that the Tribunal's work did not contribute to resilience in Ahmići, at any level. Yet, it is also important to stress that resilience was never part of the Tribunal's mandate, and this highlights a broader point. Transitional justice can potentially affect resilience, positively or negatively, in myriad ways (Wiebelhaus-Brahm, 2017). As one illustration, 'proponents claim transitional justice processes can promote such outcomes as reconciliation, trust, and the rule of law, which development practitioners associate with more resilient societies' (Wiebelhaus-Brahm, 2017: 142). It is striking, therefore, that the concept of resilience remains heavily neglected within the ever-growing field of transitional justice, including within the extensive body of scholarship that exists on the ICTY's work. Several authors have explored whether the Tribunal's work aided reconciliation (see, e.g., Clark, 2014; Hodžić, 2011; Meernik and Guerrero, 2014) – but not resilience. This section emphasises resilience as a new lens that brings an important systemic dimension to discussions about the Tribunal's impact and legacy – and about transitional justice more broadly.

According to the ICTY (n.d.), for example, one of its achievements was that it 'established beyond a reasonable doubt crucial facts related to crimes committed in the former Yugoslavia'. This is a deeply myopic assertion that overlooks critical systemic factors that have hindered and obstructed social acceptance of those facts. It would be equally myopic, however, to simply criticise the ICTY in this regard. Its claim exposes a more intrinsic and larger

Tribunal is whether crimes were committed during the conflict and by whom' (Prosecutor *v.* Blaškić, 2004. para. 427).

[11] In 2000, a Trial Chamber of the ICTY sentenced Vlatko Kupreškić and his two cousins, brothers Mirjan and Zoran Kupreškić, to prison terms of six, eight and ten years respectively for crimes against humanity in Ahmići. All three men were members of the HVO in Central Bosnia. A year later, the Appeals Chamber overturned these convictions, finding that a miscarriage of justice had occurred (Prosecutor *v.* Kupreškić et al., 2001: para. 245; see also para. 304). Josipović was also a member of the HVO in Central Bosnia. In the same trial, he was convicted of crimes against humanity and sentenced to fifteen years' imprisonment. On appeal, his sentence was reduced to twelve years, to reflect errors made by the Trial Chamber (Prosecutor *v.* Kupreškić et al., 2001: para. 361). He was granted early release in January 2006.

issue with transitional justice itself, as both a theory and a practice. Transitional justice processes are quintessentially about 'dealing with the legacy' of past human rights violations, with the aim, inter alia, of delivering justice, establishing the truth and fostering reconciliation (United Nations, 2010: 2). Yet, their primary focus on individuals – and specifically on victims and perpetrators – means that they often neglect the wider social ecologies that critically contribute to shaping the legacies of mass human rights abuses. This chapter has demonstrated that one of the legacies of the massacre in Ahmići is a broken and disjointed community.

The essential point is that, in order to understand this legacy, it is not sufficient only to focus on the crime itself or on the ICTY's shortcomings. It is also imperative to take account of broader systemic factors, as explored in the previous section, that have influenced how people in Ahmići have dealt with the past – and how they responded to the ICTY's work. Ultimately, what is needed is a social-ecological reframing of transitional justice that better reflects the realities of complex individual – environment interactions (Clark, 2020b). Such a reframing, in turn, has important implications for developing adaptive peacebuilding.

SOCIAL-ECOLOGICAL TRANSITIONAL JUSTICE AND ADAPTIVE PEACEBUILDING

Various scholars have written about the relationship between transitional justice and peacebuilding. Baker and Obradovic-Wochnik (2016: 282), for example, note that '[t]he idea that one will lead to the other is often the underlying logic of external intervention, even though it is not always clear how the two practices ought to shape each other'. In her work on the Democratic Republic of Congo, Arnould (2016: 323) finds that 'actors attach very different meanings and goals to transitional justice that are deeply embedded in broader peacebuilding goals', thus underscoring how 'deeply intertwined' the two concepts are in practice. Pointing to the importance of strengthening the relationship between the two concepts, Muvingi (2016: 20) has emphasised the need 'to reconfigure TJ [transitional justice] as processes of inclusion that facilitate and support societies affected by violence to address the legacies of the violence and chart pathways for more just and peaceable futures'.

Both in theory and in practice, liberalism – and more specifically the idea of 'liberal peace' – has frequently shaped discussions about peacebuilding and peacebuilding agendas (see, e.g., Joshi et al., 2014). de Coning (2018: 305), however, has pointed to a 'pragmatic turn in peacebuilding' at the UN level, marked by a shift away from liberal peace and a new focus on 'identifying and supporting the political and social capacities that sustain peace'. His 'adaptive peacebuilding' (de Coning, 2018: 305) seeks to operationalise this new emphasis. It also provides a framework for rethinking the relationship between transitional justice and peacebuilding in a way that promotes resilience (see also Chapter 11).

Of critical importance in this regard is adaptive peacebuilding's systemic approach, informed by complexity theory and its emphasis on the interactions and dynamics between complex and multi-layered systems (see, e.g., Norberg and Cumming, 2008). de Coning (2018: 305) underlines that '[i]nsights from complexity theory about influencing the behaviour of complex systems, and how such systems respond to pressure, should thus be very instructive for peacebuilding'. An approach to peacebuilding that highlights complex systems is similarly instructive for transitional justice, and more specifically for the development of new social-ecological ways of operationalising transitional justice.

McAuliffe (2017: 250) argues that '[t]he vigorously contested process of expanding the interdisciplinary spaces within transitional justice (and hence its ultimate goals) has taken precedence over study of actual post-conflict ecologies'. Foregrounding these ecologies, and the intersecting systems which form part of them, is essential for developing more sustainable ways of doing transitional justice that extend beyond dealing with the past to building more resilient systems and societies. In other words, the relationship between adaptive peacebuilding and transitional justice is symbiotic. The systemic approach that characterises adaptive peacebuilding is highly relevant for developing new social-ecological ways of doing transitional justice. Equally, the need to think 'innovatively and creatively' about transitional justice (International Center for Transitional Justice, n.d.) can contribute to actualising adaptive peacebuilding in practice.

In Ahmići, intersecting systems critically limited the on-the-ground impact of the ICTY's work. A social-ecological reframing of transitional justice requires giving far greater attention to these broader systems, yet it is not about simply 'correcting' them through administrative reforms or lustration measures. Most importantly, it is about helping to foster resilient systems that can effectively and positively adapt to adversity. In this regard, de Coning (2018: 314–315) notes: 'Adaptive peacebuilding recognises that conflict is a normal and necessary element of change. Its focus is on supporting the ability of communities to cope with and manage this process of change in such a way that they can avoid violent conflict'. Part of operationalising the synergy between adaptive peacebuilding and transitional justice, therefore, is to explore ways of fostering resilience within often-overlooked community-level systems.

In my previous work, I have emphasised the need for transitional justice processes to promote and harness fundamental connectivities between people, including common emotions, feelings and shared values (see, e.g., Clark, 2020a, 2020c). In Cambodia, for example, Phka Sla is an innovative and creative form of transitional justice that tells the stories of victims through the medium of dance. The power of movement, and its cultural resonance within Cambodia's classical dance tradition, creates emotional connectivity and understanding in a way that words alone may not. Commenting on this, Shapiro-Phim (2020: 212) notes that 'experiences that had in some instances triggered shame and whose suppression had kept people feeling isolated, now generate empathy and a sense of dignity and connection, along with contributions to the historical record'. In other words, a social-ecological reframing of transitional justice is partly about exploring and raising awareness of the core systems that connect people, and thus of strengthening local capacity to advocate for and exert pressure for broader systemic change as part of adaptive peacebuilding.

CONCLUSION

Žarkov discusses the British television drama *Warriors* (1999), which focuses on events in Ahmići and on a British battalion based in Central Bosnia. Warriors, she argues, 'creates two ontological worlds: one for the male, Serb/Croat military Other who is totally dehumanized, and with whom no similarity is allowed; another for the UK soldiers and their families whose very humanity and ethics stand in the way of understanding or relating to the former' (Žarkov, 2014: 190). War events in Ahmići and their filtering through, and instrumentalisation by, different interconnected systems have contributed to essentially creating two worlds in the sense that Bosniaks and Croats remain deeply divided about those events. The absence of any common narratives, in turn, has contributed to undermining the community's resilience as a whole.

While the ICTY's trials had little positive impact in this regard, this chapter has reflected on how a social-ecological remodelling of transitional justice – as part of developing adaptive peacebuilding – might target the systems (including political and education systems, attitudes and value systems) that both hinder and potentially facilitate resilience. de Coning (2020) emphasises that 'complex systems cope with challenges posed by changes in their environment by co-evolving together with their environment in a never-ending process of adaptation'. A major challenge is for transitional justice and adaptive peacebuilding to evolve together to promote positive adaptation in systems that are seemingly resilient to change.

REFERENCES

Abramušić, V. (2016). U Vitezu smanjen broj stanovnika za 7,2 posto. www.vecernji.ba/v ijesti/u-vitezu-smanjen-broj-stanovnika-za-72-posto-1100284 (accessed 22 January 2020).

Anadolija (2019). U Sarajevu održana konferencija o ratnim zločinama u Ahmićima. https://radiosarajevo.ba/vijesti/bosna-i-hercegovina/u-sarajevu-odrzana-konferencija -o-ratnim-zlocinima-u-ahmicima/333548 (accessed 21 February 2020).

Arnould, V. (2016). Transitional justice in peacebuilding: Dynamics of contestation in the DRC. *Journal of Intervention and Statebuilding*, 10(3), 321–338.

Baker, C. and Obradovic-Wochnik, J. (2016). Mapping the nexus of transitional justice and peacebuilding. *Journal of Intervention and Statebuilding*, 10(3), 281–301.

Belak-Krile, A. (2019). Ovo je Dario Kordić: Osuđen je zbog masakra u Ahmićima u kojem je ubijeno 116 civila, najmlađa žrtva imala je samo tri mjeseca; Za zločin se nikada nije ispričao, niti pokazao pokajanje. https://slobodnadalmacija.hr/vijesti/hr vatska/ovo-je-dario-kordic-osuden-je-zbog-masakra-u-ahmicima-u-kojem-je-ubijeno-116-civila-najmlada-zrtva-imala-je-samo-tri-mjeseca-za-zlocin-se-nikada-nije-ispri cao-niti-pokazao-pokajanje-597090 (accessed 2 February 2020).

Berkes, F. and Ross, H. (2013). Community resilience: Toward an integrated approach. *Society and Natural Resources: An International Journal*, 26(1), 5–20.

Bose, S. (2005). The Bosnian state a decade after Dayton. *International Peacekeeping*, 12 (3), 322–335.

Chaskin, R. J. (2008). Resilience, community and resilient communities: Conditioning contexts and collective action. *Child Care in Practice*, 14(1), 65–74.

Clark, J. N. (2012). Reflections on trust and reconciliation: A case study of a central Bosnian village. *International Journal of Human Rights*, 16(2), 239–256.

Clark, J. N. (2014). *International Trials and Reconciliation: Assessing the Impact of the International Criminal Tribunal for the Former Yugoslavia*. Abingdon: Routledge.

Clark, J. N. (2019). 'Leaky' bodies, connectivity and embodied transitional justice. *International Journal of Transitional Justice*, 13(2), 268–289.

Clark, J. N. (2020a). Emotional legacies, transitional justice and alethic truth: A novel basis for exploring reconciliation. *Journal of International Criminal Justice*, 18(1), 141–165.

Clark, J. N. (2020b). The COVID-19 pandemic and ecological connectivity: Implications for international criminal law and transitional justice. *Journal of International Criminal Justice*, https://doi.org/10.1093/jicj/mqaa057

Clark, J. N. (2020c). The ICTY, truth and reconciliation: A meta reconceptualization. In C. Stahn, C. Agius, S. Brammertz and C. Rohan (eds.), *Legacies of the International Criminal Tribunal for the Former Yugoslavia: A Multidisciplinary Approach*. Oxford: Oxford University Press, pp. 583–600.

Comes, T., Meesters, K. and Torjesen, S. (2019). Making sense of crises: The implications of information asymmetries for resilience and social justice in disaster-ridden communities. *Sustainable and Resilient Infrastructure*, 4(3), 124–136.

Dajić, M. (2017). Za miran život u Ahmićima. www.oslobodjenje.ba/vijesti/bih/za-miran-zivot-u-ahmicima (accessed 31 January 2020).

de Coning, C. (2018). Adaptive peacebuilding. *International Affairs*, 94(2), 301–317.

de Coning, C. (2020). Insights from complexity theory for peace and conflict studies. In: O. Richmond and G. Visoka (eds.), *The Palgrave Encyclopedia of Peace and Conflict Studies*. Cham: Palgrave Macmillan, http://doi.org/10.1007/978-3-030-11795-5_134-1

Dnevnik. (2019). Dario Kordić govorio o vjeri na skupu don Stojića, aktivisti mu vikali: 'Ti si ratni zločinac!' https://dnevnik.hr/vijesti/hrvatska/dario-kordic-pricao-o-vjeri-na-skupu-don-stojica-studenti-mu-vikali-ti-si-ratni-zlocinac—555528.html (accessed 27 February 2020).

Ellis, B. H. and Abdi, S. (2017). Building community resilience to violent extremism through genuine partnerships. *American Psychologist*, 72(3), 289–300.

Fletcher, L. E. and Weinstein, H.M. (2002). Violence and social repair: Rethinking the contribution of justice to reconciliation. *Human Rights Quarterly*, 24(3), 573–639.

Hina. (2019). Džaferović optužio Grabar-Kitarović da vrijeđa Bošnjake i potiče podjele u BiH: 'To ne rade ozbiljni političari'. www.jutarnji.hr/vijesti/hrvatska/dzaferovic-optuzio-grabar-kitarovic-da-vrijeda-bosnjake-i-potice-podjele-u-bih-to-ne-rade-ozbiljni-politicari/9683908 (accessed 6 February 2020).

Hoare, A. (1997). The Croatian project to partition Bosnia-Hercegovina, 1990–1994. *East European Quarterly*, 31(1), 121–138.

Hobfoll, S. E. (2001). The influence of culture, community and the nested-self in the stress process: Advancing conservation of resources theory. *Applied Psychology: An International Review*, 50(3), 337–421.

Hodžić, R. (2011). A long road yet to reconciliation: The impact of the ICTY on reconciliation and victims' perceptions of criminal justice. In R. H. Steinberg (ed.), *Assessing the Legacy of the ICTY*. Leiden: Brill, pp. 115–119.

ICTY. (n.d.). Achievements. www.icty.org/en/about/tribunal/achievements (accessed 2 February 2020).

ICTY. (2004). View from The Hague: Croats celebrated, only Blaškić showed remorse. www.icty.org/x/file/Outreach/view_from_hague/balkan_040910_en.pdf (accessed 11 October 2019).

International Center for Transitional Justice. (n.d.). What is transitional justice? www.ictj.org/about/transitional-justice (accessed 12 December 2019).

Joshi, M., Lee, S. Y. and Mac Ginty, R. (2014). Just how liberal is the liberal peace? *International Peacekeeping*, 21(3), 364–389.

Laketa, S. (2019). The politics of landscape as ways of life in the 'divided' city: Reflections from Mostar, Bosnia-Herzegovina. *Space and Polity*, 23(2), 168–181.

Liebenberg, L. and Moore, J. C. (2018). A social ecological measure of resilience for adults: The RRC-ARM. *Social Indicators Research*, 136, 1–19.

Luthar, S. S., Cicchetti, D. and Becker, B. (2000). The construct of resilience: A critical evaluation and guidelines for future work. *Child Development*, 71(3), 543–562.

Magis, K. (2010). Community Resilience: An indicator of social sustainability. *Society and Natural Resources*, 23(5), 401–416.

McAuliffe, P. (2017). Reflections of the nexus between justice and peacebuilding. *Journal of Intervention and Statebuilding*, 11(2), 45–260.

Meernik, J. and Guerrero, J. R. (2014). Can international criminal justice advance ethnic reconciliation? The ICTY and ethnic relations in Bosnia-Herzegovina. *Southeast European and Black Sea Studies*, 14(3), 383–407.

Muvingi, I. (2016). Donor-driven justice and peacebuilding. *Journal of Peacebuilding and Development*, 11(1), 10–25.

Nielsen, C. A. (2013). Surmounting the myopic focus on genocide: The case of the war in Bosnia and Herzegovina. *Journal of Genocide Research*, 15(1), 21–39.

Norberg, J. and Cumming, G. S. (eds.) (2008). *Complexity Theory for a Sustainable Future*. New York: Columbia University Press.

Nuwaydid, I., Zurajk, H., Yamout, R. and Cortas, C. S. (2011). Summer 2006 war on Lebanon: A lesson in community resilience. *Global Public Health*, 6(5), 505–519.

Olson, D. H. (2000). Circumplex model of marital and family systems. *Journal of Family Therapy*, 22(2), 144–167.

Orentlicher, D. (2018). *Some Kind of Justice: The ICTY's Impact in Bosnia and Serbia*. Oxford: Oxford University Press.

OSCE. (2018). 'Two schools under one roof': The most visible example of discrimination in education in Bosnia and Herzegovina. www.osce.org/mission-to-bosnia-and-herzegovina/404990?download=true (accessed 16 February 2020).

Piersma, M. J. (2019). 'Sistem te laze!' The anti-ruling class mobilisation of high school students in Bosnia and Herzegovina. *Nations and Nationalism*, 25(3), 935–953.

Prosecutor v. Tihomir Blaškić. (2000). ICTY Trial Chamber Judgment, IT-95-14-T, 3 March 2000.

Prosecutor v. Tihomir Blaškić. (2004). ICTY Appeals Chamber Judgment, IT-95-14-A, 29 July 2004.

Prosecutor v. Miroslav Bralo. (2006). ICTY Sentencing Judgment, IT-95-17-S, 7 December 2005.

Prosecutor v. Dario Kordić and Mario Čerkez. (2001). ICTY Trial Chamber Judgment, IT-95-14/2-T, 26 February 2001.

Prosecutor v. Dario Kordić and Mario Čerkez. (2001). ICTY Appeals Chamber Judgment, IT-95-14/2-A, 17 December 2004.

Prosecutor v. Zoran Kupreškić, Mirjan Kupreškić, Vlatko Kupreškić, Drago Josipović, Dragan Papić and Vladimir Šantić. (2000). ICTY Trial Chamber Judgment, IT-95-16-T, 14 January 2000.

Prosecutor v. Zoran Kupreškić, Mirjan Kupreškić, Vlatko Kupreškić, Drago Josipović, Dragan Papić and Vladimir Šantić. (2001). ICTY Appeals Chamber Judgment, IT-95-16-A, 23 October 2001.

Radio Sarajevo. (2010). Ivo Josipović jučer u Ahmićima i Križančevom Selu. https://radiosarajevo.ba/vijesti/bosna-i-hercegovina/ivo-josipovic-jucer-u-ahmicima-i-kri zancevom-selu/24126 (accessed 2 February 2020).

Radio Sarajevo (2019). Grabar-Kitarović poručila: Hrvatima u BiH niko drugi ne smije birati predstavnike. https://radiosarajevo.ba/vijesti/bosna-i-hercegovina/grabar-kitarovic-iz-mostara-porucila-hrvatima-u-bih-vise-niko-drugi-ne-smije-birati-predstavnike/358762 (accessed 11 February 2020).

SENSE Centre. (2019). Ahmići – 48 hours of ashes and blood; TV reports [1993] introduced into evidence on Ahmići massacre trials. www.ahmici.sensecentar.org (accessed 8 December 2019).

Shapiro-Phim, T. (2020). Embodying the pain and suffering of others. *International Journal of Transitional Justice*, 14(1), 209–219.

Southwick, S. M., Bonanno, G. A., Masten, A. S., Panter-Brick, C. and Yehuda, R. (2014). Resilience definitions, theory and challenges: Interdisciplinary perspectives. *European Journal of Psychotraumatology*, 5(1), 1–14.

State Court of BiH. (2019). Potvrđena optužnica u predmetu Ibrahim Purić i dr. www.sudbih.gov.ba/vijest/potvrena-optunica-u-predmetu-ibrahim-puri-i-dr-21038 (accessed 27 October 2020).

Stiles, A. S., Wilson, D. and Thompson, K. (2009). Description and application of personal boundary theory in traumatized adults through the use of Russian stacking dolls. *Traumatology*, 15(2), 60–77.

Swimelar, S. (2013). Education in post-war Bosnia: The nexus of societal security, identity and nationalism. *Ethnopolitics*, 12(2), 161–182.

Telhami, S. (2007). Lebanese identity and Israeli security in the shadows of the 2006 war. *Current History*, 106(696), 21–26.

Tuathail, G. O. and O'Laughlin, J. (2009). After ethnic cleansing: Return outcomes in Bosnia-Herzegovina a decade beyond war. *Annals of the Association of American Geographers*, 99(5), 1045–1053.

Ungar, M. (2008). Resilience across cultures. *British Journal of Social Work*, 38(2), 218–235.

Ungar, M. (2017). Which counts more: Differential impact of the environment or differential susceptibility of the individual? *British Journal of Social Work*, 47(5), 1279–1289.

Ungar, M. and Liebenberg, L. (2011). Assessing resilience across cultures using mixed methods: Construction of the child and youth resilience measure. *Journal of Mixed Methods Research*, 5(2), 126–149.

United Nations. (2010). Guidance note of the Secretary-General: United Nations approach to transitional justice. www.un.org/ruleoflaw/files/TJ_Guidance_Note_March_2010FINAL.pdf (accessed 31 January 2020).

Valent, P. (1998). Resilience in child survivors of the Holocaust: Toward the concept of resilience. *The Psychoanalytic Review*, 85(4), 517–535.

Vladisavljević, A. (2019). Catholic church encroaches on higher education in Croatia. https://balkaninsight.com/2019/04/01/catholic-church-encroaches-on-higher-educa tion-in-croatia (accessed 22 February 2020).

Wiebelhaus-Brahm, E. (2017). After shocks: Exploring the relationships between transitional justice and resilience in post-conflict societies. In R. Duthie and P. Seils (eds.), *Justice Mosaics: How Context Shapes Transitional Justice in Fractured Societies*. New York: International Center for Transitional Justice, pp. 140–165.

Winton, M. A. (2008). Dimensions of genocide: The circumplex model meets violentization theory. *Qualitative Report*, 13(4), 605–629.

Winton, M. A. and Unlu, A. (2008). Micro-macro dimensions of the Bosnian genocides: The circumplex model and violentization theory. *Aggression and Violent Behavior*, 13(1), 45–59.

Žarkov, D. (2014). *Warriors*: Cinematic ontologies of the Bosnian war. *European Journal of Women's Studies*, 21(2), 180–193.

Zdeb, A. (2017). Prud and Butmir processes in Bosnia and Herzegovina: Intra-ethnic competition from the perspective of game theory. *Ethnopolitics*, 16(4), 369–387.

4

Transitional Justice as Interruption: Adaptive Peacebuilding and Resilience in Rwanda

Jennie E. Burnet

INTRODUCTION

More than twenty-five years after the 1994 genocide of Tutsi, Rwanda and its people still struggle with its long-term consequences. Applying resilience theory to recovery from genocide poses several conceptual and moral problems. Many resilience approaches emphasise 'a community's ability to cope with crisis, adapt to hazards, and bounce back with minimal loss and disturbance' (Barrios, 2016: 28; Cutter et al., 2008). Genocide, however, breaks society in a way that can never be repaired. The dead cannot be brought back to life. Women and girls cannot be unraped. Survivors cannot forget the violence they experienced. Genocide makes 'bouncing back with minimal loss and disturbance' impossible. Furthermore, in a society where interdependence, kinship relations, reciprocity and communal forms of life are foundational, mass death destroys far more than lives.

This chapter's case study of the Rwandan genocide and its aftermath highlights how a contextualised resilience model of recovery raises questions about the notion of resilience itself. Anthropological critiques of resilience often focus on the variability of the term and its vague definitions (see, e.g., Barrios, 2016; Foxen, 2010). This volume avoids this trap as all authors proceed from Michael Ungar's definition in Chapter 1: 'When referring to biological, psychological, social and institutional aspects of people's lives, the term "resilience" is best used to describe processes whereby individuals interact with their environments in ways that facilitate positive psychological, physical and social development'. Ungar's definition incorporates individual and systemic components of change in response to violent conflict, crimes against humanity or other gross human rights violations. Yet, it is still largely grounded in conceptions of resilience emerging from trauma theory, which emphasise 'the qualities or characteristics that allow a community to survive following a collective trauma' (Sherrieb et al., 2010: 228). While Ungar's definition embraces complex multi-level systems of interaction, it fails to capture how post-genocide recovery and transitional justice are politicised. Thus, it risks 'depoliticize[ing] processes that are, at heart, deeply political' (Barrios, 2016: 30).

In Rwanda, politics produced the 1994 genocide, so it is no surprise that politics deeply shaped recovery processes. This recovery may have increased resilience by improving ordinary citizens' mental health, creating social institutions that mitigate conflict in non-violent ways and providing 'individuals with the internal and external resources necessary to cope with exceptional and uncommon stressors' (Ungar, Chapter 1). Yet, it also built a strong, centralised state dominated by a single political party and president, both of which were factors that made genocide possible in 1994 (Uvin, 1998). This strong centralised state exemplifies how macro-level systemic change seeks 'to avoid future exposure to stress' that Ungar identifies as central to resilience (Chapter 1). Yet, this transformation risks reinforcing inequalities that already exist and perpetuating vulnerabilities (Barrios, 2016: 32; Holling 1973: 14). In Rwanda, poverty created the context where genocide was possible, and it continued after the genocide with long-term physical and psychological consequences. As anthropologist Barrios (2016: 33) points out, 'postdisaster contexts are moments when political elites and culturally dominant groups attempt to define disaster recovery in ways that align with their socioeconomic interests and sensibilities'. Systemic factors often privilege recovery for some in society over others. In Rwanda, this reality has led to increasing divides between the wealthy and poor, which may overlap with divides between Tutsi and Hutu, and has solidified the Rwandan Patriotic Front (RPF) political party's control over the state and economy. Whether this result constitutes resilience is an open question.

This chapter also considers the implications of adaptive peacebuilding and transitional justice for post-genocide recovery. de Coning (2020: 10) defines adaptive peacebuilding as actively engaging 'in a structured process to sustain peace and resolve conflicts by employing an iterative process of learning and adaptation'. This definition of adaptive peacebuilding implicitly mobilises key aspects of Galtung's concept of positive peace. For Galtung (1969: 183), 'negative peace' is the 'absence of personal violence', which is an incomplete peace. 'Positive peace', on the other hand, is a complete peace where personal violence, structural violence and cultural violence are absent and society is integrated (Galtung, 1969: 190). In this chapter, I extend de Coning's definition of adaptive peacebuilding to encompass local, grassroots initiatives that contribute to building positive peace and resilient communities. I primarily consider initiatives led by local non-government organisations (NGOs) and church-based groups as examples of adaptive peacebuilding in Rwanda's post-genocide period. These efforts exemplify adaptive peacebuilding because they emerged from the genocide and focused on 'process not end-states' (de Coning, 2018: 315–317). Furthermore, they responded directly to ordinary people's immediate needs without promoting other political agendas. This evidence from Rwanda validates the need for peacebuilding approaches that focus on broader notions of positive peace instead of state-building (Autesserre, 2014).

Finally, I examine the disruptive nature of transitional justice for locally 'adaptive peacebuilding' initiatives and the state's use of transitional justice to impose a new, stable (and thus 'resilient') social order on Rwandan society. Yet, this resilience fosters inequality and leaves many important issues related to recovery and long-term peace unresolved. Rwanda is an important case study for understanding the relationships between resilience, adaptive peacebuilding and transitional justice because it became 'emblematic of how peacebuilding and reconciliation emerged as global master narratives of the late twentieth century' (Doughty, 2016: 3). The International Criminal Tribunal for Rwanda (ICTR) became the model for numerous international transitional justice mechanisms, and Rwanda's grassroots courts that prosecuted genocide crimes locally have been held up as models for transitional justice predicated on restorative justice and reconciliation.

THE 1994 GENOCIDE OF TUTSI

During the genocide, approximately 77 per cent of the Rwandan Tutsi population inside the country was killed between 6 April and 14 July 1994 (Des Forges, 1999: 15). The genocide's triggering event was the assassination of President Habyarimana on the evening of 6 April 1994 when his plane was shot down as it approached to land in Kigali, the capital city. Within hours, special forces units from the Rwandan Armed Forces (RAF) erected roadblocks across Kigali, and Interahamwe militiamen fanned out across the city, hunting down opposition political party leaders and prominent Tutsi politicians. On the morning of 7 April, Interahamwe militias began attacking and killing ordinary Tutsi civilians in Kigali and several other places in the country. By 12 April, genocide had become a nation-wide policy. Between 7 April and 14 July 1994, an estimated 800,000 Rwandans lost their lives in the genocide or ongoing armed conflict between the RAF and the RPF rebel group (United Nations, 1999). The genocide ended when the RPF seized the majority of the country's territory, sending the government responsible for the genocide, along with the Interahamwe militias and two million civilians, into exile in neighbouring countries.

Genocidal violence in Rwanda involved enormous amounts of hand-to-hand killing as the primary weapons used to dispatch victims were farming tools, such as machetes, hatchets, pruning knives and hoes, or traditional weapons such as spears, arrows and clubs. Local government officials organised and recruited ordinary Hutu civilians to find and kill their Tutsi kin, friends and neighbours. Additionally, perpetrators pillaged property, destroyed homes (see Figure 4.1) and slaughtered stolen livestock. Sexual violence and torture featured centrally in the violence. Post-mortem mutilation of bodies and other public displays of gruesome symbolic violence terrorised victims and potential rescuers while fuelling the passions of the most violent killers among the genocidal mobs.

The genocide took place in the midst of a civil war that began in October 1990 when the RPF, which was founded in Uganda, attacked the country in order to overthrow the government and allow tens of thousands of Rwandan refugees to return home. In 1994, civilians experienced active combat between the RAF and RPF that included heavy artillery in many places, particularly around the capital city. As the RPF took territory, allegations emerged of reprisal killings against Hutu civilians, extrajudicial killings of alleged genocide perpetrators and massacres at public meetings (Des

FIGURE 4.1 Destroyed house. Photo by the author.

Forges, 1999: 542–545). Although some scholars have alleged a 'double geno-cide', the scale and scope of these killings were incomparable to the genocidal killings that preceded them and have been disproven by at least one study (Verwimp, 2003). Nonetheless, civilian killings by the RPF have largely remained unaddressed through transitional justice mechanisms or public memory institutions.

RELIGIOUS AND SPIRITUAL RESPONSES TO MASS VIOLENCE AS ADAPTIVE PEACEBUILDING

In the wake of the 1994 genocide, the transitional government faced the near insurmountable task of governing a country with no resources and a traumatised population. The withdrawing government intentionally des-troyed the country's physical infrastructure. The genocide and massive exile of civilians more than decimated the country's human resources. Much of the emergency international aid unleashed by images of Rwandan refugees dying of dysentery in eastern Congo went to support refugee camps on the borders of the country instead of the new government and civilians who remained in Rwanda. In the months after the genocide, the new RPF-led government focused on standard, state-centred peacebuilding (as opposed to adaptive peacebuilding) efforts. It sought to stop direct violence, including continued attacks against genocide survivors, reprisal killings and conflicts over property; to appoint civilian administrative authorities; to provide humanitarian relief and to re-establish the rule of law.

Religious leaders, churches and local communities stepped in between the government response and people's spiritual and emotional needs. They organ-ised memorial services and burial ceremonies to remember victims and to give people some culturally relevant means to grieve. While intended simply to respond to people's needs, these activities were forms of adaptive peacebuild-ing. These religious interventions helped stimulate processes that enabled 'self-organisation' and led to strengthening 'the resilience of social institutions that manage[d] internal and external stressors and shocks' (de Coning, Chapter 11). Barrios (2016: 30–31) calls this phenomenon of civil society stepping into the gap between the state and the people 'resilience as an antipolitics machine'.

While cultural traditions of mourning may be impossible to practise in the wake of genocide, survivors and others needed to process their grief and honour their lost loved ones. Even though many churches became massacre sites during the genocide and some clergy were responsible for genocide crimes, religious institutions were places where Rwandans of all races

(Hutu, Tutsi and Twa) came together. During the genocide, the majority of victims had been thrown into pit latrines and inhumed, entombed in mass graves or hastily buried where they lay. Most Rwandans did not know where, when or how their loved ones had died and thus could not perform the necessary religious rituals at their graves. Religious rites such as the consecration of graves remained salient; '[i]n the African context, it is unthinkable to honor the dead without religion' (Vidal, 2001: 26; author's translation). In response, many Roman Catholic Church parishes organised community mourning ceremonies for genocide victims' families, friends and neighbours. Local genocide survivor groups mobilised to gather victims' bodies that lay in the open or were discovered in shallow graves and to hold burial ceremonies where priests, pastors or imams consecrated the graves. These community and family-level ceremonies focused on mourning loved ones lost in the violence and honouring religious obligations to the dead (see Figure 4.2). These efforts emerged from local communities and fulfilled local needs (de Coning's first principle of adaptive building, Chapter 11). They were also participatory processes that required clergy, laypeople, survivors and others to cooperate in the organisation of these activities.

FIGURE 4.2 Kibuye church genocide memorial. Photo by the author.

Ordinary Rwandans and civil society leaders utilised various cultural resources to adapt to the trauma caused by the genocide and civil war. These included religious beliefs and practices, customs of social accompaniment and patience (*kwihangana*), gift giving and other forms of reciprocity and traditional conflict-resolution mechanisms. Beyond the burials, commemoration masses and prayer services, ordinary Rwandans drew on a broad range of religious resources to promote healing. Some found solace in singing gospel music and praying alone at home. Others returned to the churches where they prayed before the genocide, not a simple proposition in cases where the spaces had become massacre sites or where clergy had participated in the killings. In the genocide's wake, some survivors renounced churches implicated in the genocide. These survivors gravitated towards charismatic Christian prayer groups, healing worship services or evangelical churches. They found solace in groups that sang gospel music and danced for hours. While these services rarely addressed harm inflicted during the genocide or war, many participants found relief from their ongoing trauma symptoms through their participation in them.

Some Rwandans returned to traditional ancestor or spirit cults, whether alongside or in place of Christianity. Before the genocide, these cults, which the Roman Catholic Church had long maligned and tried to suppress, brought people together across kinship, social group or racial/ethnic lines. In some communities, practitioners of *kubandwa* or *Ryangombe* spirit cults resumed their all-night ritual sessions. These seances helped some people address the harms done in the physical realm through the metaphysical intervention of powerful spirits. In this sense, spirituality became a contextually specific resource that enhanced both individual and community resilience.

Several women's organisations, youth associations, church congregations and church-based organisations engaged in post-genocide activities that can be understood as examples of adaptive peacebuilding. Many of these organisations did not set out with reconciliation or peacebuilding as their goals (Burnet, 2012: 179–193). Instead, they intended to help victims of sexual violence, to assist genocide widows, to improve the socio-economic conditions of women or to help people worship. These NGOs recognised that, to help rebuild people's lives after the genocide and war, they must first tackle their material conditions. By addressing the structural violence of poverty, they equipped people to deal with equally vital but more abstract needs, such as psychological health, social isolation or reconciliation. These efforts embody the difference between post-conflict approaches to peacebuilding, which are 'focused on responding to identifiable risks, and the sustaining peace concept of peacebuilding, which is aimed at investing in the capacity of societies to manage future tensions themselves' (de Coning, 2018: 313).

EVERYDAY PRACTICES OF COPING AS RESILIENCE AND ADAPTIVE PEACEBUILDING

Local-level responses to the Rwandan genocide and its aftermath can be understood as organic forms of resistance and adaptive peacebuilding. In the months and years immediately after the genocide, ordinary Rwandans improvised means to put aside their grief and go on living. Some moved to new communities to avoid daily reminders of their experiences during the genocide. Others remarried or gave birth to new children, not to forget those who perished in the genocide but as a way of creating something to live for. Others buried themselves in the minutiae of everyday life; 'a life that slowly regained normalcy with the passage of time, they succeeded at least partially in keeping their memories and the negative emotions attached to them – sadness, anger, guilt, and hatred – at bay' (Burnet, 2012: 75). Despite their best efforts to forget, embodied memories embedded in everyday life, such as an empty bed, the smell of grilled meat or the sight of a machete, broke through their amnesia and transported them back to the genocide. Psychologists might classify these reactions as forms of negative coping (i.e., repressed memories, avoidance, dissociation). Yet, they were adapted to Rwandan understandings of wellness and how to deal with negative life events. Rwandan cultural norms socialise children to hide their tears from strangers because only family members love and care about them (Mironko and Cook, 1996). To be an adult in Rwanda is to be in control, and public displays of emotion are harshly judged. In the Rwandan worldview, talking about bad events from the past risks inviting the spirits that provoked them to return. Furthermore, these everyday practices of coping align with Ungar's (Chapter 1) definition of resilience as 'processes whereby individuals interact with their environments in ways that facilitate positive psychological, physical and social development'.

The genocide had shredded the social fabric. In rural communities, subsistence farmers relied on reciprocity, cooperation and patronage relationships to survive. In the wake of the genocide, these warp threads of daily life were torn. Faced with unimaginable loss and trauma, both physical and psychological, rural Rwandans began to repair the social fabric, often unwittingly, as they muddled through the dire material circumstances in which they found themselves. Women played a central role in these efforts because of their social positions in kin groups and communities (Burnet, 2012: 168–169). At first, neighbours lived together with little to no interaction, or thinly veiled hostility.

Out of necessity, some women tentatively reached out to former friends, neighbours and colleagues. Slowly, over time, communities began to establish some kind of normalcy in their everyday interactions. They exchanged terse greetings. They borrowed household items or farming equipment. In 2001, women in a rural community described to me how astounded they were that Hutu and Tutsi neighbours had sat next to each other at a recent wedding. They explained that this was unimaginable in 1997, just after many Hutu community members had returned from exile in the Democratic Republic of the Congo. Despite the progress, many survivors actively opposed these and other conciliatory efforts.

These ad hoc processes of getting by, which emerged in the wake of the genocide, can be understood as forms of resilience and adaptive peacebuilding where people adapt to new circumstances out of necessity rather than through formal state or NGO intervention. These efforts helped build social ties through an iterative process, another principle of adaptive peacebuilding (de Coning, Chapter 11). Precisely because these efforts focused on 'process not end-states' and emerged from the devastating change wrought by the genocide, they exemplify adaptive peacebuilding (de Coning, 2018: 315–317). Furthermore, they demonstrate the need for peacebuilding approaches that focus on broader notions of positive peace rather than state-building.

Social accompaniment was an important cultural resource mobilised in the wake of the genocide that helped reweave the social fabric.[1] During times of hardship, whether illness or death, Rwandans practise social accompaniment to support those facing difficulties. For example, kin, neighbours and friends will visit a sick person at home or in the hospital. These visits provide moral support to the sick and social support for the family. Visitors never come empty-handed; they bring food, beverages or money. Their gifts help the family through the hardships of lost wages or medical costs. Undergirding all Rwandan social interactions is an elaborate system of gift giving and reciprocity. All important social and life events, such as courtship, engagement, marriage, birth, illness or death, are marked by the exchange of gifts. The immense poverty and period of scarcity that followed the genocide made it very difficult for people to maintain these customs. Nonetheless, they continued them through modest or token gifts.

Rwandans also drew on the cultural concept of patience, forbearance or endurance contained in the verb *kwihangana* (to bear up under) (Burnet,

---

[1] By social accompaniment, I am referring to a local, cultural practice and not accompaniment in social work (Wilkinson and D'Angelo, 2019), pedagogy or international activism (Koopman, 2011).

2012; Zraly and Nyiranyoye, 2010). Rwandans use this term to talk about their own difficulties, and they encourage each other to endure hardship. For example, a common thing to say during a social visit to a sick person is '*Wihangane!*' This phrase, which is difficult to translate into English, literally means 'that you might bear it', or 'that you might endure'. Perhaps it is best translated into colloquial American English as 'Hang in there!' Two additional cultural-linguistic concepts of resilience relevant specifically to genocide survivors were '*kwongera kubaho*' (to return to life [from death]) and '*gukomeza ubuzima*' (to continue living) (Zraly and Nyiranyoye, 2010).

These sociocultural resources for coping with the genocide and its aftermath, as well as the everyday practices of muddling through terrible situations, fit well with a contextualised resilience model of recovery. They also establish the need for peacebuilding interventions to account for local cultural contexts and engage with grassroots actors. Yet, these micro-level modes of resilience can be hindered or completely undone by national or international interventions and the political power of elites.

NATIONAL PROCESSES OF PEACEBUILDING, SYSTEMIC HINDRANCES AND LOCAL RESISTANCE

After ending the genocide, the RPF military forces and transitional government sought to re-establish the rule of law. As citizens' basic needs began to be met, the government moved onto symbolic, social and legal forms of peacebuilding. Some of these efforts, such as removing race from bureaucracy and public discourse, resonated positively with adaptive peacebuilding efforts at the grassroots level. Other national efforts, especially those related to genocide commemoration and public memory, disrupted adaptive peacebuilding and undermined contextualised resilience in communities by interfering with local recovery efforts.

Among its first symbolic efforts to eradicate racist ideologies, the government eliminated 'race talk' from daily life. After the genocide, the government removed racial identification from all government bureaucracy, including the national identity cards that had determined many people's fates during the genocide, and discouraged use of the terms 'Hutu', 'Tutsi' and 'Twa'. In 2001, the government passed a law forbidding discussion of racial differences and the use of racial identification in public discourse (Republic of Rwanda, 2001). At face value, these policies appeared to promote positive adaptation to past violence. Racist ideologies had made genocide possible, and the national identity cards had helped identify potential victims. While these policies sought to heal the nation, they simultaneously helped the RPF political party to consolidate its power.

National unity was a foundational ideology of racial inclusion of the RPF rebel group. The RPF's ideology of national unity emphasised unifying aspects of Rwandan history and culture (i.e., shared language, culture, religious practices, etc.) and blamed racial division on European colonisers (Burnet, 2009: 84; Burnet, 2012: 151; Pottier, 2002: 109–129). In the aftermath of the genocide, the RPF-led government joined national unity and reconciliation:

> [R]econciliation is short for national unity and national reconciliation. ... We believe that reconciliation will not come through forgetting the past, but in understanding why the past led to political turmoil and taking measures, however painful and slow, which will make our 'Never Again' a reality.
>
> (cited in Burnet, 2012: 151)

National unity and reconciliation came to encompass a broad range of initiatives reorganising local government administration, formalising and nationalising genocide commemoration and mourning activities, changing the national symbols (i.e., flag, anthem, motto, shield), rewriting the constitution, creating re-education and solidarity camps and setting up grassroots courts to adjudicate genocide crimes. The RPF's approach to national unity and reconciliation was taught in schools and was ubiquitous in public discourse, 'from political speeches to NGO conferences to sporting and music events' (Doughty, 2016: 3). National unity and reconciliation thus became the foundation for the new government's state-building programme and instilled RPF policy at its heart.

The RPF's approach interfaced not only with national and local systems in Rwanda but also with international systemic approaches to peacebuilding. Many international initiatives related to peacekeeping, peacebuilding, conflict resolution and transitional justice of the twenty-first century were directly modelled after initiatives tried in Rwanda. For example, United Nations (UN) peacekeeping regulations grew to encompass the use of force to protect civilians from gross human rights abuses in response to the UN peacekeeping mission's failure during the Rwandan genocide. The former UN High Commissioner for Refugees, Sadako Ogata (1990–2000), developed her concept of peaceful coexistence and piloted the project that became 'Imagine Coexistence' in Rwanda (Ogata, 2000). The UN Security Council created the International Criminal Tribunal for the former Yugoslavia (ICTY) and the ICTR as experiments that led to the eventual creation of the International Criminal Court.

Despite these positive national and international contributions to peace-building in Rwanda, other national efforts disrupted resilience by supplanting local adaptations to past shocks and stressors resulting from mass violence. In particular, reconciliation efforts often worked against adaptive peacebuilding efforts that had emerged from civil society organisations or at the grassroots. In early 1995, Rwanda's government displaced family and community-level com-memoration efforts with its own national project of commemoration that claimed to promote reconciliation but also reinforced the power of the new state (Burnet, 2012; Vidal, 2001, 2004). In essence, this change constituted a shift from locally led adaptive peacebuilding initiatives to formalised, sys-temic approaches that utilised some local practices of reconciliation but ultimately served to consolidate the RPF's political power.

While national reconciliation efforts were clearly needed, they were not always best adapted to local needs. In April 1995, the government organised the first annual genocide commemoration ceremony at the National Amahoro Stadium in Kigali. This first ceremony represented both Tutsi and Hutu as victims of the genocide, unlike subsequent national genocide commemor-ations. In a ceremony attended by President Pasteur Bizimungu, Vice President Paul Kagame, cabinet members, parliamentarians and international diplomats based in Kigali, the participants re-interred approximately 6,000 anonymous genocide victims alongside several well-known Hutu genocide victims (Pottier, 2002: 158; Vidal, 2001: 6). A Catholic priest, a Protestant pastor and a Muslim imam consecrated the mass grave beside the national stadium. In this way, Hutu and Tutsi were given joint recognition as victims of the genocide. The decision to recognise both Hutu and Tutsi genocide victims 'had emerged after debates in the cabinet' (Vidal, 2001: 7; author's translation).

As the RPF consolidated its hold on political power, public memory of the genocide disseminated through national genocide commemoration cere-monies shifted. This change created systemic hindrances to peacebuilding and privileged the traumatic memories of certain citizens over others. State-led commemoration practices formalised the government's official history of the genocide and silenced dissent. Only certain social categories were allowed to speak publicly about the past or comment on government policies. Genocide survivor organisations spoke relatively freely in the public sphere, although the government maintained control over their leadership (Gready, 2010).

Later national genocide commemoration ceremonies globalised blame on Hutu and erected a Tutsi monopoly on suffering (Vidal, 2001: 7). Survivors of RPF-perpetrated killings were silenced, and the victims' families could not mourn their lost loved ones in public. In many cases, the victims of RPF killings were often buried in secret mass graves or in graves designated as genocide memorials. These public secrets were known by everyone but remained unspoken, creating an amplified silence surrounding RPF-perpetrated violence experienced by Rwandans of all races (Burnet, 2012: 111–112). This resounding silence around RPF violence and ongoing human rights violations hindered adaptive peacebuilding efforts in local communities and prevented victims from positively adapting or healing. Even contextualised resilience is inherently political and may not support long-term prospects for positive peace.

Beyond the amplified silence surrounding certain forms of violence that took place during the civil war and after the genocide, Rwandan government discourse about the genocide and the country's history impeded reconciliation. Even if it was intended to achieve long-term good, the suppression of the terms 'Hutu', 'Tutsi' and 'Twa' in the wake of the genocide did not magically erase their importance in Rwandans' daily lives. Thus, people substituted new words for them: genocide survivor or victim for Tutsi, and genocide perpetrator, killer or prisoner for Hutu. Because this new terminology followed an absolutist logic of good and bad, it erased the possibility for acknowledgement of Hutu genocide victims or Tutsi perpetrators of violent crimes. The silence over RPF killings and the government's dominant discourse about the genocide created a memoryscape from which Hutu victims were erased. As a result, it laid the groundwork for genocide denial to persist among some Rwandans. From their perspective, the government's denials surrounding RPF abuses and exclusion of Hutu genocide victims made *sotto voce* allegations of a 'double genocide' plausible in some circles.

Politicisation of the genocide and public memory practices undermined adaptive peacebuilding and reconciliation efforts in local communities, and numerous systemic hindrances interfered as well. One of the most significant disruptions was recurring episodes of violence – whether perpetrated by civilians, Interahamwe militias, rebel insurgents or government security forces. After the genocide ended in July 1994, the new government security forces frequently used lethal force to capture alleged genocide perpetrators or to combat insurgents. Some genocide survivors attacked alleged perpetrators seeking revenge. As the new government re-established the rule of law, this violence largely subsided. Then, between 1997 and 1999, many regions of the country faced insurgent attacks and counterinsurgency operations by government security forces. Insurgent attacks reignited survivors' traumatic memories and intensified symptoms of post-traumatic stress disorder (PTSD) or psychosocial trauma. Violent episodes hindered individuals and communities from healing their traumas and destroyed trust where some communities had made progress.

A final systemic hindrance that delayed recovery and hindered peacebuilding efforts was the extreme poverty of rural Rwandans and the marginalisation of genocide survivors. When people's basic needs (food, water, shelter, clothing) are not met, they are incapable of expending energy on healing trauma or repairing social relationships. The majority of Rwandans faced extreme poverty in the first years after the genocide; their only focus was on survival. For genocide survivors, many of whom were the sole survivor in an entire lineage, the deaths of loved ones produced traumatic memories as well as ongoing poverty and marginalisation. When I asked her about reconciliation, an elderly woman responded: 'How can you ask me about reconciliation? I'm here all alone. When I need water, there is no one to send to the spring. When I need wood for the fire, there is no one to chop it for me. When the fields need planting, there is no one to help me. I don't even have a grandchild to keep me company at night' (author interview, Rwanda, 2000).

TRANSITIONAL JUSTICE, STATE POWER AND RESILIENCE

Two particular transitional justice processes attempted to address the 1994 genocide of Tutsi in Rwanda: the ICTR – an ad hoc international court in Arusha, Tanzania – and a nation-wide system of grassroots courts in Rwanda, known as Gacaca. As conceived in their statutory and ideal form, both mechanisms came to serve as models for transitional justice worldwide. In practice, both institutions became entangled in various competing actors' political objectives. Because of its international focus, the ICTR had little impact inside Rwanda in terms of transitional justice, adaptive peacebuilding or resilience. The Gacaca courts, on the other hand, had significant impacts on the country. In the short term, they disrupted adaptive peacebuilding efforts and increased local conflict in Rwanda. In the long term, the Gacaca courts reinforced state power and RPF dominance in Rwanda, ensuring state stability but without positive peace through interpersonal reconciliation. Whether reinforcing state power constitutes resilience depends entirely on how resilience is defined and the weight given to state stability in that definition. At a minimum, transitional justice in Rwanda illustrates that resilience is an inherently political concept.

The UN Security Council created the ICTR in November 1994, 'for the sole purpose of prosecuting persons responsible for genocide and other serious violations of international humanitarian law committed in the territory of Rwanda and Rwandan citizens responsible for genocide and other such violations committed in the territory of neighbouring states, between 1 January 1994 and 31 December 1994' (UN, 1994). In its twenty-year existence, the ICTR prosecuted seventy-six people for genocide or crimes against humanity and found sixty-two of them guilty. Its most significant achievement was the first-ever conviction for the crime of genocide (Prosecutor *v.* Akayesu, 1998). The UN Security Council conceived of the ICTR as an important mechanism for ensuring 'international peace and security' (Wilson, 2011: 366). While the Tribunal is largely considered a success at the international level, it delivered limited justice to the Rwandan people. People prosecuted by the ICTR faced lesser penalties than those tried in Rwanda. Alleged perpetrators in Rwanda lived in overcrowded prisons where food and water were at times inadequate or unsanitary, while those judged by the ICTR enjoyed prisons equipped with fitness facilities, air conditioning and access to computers. The ICTR consumed vast resources, which could have been used to rehabilitate Rwanda's legal system and speed up justice efforts inside the country. The ICTR did little to promote adaptive peacebuilding in Rwanda, but it did help to ensure that several of the genocide's architects and many perpetrators who had fled the country were held accountable.

In Rwanda, the government initially set out to prosecute every single genocide perpetrator, from the leaders who organised the genocide down to the subsistence farmers who stole their neighbours' property (Waldorf, 2006: 3). This approach was formulated with the long-term goal of ensuring stability (and, perhaps, resilience) by focusing on deterrence rather than offering amnesties in exchange for truth-telling, as in the South African Truth and Reconciliation Commission process. Yet, the approach created an insurmountable backlog of cases which would have challenged any legal or penal system in the world, much less one destroyed by genocide. In 1995, the government passed a law to prosecute genocide crimes. In 1996, the first genocide trials began in Rwanda's formal courts; these cases resulted in the first convictions of genocide perpetrators and public executions in April 1997. By 1999, 150,000 prisoners accused of genocide crimes awaited trial in congested prisons that had been fashioned from warehouses or hastily expanded school dormitories (Human Rights Watch, 2000). The most optimistic analyses at the time estimated that the accused would await trial for decades. This situation undermined justice for survivors, who sought the truth about how their loved ones were killed, and the impossibly long wait for trials and abysmal detention conditions violated the rights of those accused of genocide crimes.

In the absence of state-based transitional justice interventions between 1994 and 2002, some families turned to a traditional conflict-resolution mechanism, known as *gacaca* (pronounced ga-cha-cha), to address harm inflicted during the genocide. In gacaca, local leaders called together the people in dispute, the residents of a hill and 'people of integrity' (*inyangamugayo*), who were usually respected elders, to establish the facts of the conflict and find a solution

(Burnet, 2012: 196). After the genocide, some survivors found it expedient to resolve their conflicts over genocide crimes with kin, neighbours or business partners via a traditional gacaca process. The outcomes of these cases sometimes involved the payment of money, property, goods or services, ensuring the long-term livelihoods of victims and perpetrators. While these grassroots efforts at transitional justice were not widespread, they constitute another example of adaptive peacebuilding and community resilience.

In response to the immense caseload and inhumane prison conditions, the government transformed traditional *gacaca* into a nation-wide system of Gacaca courts, where local citizens served as judges, prosecutors, defenders and witnesses. The Gacaca courts became 'a central site for promoting national unity and restoring the social fabric' in the aftermath of genocide (Doughty, 2016: 3). They became the primary mechanism of transitional justice within the country. In a little over ten years, the Gacaca courts processed almost 2 million cases, 65 per cent of which resulted in guilty verdicts (BBC, 2012). Although they cleared the massive backlog of cases, their justice was limited. In exchange for full confessions, perpetrators' sentences were cut in half. Many perpetrators became eligible for release immediately after their sentencing. Genocide survivors often found that perpetrators' sentences were too light for the crimes committed (Rafferty, 2018). The prosecution, defendants and victims were denied legal representation, which constituted a violation of international legal standards. The falsely accused had little opportunity to prove their innocence and faced a grim set of options. They could confess to crimes they had not committed and receive early release (Burnet, 2012: 137), or they could remain in prison for years, awaiting a trial with the potential of a guilty verdict.

Many legal scholars concluded that justice in Rwanda was one-sided victors' justice (Longman, 2011; Oomen, 2005; Rettig, 2008; Thomson and Nagy, 2010; Waldorf, 2006). Gacaca and civilian courts did not have jurisdiction over killings or other atrocities perpetrated by RPF soldiers. These crimes were relegated to military courts. RPF soldiers prosecuted by the military courts usually received light sentences. Senior officers were rarely court-martialed for abuses against civilians (Human Rights Watch, 1997). The victims of RPF war crimes continue to feel that they have not received justice. In some communities' Gacaca courts, they tried to raise these issues, but the courts had no jurisdiction to hear these cases. From this perspective, transitional justice in Rwanda hindered adaptive peacebuilding and harmed resilience by leaving many citizens without a feeling of justice.

Early scholarship on the Gacaca courts focused on their ideal, intended form (Daly, 2002; Longman, 2006; Ntampaka, 1995; Staub, 2004; Tiemessen, 2004; Uvin, 2003; Wierzynska, 2004). These studies largely concluded that the

Gacaca courts were an excellent model of transitional justice because they provided for truth, justice, restitution or reparations, healing, forgiveness and reconciliation. Phil Clark's study (2010) is illustrative of this mode of research. Clark (2010: 300) portrays the courts as a form of restorative justice intended to engage 'parties previously in conflict' in 'communal dialogue and cooperation', which are 'crucial to fostering reconciliation after genocide', and to punish 'those convicted of genocide and crimes against humanity . . . explicitly in order to promote reconciliation'. He acknowledged that the gacaca process retraumatised genocide survivors and others or enflamed existing tensions where compensation was given grudgingly (Clark, 2010: 98–131). He also found that gacaca 'exacerbate[d] low-level conflicts between individuals and groups in the community' (Clark, 2010: 226). He concluded, however, that, taken as a whole, gacaca achieved its goals as a form of restorative justice (Clark, 2010: 353–355). From this perspective, the Gacaca courts appear to have supported adaptive peacebuilding and enhanced resilience.

A growing body of scholarship based on in-depth, empirical research on the practices of the Gacaca courts reached far less positive conclusions (Brounéus, 2008; Buckley-Zistel, 2005; Chakravarty, 2016; Doughty, 2016; Ingelaere, 2016; Rettig, 2008; Thomson, 2011). These studies conclude that the Gacaca courts failed to support inter-personal reconciliation, increased conflict and undermined trust. In short, transitional justice harmed adaptive peacebuilding and undermined resilience in local communities.

Truth has long been predicated as the foundation of transitional justice mechanisms (Abu-Nimer, 2001; Fletcher and Weinstein, 2002; Gibson, 2004; Hinton and O'Neill, 2009). While the Gacaca courts may have delivered a forensic truth (at least some of the time), they failed to produce a 'dialogical, narrative or healing' truth required for Rwandan understandings of conflict resolution and reconciliation (Ingelaere, 2009, 2016: 5). In my own research in rural and urban Rwanda, dialogical, narrative truth was a key element of virtually all successful, adaptive peacebuilding efforts (Burnet, 2012). Rather than producing truth, testimony (or silence) in Gacaca hearings became 'a form of alliance building' (Doughty, 2016: 107). The end result in many communities was that the Gacaca courts only produced partial truths about the genocide. Furthermore, this truth finding was conditioned by the threat of state power and potential punishment (Chakravarty, 2016; Doughty, 2016; Ingelaere, 2016). The Gacaca courts became a performative site that reinforced RPF dominance.

In the short term, the Gacaca courts dramatically increased conflict and undermined trust in adaptive peacebuilding efforts. The courts were a massive imposition on ordinary Rwandans over a period of ten years. At least once, but sometimes two or three days each week, people were required to participate in day-long hearings. This imposition took them away from their agricultural fields, their homes and their livelihoods. During the hearings, attendees often heard detailed, gruesome testimony about the genocide, which triggered traumatic memories for some and risked generating new trauma through secondary exposure for others. After testifying, many witnesses faced threats or physical violence as the families of the accused sought to silence them. Some survivors discovered that neighbours or friends with whom they had re-established social ties in the ten years after the genocide had participated in the genocide or even killed their loved ones. Although the Gacaca courts relied on confession as a cornerstone and potentially restorative justice mechanism, 'once the courts were underway, they shifted from confessions to accusatory practices' (Ingelaere, 2016: 5). In their confessions, some perpetrators falsely implicated others as a way to inflict harm or seek revenge for matters unrelated to the genocide. All these effects dramatically increased mistrust, intensified conflict and even erupted into renewed physical violence.

In the long term, the Gacaca courts increased stability (and thus resilience) by reinforcing state power and RPF dominance. The Gacaca courts and their repetitive praxis over a ten-year period reinforced the ideas that conflict was bad, conciliation was good and that 'harmonious behavior [was] more civilized than disputing behavior, the belief that consensus is of greater survival value than controversy' (Nader, 1990: 2, cited in Doughty, 2016: 10). Because this view was backed by 'the threat of state punishment', including imprisonment, property forfeiture, fines, restitution to victims in the form of money or labour or compulsory community service, ordinary Rwandans conformed to the scripted reconciliation imposed through the Gacaca courts (Doughty, 2016: 10). Over time, the Hutu population acceded to this imposition because they saw no other good options. Thousands of Hutu adults actively participated in the entrenchment of RPF rule by participating in the Gacaca courts to secure reduced sentences, 'private gains in the form of personal vengeance or economic windfalls' or opportunities to secure their own political power (Chakravarty, 2016: 3). Rather than genuinely participating in a process of truth and reconciliation, they sought 'to protect or advance themselves' by submitting to RPF rule (Chakravarty, 2016: 3). Chakravarty's analysis of the Gacaca court system demonstrates how the courts reinforced RPF dominance at all levels of the state apparatus.

REPARATIONS, ADAPTIVE PEACEBUILDING AND RESILIENCE

Although the ICTR had little impact on adaptive peacebuilding and resilience in Rwanda, its successes and failures highlight the ways in which reparations, in all their diverse forms, have the potential to support adaptive peacebuilding and build resilient communities prepared to deal with intense conflict without descending into mass violence. Reparation efforts inside Rwanda provide clear evidence that reparations can support adaptive peacebuilding and enhance resilience.

In the early 1990s, international legal theory and practice had not yet discovered the fundamental importance of reparations to transitional justice. Thus, the UN Security Council failed to include reparations as part of the ICTR's mandate. Over the course of its operation and through its engagement with witnesses, the ICTR came to understand the foundational importance of victims' rights, restitution and reparations to recovery from mass violence. In 1998, the Rules of Procedure and Evidence were amended to extend the mandate of the Victims and Witness Support Unit to include 'physical and psychological rehabilitation' and short- and long-term plans for the protection of witnesses and their families (Evans, 2012: 95). The UN International Residual Mechanism for Criminal Tribunals, which took over ongoing duties when the ICTR closed in 2015, continues to provide healthcare and social services to hundreds of witnesses in Rwanda. While of minimal impact given the hundreds of thousands of Rwandan survivors, these efforts at least demonstrate an approach that incorporates restitution, reparations and victim support into international justice mechanisms. The mistakes made and lessons learned from the ICTR became the foundation for the multi-modal reparations for victims of gross human rights violations outlined in UN General Assembly Resolution 60/147 of 16 December 2005. In the eleven years between the ICTR's creation and this resolution, legal theory and empirical evidence about reparations grew exponentially. The resolution delineated the many complementary forms that reparations can take: restitution, compensation, rehabilitation, satisfaction and guarantees of non-repetition.

In the quarter century following the genocide, the Rwandan government provided many complementary forms of reparations to genocide victims, at times with support from the international community. Reparations included a variety of direct assistance programmes ranging from food aid, housing assistance, medical treatment, health insurance or tuition. Yet, only officially recognised and registered survivors benefitted from these programmes. Many survivors of mixed parentage and Hutu or Twa genocide victims did not receive anything (Burnet, 2012: 159). Perhaps more importantly, these forms of government assistance often came late, after months or years of misery. They were almost always insufficient to raise survivors out of poverty. At times, they were discontinued due to budgetary constraints.

Many international and government initiatives in Rwanda sought to rehabilitate victims physically and psychologically in the first ten years after the genocide. While these programmes helped, they were all funded through emergency humanitarian aid. Thus, the programmes often stopped after a few years or trained Rwandans in psychosocial support without creating a permanent infrastructure to employ them or provide services. For example, hundreds of trauma counsellors were trained between 1997 and 2000, but the international community only funded civil society organisations to employ them for a few years. Then, the government did not create permanent positions. As a result, few genocide victims received the ongoing psychological support that trauma survivors often need to thrive. The national genocide commemoration ceremonies and genocide memorial sites provided victims with symbolic reparations. Yet, genocide memorial sites languished for more than a decade before coming to fruition. In addition, politics entwined these symbolic reparations with state-building, thus limiting their healing effects.

The Rwandan Genocide Statute (Law No. 08/96) and the Gacaca courts provided restitution to both individual victims and communities as part of their mandates. Where judges determined that property had been looted or destroyed, perpetrators or their families were required to compensate the victims. These judgments came ten to fifteen years after the genocide. While symbolically powerful, they arrived too late for victims who were in desperate need (homeless, destitute, malnourished) between 1994 and 2004. In addition, survivors rarely received full restitution because the perpetrators and their families were too impoverished to complete the payments. The vast majority of perpetrators given reduced sentences in Gacaca were also required to complete community service projects, early on through labour camps, and later a few days each week or month from their homes.

The Gacaca courts and the ICTR both demonstrate the need for multi-modal reparations to victims of gross human rights violations and mass violence. Restitution and diverse forms of reparations can help victims build meaningful lives even if they cannot make them whole or help them to 'bounce back with minimal loss and disturbance' (Barrios, 2016: 28). This assistance must come quickly to have a significant impact on adaptive peace-building and resilience. Diverse forms of reparations, especially those that integrate the principles of adaptive peacebuilding at a community level, can help reweave the social fabric and build more resilient communities. These forms of reparations range from the symbolic – including religious mourning rituals, memorials and public commemorations – to the material – such as compensation for harm done and support to survivors – to public disclosure of the truth. To be effective, these forms of reparations must be designed and implemented through approaches that fully integrate local voices. Regional, national or international programmes must be developed to accommodate high levels of local variation.

CONCLUSION

Rwanda's post-genocide recovery and state-building reinforced RPF political, economic and social dominance. Even when multi-system change leads to greater societal stability and the ability to absorb disturbance and avoid future stress exposure, this short-term appearance of resilience may hide new hierarchies and societal divides that risk generating new conflict. Resilience as a transformational process is still conditioned by politics. Politics must not be ignored in resilience models of recovery. In Rwanda, transitional justice ultimately benefitted the nation-state at the expense of community healing and displaced local adaptive peacebuilding efforts that were often the most successful in promoting reconciliation.

The lessons learned from adaptive peacebuilding and transitional justice in Rwanda point to the importance of tending to local-level needs and concerns in post-genocide crises. Reparations must encompass all victims of gross human rights abuses to avoid creating hierarchies of suffering or new divisions within society. Emphasis on rebuilding social processes of dialogue and reciprocity can help communities heal even when these efforts are not undertaken with peacebuilding or resilience in mind. Adaptive peacebuilding's emphasis on process instead of end states adds an important dimension to resilience models of recovery. Resilience models must consider micro- and macro-level concerns and pay attention to the impact of political power on outcomes.

REFERENCES

Abu-Nimer, M. (2001). *Reconciliation, Justice, and Coexistence: Theory and Practice.* Lanham, MD: Lexington Books.

Autesserre, S. (2014). *Peaceland: Conflict Resolution and the Everyday Politics of International Intervention.* Cambridge: Cambridge University Press.

Barrios, R. E. (2016). Resilience: A commentary from the vantage point of anthropology. *Annals of Anthropological Practice,* 40(1), 28–38.

BBC. (2012). Rwanda 'gacaca' genocide courts finish work. www.bbc.co.uk/news/world-africa-18490348 (accessed 6 May 2020).

Brouneus, K. (2008). Truth-telling as talking cure? Insecurity and retraumatization in the Rwandan gacaca courts. *Security Dialogue,* 39(1), 55–76.

Buckley-Zistel, S. (2005). 'The truth heals?' Gacaca jurisdictions and the consolidation of peace in Rwanda. *Die Friedens-Warte,* 80(1–2), 113–130.

Burnet, J. E. (2009). Whose genocide? Whose truth? Representations of victim and perpetrator in Rwanda. In: A. L. Hinton and K. L. O'Neill (eds.), *Genocide: Truth, Memory and Representation*. Durham, NC: Duke University Press, pp. 80–110.

Burnet, J. E. (2012). *Genocide Lives in Us: Women, Memory, and Silence in Rwanda*. Madison, WI: University of Wisconsin Press.

Chakravarty, A. (2016). *Investing in Authoritarian Rule: Punishment and Patronage in Rwanda's Gacaca Courts for Genocide Crimes*. Cambridge: Cambridge University Press.

Clark, P. (2010). *The Gacaca Courts, Post-Genocide Justice and Reconciliation in Rwanda: Justice without Lawyers*. Cambridge: Cambridge University Press.

Cutter, S. L., Barnes, L., Berry, M., Burton, C., Evans, E., Tate, E. and Webb, J. (2008). A place-based model for understanding community resilience to natural disasters. *Global Environmental Change*, 18(4), 598–606.

Daly, E. (2002). Between punitive and reconstructive justice: The gacaca courts in Rwanda. *New York University Journal of International Law and Politics*, 34(2), 355–396.

de Coning, C. (2018). Adaptive peacebuilding. *International Affairs*, 94(2), 301–317.

de Coning, C. (2020). Insights from complexity theory for peace and conflict studies. In O. Richmond and G. Visoka (eds.), *The Palgrave Encyclopedia of Peace and Conflict Studies*. Cham: Palgrave Macmillan. https://doi.org/10.1007/978-3-030-11 795-5_134-1

Des Forges, A. (1999). *Leave None to Tell the Story: Genocide in Rwanda*. New York: Human Rights Watch.

Doughty, K. (2016). *Remediation in Rwanda: Grassroots Legal Forums*. Philadelphia, PA: University of Pennsylvania Press.

Evans, C. (2012). *The Right to Reparation in International Law for Victims of Armed Conflict*. Cambridge: Cambridge University Press.

Fletcher, L. E. and Weinstein, H. M. (2002). Violence and social repair: Rethinking the contribution of justice to reconciliation. *Human Rights Quarterly*, 24(3), 573–639.

Foxen, P. (2010). Local narratives of distress and resilience: Lessons in psychosocial well-being among the K'iche' Maya in postwar Guatemala. *The Journal of Latin American and Caribbean Anthropology*, 15(1), 66–89.

Galtung, J. (1969). Violence, peace and peace research. *Journal of Peace Research*, 6(3), 167–191.

Galtung, J. (1990). Cultural violence. *Journal of Peace Research*, 27(3), 291–305.

Gibson, J. L. (2004). Does truth lead to reconciliation? Testing the causal assumptions of the South African truth and reconciliation process. *American Journal of Political Science*, 48(2), 201–217.

Gready, P. (2010). 'You're either with us or against us': Civil society and policy making in post-genocide Rwanda. *African Affairs*, 109(437), 637–657.

Hinton, A. L. and O'Neill, K. L. (eds.) (2009). *Genocide: Truth, Memory, and Representation*. Durham, NC: Duke University Press.

Holling, C. (1973). Resilience and stability of ecological systems. *Annual Review of Ecology and Systematics*, 4, 1–23.

Human Rights Watch. (1997). Prosecuting genocide in Rwanda: A lawyers' committee report on the ICTR and national trials. www.unwatch.com/rwanda.html (accessed 13 August 2017).

Human Rights Watch. (2000). Rwanda. In: *World Report 2000*. www.hrw.org/wr2k/Af rica-08.htm#TopOfPage (accessed 19 May 2018).

Ingelaere, B. (2009). 'Does the truth pass across the fire without burning?' Locating the short circuit in Rwanda's gacaca courts. *The Journal of Modern African Studies*, 47(4), 507–528.

Ingelaere, B. (2016). *Inside Rwanda's Gacaca Courts: Seeking Justice After Genocide*. Madison, WI: University of Wisconsin Press.

Koopman, S. (2011). Alter-geopolitics: Other securities are happening. *Geoforum*, 42(3), 274–284.

Longman, T. (2006). Justice at the grassroots? Gacaca trials in Rwanda. In N. Roht-Arriaza and J. Mariezcurrena (eds.), *Transitional Justice in the Twenty-First Century: Beyond Truth versus Justice*. Cambridge: Cambridge University Press, pp. 206–228.

Longman, T. (2011). Limitations to political reform: The undemocratic nature of transition in Rwanda. In S. Straus and L. Waldorf (eds.), *Remaking Rwanda: State Building and Human Rights after Mass Violence*. Madison, WI: University of Wisconsin Press, pp. 25–47.

Mironko, C. and Cook, S. (1996). The linguistic formulation of emotion in Rwanda. In: *Texas Linguistic Forum (TLF)*, vol. 4. Austin, TX: University of Texas Press.

Nader, L. (1990). *Harmony Ideology: Justice and Control in a Zapotec Mountain Village*. Stanford, CA: Stanford University Press.

Ntampaka, C. (1995). Le retour à la tradition dans le règlement des différends: Le gacaca du Rwanda. *Dialogue*, 186, 95–104.

Ogata, S. (2000). Keynote Speech by the UN High Commissioner for Refugees, at the International Symposium on Human Security. www.reliefweb.int/report/afghanistan/k eynote-speech-mrs-sadako-ogata-un-high-commissioner-refugees-international (accessed 29 March 2020).

Oomen, B. (2005). Donor-driven justice and its discontents: The case of Rwanda. *Development and Change*, 36(5), 887–910.

Pottier, J. (2002). *Re-Imagining Rwanda: Conflict, Survival and Disinformation in the Late Twentieth Century*. Cambridge: Cambridge University Press.

Prosecutor v. Jean-Paul Akayesu. (1998). ICTR Trial Chamber Judgment, ICTR-96-4-T, 2 September 1998.

Rafferty, J. (2018). 'I wanted them to be punished or at least ask us for forgiveness': Justice interests of female victim-survivors of conflict-related sexual violence and their experiences with gacaca. *Genocide Studies and Prevention: An International Journal*, 12(3), 95–118.

Republic of Rwanda. (2001). Law No. 47/2001 of December 2001 Instituting Punishment for Offences of Discrimination and Sectarianism. *Official Gazette of the Republic of Rwanda*, Special Issue, December 2001.

Republic of Rwanda. (2004). *Denombrement des victimes du génocide*. Kigali: Ministry of Local Government, Communal Development and Social Affairs (MINALOC).

Rettig, M. (2008). Gacaca: Truth, justice and reconciliation in postconflict Rwanda? *African Studies Review*, 51(3), 25–50.

Sherrieb, K., Norris, F. and Galea, S. (2010). Measuring capacities for community resilience. *Social Indicators Research*, 99(2), 227–247.

Staub, E. (2004). Justice, healing and reconciliation: How the people's courts in Rwanda can promote them. *Peace and Conflict: Journal of Peace Psychology*, 10(1), 25–32.

Straus, S. (2006). *The Order of Genocide: Race, Power, and War in Rwanda*. Ithaca: Cornell University Press.

Thomson, S. M. (2011). The darker side of transitional justice: The power dynamics behind Rwanda's gacaca courts. *Africa*, 81(3), 373–390.

Thomson, S. M. and Nagy, R. (2010). Law, power and justice: What legalism fails to address in the functioning of Rwanda's gacaca courts. *International Journal of Transitional Justice*, 5(1), 11–30.

Tiemessen, A. (2004). After Arusha: Gacaca justice in post-genocide Rwanda. *African Studies Quarterly*, 8(1), 57–76.

Ungar, M. (2008). Resilience across cultures. *The British Journal of Social Work*, 38(2), 218–235.

United Nations. (1994). Security Council Resolution 955 [S/RES/955], Establishment of the International Criminal Tribunal for Rwanda. www.refworld.org/docid/3b00 f2742c.html (accessed 14 March 2020).

United Nations. (1999). Report of the independent inquiry into actions of the United Nations during the 1994 genocide in Rwanda. https://iccforum.com/media/back ground/reparations/2006-03-21_UN_General_Assembly_Resolution_60-147_(Englis h).pdf (accessed 15 March 2020).

Uvin, P. (1998). *Aiding Violence: The Development Enterprise in Rwanda*. Hartford, CT: Kumarian Press.

Uvin, P. (2003). The gacaca tribunals in Rwanda. In D. Bloomfield, T. Barnes and L. Huyse (eds.), *Reconciliation After Violent Conflict*. Stockholm: International IDEA, pp. 116–121.

Verwimp, P. (2003). Testing the double-genocide thesis for Central and Southern Rwanda. *Journal of Conflict Resolution*, 47(4), 423–442.

Vidal, C. (2001). Les commémorations du génocide du Rwanda. *Les Temps Modernes*, 613, 1–46.

Vidal, C. (2004). La commémoration du génocide au Rwanda: Violence symbolique, memorization forcée et histoire officielle. *Cahiers d'études Africaines*, 44, 575–592.

Waldorf, L. (2006). Mass justice for mass atrocity: Rethinking local justice as transitional justice. *Temple Law Review*, 79(1), 1–87.

Wierzynska, A. (2004). Consolidating democracy through transitional justice: Rwanda's gacaca courts. *New York University Law Review*, 79(5), 1934–1969.

Wilkinson, M. T. and D'Angelo, K. A. (2019). Community-based accompaniment and social work – A complementary approach to social action. *Journal of Community Practice*, 27(2), 151–167.

Wilson, T. Y. N. (2011). Procedural developments at the International Criminal Tribunal for Rwanda (ICTR). *The Law and Practice of International Courts and Tribunals*, 10(2), 351–380.

Zraly, M. and Nyirazinyoye, L. (2010). Don't let the suffering make you fade away: An ethnographic study of resilience among survivors of genocide-rape in Southern Rwanda. *Social Science and Medicine*, 70(10), 1656–1664.

5

Resilience, Adaptive Peacebuilding and Transitional Justice in Post-Conflict Uganda: The Participatory Potential of Survivors' Groups

Philipp Schulz and Fred Ngomokwe

INTRODUCTION

We began thinking about this case study chapter in the midst of a global pandemic. COVID-19 still has much of the world in various degrees of lockdown and presents unprecedented challenges, anxieties and concerns. In April 2020, as the global numbers of infections and the death count climbed exponentially, Uganda also began registering and reporting its first cases, responded to with drastic political measures carrying far-reaching socio-political and economic consequences for vast parts of the country's population. Yet, whereas various politicians and commentators around the world consider this epidemic to be one of the biggest challenges since World War II, in the north of Uganda the pandemic in many ways constitutes yet another episode in a series of crises and disasters. In addition to an Ebola outbreak in the early 2000s, and an influx of over one million Southern Sudanese refugees during the years prior to this crisis (bringing with it a set of socio-economic and political difficulties for refugee and host populations alike), the populace in northern Uganda also specifically suffered from the more than two-decade-long civil war between the Lord's Resistance Army (LRA) rebel group and the Government of Uganda. In the words of one of our research participants, shared via social media: 'Things are tough with Corona, but we will manage. We managed to live through the LRA-led violence, and so we will even overcome this. We *have become resilient enough*.' In this chapter, we are interested in examining what aspects, processes and capacities may play a role in fostering such resilience.

In response to the LRA war in particular, and in its immediate aftermath, for the past twelve years a wealth of instruments and processes – including criminal prosecutions, an amnesty policy, proposals for a reparations framework and traditional justice mechanisms – have been put in place, aiming to sustainably build peace and development, deliver justice and facilitate healing and reconciliation (Okello et al., 2012) – and ultimately to foster resilience among war-affected communities (Vindevogel et al., 2015). This multitude of processes makes northern Uganda a particularly interesting case for thinking about the interconnectivities between transitional justice, adaptive peacebuilding and resilience, and how these concepts and their linkages can be conceptualised, understood and utilised.

Although transitional justice and peacebuilding measures have been explicitly linked to resilience (Clark, 2020, 2021; Juncos and Joseph, 2020; Kastner, 2020), what remains under-explored is whether and how these mechanisms are equipped (or even intended) to foster conflict-affected societies' resilience, in Uganda and globally. In recent years in particular, the concept of resilience – emphasising how some individuals, communities or societies do well despite enduring adversity – has gained significant traction within conflict transformation and peacebuilding discourses globally (van Metre, 2014). Throughout the growing body of literature on these intersections, there has been a (slow) shift from thinking about resilience in neoliberal and individualistic terms towards more complex ecological, contextual and process-oriented conceptions of resilience (Ungar, 2013) that centre on interactions and relationalities and that facilitate sustainability (Kirmayer et al., 2011: 85).

Against this backdrop, in this chapter we examine what role transitional justice measures have played, directly or indirectly, in fostering resilience in post-conflict northern Uganda. For this, we specifically focus on one under-utilised element of transitional justice and peacebuilding at the micro level, namely survivors' groups. Situated within a vacuum of post-conflict services and mechanisms for conflict-affected communities at large, groups of survivors[1] in northern Uganda began crafting their own spaces and forums at the micro level, in the form of survivors' support groups. These groups – which cultivate local ownership and enable affected communities to exercise agency (Touquet and Schulz, 2020: 12–14) – contribute towards building survivors' adaptive and transformative capacities, and therefore constitute an effective and sustainable resource that conflict-affected communities in

---

[1]   Throughout this chapter, we primarily employ the terminology of survivor, rather than victim, thereby representing how the survivors identified themselves, and to reflect the active agency associated with this terminology. The same applies to survivors' groups, rather than victims' groups. The instances where we use the terminology of victim and victims' groups are cases where the individuals themselves chose that terminology – to describe themselves or their associations.

Acholiland[2] have utilised to positively adapt to various shocks and stressors caused by the armed conflict.

In particular, most existing survivors' groups in northern Uganda are involved in forms of peer-to-peer support and collective income-generating activities, which enable survivors to engage with and recover from experiences of the war as well as to adapt to the hardships of its aftermath by facilitating social (re-)integration, communal belonging and economic stability. Survivors' groups thus combine multiple systemic factors – including gender relations, sociality, communality and a shared lived reality, as well as financial stability – which facilitate local communities' resilient capacities. This, in turn, can create what we think of as a local 'ecology of resilience' (Kirmayer et al., 2012; Ungar, 2011) among members of these groups on an individual and communal level (see Williams, 2021).

In this reading, resilience within the context of the groups is understood as 'a dynamic process of social and psychological adaptation and transformation' (Kirmayer et al., 2011: 85), composed of multiple systemic factors, offering new ways to think about resilience in communal terms and beyond neoliberal individualism (Chandler, 2014: 48). Whereas previous debates about resilience in the context of peacebuilding have primarily focused on how international, external actors can foster resilience (Chandler, 2015: 25), relatively little attention has been paid to 'how local resilience is understood, mobilized and transformed *within* local communities' (Lee, 2020: 349–350). Through our focus on a local ecological understanding of resilience within the context of survivors' groups, we thereby seek to uncover what resources and processes are required by local actors for fostering resilience, in part emphasising the importance of local communities' internal capacities to deal with hardships ensuing from armed conflicts or human rights violations.

Following some methodological reflections, we commence by offering a brief recap of the conflict in northern Uganda and its manifold socio-political consequences, before describing the diverse post-conflict peacebuilding and transitional justice landscape in this context. We then concentrate on processes situated at the micro level that foster survivors' agency, and specifically on the manifold roles played by survivor support groups. To that end, the analytical core of the chapter focuses on different survivors' groups and the assistance they can offer to survivors of the war, as well as how this relates to

---

[2]   Acholiland is a sub-region in northern Uganda, home to the Acholi population, which was arguably most heavily affected by the armed conflict between the LRA and the Ugandan Government. The sub-regions of West Nile and Lango – which also belong to the greater north of Uganda – as well as Teso (in north-western Uganda) were also affected by the war.

transitional justice, adaptive peacebuilding and resilience more broadly. We close this chapter by thinking about what these insights can teach us about the communal and relational components of these interrelated concepts.

METHODOLOGY AND FIELDWORK

The reflections and arguments offered in this chapter are based upon prior experiences of working and conducting research in Acholiland since 2011 on questions of post-conflict reconstruction and transitional justice processes through a gender lens (Schulz, 2020), as well as sustained work experience with different non-governmental organisations (NGOs) in the region, including the Refugee Law Project (RLP) since 2009 (Ngomokwe). In particular, both of us have worked extensively with different survivors' groups, while one of us (Ngomokwe) continues to provide assistance to and regularly engages with different support groups across northern Uganda.

The findings and insights that we draw on in this chapter are primarily based upon research conducted jointly by the two of us over a period of seven months between January and July 2016, focused primarily on questions of transitional justice in northern Uganda. The data specifically derive from focus group discussions (FGDs) with seven different survivors' associations, comprising a total of sixty-eight group members of survivors' groups, as well as in-depth key-informant interviews with eleven individual members of such groups across the conflict-affected north of Uganda. Complementing these data are corroborative insights from ethnographic participant observation of different meetings and activities of the seven survivors' associations, including regular meetings and trainings that the groups were involved in, and conferences and workshops on the topics of peacebuilding and transitional justice. In addition, we draw on supplementary material from two separate studies – that we were both involved with respectively – that examine the roles and functioning of survivors' groups in the northern Ugandan context, with a focus on quests for justice and reparations (Akullo Otwili and Schulz, 2012) and an evaluation study of groups in relation to community healing and activism (RLP, 2016).

THE NORTHERN UGANDAN CONFLICT

Once referred to by Jan Egeland – the former United Nations (UN) Under-Secretary for Humanitarian Affairs and emergency relief coordinator – as 'the biggest forgotten, neglected humanitarian emergency in the world', the conflict between the LRA rebel group and the Government of Uganda has more recently received substantial international attention. For over two decades, between 1986 and 2006, violence by and between the rebel group and government troops resulted in large-scale human rights violations with immense civilian casualties (Finnström, 2008: 22). Tens of thousands of civilians were killed, mutilated, tortured, displaced, raped and otherwise sexually abused by both the LRA and government forces (Dolan, 2009: 39; Porter, 2016: 3). An African proverb quite adequately describes this situation of civilians being affected by and trapped in-between the two warring parties as: '*When two elephants fight, it is the grass that suffers*'.

As of the early 1990s, the LRA grew largely dependent upon forcefully abducting civilians, particularly youth, to generate a larger armed force to fight its cause. According to the United Nations Children's Fund (UNICEF), approximately 35,000–66,000 children and youths were abducted by the LRA, forced to fight as child soldiers and/or serve as sex slaves (Allen and Vlassenroot, 2010: 14). At the same time, at the height of the military conflict in the early 2000s, more than one and a half million people, or up to 95 per cent of the civilian population, were forced from their villages and homesteads into camps for internally displaced persons (IDPs) across the entire northern region. Here, civilians suffered continuous human rights violations, often at the hands of the soldiers there to protect them (Okello and Hovil, 2007: 440), and were vulnerable to constant rebel attacks – leading Dolan (2009: 1) to describe the camps as a form of 'social torture'. As a result of these intersecting dynamics and consequences, individuals within conflict-affected communities in the current post-conflict context suffer from various physical injuries and psychosocial harms, while mental health challenges and spiritual problems connected to the war are common (Williams, 2019: 22). Much of the region's basic infrastructure was destroyed during the war, and social relations largely broke down.

In many ways, the 'Ugandan government's response to the LRA has shifted back and forth between negotiation and military offensives' (Allen and Vlassenroot, 2010: 11). In addition to various military operations during the two-decade-long conflict and several (failed) attempts at talks and negotiations, the Ugandan government in 2000 issued a blanket amnesty, aimed at encouraging rebels in the bush to renounce rebellion, lay down arms and return to civilian life without fear of punishment. In addition to these efforts and developments, religious leaders and civil society representatives have long been involved in finding a mutual, peaceful end to the conflict and – often with the support of the international community and regional stakeholders – initiated various rounds of peace talks and negotiations. Out of a whole variety of non-violent means of conflict resolution and different attempts at

negotiation, the 2006–2008 Juba peace talks were seemingly the most promising initiative. The talks led to the signing of various separate agenda items of
a peace deal, although the final peace agreement was never signed by Joseph
Kony and the LRA. Following the Juba peace talks, it appears that 'an
unfamiliar degree of stability and order has been sustained in northern
Uganda' (Allen and Vlassenroot, 2010: 279).

POST-CONFLICT PEACEBUILDING AND TRANSITIONAL JUSTICE IN NORTHERN UGANDA

Even though the final peace agreement was never officially signed by the LRA,
the separately signed agenda items provided a framework for a ceasefire deal,
an Agreement on Accountability and Reconciliation (AAR) and an accord on
Demobilization, Demilitarization and Reintegration. Shortly after the signing
of the AAR in February 2008, the Ugandan government set up a Transitional
Justice Working Group (TJWG) with the aim of drafting the framework for
Uganda's process of dealing with the legacies of the violent conflict, in the
form of a national transitional justice policy.[3] Under the auspice of the Justice
Law and Order Sector (JLOS) of the Ugandan Ministry of Justice, the transitional justice policy sets out to provide 'an overreaching framework of the
Government of Uganda, designed to address justice, accountability and reconciliation needs of post conflict Uganda' (JLOS, 2019: 3) – and thus serves as
an essential tool in facilitating peacebuilding and transitional justice in this
context.

Aiming 'to ensure accountability, serve justice and achieve reconciliation'
(JLOS, 2019: 3), the policy proposes the implementation and utilisation of:
formal justice processes at the national and domestic level (the International
Crimes Division [ICD] of the High Court of Uganda) and at the international
level (the International Criminal Court [ICC]); traditional justice processes;
a truth-telling process; a reparations programme and amnesty. The policy was
passed by the Ugandan Parliament in 2019. However, it is yet to be legislated
and implemented – a process that has been further delayed by the ongoing
COVID-19 pandemic and resultant political developments.

Earlier, in late 2003, the Government of Uganda announced the referral of
the northern Ugandan situation to the ICC in The Hague. The Court in 2005

---

[3]   The drafting process has continuously been delayed, largely attributed to an apparent lack of
      political will by the Government of Uganda to initiate a holistic transitional justice approach.
      At the same time, JLOS, which is responsible for the development of the transitional justice
      policy, is heavily dependent upon external donor funds, much of which has been withdrawn in
      recent years (see MacDonald, 2014: 279).

issued five arrest warrants against top LRA cadre, including Joseph Kony and Dominic Ongwen. The latter surrendered in early 2015, and his trial commenced in December 2016. Trial Chamber IX of the ICC delivered its judgment on 4 February 2021 (Prosecutor *v*. Ongwen, 2021).[4]

Uganda, therefore, constitutes a poignant example of a relatively diverse transitional justice landscape, including international criminal proceedings by the ICC, national prosecutions by the ICD (see MacDonald and Porter, 2016), traditional justice processes (see Baines, 2007) and proposals for a state-driven and government-led national transitional justice policy. Yet, whether and to what extent these (and other) measures can be deemed successful in helping communities in northern Uganda transition from war to peace, as well as in facilitating justice, healing and reconciliation, remains a subject of continuing debate and indeed criticism (MacDonald, 2019: 226). Ultimately, most of these processes (perhaps with the general exception of some traditional processes) are top-down, elite-driven and often externally funded or supported, situated at the macro level, with little participation and ownership of local stakeholders or communities. Even more locally owned traditional mechanisms are often mediated or facilitated through external NGOs or actors and thus do not necessarily accommodate victims' and survivors' agency (Baines, 2007: 91; also see Kent, 2014: 290). These multi-systemic factors – that is, the lack of local ownership and participation and the externally driven character of most processes – in many ways hindered a successful transition from war to sustainable peace and the facilitation and delivery of justice at a societal, macro level.

Indeed, the result of these (and other) dilemmas is a vacuum of post-conflict assistance, justice and redress for large parts of the conflict-affected populaces across northern Uganda, particularly at the community level and in rural areas (Schulz, 2021: 55). Situated in this vacuum, groups of survivors inevitably need to turn to alternative and often more creative processes at the micro level as a means to address their experiences of harm and suffering. This turn to the local and the micro level in the absence of effective measures at the state or macro level has previously been documented by scholars across post-conflict terrains (Shaw and Waldorf, 2010: 3), including in northern Uganda (Baines, 2007: 91). In the Ugandan case, such micro-level measures include, for instance, civil society-led truth-seeking initiatives (Anyeko et al., 2012: 108) or localised memorials (Hopwood, 2011: 19). All of

---

[4]   The ICC faced much criticism for only issuing arrest warrants against LRA commanders, while failing to investigate crimes committed by national army soldiers and relying heavily on support, intelligence and information provided by the government.

these constitute avenues and measures by which communities in northern Uganda seek to engage with their war-related experiences and harms in creative and participatory ways outside the purview of the state and official, formalised institutions. Another such example of processes at the micro level is survivors' support groups, in which diverse groups of survivors organise themselves to collectively address different harms and experiences as a result of conflict-related experiences. These groups and organisations have a relatively rich tradition in Acholiland but take on new roles and prominence in the contemporary post-war context, including with regards to peacebuilding, transitional justice and resilience.

SURVIVORS' SUPPORT GROUPS

We begin this section by setting out the roles of survivors' groups in relation to peacebuilding and transitional justice on a more general level, before focusing specifically on different roles and constellations of support groups that exist in post-war northern Uganda. We then examine different activities by these groups, focusing on peer-to-peer support and income-generating activities, to then explore how these aspects link to adapting to peace, facilitating a sense of justice and fostering resilience.

Even though the fields of peacebuilding and transitional justice are increasingly becoming more victim-centric (Robins, 2009: 322), thus far 'not much research has been conducted on organized victims-survivors of human rights violations' (de Waardt, 2016: 434) and specifically on survivors' groups (Rudling, 2019: 460). Nevertheless, some analyses exist, often focused on the more prominent and larger groups, such as the *Khulumani Victim Support Group* in South Africa, or the *Madres de Plaza de Mayo* in Argentina (Hamber, 2009). In particular, previous studies began to analyse how survivors in groups engage with wider, macro-level peacebuilding and transitional justice processes. For instance, Humphrey and Valverde (2008: 84–85) show that groups in Argentina and South Africa aid survivors in demanding recognition from the state. Utilising post-genocide Rwanda as a case study, Rombouts (2004: 7) similarly unveils the manifold roles of survivors' organisations in advocating for reparations. Together, these studies demonstrate that by uniting individual survivors under the umbrella of an association, groups facilitate an environment that enables survivors to collectively participate in and engage with external processes of dealing with the past (Strassner, 2013: 331). Fewer studies have examined more closely how groups can offer active coping strategies and may facilitate healing and contribute to recovery. For instance, work by Robins (2009: 320) shows how, in Nepal and East Timor, groups of families of the disappeared aid victims in reconstructing their identities that have been impacted by conflict-related disappearances.

Despite these positive aspects of survivors' groups with regards to facilitating agency and contributing to peacebuilding and transitional justice, survivors' groups also face different sets of challenges and are characterised by certain limitations. For instance, victim-survivor associations are frequently shaped by hierarchies between survivors (de Waardt, 2016: 434). Membership in survivors' groups is often characterised by stark power discrepancies between different members who exercise diverging levels of influence. Yet another commonplace challenge is that survivors' groups are often established or supported by external actors, and hence an inherent danger of dependency on outside bodies can result from these relations. As argued by Kent (2011: 447–448) in the context of East Timor, 'the agency, autonomy and "home grown" nature of victims' groups should not be overstated [. . .]. Victims' groups have been intensively cultivated by national and international NGOs. Without this support, it is likely that many of their activities would not be sustainable'. This absolutely applies to the context of northern Uganda, where many groups at the community level are established through, or supported by, NGOs.

Yet, despite these emerging engagements with survivors' associations in relation to post-conflict reconstruction efforts, existing studies thus far have largely neglected survivors' groups as constituting pathways to and forms of justice-making and peacebuilding at the micro level, with only a few noteworthy exceptions (see, e.g., Edström and Dolan, 2018; Schulz, 2019). Specifically, insufficient attention has been paid to how these survivor support groups can contribute towards fostering communities' resilience.[5]

SURVIVORS' GROUPS IN NORTHERN UGANDA

As in other post-war contexts globally, in northern Uganda a variety of survivors' groups exist in different forms and with diverging mandates, objectives and foci, as well as variations in size, activities and levels of organisation. Most of these groups unite survivors of the LRA conflict and assist victims in advocating for their demands and pursuing their quests for justice, but they also provide more practical assistance – including peer support, income-generating activities or shared finance schemes, such as Village Savings and Loan Associations (VSLA). While smaller groups at the community level primarily engage in these forms of immediate practical support for survivors,

---

[5] Also focused on northern Uganda, Williams (2021) has examined how small religious groups can foster an ecology of resilience, which is indeed similar to the argumentation we offer here.

FIGURE 5.1 Signpost of Acholi War Debt Claimants' Association in Gulu town.
Photo by the author.

quests for justice and reparations have mostly been taken up by larger claimants' associations, such as the Acholi War Debt Claimants' Association
(AWDCA) (see Figure 5.1), thereby creating hierarchies between different
types of groups.

By uniting larger numbers of conflict-affected populaces, such groups
enable survivors to more widely disseminate their demands and needs. As
articulated by a member of one survivors' group, '[w]hen we organise ourselves we can raise our voices and make them be heard by the government in
order to receive help' (Akullo Otwili and Schulz, 2012: 2). As shown above,
the post-conflict context in northern Uganda continues to be characterised
by restrained access to services for most conflict-affected communities.
Many survivors often do not benefit from any of the developmental programmes implemented by either the Ugandan government (such as the
Peace and Recovery Development Plan [PRDP]) or by the countless non-
governmental agencies, mainly due to a lack of practical measures or their
inaccessibility for rural communities in particular. This creates a lack of
provisions and assistance for the majority of survivors of the conflict, as
attested above.

In light of this, and in attempts to respond to their war-related challenges, survivors across the sub-region began to construct their own forums to articulate their voices and advocate for their needs and demands. As a recent evaluation of different survivor support groups conducted by the RLP points out, one of the key motivations for forming such groups is this potential for survivors to collectively mobilise within groups in order to jointly deal with war-related challenges, as well as to access services and assistance (RLP, 2016: 5). To further illustrate this, and as summarised in a similar evaluation study on survivors' groups' quest for reparations conducted by the Justice and Reconciliation Project (JRP; Akullo Otwili and Schulz, 2012), one member of a survivors' association explained that 'as a group, you can easily access people who have an interest in you. Some people come and say they want to give support but in most cases they just give it to established groups' (Akullo Otwili and Schulz, 2012: 13).

Varying in their composition, some groups bring together different categories of survivors within one association, while other groups primarily unite specific (sub-)categories of survivors. As a result, a variety of associations exist, including groups of families of the disappeared,[6] groups of disabled war victims and survivors, of formerly abducted persons (FAPs) or of torture survivors. Focusing on gender, some groups – such as the Women's Advocacy Network (WAN) or *Watye ki Gen* – provide a platform for conflict-affected women who have returned from LRA captivity with children born as a result of rape (Amony, 2015; Stewart, 2015), in addition to several groups of female and male survivors of conflict-related sexual violence (Apiyo and McClain Opiyo, 2015: 9; Edström and Dolan, 2018: 178). These survivors' support groups exist alongside numerous small Christian churches in rural northern Uganda that similarly offer 'a variety of social practices' (Williams, 2021).

All of these groups engage in a variety of different activities, including psychosocial peer support, collective income-generating activities and joint financial schemes, in the form of VLSAs. Locally referred to as *bol cup*, various forms of savings and farmers groups existed historically in Acholiland and took on similar roles and activities, albeit in a different context (Allen, 1987). The current post-conflict groups thereby qualify as a 'continuation of local methods of self-help and income generation', although their function 'now extends to providing some form of non-material comfort too' (MacDonald, 2014: 256). In many ways, groups therefore constitute key avenues 'in which communities [are] coping with the legacy of the conflict' (MacDonald, 2014: 255).

---

[6]   These groups include primarily family members of abducted children and youth.

SOCIAL BELONGING AND FINANCIAL STABILITY: NURTURING A LOCAL ECOLOGY OF RESILIENCE IN SURVIVORS' GROUPS

It is primarily the aforementioned types of activities and social practices – offering mutual support and counselling, as well as collective economic activities – and their ensuing effects that fundamentally assist survivors in their contemporary post-conflict situations. In this way, they constitute an effective resource for survivors to engage with conflict-related harms, thereby contributing towards facilitating a local ecology of resilience (Ungar, 2011; Williams, 2021). Elsewhere, one of us has previously examined how groups facilitate spaces for survivors to exercise agency (Touquet and Schulz, 2020: 12–14) and thereby serve as a conduit for these individuals to attain a sense of justice on their own terms (Schulz, 2019: 178).[7] Here, we want to extend that line of argument and focus on how, through these different social practices and their agentive capacities (Schulz, 2021: 118–128), groups can also contribute towards fostering resilient capacities of conflict-affected communities.

In essence, we argue that through these activities (of peer support and income-generation) and their respective impacts on survivors and their communities, groups facilitate spaces and processes for survivors to support each other, to recover from violence and to adapt to the effects of violence – including trauma, psychosocial effects and socio-economic impacts – in sustainable and locally owned ways. Groups thereby enable survivors to interact with their wider socio-ecological environments on their own terms and 'in ways that facilitate positive psychological, physical and social development' (Ungar, Chapter 1), as well as aid recovery, adaptation and transformation. The groups thereby comprise multiple systemic factors – including, most importantly, communality and a sense of social belonging, re-negotiated gender identities as key markers of identity and economic support – which facilitate resilience among members of the groups. These aspects, in turn, form a necessary part of transitional justice work and adaptive peacebuilding and contribute towards fostering resilience (Chandler, 2012).

In line with the approach adopted in this edited volume, we conceive of adaptive peacebuilding and resilience as multi-faceted and multi-factoral processes that require relationality and local ownership and which embrace the complexities and diversities of post-conflict and post-disaster lived realities (Chandler, 2012; de Coning, 2018; Ungar, Chapter 1). Our understanding of

---

[7] These examinations focused primarily on groups of male sexual violence survivors.

resilience specifically emphasises a communal and group perspective, following Kirmayer et al. (2012: 400), who suggest that:

> [R]esilience may reside in the durability, flexibility and responsiveness of *relationships* that constitute extended families or *wider social networks* [...]. The individualistic models [of resilience], therefore, need to be enlarged to take into account the *dynamic systems that may offer resilience of individuals, communities and whole people*. Indigenous concepts can provide ways to approach a more dynamic, systemic, ecological view of resilience.
>
> (emphasis added)

As de Coning (2018: 307) further elaborates, 'in the adaptive peacebuilding approach, the core activity [...] is one of process facilitation. Peacebuilding in the sustaining peace context is about stimulating those processes in a society that enable self-organization and that will lead to strengthening the resilience of the social institutions that manage internal and external stressors and shocks'. By setting in place processes for survivors to engage with their experiences on their own terms – structured around self-organisation, local ownership and internal capacities as well as relationality and social networks – survivor groups contribute towards adaptively building peace and fostering resilience at the local level and among their members, facilitating their capacities for recovery from violence and transformation of post-conflict circumstances.

PEER-TO-PEER SUPPORT

Most of the extant groups in northern Uganda engage in various forms of individual and collective psychosocial peer-to-peer support. During their (semi-)regular meetings, members in the groups frequently share their experiences and stories with one another, mostly in small group-based settings, and thereby offer mutual support, counselling and solace. 'When we meet and sit together, we can talk freely about what happened to us, because everyone understands and has the same experience', one member of a male sexual violence survivors' support group explained (Schulz, 2021: 148). These forms of peer support and psychosocial assistance – of sharing stories and an open ear – help survivors to engage with their prior experiences of violence and armed conflict, and to deal with many of the after-effects ensuing from these experiences, such as mental health problems or stigmatisation.

As Edström et al. (2016: 17) underline:

> The concept and methodology of "peer support" focuses on groups of people with shared challenges, who support each other and collectively develop

a critical awareness (or shared critical consciousness) about their situation. This can be achieved through mutual support and training in groups. In developing a critical awareness through peer support, people explore their experiences (such as stigma [...]) and they can unpack the causes and impacts of these experiences. In turn, this promotes individual and collective development of new skills, which contributes to changes at personal, inter-personal and – potentially – societal levels [...].

This mode of peer support is based on and reflects a theoretical-conceptual model of positive psychology (see Joseph and Linley, 2008) that seeks to facilitate collective healing and 'takes into account the role of *social inter-actions and support* in how people process traumatic events' (Edström et al., 2016: 17, emphasis added). This approach 'enables us to perceive a person's struggles in relation to their environment, and to conceptualise support in socially contextualised terms using educational, relational, social and political strategies' (Edström et al., 2016: 17). The emphasis thereby primarily rests on personal psychological recovery, 'as linked to supportive and enabling social environments' (Edström et al., 2016: 17), which implies a clear ecological dimension. As Edström et al. (2016: 18) further argue, 'collective healing is often cast as a linear journey from "vulnerability" to "resilience" and "coping", rather than a dynamic evolution of agency towards changing norms and establishing new communities'. This focus thereby implies numerous cross-overs with resilience discourses, which focus on the inherent strengths and resources of people and the intent to shift attention away from vulnerability and pathology (Kirmayer et al., 2012: 402) towards agency, recovery, adaptation and transformation.

By focusing on psychosocial dynamics, interactions with environments as well as agency and collective healing, the groups' peer-to-peer support and collective sharing of stories and experiences thus carry numerous conceptual and analytical commonalities with adaptive peacebuilding and resilience, while at the same time offering new and creative ways to think about resilience beyond neoliberal and individualistic paradigms (Brassett et al., 2013: 222). In particular, the understanding of peer support as a *process* that is embedded in relation to wider socio-political environments speaks to the conceptual and analytical foundations of adaptive peacebuilding and resili-ence as measures that require interaction between individuals and commu-nities with their immediate environments (de Coning, 2018: 305; Ungar, Chapter 1).

This raises the important question of how some of these dynamics actually play out in practice. Through the collective sharing of experiences and related peer-to-peer support, survivors in groups develop 'a critical awareness about their situation' which, in turn, can facilitate a mutual, collective process of 'unpack[ing] the causes and impacts of these experiences' (Edström et al., 2016: 28). Engaging with these effects 'has a deep and liberating influence on [their] individual sense of personhood and self-worth' (Edström et al., 2016: 28). As one member of a support group shared with us, 'when we come together in a group, it is easy to share experiences and memories and we can try to at least better accept it together as a group' (joint author interview, northern Uganda, 13 May 2016). Kirmayer et al. (2012: 408) similarly emphasise this narrative dimension of resilience at a group and community level, by arguing that sharing stories within small group settings 'amplifie[s] our capacity for social cognition, communal cooperation and creative imagination'. Building on this, Williams (2021) thus concludes that 'upholding specific narratives together' – as survivors in groups certainly do – 'enables people to co-create a social landscape in which they can establish and uphold identities together'. In a similar line of argument, Clark (2020) likewise draws out linkages between storytelling and resilience, implying the potential to move 'transitional justice in a new ecological direction'.

In the context of male sexual violence specifically, members of survivors' groups create a new 'critical awareness' about their experiences, as Edström et al. (2016: 28) frame it, which can contribute towards re-negotiating their masculine identities that were previously impacted through the sexual violations (Schulz, 2018: 1102). Across time and space, as well as context – specifically in northern Uganda – sexual violence strikes at multiple levels of what it means to be a man within society, thereby displacing male survivors from their gendered identities. These experiences, however, are potentially variable, fluid and malleable through different socio-political measures or interventions, and survivors can re-negotiate their gender identities, and even form new understandings of masculinities in the aftermath of their violent experiences (Schulz, 2021: 4). One way for survivors to engage with their experiences and re-negotiate their gendered identities unfolds through the groups, including through the collective unpacking of their lived realities. Indeed, and further aided through other aspects and activities of the groups – such as, for instance, joint agricultural activities, as examined below – collectively coming to terms with their experiences and creating that critical awareness about their violations allowed survivors to re-establish a sense of social identity and belonging. Statements by male survivors who are members of survivors' groups attest to these dynamics. As articulated by one survivor, 'before we came together in the group, we had a lot of feelings of being less of a man but since being in a group, the feelings [...] have reduced' (author interview, northern Uganda, 22 June 2016). Dr Chris Dolan, the director of RLP who closely collaborates with these groups of male survivors, similarly attests that the group-based peer-support activities 'help to give back a sense of being recognized as an adult and as a man' (Select Committee on Sexual Violence in Conflict, 2016: 3).

Across other survivors' groups in northern Uganda, the peer-support activities registered similar effects with regards to rehabilitating and supporting individual members, thereby aiding processes of recovery and transformation (see Figure 5.2). Members across a variety of sub-groups repeatedly emphasised the rehabilitative and transformative effects of these activities and the sense of social belonging and community that is being nurtured through these groups. As one member of a torture survivor group explained, 'being in a group psychologically rehabilitated us and really empowered us' (author interview, northern Uganda, 22 March 2016). By doing so, the groups not only contribute towards rebuilding survivors' selves, personhood and subjectivities, but also their relationships with families and communities, which, in turn, carries important implications for survivors' capacities to participate in post-conflict communal life and subsequent recovery from the effects of violence.

FIGURE 5.2 Meeting of survivor group of formerly abducted women in Awach sub-county, northern Uganda. Photo by the author.

COLLECTIVE INCOME-GENERATING ACTIVITIES

In addition to peer support, survivors' groups across northern Uganda also engage in different types of collective income-generating activities (Akullo Otwili and Schulz, 2012: 2). These primarily include communal agricultural work – such as mutual farming on shared pieces of land, cultivating small animal farms or harvesting honey from bee-hives – as well as joint saving schemes, such as VSLAs (see above). The profits that derive from these agricultural activities are used in a variety of ways and for different purposes. For instance, the profits may be used to invest in new food crops for future harvests; to buy animals and livestock for the groups for additional agricultural profits; invested into joint saving schemes; or distributed among members of the group to meet their respective day-to-day survival needs.

According to survivors, such activities have helped them to respond to their everyday post-conflict challenges, including poverty and dependency. The chairperson of one survivor group explained that 'the members of the group have decided that they should not be spoon-fed but that they can stay on their own and fend for themselves without living in poverty like before' (author field notes, northern Uganda, 2 June 2016). In many ways, this sentiment highlights the socio-political and economic context in which these groups, their immediacy and their primary activities arise. As indicated above, because of a lack of both governmental and non-governmental assistance for mostly rural-based communities, groups of survivors get together and form associations to collectively address their needs on their own terms. As one member of a survivor organisation explained: 'we still need that support from the government, but you never know what will happen. That is why we (the groups) do (our own) small income-generating activities' (Akullo Otwilli and Schulz, 2012: 4). The groups thus envisage and push for (social) change to be led by social actors themselves, rather than focusing on external structures and institutions to create that change, which Chandler (2014: 62) conceptualises as a key characteristic of resilience.

The joint income-generating and agricultural activities thus assist survivors in numerous ways and on different levels. For some survivors who were physically impacted by the war – including landmine survivors, people with disabilities or survivors with long-lasting physical impairments as a result of different types of violations – these collective activities constitute unique avenues for them to conduct manual, agricultural labour and to generate an income, which they cannot sufficiently do on their own.

Here, we once again refer to the example of male sexual violence survivors' groups in northern Uganda. As one of us has previously explored, most male survivors of sexual violence in the current post-war context are unable to carry out agricultural and manual labour, mostly caused by the after-effects and physical injuries of the violations committed against them (Schulz, 2018: 1115). This is further compounded by the fact that most male survivors, who were victimised in the late 1980s and early 1990s, are now elderly and thus unable to carry out heavy work. As a result of these consequences, and exacerbated by various intersecting factors, male survivors are often unable to provide for their families and communities, which carries implications for their abilities to live up to normative hegemonic expectations of masculinities. In this context, these groups of male survivors carry out income-generating activities such as cultivating beehives and operating saving schemes, which enable them to generate a small income. Male survivors are thereby given new opportunities to contribute to the provision of their families, as they are socially expected to do according to hegemonic masculinities constructions. The groups' income-generating activities thus aid a longer and multi-faceted process of re-configuring male survivors' previously impacted gender identities (Schulz, 2021: 118).

The numerous positive aspects and influences of these types of activities also carry certain wider societal and ecological implications. For instance, by being able to provide for their families, survivors are able to rebuild not only their selves and subjectivities but also their relations with their families and communities. This, in many ways, facilitates processes of re-creating and transforming social bonds and interactions between and among conflict-affected communities, as well as with their wider socio-political environments – which constitute key aspects of both adaptive peacebuilding and resilience processes. Discussing how conflict-affected communities in Sierra Leone 'were able to find peace by regaining a sense of normality [...] through everyday practices', Martin (2016: 401) likewise shows how 'groups can provide a space for rebuilding relationships and re-establishing social connections'; and how these 'seemingly mundane interactions aided people in moving away from feelings of isolation [...] towards feeling a greater sense of community' (Martin, 2016: 409–410). This constitutes an often unrecognised element of transitional justice and peacebuilding work. Facilitating and creating these environmental, communal and social interactions and relationships and a sense of community, of belonging, in the midst of war-related hardships and suffering in many ways constitutes a crucial pre-condition and component of adaptive peacebuilding and resilience.

BUILDING A LOCAL ECOLOGY OF RESILIENCE AT THE MICRO LEVEL

As we have shown, survivors' groups in northern Uganda constitute effective resources for survivors to deal with conflict-related experiences and shocks, and to recover from and transform the struggles and effects of war and its aftermath. In particular, through peer-to-peer counselling and joint income-generating activities, groups enable survivors to make sense of their experiences, to renegotiate their own identities and to recognise a shared lived reality as well as to socially reintegrate within their families and communities. Furthermore, groups enable conflict-affected communities to develop new skills – of counselling, adaptation and income-generation – that are geared towards recovery and transformation.

In their existence and activities, groups thereby embody a sense of local ownership, of crafting social relationships and networks and of nurturing adaptive and transformative capacities – all of which are key requisites for adaptive peacebuilding, transitional justice and resilience. In this reading, the groups combine multiple systemic factors – including gender identities, and in particular masculinities constructions, social relationalities and socio-economic components – which contribute towards facilitating survivors' resilient capacities within group settings and at the micro level. Hence, the type of resilience that can be fostered through survivors' groups should not be understood as a set of static character traits that are inherent in individuals or in groups, but, rather, as 'an adaptive process inculcated through specific practices' (Williams, 2021).

By teasing out these participatory capacities of survivors' groups and their ensuing linkages to peacebuilding, transitional justice and resilience, it is not our intention to paint an idealised or romanticised picture of these groups, their activities and effects. Instead, we recognise the challenges and limitations of these groups, including inherent hierarchies within them as well as dependencies and restrictions in scope and reach. Concerning the groups' potential to foster a local ecology of resilience, it is important to differentiate between resilience at different levels of social organisation (Brassett et al., 2013: 223), and to emphasise that the dynamics we have analysed here primarily apply at the micro level, among individuals and smaller groups and communities of survivors.

Groups can thus contribute towards facilitating resilience at an individual and communal level, but not necessarily at a wider regional or societal level. For this, additional transitional justice and peacebuilding measures and processes at other levels of social organisation – and with wider reach in an inclusive and participatory manner – are necessary to ultimately compose a multi-systemic framework for fostering resilience at a societal and regional level.

CONCLUSION

In this chapter, we have sought to demonstrate how, within a vacuum of transitional justice and peacebuilding measures at the macro level in northern Uganda, survivors began crafting their own spaces in the form of survivors' support groups. These groups have enabled survivors to exercise different forms of agency by way of engaging with their war-related experiences and harms. This, in turn, positions survivors' groups as important vehicles of post-conflict peacebuilding and justice-making at the local level. Here, we have specifically focused on examining how, through these dynamics, survivor groups can contribute towards processes of fostering conflict-affected communities' resilient capacities and creating a local ecology of resilience.

Our discussion shows how these groups – in particular through psychosocial peer-to-peer support and collective income-generating activities – facilitate survivors' adaptive and transformative capacities, which enable them to positively respond to shocks and stressors resulting from mass violence and its after-effects. Taken together, these groups help survivors to relationally engage with their experiences of harms as well as with their socio-economic environments in new and creative ways, which are fundamental pre-conditions for adaptive peacebuilding, transitional justice and resilience. In the context of support groups, survivors thus develop new capacities that ultimately offer pathways to a resilient system at the communal level. This local ecology of resilience is focused on recovery and transformation and is centred around individuals' and communities' self-organisation, agency and self-empowerment (Chandler, 2015: 28; Zebrowski, 2013: 161).

Our case study analysis thereby illuminates what a local ecology of resilience can look like in practice in northern Uganda, and how locally owned processes can foster resilient capacities. This focus on processes and dynamics at the communal and group level enables us to divorce the concept of resilience from its often neoliberal and individualistic focus, and instead to utilise its relational and communal elements. It is particularly through the locally owned nature of these groups, and the collectivism and communality that underpin their activities, that a local ecology of resilience can be nurtured.

REFERENCES

Akullo Otwili, E. and Schulz, P. (2012). *Paying Back What Belongs to Us. Victims' Groups in Northern Uganda and their Quest for Reparations. JRP Field Note XVI.* Gulu: Justice and Reconciliation Project (JRP).

Allen, T. (1987). *Kwete and Kweri: Acholi Farm Work Groups in Southern Sudan.* Manchester: Department of Administrative Studies, University of Manchester.

Allen, T. and Vlassenroot, K. (2010). *The Lord's Resistance Army: Myth and Reality*. London: Zed Books.

Amony, E. (2015). *I am Evelyn Amony. Reclaiming my Life from the Lord's Resistance Army (LRA)*. Madison, WI: University of Wisconsin Press.

Anyeko, K., Baines, E., Komakech, E., Ojok, B., Ogora, L. O. and Victor, L. (2012). 'The cooling of hearts': Community truth-telling in northern Uganda. *Human Rights Review*, 13(1), 107–124.

Apiyo, N. and McClain Opiyo, L. (2015). *My Body, A Battlefield: Survivors' Experiences of Conflict Sexual Violence in Koch Ongako. JRP Field Note 22*. Gulu: Justice and Reconciliation Project.

Baines, E. (2007). The haunting of Alice: Local approaches to justice and reconciliation in Northern Uganda. *International Journal of Transitional Justice*, 1 (1), 91–114.

Branch, A. (2011). *Displacing Human Rights: War and Intervention in Northern Uganda*. Oxford: Oxford University Press.

Brassett, J., Croft, S. and Vaughan-Williams, N. (2013). Introduction: An agenda for resilience research in politics and international relations. *Politics*, 33(4), 221–228.

Chandler, D. (2012). Resilience and human security: The post-interventionist paradigm. *Security Dialogue*, 43(3), 213–229.

Chandler, D. (2014). Beyond neoliberalism: Resilience, the new art of governing complexity. *Resilience*, 2(1), 47–63.

Chandler, D. (2015). Resilience and the 'everyday': Beyond the paradox of liberal peace. *Review of International Studies*, 41, 27–48.

Clark, J. N. (2020). Storytelling, resilience and transitional justice: Reversing narrative social bulimia. *Theoretical Criminology*, https://doi.org/10.1177%2F1750698020959813

Clark, J. N. (2021). Thinking systemically about transitional justice, legal systems and resilience. In M. Ungar (ed.), *Multisystemic Resilience: Adaptation and Transformation in Contexts of Change*. New York: Oxford University Press, pp. 530–550.

de Coning, C. (2016). From peacebuilding to sustaining peace: Implications of complexity of resilience and sustainability. *Resilience*, 4(3), 166–181.

de Coning, C. (2018). Adaptive peacebuilding. *International Affairs*, 94(2), 301–317.

de Waardt, M. (2016). Naming and shaming victims: The semantics of victimhood. *International Journal of Transitional Justice*, 10(3), 432–450.

Dolan, C. (2009). *Social Torture: The Case of Northern Uganda, 1986–2006*. Berghahn Books.

Dolan, C., Shahrokh, T., Edström, J. and Kabafunzaki, D. K. (2017). Engaged excellence or excellent engagement? Collaborating critically to amplify the voices of male survivors of conflict-related sexual violence. *IDS Bulletin*, 47(6), 1–23.

Edström, J., Dolan, C., Shahrokh, T. and David, O. (2016). Therapeutic activism: Men of hope refugee association Uganda breaking the silence over male rape in conflict-related sexual violence. *IDS Evidence Report 182*. Brighton: Institute for Development Studies.

Edström, J. and Dolan, C. (2018). Breaking the spell of silence: Collective healing as activism amongst refugee male survivors of sexual violence in Uganda. *Journal of Refugee Studies* 32(2), 175–196.

Finnström, S. (2008). *Living with Bad Surroundings: War, History, and Everyday Moments in Northern Uganda*. Durham, NC: Duke University Press.

Hamber, B. (2009). *Transforming Societies after Political Violence: Truth, Reconciliation, and Mental Health.* New York: Springer.

Hopwood, J. (2011). *We Can't Be Sure Who Killed Us: Memory and Memorialization in Post-conflict Northern Uganda.* New York: International Center for Transitional Justice (ICTJ).

Humphrey, M. and Valverde, E. (2008). Human rights politics and injustice: Transitional justice in Argentina and South Africa. *International Journal of Transitional Justice*, 2(1), 83–105.

Joseph, S. and Linley, P. A. (2008). Positive psychological perspectives on posttraumatic stress: An integrative psychosocial framework. In S. Joseph and P. Linley (eds.), *Trauma, Recovery, and Growth: Positive Psychological Perspectives on Posttraumatic Stress.* New Jersey: John Wiley and Sons, pp. 3–20.

Juncos, A. and Joseph, J. (2020). Resilient peace: Exploring the theory and practice of resilience in peacebuilding interventions. *Journal of Intervention and Statebuilding*, 14(3), 289–304.

Justice Law and Order Sector (JLOS). (2019). *National Transitional Justice Policy.* Prepared by the National Transitional Justice Working Group. Kampala: Justice Law and Order Sector, Ministry of Justice of the Republic of Uganda.

Kastner, P. (2020). A resilience approach to transitional justice? *Journal of Intervention and Statebuilding*, 14(3), 368–388.

Kent, L. (2011). Local memory practices in East Timor: Disrupting transitional justice narratives. *International Journal of Transitional Justice*, 5(3), 434–455.

Kent, L. (2014). Narratives of suffering and endurance: Coercive sexual relationships, truth commissions and possibilities for gender justice in Timor-Leste. *International Journal of Transitional Justice*, 8(2), 289–313.

Kirmayer, L. J., Dandeneau, S., Marshall, E., Phillips, M. K. and Williamson, K. J. (2011). Rethinking resilience from indigenous perspectives. *The Canadian Journal of Psychiatry*, 56(2), 84–91.

Kirmayer, L. J., Dandeneau, S., Marshall, E., Phillips, M. K. and Williamson, K. J. (2012). Toward an ecology of stories: Indigenous perspectives on resilience. In M. Ungar (ed.), *The Social Ecology of Resilience: A Handbook of Theory and Practice.* New York: Springer, pp. 399–414.

Lee, S. Y. (2020). Local resilience and the reconstruction of social institutions: Recovery, maintenance and transformation of Buddhist Sangha in Post-Khmer-Rouge Cambodia. *Journal of Intervention and Statebuilding*, 14(3), 349–367.

MacDonald, A. (2014). *Justice in Transition? Transitional justice and its discontents in Uganda.* PhD Dissertation, Department of War Studies, King's College London.

MacDonald, A. (2019). 'Somehow this whole process became so artificial': Exploring the transitional justice implementation gap in Uganda. *International Journal of Transitional Justice*, 13(2), 225–248.

MacDonald, A. and Porter, H. (2016). The trial of Thomas Kwoyelo: Opportunity or spectre? Reflections from the ground on the first LRA prosecution. *Africa*, 86(4), 698–722.

Martin, L. (2016). Practicing normality: An examination of unrecognizable transitional justice mechanisms in post-conflict Sierra Leone. *Journal of Intervention and Statebuilding*, 10(3), 400–418.

Okello, M.K. and Hovil, L. (2007). Confronting the reality of gender-based violence in northern Uganda. *International Journal of Transitional Justice*, 1(3), 433–443.

Okello, M. C., Dolan, C., Wande, U., Mncwabe, N., Onegi, L. and Oola, S. (2012). *Where Law Meets Reality: Forging African Transitional Justice*. Cape Town: Pambazuka Press.

Porter, H. (2016). *After Rape: Violence, Justice and Social Harmony in Uganda*. Cambridge: Cambridge University Press.

Pouligny, B. (2014). State of the art: The resilience approach to peacebuilding – A new conceptual framework. *Insights: Newsletter of the US Institute for Peace (USIP)*, 4–6.

Prosecutor *v*. Dominic Ongwen. (2021). ICC Trial Chamber Judgement, ICC-02/04-01/15, 21 February 2021.

Refugee Law Project (RLP). (2016). *Victims' collective journey to survivorhood and activism: An evaluation of the efficacy of victim support group initiatives in facilitating individual and community healing in post-conflict northern Uganda – A case of the 6 victim support groups being supported by RLP*. Kampala: Refugee Law Project, School of Law, Makerere University.

Robins, S. (2009). Whose voices? Understanding victims' needs in transition: Nepali voices – Perceptions of truth, justice, reconciliation, reparations and the transition in Nepal. *Journal of Human Rights Practice*, 1(2), 320–331.

Rombouts, H. (2004). *Victim Organisations and the Politics of Reparation: A Case-Study on Rwanda*. Cambridge: Intersentia.

Rudling, A. (2019). What's inside the box? Mapping agency and conflict within victims' organizations. *International Journal of Transitional Justice*, 13(3), 458–477.

Schulz, P. (2018). Displacement from gendered personhood: Sexual violence and masculinities in northern Uganda. *International Affairs*, 94(5), 1101–1119.

Schulz, P. (2019). 'To me, justice means to be in a group': Survivors' groups as a pathway to justice in Northern Uganda. *Journal of Human Rights Practice*, 11(1), 171–189.

Schulz, P. (2020). Towards inclusive gender in transitional justice: Gaps, blind-spots and opportunities. *Journal of Intervention and Statebuilding*, 15(5): 691–710.

Schulz, P. (2021). *Male Survivors of Wartime Sexual Violence: Perspectives from Northern Uganda*. Berkeley, CA: University of California Press.

Select Committee on Sexual Violence in Conflict. (2016). *Sexual Violence in Conflict: A War Crime. Report of Session 2015–16*. HL Paper 123. London: UK Parliament, House of Lords.

Shaw, R. and Waldorf, L. (2010). *Localizing Transitional Justice: Interventions and Priorities after Mass Violence*. Redwood City, CA: Stanford University Press.

Stewart, B. (2015). *We Are All the Same. Experiences of Children Born into LRA Captivity*. JRP Field Note 23: Gulu: Justice and Reconciliation Project.

Strassner, V. (2013). From victimhood to political protagonism: Victim groups and associations in the process of dealing with a violent past. In T. Bonacker and C. Safferling (eds.), *Victims of International Crimes: An Interdisciplinary Discourse*. London: Springer, pp. 331–344.

Touquet, H. and Schulz, P. (2020). Navigating vulnerabilities and masculinities: How gendered contexts shape the agency of male sexual violence survivors. *Security Dialogue*, https://doi.org/10.1177%2F0967010620929176

Ungar, M. (2011). The social ecology of resilience: Addressing contextual and cultural ambiguity of a nascent construct. *American Journal of Orthopsychiatry*, 81(1), 1–17.

Ungar, M. (2013). Resilience, trauma, context and culture, *Trauma, Violence and Abuse*, 14, 255–266.

van Metre, L. (2014). Resilience as a peacebuilding practice: To realism from idealism. *Insights: Newsletter of the US Institute for Peace (USIP)*, 1–6.

Vindevogel, S., Ager, A., Schiltz, J., Broekaert, E. and Derluyn, I. (2015). Toward a culturally sensitive conceptualization of resilience: Participatory research with war-affected communities in northern Uganda. *Transcultural Psychiatry*, 52(3), 396–416.

Williams, L. (2019). *In Search of a Stable World. Contamination of Spirits and Mental Disorder in Post-Conflict Northern Uganda*. Aarhus: Arhus University.

Williams, L. (2021). Building an ecology of resilience through religious practice and community in northern Uganda. *Civil Wars* (in press).

Zebrowski, C. (2013). The nature of resilience. *Resilience*, 1(3), 159–173.

6

The *Birangonas* (War Heroines) in Bangladesh: Generative Resilience of Sexual Violence in Conflict through Graphic Ethnography

Nayanika Mookherjee

INTRODUCTION

We cried and laughed on reading this book and seeing this film. It should be read and seen by all children and their parents. By reading this book and seeing this film children will not question the war again. No one will question who fought and no one will ever give khota/scorn to birangonas. Along with children, their parents would read, their mothers would read and they would get to know about the war. All our stories are here in this book and I want this book to be in every school in Bangladesh so that all children know about us (discussion with rural birangonas and their children, 2020).

In May 2020, in a WhatsApp conversation across the United Kingdom (UK), rural Bangladesh and the capital city Dhaka, we are having a collective discussion about a graphic novel[1] and animation film that I co-authored and which the *birangona* (war heroine) *chachis* (the term I use, meaning 'aunts', to refer to the women, following the norms of fictive kinship of South Asia) have just read and watched. *Birangona: Towards Ethical Testimonies of Sexual Violence during Conflict* (Mookherjee and Keya, 2019, 2020) draws on my book *The Spectral Wound: Sexual Violence, Public Memories and the Bangladesh War of 1971* (Mookherjee, 2015). Sundori, Moyna's youngest daughter whom I have known for the last two decades, is also joining us in the call from Dhaka and has been pivotal in getting the graphic novels delivered and ensuring the *chachis* have seen the film before it is finalised. They have all gathered in Moyna's house and are sitting in the shade of a mango tree in the midst of the scorching May sunshine. Sundori is in her small apartment in Dhaka, which she shares with her husband who works in the garment factory, and her two children are also hovering around her as

---

[1] A graphic novel is an illustrated account in comic-strip form of a work of fiction.

we catch up with their grandmother and her *birangona* friends in rural Bangladesh.

I am in the UK in the middle of lockdown, as are Sundori and her family in Dhaka. Hearing the *birangonas*' response to the graphic novel and film, my heart leapt with joy, and I am particularly struck by the strength of their validation that everyone should know about the subject matter and their conviction that it should be taught in schools. This is a long way from the processes of public secrecy (Mookherjee, 2006) from two decades ago, through which they revealed to me fragments of their experiences of the war of 1971.

In December 1971, East Pakistan became the independent nation of Bangladesh after a nine-month war with West Pakistan and its local Bengali collaborators. Rape was common during this conflict. Faced with a huge population of rape survivors, the new Bangladeshi government in December 1971 – six days after the war ended – publicly designated any woman raped in the war as a *birangona* (meaning a brave or courageous woman); the Bangladeshi state uses the term to mean 'war heroine' (Mookherjee, 2015, 2019). Even today, the Bangladeshi government's bold, public effort to refer to the women raped during 1971 as *birangonas* is internationally unprecedented, yet it remains unknown to many besides Bangladeshis.

The issue of rape during the war was widely reported in the press from December 1971 until mid-1973. Thereafter, it was relegated to oblivion in government and journalistic consciousness until it re-emerged in the 1990s. Since then, a large number of Bangladeshi feminist and human rights organisations have also been documenting the testimonies of *birangonas*, to bring to justice those Bengali men who collaborated with the Pakistani army in perpetrating the rapes and deaths in 1971. Hence, over the last nearly fifty years in Bangladesh, there has existed a public memory of wartime rape through various literary, visual (films, plays, photographs) and testimonial forms, ensuring that the raped woman endures as an iconic figure. My previous research (including the aforementioned graphic novel and animation film) ethnographically engaged with the public memories of sexual violence of the Bangladesh war of 1971 among survivors, their family members, human rights activists and state officials, and triangulated these findings with extensive archival, literary and visual representations.

The omnipresence of rape in various conflicts has made it imperative to 'recover' and document voices of survivors, these 'untold stories' of a 'real past', by means of oral history and testimonies, facilitated by feminists and human rights activists in their efforts to seek justice for these crimes. However, these experiences of wartime sexual violence are often explained through the limited lenses of silence, voice, shame, honour, gender, patriarchy, stigma, trauma and ostracisation, which help to create the figure of the horrific raped woman. In using this term 'horrific raped woman', I refer to the ways in which *birangonas* are assumed to have a horrific life trajectory, reflected in physical 'evidence' of muteness, dishevelled hair and social evidence of the notion that all women are ostracised by their communities and families.

The testimonial processes through which narratives of sexual violence are recorded call into question the role of external actors – those collecting testimonies – as peacebuilders in these contexts. These narratives, which suggest vulnerability, may in fact undermine the very resilience that characterises many of the women who were raped. A more generative resilience, which is the focus of this chapter, would honour a different narration of sexual violence – one that emphasises women's abilities to continue to live with and pass on the experiences of sexual violence in ways that are uniquely relational. It is this contextualised and social-ecological understanding of resilience (Ungar, 2011) that needs to inform adaptive peacebuilding, in order to foster a nuanced understanding of the effects and transmissions of the experiences of rape as a weapon of war.

Ideas of 'resilience' linked to the 'voicing' of the violent encounter of sexual violence are called into question through the dominant horrific figuration of the raped woman. In contrast, this chapter explores the idea of generative resilience, drawing from my ethnography and as represented in the visual motifs of the aforementioned graphic novel and animated film. Generative resilience allows us to highlight the violence that is embedded in different patterns of sociality, 'the everyday sociality' (Mookherjee, 2015: 108), through which *birangonas* have navigated their life trajectories. It also critiques the lenses, simultaneously both overly wide and limited, of concepts of silence, voice, shame, honour, gender, patriarchy, stigma, trauma and ostracisation through which sexual violence in conflict is commonly understood. The chapter additionally interrogates the ways in which graphic novels can be like 'adaptive peacebuilders', in the sense of 'strengthening the resilience of social institutions, and investing in social cohesion and capacities that assist societies to self-sustain their peace processes' (de Coning, 2018: 317). This will allow us to reflect on the theorisations of long-term 'transitional justice' and reconciliation within historical and contemporary contexts. In the process, the chapter draws on my own work to interrogate the idea of 'resilience'. It begins with a brief overview of the country's transitional justice process.

GRIHOJUDDHO (THE WAR AT HOME) AND THE WAR CRIMES TRIBUNAL IN BANGLADESH

In Bangladesh, a process of accountability was initiated in March 2009, nearly forty years after the war of 1971. Given the lack of acknowledgement of the killings and rapes committed by the Pakistani army, the Bangladeshi government announced that a national war crimes tribunal would be set up to try local collaborators and Pakistani military personnel. The tribunal was set up in 2009 by the current Awami League (AL) government (deemed to be left-liberal, secular) but was first constituted under the International Crimes Tribunals Act of 1973, formulated in Bangladesh and amended in 2009. The current Awami League government is headed by Sheikh Hasina, whose father – Sheikh Mujib – was the first prime minister of Bangladesh and was assassinated in 1975. In 2009, the government executed those who killed Sheikh Mujib. Only after successfully trying her father's killers did Sheikh Hasina take steps to set up the tribunal from March 2010, a year after the initial announcement.

During the fifteen years of military rule (1975–1990) in Bangladesh, those who collaborated with the Pakistani army enjoyed political impunity and continued to hold positions of power. After nearly forty years of Bangladeshi independence, this national tribunal charged seventeen individuals. Of these, fourteen individuals were arrested and detained in prison, two were charged in absentia for their role during the Bangladesh war and six were ultimately executed. Many of these individuals were linked to the Jamaat-e-Islami party and the opposition Bangladesh National Party, and all were deemed to have collaborated with the Pakistani army in 1971 (Shaon, 2018). The Pakistani National Assembly inflamed the situation when, on 17 December 2003, it passed a resolution heralding one of the collaborators as a 'friend of Pakistan', condemning his execution and warning Bangladesh against 'resurrecting 1971'. This, in turn, has led to fresh demands for Pakistani army personnel to stand trial for crimes perpetrated in 1971.

Transitional justice is fundamentally about 'dealing with' the past, with the aim of enabling societies to move on. Bangladesh's attempted juridical redress through the tribunal and its death penalties, however, is not only an attempt to seek accountability. It is also an attempt to keep the wounds of 1971 open, in the context of nearly fifty years of unacknowledged genocidal crimes by the Pakistani authorities and long-term impunity of collaborators and the Pakistani military. Paradoxically, thus, Bangladesh is undertaking processes of transitional justice in order to keep the past alive. The tribunal itself has faced extensive international criticism for its lack of transparency, flouting of the rule of law and its use of the death penalty.

Reconciliation is often assumed to be a natural framework and trajectory for a post-conflict society (United Nations [UN], 2004). Following South Africa's Truth and Reconciliation Commission (TRC) (1996–1998), reconciliation has been a recurrent theme in debates about violent pasts, seeking 'closure' and 'moving forward'. The idea of reconciliation has an inherent linearity of transitioning from authoritarian to liberal democratic structures as a solution, and moving forward at the cost of closing problematic debates about the past for those most affected (see Turner, 2016, for a critical discussion of the concept). Reconciliation is thus meant to enable 'renewal of applicable relations of persons who have been at variance' (Gallimore, 2008: 251) – and thereby return a measure of social resilience during a period of recovery and growth. The dialogical process of giving and hearing testimonies is also deemed to contribute to reconciliation, as in the case of the International Criminal Tribunal for Rwanda (ICTR) (Eltringham, 2009, 2019; Gallimore, 2008).

Reconciliation is not an aim of the Bangladesh tribunal, and indeed the example of Bangladesh fundamentally problematises any assumed or posited relationship between 'justice' and reconciliation. First, the issues relating to the genocide in 1971 remain unresolved. They have not been addressed either by Pakistan or at the international level. Second, the country itself remains 'at war' within its borders. Highlighting this, the war crimes tribunal enjoys enormous support among Bangladeshis (many of whom also supported the execution of well-known collaborators of the war) and it has strengthened the government, while it has also opened 'a can of worms' based on unresolved issues from the past and *Grihojuddho.*

During my fieldwork, Bangladeshis would often ask 'Peace for whom?' 'Reconciliation for whom?' Ultimately, what the Bangladesh case illustrates is that peace and reconciliation can only be addressed after the process of justice has run its course. In the absence of these normative, post-conflict processes of reconciliation and peace – the limited frameworks of 'transitional justice' which Bangladesh has not adhered to – this chapter directs attention to the *birangonas* and to what they can bring to our understandings of transitional justice. For some of the *birangonas* themselves, the process of keeping the wounds of the past open has been important, and it is in this context that they transmit what this chapter calls generative resilience. In short, it is the horrific figure of the *birangona*, alongside the presence of the collaborator, that keeps alive the need to seek justice.

THE HORRIFIC *BIRANGONA*

Doing my research in the late 1990s on the public memories of wartime rape during the Bangladesh war of 1971 (Mookherjee, 2015), I came across various personal accounts of war among a large number of people in cities, suburban towns and villages. These accounts would feature 'knowing' a woman who had been raped in 1971, 'who lived next door', 'in the same road', 'in the neighbouring locality/village'. The woman in question would always be remembered through the *bhoyonkor drishsho* (horrific scene) marked by her 'dishevelled hair', 'her loud laughter' or her 'quietness', 'muteness'; she was 'the one who stares into space' with 'deadened-eyes'. These descriptions would often end with the phrase *she ki bhoyonkor drishsho* (what a horrific scene it was). Apart from encountering the raped women after the war, there would be various narrations about their whereabouts during the war and how long they were staying 'away' at an 'uncle's' place afterwards, the latter signifying the possibility that they had become pregnant as a result of being raped during the war. Suspicion and speculation about the possibility of young and attractive women being raped in 1971 are rife in the rumours of the post-war whereabouts of these women.

These oft-cited post-war rumours and the formation of an idea of the *birangona* resonates powerfully with the famous *oi chuler chobi* (that hair photograph) of a war heroine, depicted by unkempt hair and a pair of bangle-clad fists covering a woman's face (discussed at length in Mookherjee, 2015). Giving an interview about this photograph, the photographer Naibuddin Ahmed narrated that the image was smuggled out of Bangladesh and was first published in the *Washington Post* (Masud, 1998), which drew international attention to the events of the Bangladesh war. In April to May 2008, this photograph was chosen to be the last image to mark the end of a photographic exhibition in London, entitled 'Bangladesh 1971'. This photograph of the war heroine is the visual trace of the raped woman of 1971. The caption of the photograph was: 'One of the estimated 400,000 *birangona*, meaning "brave women", who were raped during the war'.[2] The novelist Tahmima Anam (author of *Golden Age* from 2007), writing in *The Guardian* on 10 April 2008, described this photograph as 'one of many haunting images that make up Bangladesh 1971' (Anam, 2008).

The widespread use of rape and other forms of conflict-related sexual violence has made it imperative to 'recover' and document the voices of survivors as part of the pursuit of justice for these crimes. However, this redemptive and emancipatory aesthetics often ascribes a permanently raped and *bhoyonkor* (horrific) status to a war heroine, and hence fails to highlight how she has lived with the horror of wartime rape in independent Bangladesh. How does this universal desire for justice and the will to explain violence work

[2] Estimates of the numbers of women raped vary hugely from 25,000 to 400,000 in different contexts (see, e.g., Hasan, 2002).

to reproduce the very violence that feminists and human rights activists seek to condemn (Hanssen, 2000)? At what cost are these stories being re-narrated, and what is the nature of this justice? Sarkar (2006: 140), for example, notes that '[p]opular memory, has come to be increasingly important as an alternative, oppositional archive that allows access to "untold stories" of a "real past" that can presumably be tapped into by simply posing the right questions'. Das (2006: 57), moreover, reflects:

> It is often considered the task of historiography to break the silence that announces the zones of taboo. There is even something heroic in the image of empowering women to speak and to give voice to the voiceless. I have myself found this a very complicated task, for when we use such imagery as breaking the silence we may end up using our capacity to "unearth" hidden facts as a weapon.

Images of the *birangona* are also complemented in contemporary Bangladesh by various testimonies of wartime rape by the women survivors themselves. Mosammad Rohima Nesa, Kajoli Khatoon, Moyna Karim and Rashida Khatoon,[3] like many other women, were raped by West Pakistani soldiers in their homes during the Bangladeshi liberation war of 1971. When attempting to narrate their experiences of 1971 in the 1990s, they would say to me '*Ha, amader mela itihash, chorom itihash ache*' (Yes, we have a lot of history, a severe history). They would refer to the 'poison' of the 1971 'history' that they carry, the 'spillages' and 'excesses' of their experiences from the 1970s to the 1990s.

These four poor, landless women have lived since 1971 with their husbands and children in villages (Enayetpur [anonymised] and its neighbour) in a western district in Bangladesh where I spent eight months of my year-long multi-sited fieldwork. During this fieldwork, whenever I would return to Dhaka from Enayetpur, people – activists from non-governmental organisations (NGOs), human rights lawyers, intellectuals, writers, journalists, academics, feminists who knew about my research – would invariably ask the following questions about the war heroines: Are they married? Do they have a family, children, *kutumb*? Did their husbands know of the incident of rape? My answer to these questions would amaze them: the poor, rural and illiterate women continue to be married to their landless husbands with whom they were married even before 1971, *in spite of* the rape. These frequently occurring, repetitive questions point to a sedimented imaginary of the war heroine among the activist community. Just as the image in the hair photograph

---

[3] All the names of *birangonas* and places have been anonymised.

gives an idea of the *birangona* as 'abnormal', various literary and visual representations have contributed to the perception that the war heroine's kin networks have abandoned her and her family has not accepted her as a result of the rape.

The phrase of the Enayetpur women with whom I worked – 'a lot of history, a severe history' – further resonates with Shiromoni Bhaskar's representation and articulation of her own experience of the Bangladesh war of 1971. In 1998, Shiromoni, a famous Bangladeshi artist, acknowledged publicly that she had been raped during the war by Pakistani officials and Bengali collaborators. As a raped woman from a middle-class background, her testimonies and photographs have been central to various national commemoration programmes marking 1971. As a middle-class *birangona*, Shiromoni dismantled the prevalent stereotype that all *birangona*s are ashamed and invisible as a result of their rape.

This public memory contradicts the prevalent assumption that there is silence regarding wartime rape. It is incorrectly assumed by many that, since Bangladesh is a 'Muslim' country, the traditions and practices of Islam – and its assumed association with ideologies of gender, patriarchy, honour and shame – ensure the preservation of silence about wartime rape (see, e.g., Brownmiller, 1975, 1994). My ethnography highlights the various socio-economic dynamics within which the ideologies of gender, honour and shame are practised among the *birangona*s. It shows that the public memory of wartime rape manifests in Bangladesh in three ways: first, the state category that designates the raped women as *birangona*s; second, an extensive archive of visual and literary representations dating back to 1971; and, third, human rights testimonies of poor and middle-class *birangona*s since the 1990s.

To date, around 100 war heroines have publicly acknowledged their history of rape during 1971, including the earlier-mentioned four women from western Bangladesh whose testimonies and photographs have been part of a number of national commemorative programmes. These testimonies started being collected by the Bangladeshi left-liberal activist community in the 1990s as evidence of injustices and what many would consider as genocidal acts[4] committed through the rapes and killings of 1971.

Within human rights narratives, there is a predetermined focus on documenting and presenting the *birangona*s' account as only a horrific one.

---

[4]   In Bangladesh, the events of 1971 are considered to be genocide based on mass killings, impositions on culture, language, religion and national feelings. For varied accounts of the Bangladesh War of 1971, see Ahmed (1973); Hasan (2002); S. Islam (1992); Muhith (1992); Totten (1997); Williams (1972).

Inadequate attention is given to the ways in which the war heroines themselves want to articulate their experiences, not only of 1971 but also of the trajectory of their subsequent post-conflict lives. Focusing on the post-conflict lives of these women not only gives us an in-depth account of the impact of wartime rape but also highlights the complex ways in which women and their families have dealt with the violence of rape over time. By giving due emphasis to the concerns of *birangonas*, one can also attempt to ethically document and care for the informants whose violent narratives and experiences are possible evidence of the occurrence of genocide in 1971.

If we open up questions about the complex realities of experiences of wartime rape among the women and their families, we could locate their accounts within a wider local politics and the political economy of their post-war appropriation in the public sphere of Bangladesh. These testimonial cultures (Ahmed and Stacey, 2001) of state and civil society, as multi-systemic factors and processes, have exacerbated the process for war heroines of living with their experience of sexual violence through the reiteration of a horrific image. As a result, representational politics and choices become central to identifying how resilience needs to be understood for the *birangonas*. This is where we turn to generative resilience to identify the 'socialities of violence' (thereby avoiding the empty global signifier of 'trauma') for the *birangonas*.

GENERATIVE RESILIENCE AND GRAPHIC ETHNOGRAPHY

In instances of violent events particularly related to sexual violence, it is often assumed that memories of atrocities are shrouded in silence. Memory-making thereby becomes the resistive process through which these untold stories can be brought to the surface and a suppressed, even subaltern account can be made part of history. These processes are synonymous with resilience, understood as strategies to overcome adversity and cope in the best possible ways given the cultural and contextual constraints facing the *birangonas*. Memory-making as resistance can occur through interviews and oral history projects. The accounts arising from these methods are then made part of objects, which are seen to represent these memories. For example, intergenerational family memories, Holocaust and World War II memories can be transmitted orally through stories and interviews. They can also be located in language, bodily practices and rituals. These accounts can additionally be represented through various material and external memories, including as objects of memory like the poppy. Photographs, films and literature – as well as structures and organisations such as memorials, museums and archives – can come to represent and/or exhibit different aspects of these memories. The processes of preserving memories, whether through remembering, silences, forgettings, contestations, reconciliation or redress, also highlight the objective of this memory-making. Finally, processes of memory-making seek to establish the relationship between meaning and identity as expressed, claimed and contested through representation of the past in voice and text.

What is the role of visuality in this memory-making process? Does a visually rich object, like a graphic ethnography, enable stronger memorialisations, particularly when the memories of violent pasts are in question? I explore the graphic novel in representing the memory of sexual violence perpetrated during the Bangladesh war of 1971 as a form of transmission and circulation of vicarious memory across generations when memory is not experienced personally by Labonno, the girl in the graphic novel. This leads to what I refer to as generative resilience.

The graphic novel and film that I co-authored emerged from the development of guidelines drawn from the ethnography of *The Spectral Wound*, which shows how adaptive peacebuilding can be a flawed process without adequate consideration being given to the ethical dilemmas that accompany such peacebuilding efforts. In the text, Labonno/Labony needs to do a school project on family memories of 1971, the Bangladesh War. When coming to ask her grandmother, she wakes the latter from one of her frequent nightmares. What follows is her grandmother's (Nanu/Rehana) narration of the history of *birangona*. Her mother, Hena, also tells her of the Oral History Project through which they tried to collect testimonies. This leads them to talk about the various points that need to be covered in the development of ethical guidelines to record testimonies of sexual violence during conflict. Hidden in these discussions of the guidelines, Labonno discovers an intricate secret family history. This family history is that of the grandmother Rehana (affectionately referred to as Nanu by Labony), who is also a *birangona*. She narrates her story (see Figure 6.1).

> *I was visiting my uncle's house in a village in Pabna during the war and got captured by the Pakistani army. I was in a camp for three months and got raped by the army. We became free after a group of Liberation Fighters stormed the camp and set us free near the end of the war. I have erased the memories of those three months as I don't feel well when I remember them. A liberation fighter wanted to marry me after the war but I did not want to marry.*
>
> *A year later I met your grandfather and we got married. He was away in Kolkata during the war and cried on hearing my story. He would say: "Rehana, would my love make you forget those horrible days?" But your grandfather's*

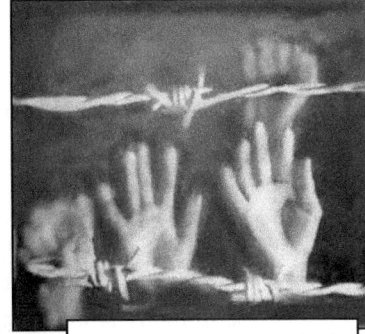

Photographed by Nayanika Mookherjee: Working Women's Hostel in New Eskaton, Dhaka. Bangladesh Central Women's Rehabilitation Organisation. Established in 1972.

FIGURE 6.1 Generative resilience – Nanu/Rehana's story

family used to scorn me and so we left it. Hence we did not get a share of your great grandfather's property. Remember Hena said all forms of stigma have an economic reason. After your grandfather's sudden death after the war I was

*heartbroken. But my government job gave me a lot of strength and I could bring
up Hena alone.*

The government rehabilitation centre that Rehana talks about reminds us of
the extensive programme set up by the Bangladeshi government to address
the concerns of the *birangonas* in the newly formed nation. Abortions were
performed and adoptive families in western countries were found for children born of rape. The rehabilitation centre also tried to marry off the
women and gave them jobs – the two aspects that I will discuss here in my
understanding of generative resilience. In 1972, the head of the state, Sheikh
Mujib, announced: 'The raped women are my mother, sister and daughter
and many of you will have to marry. I shall arrange for such a marriage'
(Banglar Bani, 1972a).

Following this announcement, newspapers carried images of these marriages, which were deemed to be an 'inspirational example and noble character', to exhibit 'unprecedented patriotism and magnanimity' on the part of
youths (as the future of the young nation) and to 'enable society to move
towards progress' (Banglar Bani, 1972a). While 9,000 applications were
received for these marriages, newspapers also reported that men were seeking
18,000 taka (equivalent to 180 British Sterling) as dowry to marry the
birangonas. However, the Rehabilitation Board clarified that 'any individual
who is seeking to marry *birangonas* in the hope of receiving dowries in the
form of red Japanese cars, houses, publication of unpublished poems, permits
or license is the last person to whom the war-heroines should be married. The
opportunities for the war-heroines are not a dowry of money, houses, cars, jobs.
Instead, they constitute of education and specific training opportunities'
(Banglar Bani, 1972b; Brownmiller, 1975: 83; Purbodesh, 1972).

With *birangonas* also exhibiting disinterest in marriage (Doinik Bangla,
1972), the Rehabilitation Board wrote in newspapers to ask prospective
grooms to stop making enquiries. In negating the demands for dowry, the
rehabilitation centre was reminding prospective grooms that they were
getting educated and vocationally trained wives. However, the refusal of
birangonas to marry following the dictates of the state point to the failure
of the marrying-off processes, through which the state was hoping to dictate
rules of conjugality and choice of partner based on patriotism. Outside the
purview of the state, there were also various practices of practical kinship
among communities. As previously noted, most of the women I worked with
were still with their husbands after being raped. This precisely exhibits the
prevalence of practical kinships and contingencies within families, which
absorbed raped women. It was, therefore, often the family system's resilience

which created the sustaining relations and social security required for acceptance, even in the absence of community recognition for the plight of the *birangonas*.

Rehabilitation in all its many forms not only created a framework of legitimacy for the state but also ensured that the *birangonas* could make claims on the newly formed government. *Birangonas* who were reluctant to get married instead demanded jobs from the state as part of their rehabilitation. Hosneara's unwillingness to take help from her family, instead demanding a job and help from the state (Akhtar et al., 2001), shows that *birangonas* were not passive recipients of state policy or satisfied with being sheltered by their families. Rather, they were actively involved in the idea of state responsibility and were thereby defining the framework for citizenship and what social resilience would look like. This compelled the government 'to reserve 10% vacancies for affected women in all government, semi-government, autonomous and semi-autonomous organization' (People, 1972), a strategy that seems to have improved these women's ability to cope despite their adversity.

The Rehabilitation Board (see Figure 6.2) thus became an important launching pad to provide 'self-sufficiency and independence' to women who constituted one-fourth of the population (Observer, 1972). Literate women gained training in 'useful professions' like secretarial work, nursing, family planning, midwifery, teaching, stenography, accounts and office management. In 1972, some of these women became the lady village workers who promoted family planning techniques. This also laid the foundation for the 'NGO-isation' of women's health (Mookherjee, 2007) in Bangladesh, which continues to this day. Illiterate women were given vocational training in handicrafts, like tailoring, embroidery, weaving, pottery, clay modelling, jute and leather crafts, printing, embroidery, rice husking, spice-making, making various food products, cooking lunch for offices and poultry raising. Shops called *Komolkoli* and *Unmesh* (awakening) were set up through which these handicrafts and items could be sold. The various photographs of women engaged in different vocational trainings were testimony to the Rehabilitation Board's aim of emancipating women. As a result, newspapers were full of photographs of rehabilitated women, and these were juxtaposed to the aforementioned horrific Naibuddin Ahmed image of the raped woman with hair over her face. The horrific wound had been dealt with; it had been rehabilitated into legitimate mothers, productive, classed workers for the new nation.

Large numbers of women were absorbed into various government departments and continued to work in them until they retired. In the early days of my research, one of the feminist organisations that was conducting an oral history

The Women's Movement in Bangladesh

FIGURE 6.2 Generative resilience – rehabilitation and the women's movement in Bangladesh

project suggested that I should meet some officials working in specific government departments. Arriving for my scheduled appointment, I was informed
that the Director was double-booked and that I should talk to her deputy,
Shireen Ahmed (also depicted in the graphic novel/film; Mookherjee, 2019:
10). On being asked whether there are any government documents related to
the rehabilitation programme, Shireen sharply admonished me and said:
'What will you do with these documents? These are such painful events –
you think you can find them in documents, that too in government documents,' suggesting that government documents would misrepresent the
experiences of war heroines. I did not know what to say as I did not know
who this woman was. She continued and talked about the oral history project
conducted by the feminist organisation: 'They came and talked to me and
every day after talking to them I would go home and just sit with the Koran
Sharif and pray for hours. That is all I can do. My current husband keeps on
asking me why I am doing my prayers for so long'.

Shireen continued to narrate that during the war, she was pregnant. She
was newly married that year. She added that her husband was good
looking and they really loved each other. One day the army came to her
home when her husband, a liberation fighter, had come home to visit her.
Before he opened the door of the house, he asked her to flee as she was
pregnant. She stayed behind a wall and saw the army beat him up,
bayonet him. They also found her hiding. At this point, she fidgets with
the paperweight on her table of files and papers. She continues:

> After the war I got this job and later I married my cousin and you know what the
> pain is? I cannot mention my first husband to my second husband as he
> considers that as a betrayal. But he knows I love my first husband more and
> he cannot stand it. He knows I remember him when I am praying and that is
> why he asks me why I am spending so much time with Koran Sharif. Now that
> I have told you all these things I want to pray again.

Shireen's spontaneous outburst had left me completely dumbstruck. She then
went to her filing cabinet and got out a document which she photocopied for
me. She said that there are many women like her who have sought refuge and
spent their lives in these government jobs. Shireen's story parallels Nanu's
story in the graphic novel. The newly formed Bangladeshi government
attempted to re-member *birangonas* into families, marriages and the labour
market through the rehabilitation project. The professionalisation of family
planning and social work engendered through the rehabilitation programme
allowed many middle-class women to restructure their lives outside the paradigms of marriage but within the cultural norms of femininity. The entire

process of the rehabilitation programme is thereby rooted in what Spivak referred to (Mookherjee, 2012: 212) as 'reproductive heteronormativity – the para-reasonable assumption that producing children by male-female coupling gives meaning to any life', and its re-centring in post wartime Bangladesh. Truly, reproductive heteronormativity is 'a tacit globaliser' (Mookherjee, 2012: 212) within which war and rape belong.

The varied programmes of rehabilitation aimed at providing women with jobs bring out the class dimension linked with access to literacy, as well as a certain urban/rural divide. Where each woman is also indicates her broad social position outside the rehabilitation programme. The rehabilitation programme thereby intrinsically hinged on reproductive heteronormativity and governmentality, which reallocated women in their class locations. The juxtaposition of the call for rehabilitation with the images of the rehabilitated women and the Naibuddin Ahmed photograph of the raped woman with her face covered with hair highlights the therapeutic, reformist, parental and modernist basis of the rehabilitation project. The raped woman as the wound can only be brought back into the new nation through the rehabilitation programme and the 'clean' images of those rehabilitated. The reformist and modernist agenda of the rehabilitation programme in fact pathologises *birangonas* and aims to expunge them of their ills. A more resilience-promoting strategy narrates their stories to prevent future atrocities and support calls for justice.

Nanu's story, captured through the graphic novel to Labony, is what I have referred to as generative resilience. It is also intersectional, as when she says: 'But I am not only a *birangona*. I am your nanu, I worked for many years in my government job, brought up my daughter Hena, your mother.' The role of the government in providing jobs and a pathway to self-sufficiency for *the birangonas* is well exhibited through Nanu's narrative. It also shows how the exercise of stigma towards Nanu has an intrinsic socio-economic basis. Hence, the socialities of violence that she has lived with are based on how she is excluded from property rights by her in-laws, who stigmatise her for her experience of sexual violence. The systemic aspects of resilience are intertwined with these economic factors, which get articulated through the rhetoric of stigma and shame.

We also find that the generative resilience imparted to Labony by Nanu draws on the energy and strength derived from social movements, international tribunals and protagonist figures who have experienced sexual violence during wars. Hence, Nanu narrates:

Yes, in 1992 when the three women from Kushtia were testifying, I was scared and thrilled and wanted to say aloud that I am a birangona, but kept quiet.

I was nearly fainting there. The women's movement in Bangladesh has waged a huge campaign to bring these debates to the forefront.

Yes and when Ferdousy Priyobhashini told her story of 1971, I felt so proud and strong but I acknowledged it quietly inside me. Soon many more of us were openly saying I am a birangona.

In 2000, Ferdousy Apa also spoke at the Tokyo Tribunal and she met a ninety-year-old Korean comfort woman and they held hands and said: 'You, me, we are the same, our pain is the same.' The *birangonas* who testified in 1992 suffered a lot as the testimonial process was another violation for them. In August 2018, they launched an ethical guideline meant for all those who are working with *birangonas*.

The graphic ethnography allows us to capture the emotions and to visibilise this generative resilience through the moment when Labony realises in the car that her grandmother is a *birangona*. The image of the tears of all the individuals in the car and the clasped hands allow the ethnography to be communicated without any text. In the last page of the graphic novel, when the family visits the Meherpur war memorial, this generative resilience comes together through the role of memorials, family acknowledgement of this history and pedagogy when Nanu says:

Labony, your generation has to bring out the stories of losses of men, women, birangonas and war babies which is not known. You have to make space for them to either speak (if they wish to) or keep quiet. Survivors need that space of safety, trust and empathy. Your generation has to implement these guidelines and ethically record testimonies of sexual violence when needed. Labony responds and says, I will tell everyone in school – my friends and teachers – about these guidelines. I am so proud to have you as my Nanu, Ammu and Abbu.

Hence, rather than thinking of gender and patriarchy as systemic, we need to reconceptualise resilience as generative. It not only allows us to show how memories are transmitted intergenerationally. It also highlights how, within the realms of patriarchy and nationalism, other demands can be made on it so that resilence – and its systemic mechanisms – is reconfigured in the process.

CONCLUSION

'Bangladesh is not a conflict'. This is what I was told in 2014 (Mookherjee, 2014) by the Special Representative of the UN Secretary-General at the Global Summit to End Sexual Violence in Conflict, at a time when the Bangladesh War Crimes Tribunal was underway. She said that the history of wartime rape during the Bangladesh war of 1971 could not be included in the summit, which took as its starting point the Bosnian war of 1992–1995. In effect, it was a summit without history, excluding all examples of sexual violence in conflict prior to 1992. It also excluded all instances of sexual violence perpetrated by soldiers from the United States and the UK.

While the summit wanted to end sexual violence in conflict, it did not attempt to end conflict as the first starting point, given the close connections that governments have with the arms and extractive industries. As evident in Kamari Clarke's book *Affective Justice* (2019), the anti-impunity debate and the rhetoric around sexual violence in conflict are the new tools of global control and soft power today, aimed specifically at the African sub-continent. The structural adjustments proposed for various African countries by the World Bank and International Monetary Fund (Clarke, 2019: 104) also included the ratification of the Rome Statute. This shows how law, while being a tool of social change, is also a renewed tool of historical subjection and structural injustice.

This volume places a strong emphasis on the concept of adaptive peace-building, as articulated by de Coning (2018; see also Chapter 11). This chapter has shown that any process of peacebuilding, including adaptive peacebuilding, can be inherently flawed if ethical practices are not adhered to when recording testimonies of sexual violence. In particular, the reiteration of the horrific figure of the *birangona* has disallowed insights into the socialities of violence through which survivors of wartime sexual violence, their families and communities have continued to live with their encounters of wartime rape folded into their everyday. Moyna and the other *birangona*s with whom I started this chapter have continued to be reminded of their wartime experience by their embodied memory and objects within their environment. Moyna's experience in the graphic novel (Mookherjee and Keya, 2019) illustrates this experience:

> Moyna Karim (anonymised) (a landless, rural woman):
> *During the war, she was raped by the Pakistani army in the courtyard of her own home. She was cutting fish when she was captured. Holding on to the wooden pole of her house, she thought I will give my life but not my honour. After the war, her husband took on the responsibility of cutting fish, and after her son got married this job was passed on to her daughter-in-law. Moyna hasn't cut fish since the war. Holding on to the wooden pole of her house, she says that the pole is the witness to her event. Whenever she sees this pole, she clearly sees the events of that day. In 1992, Moyna gave witness against the war criminals at the People's Court. Today, she is appealing to the government to give jobs to her sons and daughters.*

The call of the *birangona*s to include the graphic novel in schools is the ultimate resonance of generative resilience as they want it to be studied and known – not only by children but also by their parents and teachers. This is even more significant given the frail health and ages of the *birangonas*. It is this assertion and validation that gets passed on, not only within their families but also in their communities and beyond. The concept of generative resilience emerging from my ethnography highlights that adaptive peacebuilding, while attempting to strengthen the resilience of social institutions, needs to disinvest from the idea of social cohesion. Instead, generative resilience shows us how survivors of wartime sexual violence negotiate their violent experiences through everyday socialities of violence. It is these infractions and their transmission through generative resilience that adaptive peacebuilding needs to focus on, because it is not possible to self-sustain one's peace processes when past injustices remain unresolved.

The remit of this edited volume asks us, as contributing authors, to 'think about resilience as a systemic process that brings about stability and sustainability, as well as individual well-being, and to examine how different systems interact with each other'. While this is laudable on one level, we need to hope that the need for resilience does not come to us. We hope not to have to face traumatic experiences, catastrophic events and be vulnerable to threat, injury and loss. I share Evans and Reed's (2014: 4) concern in asking whether resilience is 'a neo-liberal deceit that works by disempowering endangered populations of autonomous agency', and whether its consequences 'represent a profound assault on the human subject whose meaning and sole purpose is reduced to survivability'. Is resilience not calling for the optimising of the capacities of the individual and environment, such that we would only then have generative resilience to fall back on? The complexity-informed approach, reflected in de Coning's adaptive peacebuilding, and its call for resilient capacities for self-organisation might not even leave us and the environment the resources with which to enable such self-mobilisation. The time has come to rethink our current over-reliance on resilience.

REFERENCES

Akhtar, S., Begum, S., Hossein, H., Kamal, S., and Guhathakurta, M. (eds.) (2001). *Narir Ekattor O Juddhoporoborti Koththo Kahini* (Oral History Accounts of Women's Experiences During 1971 and After the War). Dhaka: Ain-O-Shalish-Kendro (ASK).

Ahmed, F. (1973). The Structural Matrix of the Struggle in Bangladesh. In K. Gough and H. P. Sharma (eds.), *Imperialism and Revolution in South Asia*. London: Monthly Review Press, pp. 419–448

Ahmed, S. and Stacey, J. (2001). Testimonial cultures: An introduction. *Cultural Values*, 5(1), 1–6.

Anam, T. (2008). The war that time forgot. www.theguardian.com/world/2008/apr/10/ bangladesh.photography (accessed 25 April 2008).

Brownmiller, S. (1975). *Against Our Will: Men, Women and Rape*. London: Secker and Warburg.

Brownmiller, S. (1994). Making Female Bodies the Battlefield. In A. Stiglmayer (ed.), *Mass Rape: The War Against Women in Bosnia*. Translations by Marion Faber. Lincoln, NE: University of Nebraska Press, pp. 180–182.

Clarke, K. (2019). *Affective Justice: The International Criminal Court and the Pan-Africanist Pushback*. Durham, NC: Duke University Press.

Das, V. (2006). *Life and Words: Violence and the Descent into the Ordinary*. Foreword by Stanley Cavell. Berkeley, CA: University of California Press.

de Coning, C. (2018). Adaptive peacebuilding. *International Affairs*, 94(2), 301–317.

Eltringham. N. (2019). *Genocide Never Sleeps: Living Law at the International Criminal Tribunal for Rwanda*. Cambridge: Cambridge University Press.

Eltringham, N. (2009). Introduction: Identity, justice and 'reconciliation' in contemporary Rwanda. *Journal of Genocide Research*, 11(1), 5–10.

Evans, B. and Reed, J. (2014). *Resilient Life: The Art of Living Dangerously*. Cambridge: Polity Press.

Gallimore, T. (2008). The legacy of the International Criminal Tribunal for Rwanda (ICTR) and its contributions to reconciliation in Rwanda. *New England Journal of International and Comparative Law*, 14(2), 239–266.

Hanssen, B. (2000). *Critique of Violence: Between Poststructuralism and Critical Theory (Warwick Studies in European Philosophy)*. Abingdon: Routledge.

Hasan, M. A. (2002). *Juddho O Nari (War and Women)*. Dhaka: War Crimes Facts Finding Committee (Trust) and Genocide Archive and Human Studies Centre.

Islam, S. (1992). *History of Bangladesh, 1704–1971, Volumes I and II*. Dhaka: Asiatic Society of Bangladesh.

Masud, M. (1998). *Ki bhabe tola muktijuddher ei chobi?* (How is this photograph of the liberation war taken?) Dhaka: Prothom Alo.

Mookherjee, N. (2006). 'Remembering to forget': Public secrecy and memory of sexual violence in Bangladesh. *Journal of Royal Anthropological Institute*, 12(2), 433–450.

Mookherjee, N. (2007). Available motherhood: Legal technologies, 'state of exception' and the dekinning of 'war babies' in Bangladesh. *Childhood: A Journal of Global Child Research*, 14(3), 339–354.

Mookherjee, N. (2012). Reproductive heteronormativity and sexual violence in the Bangladesh War of 1971: A discussion with Gayatri Chakravorty Spivak. *Social Text*, 111, 123–131.

Mookherjee, N. (2014). The 'war heroines' of Bangladesh: Lessons for fighting sexual violence in conflict. *The Conversation*, http://theconversation.com/the-war-heroines-of-bangladesh-lessons-for-fighting-sexual-violence-in-conflict-29232 (accessed 20 September 2020).

Mookherjee, N. (2015). *The Spectral Wound: Sexual Violence, Public Memories and the Bangladesh War of 1971*. Foreword by Veena Das. Durham, NC: Duke University Press.

Mookherjee, N. and Keya. N. (2019). *Birangona: Towards Ethical Testimonies of Sexual Violence during Conflict*. Durham: University of Durham. www.ethical-testimonies-svc.org.uk/how-to-cite/ (Graphic Novel, Animation Film) (accessed 20 September 2020).

Muhith, A. M. A. (1992). *Bangladesh: Emergence of A Nation*. Dhaka, Bangladesh: University Press Limited.

Rosoux, V. (2009). Reconciliation as a peace-building process: Scope and limits. In J. Bercovitch, V. Kremenyuk and I. W. Zartman (eds.), *The SAGE Handbook of Conflict Resolution*. London: SAGE, pp. 543–560.

Sarkar, M. (2006). Difference in memory. *Society for Comparative Study of Society and History*, 48(1), 139–168.

Shaon, A. I. (2018). Eight years of war crime trials. www.dhakatribune.com/bangladesh/war-crimes/2018/08/18/eight-years-of-war-crimes-trials (accessed 2 August 2020).

Totten, S., Parsons, W. S. and Charny, I. W. (eds.) (1997). *Century of Genocide: Eyewitness Accounts and Critical Views*. London: Routledge.

Turner, C. (2016). *Violence, Law and the Impossibility of Transitional Justice*. London: Routledge.

Ungar, M. (2011). The social ecology of resilience. Addressing contextual and cultural ambiguity of a nascent construct. *American Journal of Orthopsychiatry*, 81, 1–17.

United Nations. (2004). *The Rule of Law and Transitional Justice in Conflict and Post-Conflict Societies: Report of the Secretary-General*. www.un.org/ruleoflaw/blog/document/the-rule-of-law-and-transitional-justice-in-conflict-and-post-conflict-societies-report-of-the-secretary-general/ (accessed 2 October 2020).

Williams, R. (1992). *The East Pakistan Tragedy*. London: Tom Stacey.

Newspapers cited

Banglar Bani (1972a) (Dhaka, Bangladesh) Sheikh Mujib makes announcements for birangonas (28 February 1972).

Banglar Bani (1972b) Applications received from youths (Dhaka, Bangladesh) (22 April 1972).

Doinik Bangla (1972) (Dhaka, Bangladesh) Birangonas not willing to marry (21 April 1972).

Observer (1972) (Dhaka, Bangladesh) Self Sufficiency for Women (9 October 1972).

People (1972) (Dhaka, Bangladesh) 10% vacancies for affected women (26 April 1972).

Purbodesh (1972) (Dhaka, Bangladesh) Many marriage applications received (20 April 1972).

7

Resilience in Post-Khmer Rouge Cambodia: Systemic Dimensions and the Limited Contributions of Transitional Justice

Timothy Williams[1]

INTRODUCTION

Since the 70s, I have thought that Cambodia had no more peace [...] There are only the strong people, the weaker ones will be dead. That's it. [...]. It is only the leaders who live happily while the normal people don't. They decide on when and who will be alive, who will be dead and who will become the leader. [...] It's quite similar [to the Khmer Rouge period ...]. But this society is different since there are computers, spacecraft and Facebook. That's what is different. [... But it is] the same worry, just a different regime. It's still difficult but just different difficulties.

These words were spoken by an elderly Cambodian man who leads a life of poverty in the rural province of Kampong Cham.[2] The man is a victim of the totalitarian and genocidal Khmer Rouge regime that turned the country upside down in the 1970s. His life has continued to be extremely hard since the end of the regime; and indeed much evidence suggests that life since the liberation in 1979 has remained difficult for many victims, characterised by poverty, limited (although growing) economic and social opportunities, corruption and nepotism and the hegemony of an authoritarian ruler.

[1] The research underlying this chapter was funded by two research grants: 'Victimhood after Mass Violence' (funded by the German Federal Ministry of Economic Cooperation and Development) and 'The Cultural Heritage of Conflict' (funded by the Swedish Research Council under grant number 2016–01460). I would like to thank Roland Kossler for his assistance, as well as Julie Bernath, Roddy Brett, Kirsty Campbell, KEO Duong, Jonathan Leader Maynard, Jan Reinermann, David Simon, SIRIK Savina and Manuel Vogt for their valuable feedback on a draft version of this chapter.
[2] Some interviews referred to in this chapter were conducted in 2018 by Julie Bernath in the context of a joint project 'Victimhood after Mass Violence'. These interviews are labelled (JB). All other interviews were conducted by the author.

Nevertheless, in the aftermath of Democratic Kampuchea and the civil wars that preceded and succeeded it, victims have rebuilt their lives, demonstrating a desire and capacity to survive in the face of extreme hardship. This chapter assesses resilience in post-Khmer Rouge Cambodia through this edited volume's social-ecological lens (Ungar, 2018) to explore how various systems interact to provide resources that enable and foster resilience among victim populations. It demonstrates that while some resources are generated in this resilience process, the political system actually limits them and undermines resilience in exerting political and economic dominance. Fundamentally, systems related to political empowerment, economic opportunity, social structure, rule of law and others interact with each other to promote or undermine the provision of resources.

The chapter also analyses how transitional justice work in Cambodia has affected resilience. It focuses particularly on the Extraordinary Chambers in the Courts of Cambodia (ECCC) – the hybrid Cambodian-United Nations (UN) tribunal that was created to deliver justice for the Khmer Rouge period – and its programme of victim participation and moral and collective reparations. I argue that while the ECCC has the potential to contribute to resilience (and does for some victims), its design and procedures constrain it in this regard, even inadvertently reinforcing broader marginalising systemic dynamics. This does not paint a bright picture of the relationship between transitional justice and adaptive peacebuilding (see de Coning, 2018). The key point, however, is that national actors in Cambodia recognise that they can gain significant advantages through corrupt practices and autocratic power (Un, 2019), and thus they have used transitional justice strategically to undermine peacebuilding (Gidley, 2019; Killean, 2018; Manning, 2017).

Pursuing a multi-systemic approach means that this chapter's engagement with social-ecological resilience is complex and at times messy. Nevertheless, I endeavour to portray the interlinkages between the systems as clearly as possible, using empirical data. First, I utilise data from a nation-wide survey conducted in 2018 with 439 victims of the Khmer Rouge, most of whom had participated in transitional justice processes in some form, as well as follow-up interviews with sixty seven of them (for more details, see Williams et al., 2018). Second, I draw on interviews conducted with international and Cambodian transitional justice and memory actors from the same project and a further project on the politics of memory. Third, my own insights on national political dynamics from regular fieldwork engagement since 2014 complement the above data.

This chapter begins with a brief historical introduction to the Khmer Rouge past. It moves on to discuss resilience and the utility of this volume's multi-systemic approach. It proceeds to analyse how different systems have contributed to or undermined resilience, with a particular focus on the ECCC, its victim participation programme and its moral and collective reparations. The chapter ends with a discussion of what the case study of Cambodia means for our understanding of adaptive peacebuilding.

THE KHMER ROUGE AND THE LONG SHADOW OF THE PAST

In 1953, King Norodom Sihanouk secured Cambodia's independence from France and separation from the rest of colonial Indochina (Kiernan, 1985). Sihanouk remained Cambodia's strongman and positioned Cambodia neutrally in the neighbouring Vietnam War (Chandler, 2008a: 233–254; Kiernan, 1996: 17). In opposition to this policy, Prime Minister General Lon Nol led a coup against Sihanouk and realigned foreign policy in a pro-United States (US) direction, allowing bombardment of Viet Cong troops inside Cambodian territory.

In a pragmatic liaison, King Sihanouk drew on his unwavering popularity among the rural population to call upon his subjects to 'come to the jungle' and join a hitherto small and relatively unknown group, later to be known as the Khmer Rouge (Chandler, 1999: 88). The subsequent five-year civil war and US bombardments killed 500,000 people (Chandler, 2008a: 256) and internally displaced large parts of the rural population who fled from the countryside to the cities.

The Khmer Rouge took Phnom Penh on 17 April 1975, winning the civil war, and were welcomed enthusiastically by a war-weary population. However, the Khmer Rouge immediately evacuated the cities (Chandler, 2008a: 256; Kiernan, 1996: 8) and began to implement their vision of a peasant revolution, according to a radical Maoist model. They pledged to take the country back to the 'Year Zero' and rebuild it independently of the imperialist and capitalist West through intense rice production and large-scale irrigation construction (Chandler, 2000: 14; Chandler, 2008a: 264). A quota of three tonnes of rice to be harvested per hectare of land was instituted, a substantial overestimation of realistic productivity levels for most of the country's land. Local leaders were torn between three priorities: first, delivering the quota; second, saving seed for planting next season; and, third, feeding the population. In the end, many local leaders followed strategies that maximised their own security and de-prioritised feeding the population, causing mass starvation (Hinton, 2005: 11; on famine, see DeFalco, 2014).

After taking power, the Khmer Rouge sought to eradicate anyone associated with the former Lon Nol regime (Chandler, 2000: 45); and, as the revolution failed to meet its targets, the leadership around Pol Pot identified 'microbes' within the regime intent on undermining the revolution (Chandler, 2000: 45–76). The regime became ever more fixated on rooting out these internal enemies, interning, interrogating and executing anyone suspected of trying to jeopardise the revolution, with even minor dissent or rule-breaking classed as anti-revolutionary. Furthermore, the Khmer Rouge understood itself in strongly nationalistic terms, targeting ethnic minorities for annihilation, too. Ultimately, between 1.7 and 2.2 million people died during Democratic Kampuchea, about half from violent deaths and the other half from exhaustion, overwork, sickness or starvation (Tabeau and Kheam, 2009: 19).

Democratic Kampuchea finally ended on 7 January 1979 when defected Khmer Rouge units, supported by Vietnamese troops, invaded and liberated the country. The Khmer Rouge retreated to the Northern and Western borders with Thailand, along with hundreds of thousands of refugees, throwing the country into another civil war wherein multiple factions developed in resistance to the new rulers and Vietnamese occupation of the country (Chandler, 2008a: 277–295). Cambodia remained internationally isolated throughout the 1980s due to international hostility towards Vietnam in the aftermath of US defeat in the Vietnam War (Chandler, 2008a: 277–295), until the Paris Peace Agreement of 1991 and the UN peacekeeping intervention, UNTAC (UN Transitional Authority in Cambodia). With the defection of increasing numbers of Khmer Rouge (and other factions) through the promise of amnesty as part of the government's 'win-win policy', the civil war drew to a close in the late 1990s. Subsequently, there was an economic opening to a liberal market economy and democratic reforms. In this new environment, Prime Minister Hun Sen – who had been part of the liberating forces and rose to power in 1984 – was able to quash political threats. He remains in power to this day, reaping significant economic benefits through corruption, land-grabbing and favourable concessions (Global Witness, 2016).

Although the government propagated hatred against the Khmer Rouge during the civil war, once hostilities ended Hun Sen urged people to 'dig a hole and bury the past' (cited in Chandler, 2008b: 356). However, this envisaged 'induced amnesia' (Chandler, 2008b) was ultimately less important to the government than the potential international political capital to be gained from supporting transitional justice. Established in 2003, the ECCC applies international law within the context of the Cambodian judicial system and fills all positions with both international and Cambodian counterparts (for an introduction to the ECCC, see Gidley, 2019; Hughes, 2015; Killean, 2018; Manning, 2017). The judicial mandate of the ECCC is to try the senior leaders and those most responsible for the crimes committed during Democratic

Kampuchea. As such, and compared with other tribunals, the ECCC has tried relatively few individuals, with verdicts handed down for only three individuals. Further cases are unlikely to go forward due to government pressure to limit the ECCC's activities to the cases already tried. Beyond the ECCC, the broader transitional justice process in Cambodia encompasses considerable non-governmental organisation (NGO) activity, although most of this work is thematically tied to the ECCC (see Hinton, 2018: 43). Many NGOs feed into the tribunal directly, supporting its internationally innovative yet poorly financed victim participation programme (Ryan and McGrew, 2016: 92; Sperfeldt, 2012a).

A MULTI-SYSTEMIC APPROACH TO RESILIENCE AND MULTI-SYSTEMIC CHALLENGES IN CAMBODIA

This volume approaches resilience as 'processes whereby individuals interact with their environments in ways that facilitate positive psychological, physical and social development' (Ungar, Chapter 1). More than just an individual trait, resilience thus incorporates important social-ecological dimensions, drawing attention to the broader social environment in which the individual is embedded and which, through the resources and opportunities that it offers or fails to provide, fosters or undermines the individual's development. This social environment is diverse, formed of various systems that affect the individual and interact with each other. Hence, resilience is about the interactions between the individual and the social environment, with responsibility for an individual's development partly explained by the quality of a system's functioning (see Ungar, 2018).

In this chapter, I foreground several inter-linked systems. The *political system* can provide resources to equip individuals with political agency and the ability to shape the contextual structure of their lives. This is closely connected to the *legal system*, which can provide resources in terms of individual rights and the rule of law, supporting resilience through legal security. The *economic system* mediates resources through access to economic opportunities that lay the foundation for individual development and the provision of the means to earn a living and secure shelter, as well as more advanced economic goals. Each of these systems can provide resources to individuals, allowing for resilience, but they can also remove these resources or even undermine resilience. Within the scope of this chapter, I demonstrate some of the key interactions between these systems and their repercussions for resilience, before specifically exploring their impact within the context of the ECCC's work.

Political system

Political developments over the past four decades since the end of Democratic Kampuchea have had a significant impact on social-ecological resilience in Cambodia. Key to understanding this is the *political system* itself. Since the 1980s, Cambodia's political system has been dominated by Prime Minister Hun Sen and his Cambodian People's Party (CPP; known until 1991 as the Kampuchean People's Revolutionary Party), with gradual liberalisation beginning with the UNTAC mission and supported by broad peacebuilding efforts in subsequent years. However, while formal democratic institutions are in place, the system is fundamentally illiberal; and, in recent years, there has been a concerted political effort by the government to close the political space, reduce political freedoms and limit the political opposition (Un, 2019). There is direct targeting of opposition politicians, human rights activists and civil society organisations, but the fear of personal repercussions for political dissent also affects the broader population. For example, a female interviewee from Kratie province revealed: 'nowadays people are only scared of the people who hold power. Their relevant institutions. [...] The people dare not to say [anything negative, but] just agree with everything [...] in order to avoid being accused like this or like that'.[3] While 46 per cent of respondents in a 2018 nation-wide survey felt that they were able to participate to improve things in their community,[4] the previous quote demonstrates that clear limitations exist for people to exercise their agency.

Moreover, political repression goes beyond just the targeting of politically unfavourable individuals and structural limitations placed on political freedoms and relevant political resources. In 2017, for example, the country's main opposition party, the Cambodian National Rescue Party (CNRP), was dissolved in the run-up to local elections, after significant gains by the opposition in the 2013 national elections (Un, 2019). Furthermore, there has been a crackdown on the free press, with several newspapers being forced to close due to supposedly unpaid tax bills, as well as stricter laws on international funding (Un, 2019), severely limiting the population's access to politically unbiased reporting in print and radio – and thereby weakening resources for the development of political agency. This illiberal backlash also includes a curtailing of NGO activities through the Law on Associations and Non-Governmental Organizations (LANGO), which allows tighter controls on NGOs and has led to several organisations being shut down. Given that many fundamental services are provided by NGOs, this encroachment on the civil society sector not only

---

3 The interview was conducted in Kratie province in 2018 (JB).
4 Unpublished statistics, used by Williams et al. (2018).

restricts access to support for human rights violations but also affects many other systems, including community services, business and agriculture, education and physical and mental health. As such, the transformative potential for other systems through NGO work is curtailed. Furthermore, political participation and agency are a key resilience resource (Comes et al., 2019), and hence increasing political disempowerment significantly limits the development of resilience for a large part of the population. Nonetheless, some activists are still able to use alternative spaces, such as social media or radio programmes, to circumvent government control and develop agency, even though these spaces continue to shrink (see Human Rights Watch, 2019).

A further facet of the political system that engages other systems is the issue of corruption. Transparency International rates Cambodia as one of the most corrupt countries worldwide (with 162 out of 180 countries exhibiting less corruption in 2019) (Transparency International, 2019). Corruption is plainly manifest in the extraordinary wealth of government officials, in particular Prime Minister Hun Sen's family; it is estimated to be worth between half and one billion US dollars, owning a network of lucrative companies and holdings. Additionally, Hun Sen's family members occupy various key positions in the administration, military and police (Global Witness, 2016). Corruption also exists in every aspect of public life, with payment of bribes routinely expected for bureaucratic action, police assistance or even access to healthcare. Access to land, contracts and permits is also structured through corruption and nepotism (Hennings, 2016: 226).

Legal system

Corruption also interacts with the *legal system*, significantly undermining access to justice and rule of law. For example, a female interviewee from Kampong Cham province explained that one of her nieces, a seven-year-old girl, was raped. The accused 'was detained, but later was bailed out after his mother bribed the authorities'.[5] In more general terms, a villager from Takeo province explained his perspective on courts in the Cambodian justice system: 'The court sees only the one side that is powerful and rich, so there is no justice to change the society. If a person is poor [. . .] and he/she is innocent, the rich person wins the case; thus, our society does not change and it becomes more corrupt'.[6]

---

[5] The interview, with a civil party of case 001 at the ECCC, was conducted in Kampong Cham province in 2018 (JB).

[6] The interview, with a civil party representative at the ECCC, was conducted in Kampong Cham province in 2018 (JB).

These injustices permeate various issues and interact with the political system when human rights violations are not prosecuted, or when land-grabbing in the economic system is judicially legitimated. This intersection of systems and their cumulative effects limit resilience and access to potential resources that could, in theory, support resilience.

While corruption is structurally inefficient from a social-ecological perspective on resilience, one way that people deal with it is through participation in patronage networks, in which patrons provide access to resources and security to their clients who, in turn, support the patrons with loyalty and service (Springer, 2011; Un, 2019). This often means that patrons will secure positions for their clients, and a significant part of the money made through corruption and bribes is then passed upwards. These patron–client networks are expansive and extend over many levels, including the state bureaucracy and party structures throughout the country, as well as many other societal and economic relations. This provides an alternative option for individuals to develop resilience and gain access to key resources. For example, the Union of Youth Federations of Cambodia is an influential actor headed by Hun Sen's son, Hun Many, and offers a variety of opportunities to individuals associated with it. However, these patron networks systematically marginalise those who are not well positioned to take advantage of them. Patronage networks also play a role in transitional justice, as discussed in the next section.

Economic system

Corruption and government control strongly affect the *economic system*, which is characterised by an absence of any engaged provision of services, particularly in the provinces. Compared with the mass starvation, dire poverty and lack of individual ownership (due to collectivisation) under the Khmer Rouge, and the difficulties of the civil war period, today's residents of Cambodia enjoy a higher degree of economic development and wealth. Nonetheless, the country remains poor; and in a 2018 nation-wide survey of victims of the Khmer Rouge, just over half of respondents 'stated that they did not earn enough to make a living' (Williams et al., 2018: 28). Highlighting this marginal progress, a male interviewee from Kampong Cham province lamented: 'In the past, it was very difficult for us but today it's difficult in the way that we have something to eat, but we don't have a house to live in'.[7] While part of this poverty can be traced back to the long-term effects of the

---

[7]   The interview, with a rejected civil party at the ECCC, was conducted in Kampong Cham province in 2018.

Khmer Rouge regime's economic policies, the mass killing of intellectuals and the subsequent civil wars, it is also a product of the corrupt and extractive government policies, described above, which lead to a highly unequal distribution of wealth.

Cambodia's economy is industrialising, but it remains dominated by the agricultural sector and three-quarters of the population is rural (World Bank, 2020). This makes insecurities surrounding land rights and increasing cases of land-grabbing highly pertinent issues to resilience in the context of a survival economy that depends on access to land. While increasing industrialisation is providing jobs, foreign investment is predominantly Chinese, de-emphasising human and labour rights and exporting profits in an increasingly extractive way (with the exception of the substantial pay-offs that the government presumably benefits from). This extractive economic tendency, as well as the increased presence of Chinese investors in Cambodia – 43 per cent of foreign direct investments are Chinese (National Bank of Cambodia, 2020) – has led to an upsurge of anti-Chinese sentiment throughout the country (Po and Heng, 2019), an interaction between the economic system and social system that reduces social cohesion.

An alternative strategy to enhance resilience in the economic system can be found in migrant labour. The high proportion of young people in the country facilitates this; 65.3 per cent of the population is under 30 (United Nations Development Programme, 2020). Migrant labour occurs both within the country, to urban factories, as well as abroad, through agricultural positions and menial labour, particularly in Thailand (see Parsons et al., 2014). While this migration – which the COVID-19 pandemic has significantly affected (Olsen and Vorn, 2020) – enables resilience through access to economic resources, it has inter-systemic fallout through its effects on the social system of families. In particular, it can contribute to weakening family ties and decentralising them, often leaving young children with elderly relatives while the still young parents migrate for most of the year.

Other relevant systems that go beyond the scope of this chapter could include physical security or spiritual practices in Buddhist traditions (Bennett, 2018; Ledgerwood, 2012). What this section has specifically sought to demonstrate, however, are the complex ways in which three particular systems interact with each other to restrict political agency and access to resilience-supporting resources. The key point is that the lack of resilience is not due to structural deficits, chance or exogenous shocks, such as natural disasters. Rather, it is built into the system to advance personal and political interests. While some access to resources can be traced within each system, for the most part powerful actors use their positions to structurally limit access across systems for their own personal benefit.

TRANSITIONAL JUSTICE AND ITS OVERALL LIMITED CONTRIBUTIONS TO RESILIENCE

Within the political and legal context of Cambodia, there have been various efforts over the years to come to terms with the violent Khmer Rouge past, including the largest transitional justice intervention, the ECCC. While hopes for transitional justice processes are often very high, they also necessarily unfold within the constraints and opportunities of the broader context in which they are structurally embedded. While resilience was not a stated part of the ECCC's mandate, this section highlights the contributions that transitional justice can and has made to resilience in Cambodia while also underlining its significant limitations in this regard. Victims of the Khmer Rouge nevertheless appear to positively assess the impact of transitional justice, despite these limitations. For example, two-thirds of victims in a 2018 nationwide survey opined that the ECCC had brought justice for the victims of the Khmer Rouge regime and their families, while about a quarter believed that the ECCC had delivered justice in conjunction with other factors (Williams et al., 2018: 42).

The Effect of the ECCC's Mandate on Attributing Responsibility

Undoubtedly, the ECCC's cases to date have contributed to providing justice for the crimes of the Khmer Rouge, even though only three people have been sentenced. This narrow focus on individual criminal responsibility avoids the generalisation of guilt to entire groups – a key aim of international criminal justice more generally – which potentially affects the resilience of social systems in the sense of improving relations in local communities. The focus on a few key individuals arguably also gives judicial credence to a narrow attribution of responsibility that has been politically pursued since the mid-1990s alongside the integration of former Khmer Rouge, as does the inclusion of former Khmer Rouge as civil parties at the tribunal (Bernath, 2016). Relatedly, the narrow approach to responsibility for violence has allowed almost all low- and mid-level cadres to claim victimhood under the Khmer Rouge (Williams, 2018a, 2019). This was exemplified by a male interviewee from Kampong Cham province who said: 'I cannot hate them since they just followed the orders; even the commune chief in Pol Pot regime also got killed.

The officers got killed more than normal people. How can we hate them since they also received the order as well'.[8]

This broad classification of victimhood can lead to tensions in certain communities where former Khmer Rouge who committed atrocities continue to live. However, for the most part, cadres were assigned to work in other areas (Williams, 2018b), allowing the frame of broad victimhood and narrow culpability to appear plausible, thereby aiding the ECCC's contribution to consolidating community relations (Williams, 2018a) – and strengthening resilience resources within social systems.

The Politicisation of the ECCC

The ECCC's creation came at the end of protracted negotiations and political interference in its work has always existed (Manning, 2017; Orentlicher, 2020; Ryan and McGrew, 2016: 72; Un, 2019; Williams et al., 2018: 45). The government, for example, appoints national staff from within its patronage networks, and these staff have blocked international attempts to progress prosecutions in Cases 003 and 004, even though more than 80 per cent of victims support these prosecutions (Williams et al., 2018: 62).[9]

The politicised nature of the tribunal has also stymied hopes that it would positively benefit the rule of law and jurisprudence in Cambodia, and contribute to the consolidation of resources within the legal system (Gidley, 2019). Slightly tangential to this, the work of the tribunal has inadvertently masked ongoing human rights violations; it focuses on past 'injustice', even though two-thirds of victims believe that today's problems are more important (Williams et al., 2018: 31). Moreover, by virtue of its embeddedness within the Cambodian legal system, the ECCC provides a degree of legitimacy and normalcy to government intervention in, and control of, the legal system. As such, for the most part, the ECCC has largely failed to positively influence the legal system vis-à-vis the right to legal representation, despite some limited contributions (Soy and Hing, 2019). It has not enabled easier access to justice for victims of today's human rights violations in a national court system that remains rampantly corrupt, and it has accorded greater legitimacy to this national system and to the political interference that occurs within it (DeFalco, 2018).

---

[8] The interview, with a rejected civil party at the ECCC, was conducted in Kampong Cham province in 2018.
[9] Notwithstanding political influence, it appears that basic fair trial procedures have not been undermined (Orentlicher, 2020).

Trials at the ECCC focus, unsurprisingly, on the violence of the Khmer Rouge regime, while giving little space to the broader structures of repression and economic exploitation that are important to some victims in their memory of the past (Williams et al., 2018: 41). The focus of the tribunal's mandate aids the government in its efforts to highlight how it ended Khmer Rouge violence, while deflecting attention from any form of illiberal continuity. In this way, the ECCC is both shaped by and advantageous to the political system. Similarly, the absence within the tribunal's mandate of issues pertaining to economic exploitation precludes debates about ongoing economic marginalisation today, thereby normalising and hiding the lack of resilience resources available. However, the addition of particular topics to the ECCC's work has also provided resilience resources. For example, through the efforts of international civil party lawyer, Silke Studzinsky, forced marriage was recognised as a crime to be addressed by the ECCC. This, in turn, had important repercussions for the social system, where victims were able to understand what happened to them specifically as a crime (Strasser et al., 2015).

Victim Participation

When it was created, one of the ECCC's most innovative features was that it included a strong degree of victim participation. Victims were able to participate in proceedings not only in the form of witness testimony but also as civil parties and complainants. While the latter only filed a complaint to the ECCC and received recognition of this, civil parties were actual parties to the proceedings, represented by international and national lawyers and afforded various rights – albeit gradually diminished over time – in co-operation with the prosecution (Killean, 2018). They also had the right to apply for moral and collective reparations (discussed below). This provided an opportunity to embed a 'victim-centred' approach (Robins, 2011) at the core of the transitional justice project.

In total, 94 people applied to be civil parties in Case 001 (of whom 76 were accepted) and 4,128 in Case 002 (of whom 3,865 were accepted). A further 645 and 2,008 have applied to participate in Cases 003 and 004, respectively, notwithstanding uncertainties about whether these trials will proceed.[10] In the context of this chapter, it is also significant that various NGOs offered services and programmes for victims who were officially participating, providing resources for resilience across a range of projects – including psychological

---

[10] All statistics were provided by the ECCC's Victim Support Section in private correspondence (see also Williams et al., 2018: 14).

counselling, interpersonal dialogues or spaces to share their stories. This strong degree of victim participation could be an important opportunity for transitional justice processes to positively contribute to resilience.

A 2018 nation-wide survey of victims showed that considerable mental health benefits accrued from participating in transitional justice (Williams et al., 2018: 101), which is important in a population that still suffers from the long-term effects of the violent past.[11] For example, '69.3% of civil party respondents agreed that their participation helps them cope with the Khmer Rouge past (compared with 38.5% of complainants) [... and] 74.7% of civil party respondents agreed that being a civil party helps them to feel mentally stronger (complainants: 40.9%)' (Williams et al., 2018: 101). One civil party representative from Kandal province talked about meeting other civil parties in the context of the tribunal: 'I was very happy not because of money but I got to meet others, so that I could feel relieved and reduce my stress.'[12] Many victims emphasise the therapeutic value of being able not just to meet and talk to others, but also to share stories with them (Williams et al., 2018: 102). A male interviewee from Kampot province who participated in a reparations project reported: 'after I got to talk, I felt very released, especially my anger, as I got to share it with other people, so it made me feel better'.[13]

Besides being able to tell their story and find a voice, material interests are relevant for victim participation, aiding resilience. While economic reparations are not accessible through the ECCC (see the next subsection), civil parties are provided with per diems when participating in programmes or visiting the court. Most interviewees emphasised that these were important and that they would eat as little as possible or share guesthouse rooms in order to save money to take home to their families (Williams et al., 2018: 79). This practice speaks as much to their poverty as it does to the meagre but subjectively important resources it provides in bolstering their economic security and allowing a degree of resilience.

However, three key dynamics structurally limit the potentially positive impact of victim participation. First, victims are only included in the implementation phase of transitional justice and not in its design, meaning that their participation is not on their own terms and thus falls short of a more

---

[11] While reports of post-traumatic stress disorder (PTSD) are low (Sonis et al., 2009: 532), localised concepts, such as *baksbat* (literally: broken courage), can be more helpful in understanding psychological suffering in Cambodia (Chhim, 2013).

[12] The interview, with a civil party representative at the ECCC, was conducted in Kandal province in 2018 (JB).

[13] The interview, with a man who participated in an ECCC reparations project, was conducted in Kampot province in 2018 (JB).

substantive empowerment (Williams et al., 2018: 54). This is most obvious vis-à-vis reparations (Sperfeldt, 2012b: 475; Williams et al., 2018: 117), discussed later. Second, participation in events and programmes, as well as visits to court, is theoretically open to all civil parties. However, in practice, these activities are organised by the supporting NGOs, and invitations often run through local focal points (civil party representatives). It is regularly reported that people closest to these key individuals are more likely to be invited; others cannot afford to participate as they need to engage in agricultural or caregiving work. Thus, access to participation opportunities in transitional justice appears to be mediated by power structures and patronage networks, as well as economic position, thereby reinforcing patterns of societal marginalisation visible in the political, legal and economic systems.

Third, not all victims were even able to register and be accepted as civil parties at the ECCC. Of those victimised by the Khmer Rouge, the vast majority are not registered as civil parties. This non-participation is unproblematic when it is voluntary; for example, due to individuals being uninterested or not seeing the benefits of participation. However, non-participation is mostly involuntary; some people did not know that they could apply or how to go about this, and others felt afraid or did not have sufficient resources (time and money) (Williams et al., 2018: 92–93). Most people were registered by NGOs, meaning that those individuals who were not already part of projects had a much slimmer chance of understanding how to register, with potential implications for mental health and other support. Furthermore, even if they did register, 276 out of 4,222 civil party applicants were rejected in the first two cases at the ECCC. Rejection of civil party status is psychologically very difficult for victims, leading to great disappointment, feelings of hopelessness and guilt, and even fears that others will now see them as lesser victims. This underscores that a technical, legal decision has very real consequences for the affected parties (Williams et al., 2018: 86–87).

The differentiation between types of participation (e.g., civil party or complainant) and the varying degree of opportunity to participate due to patronage systems and access create hierarchies of access to justice for victims (Williams et al., 2018: 83). As such, the key resources for resilience that transitional justice processes can provide – in particular the aforementioned mental health benefits, social exchanges with others and limited access to economic benefits – are accessible only to those who can actually participate in them. Not only are there just a few thousand civil parties at the ECCC, but even within the victim participation system access varies significantly (Williams et al., 2018: 69, 107).

Collective and Moral Reparations

One aspect of the ECCC's victim participation programme includes access for civil parties to 'collective and moral' reparations.[14] Even though monetary reparations are explicitly excluded from the ECCC's mandate, they were by far the most requested type of reparations in a 2018 nation-wide survey among victims (Williams et al., 2018: 110). In this sense, 'victim participation in internationalised criminal tribunals provides a stage for the putting of collective claims in otherwise politically impoverished post-conflict contexts' (Hughes, 2016: 144), thus highlighting how the (lack of) resources in the political system influences how transitional justice is approached. The economic system is also implicated, as poorer respondents were statistically more likely to demand individual financial reparations (Williams et al., 2018: 111). This reflects to some degree the disconnect between, on one hand, the central importance of social and economic rights in understanding the cause of conflict and victims' needs and, on the other hand, their marginalisation in transitional justice processes (McEvoy and McConnachie, 2013; Robins, 2017).

While some victims expected individual payments to compensate for specific material losses, in order to then be able to build homes, many others emphasised the need for money to perform Buddhist ceremonies (Williams et al., 2018: 112). In the words of one civil party: 'We cannot perform religious ceremonies without money. When we demand something like this [individual financial reparations], it seems like it is all about money, money, money. It does not mean that I want that money to be rich. I just want to pay respect to the deceased, for them to feel at ease'.[15] These ceremonies are crucial for people to deal with the past as they are needed to support the spirits of the dead in their quest for re-birth (Arensen, 2017). As such, the spiritual system interacts strongly with a perception of limited resources in the legal and economic systems, undermining resilience.

Besides direct financial payments, some victims suggest that they would like all victims to be given rice to help them survive or free health care, arguing that their health 'was destroyed by the Khmer Rouge regime due to the lack of food and medical care'.[16] Both demands illustrate how a lack of resources for resilience in the economic system shapes what people need from transitional justice – and their frustrations relating to participation.

---

[14]   These reparations are 'collective and moral', meaning that they are to be symbolic and 'a) acknowledge the harm suffered by Civil Parties as a result of the commission of the crimes for which an Accused is convicted and b) provide benefits to the Civil Parties which address this harm. These benefits shall not take the form of monetary payments to Civil Parties' (ECCC, 2015: 26).

[15]   The interview, with a civil party at the ECCC, was conducted in Phnom Penh in 2018.

[16]   The interview, with a civil party of case 002 at the ECCC, was conducted in Kampong Cham province in 2018 (JB).

FIGURE 7.1 Memorial to those killed after being incarcerated at the S-21 security
centre, one of the ECCC reparation projects. Photo by the author.

Turning now to the actual collective and moral reparations that are designed
and implemented by NGOs (ideally in consultation with the civil parties),
multiple reparations projects exist. These include testimonial therapy programmes, a memorial (see Figure 7.1), a national remembrance day, the listing
of names in ECCC judgments, a play about moral courage and a traditional
apsara dance performance about forced marriage (see Hughes, 2016: 158–160;
Jasini, 2016: 41–46). The reparations are similar to many other projects implemented to deal with the past outside the judicial setting, possibly explaining why
the vast majority of victims, even those who had taken part in the programmes,
did not know that they were actually even participating in reparative projects
(Sperfeldt et al., 2016: 57; Williams et al., 2018: 116). While there is little rigorous
evaluation of the impact of the reparations, interviews and participant observation
of the events connected to these reparations projects would suggest that they are
indeed meaningful for the participants. In particular, many interviewees mentioned the Transcultural Psychological Organization (TPO) as having provided
significant relief and contributed to resilience by improving their mental health
and allowing people to better deal with their past and participate in community
life today.

One example of a reparations project that is particularly interesting as a broad collaboration of four organisations[17] is the dance theatrical performance *Pka Sla Krom Angkar* (see Grey et al., 2019; Shapiro-Phim, 2020). It was choreographed by Sophiline Cheam Shapiro and originally initiated by Theresa de Langis, whose interview-based research informs the performance (de Langis et al., 2014). The dance performance (see Figure 7.2) deals with the crime of forced marriage and tells the story of one particular couple, Kesar and Mony, although this is interlaced with the stories of other couples forced to marry.[18] Most scenes are set during Democratic Kampuchea but commented upon by Kesar and Mony from today's perspective. It is a particularly important project given that many victims were not even aware that state-led forced marriage constituted a crime in a culture where arranged marriages are common. As such, the dance performance, as well as the trial in Case 002/ 02 at the ECC, rendered visible the trauma that forced marriages had caused,

FIGURE 7.2 Pka Sla Krom Angkar dance performance. Photo by the ECCC, available under a creative commons license.[19]

[17] The four collaborating organisations are the TPO, Kdei Karuna and Bophana Audiovisual Resource Center, all of which have worked extensively on dealing with the Khmer Rouge past, and Khmer Arts, a cultural organisation.

[18] I was able to observe both the premiere live in January 2017 and a subsequent recording and panel discussion.

[19] See www.flickr.com/photos/krtribunal/3248980378o/.

allowing the suffering to be expressed and articulated. The success of this reparations project from the social-ecological resilience perspective of this chapter is that it ties into other systems, connecting cultural dealings with the past to social systems that can be repaired after forced marriage.

THE LIMITATIONS OF TRANSITIONAL JUSTICE FOR ADAPTIVE PEACEBUILDING IN CAMBODIA

While some of the limitations discussed in the previous section are due to the way that transitional justice was designed, most are rooted in its relationships with other systems, including how these systems affected its design in the first place. Specifically, in Cambodia, transitional justice interacts with dysfunctional and resource-depleted political, economic and legal systems, which, in turn, constrain its full transformative potential. In this final section, I turn to one of the key interests of this volume, namely the relationship between transitional justice and adaptive peacebuilding – and how the former might aid the latter.

Adaptive peacebuilding centres around three elements of complexity theory, namely adapting to uncertainty, focusing on means rather than ends and emphasising change as opposed to working against it. These elements are significant in evaluating how transitional justice can support adaptive peacebuilding in Cambodia. On the issue of adapting to uncertainty, adaptive peacebuilding (de Coning, 2018) sees conflict not as juxtaposed to peacebuilding but as an inherent part of it, and it emphasises that the avoidance of violence and good management of conflict are key. In this sense, it ties in well with the concept of social-ecological resilience and how conflict can be mitigated and contained through the interactions and collaborations of various systems. While Cambodia's transitional justice process is implemented in a context of relative uncertainty, it has avoided stoking larger conflicts. However, it has fuelled conflict at the local level about who can participate in the ECCC's proceedings, linked to the aforementioned patronage-based networks. In this sense, it has not optimally adapted to the individual-level uncertainties that exist within the illiberal political system. There is also some degree of conflict around disappointed hopes, in particular related to the absence of individual financial reparations. At the same time, transitional justice has made positive contributions to Cambodian society, for example, by reinforcing the aforementioned government narrative of universal victimhood that allows for easier reconciliation through emphasis on the victimhood of former low-level Khmer Rouge cadres and enabling adaptation to deep-seated uncertainty about how to handle local relations (Williams, 2018a).

Regarding the second element of adaptive peacebuilding – accentuating means rather than ends – transitional justice also helps by shifting the focus from a defined liberal end point to the actual implementation of the justice project. In Cambodia, it has been particularly necessary in the context of implementing transitional justice to pragmatically compromise on some higher-order goals in order to accommodate the regime's political interests. For example, the acceptance of patronage networks in staffing the ECCC or in structuring victim participation plays to key political interests while still forwarding a transformative agenda.

It is particularly in relation to the third element of adaptive peacebuilding, the focus on change, where we can see an undermining of transitional justice's broader impact on adaptive peacebuilding. Transitional justice is inherently embedded in the idea of transition and change. In Cambodia, however, any transformative potential is severely limited through transitional justice inter-actions with other systems, such as the political system of oppression and a lack of democracy in which the government forwards its own agenda, as well as economic systems of corruption and patronage. Furthermore, with inter-national engagement in the country focused so heavily on the horrific past, transitional justice and the changes that have occurred since Democratic Kampuchea, this contributes to legitimising today's government (as a positive contrast to the past). Here, the necessity for change becomes less important, and the past masks many of the current regime's illiberal practices and today's conflicts, particularly around the violation of land rights and human rights, or the increasing constraints on the political opposition.

According to Ungar, '[w]hen one component fails, a justice system can still maintain its resilience and function properly despite an unanticipated (or anticipated) stressor' (Chapter 1). This 'reliability' of the system also works in the opposite direction. In short, transitional justice cannot positively influence other systems when it remains constrained by corruption, nepotism, political illiberalism and hegemony.

CONCLUSION

In this chapter, I have argued that, in Cambodia, transitional justice's contri-bution to social-ecological resilience and adaptive peacebuilding is limited. While resources for resilience have been successfully carved out in various private systems (including social systems of the family, as well as spiritual systems), in several more public systems – notably the political, economic and legal systems – there are few resources provided for resilience. Transitional justice would have the potential to contribute to resilience (and does so for a limited number of people), but its design and implementation are strongly embedded in these other systems – and at times even reinforce them.

In this context, the government largely fails to provide resources to deal with stressors in other systems; and indeed, for parts of the population it could itself be regarded as an additional stressor. As such, politics is very much at the centre of understanding the prospects for resilience (Joseph, 2018). Political gain can be found in not engaging in adaptive peacebuilding as the government derives greater benefits from maintaining systems of corruption and autocratic power, meaning that national actors in Cambodia have used transitional justice strategically to undermine peacebuilding.

REFERENCES

Arensen, L. J. (2017). The dead in the land: Encounters with bodies, bones and ghost in Northwestern Cambodia. *The Journal of Asian Studies*, 76(1), 69–86.

Bennett, C. (2018). Karma after Democratic Kampuchea: Justice outside the Khmer Rouge Tribunal. *Genocide Studies and Prevention: An International Journal*, 12(3), 68–82.

Bernath, J. (2016). 'Complex political victims' in the aftermath of mass atrocity: Reflections on the Khmer Rouge Tribunal in Cambodia. *International Journal of Transitional Justice*, 10(1), 46–66.

Chandler, D. P. (1999). *Brother Number One: A Political Biography of Pol Pot*. Boulder, CO: Westview.

Chandler, D. P. (2000). *Voices from S-21: Terror and History in Pol Pot's Secret Prison*. Chiang Mai: Silkworm.

Chandler, D. P. (2008a). *A History of Cambodia*, 4th ed. Boulder, CO: Westview.

Chandler, D. P. (2008b). Cambodia deals with its past: Collective memory, demonisation and induced amnesia. *Totalitarian Movements and Political Religions*, 9(2), 355–369.

Chhim, S. (2013). Baksbat (broken courage): A trauma-based cultural syndrome in Cambodia. *Medical Anthropology*, 32(2), 160–173.

Comes, T., Meesters, K. and Torjesen, S. (2019). Making sense of crises: The implications of information asymmetries for resilience and social justice in disaster-ridden communities. *Sustainable and Resilient Infrastructure*, 4(3), 124–136.

de Coning, C. (2018). Adaptive peacebuilding. *International Affairs*, 94(2), 301–317.

DeFalco, R. (2014). Justice and starvation in Cambodia. The Khmer Rouge famine. *The Cambodia Law and Policy Journal*, 3, 45–84.

DeFalco, R. (2018). The uncertain relationship between international criminal law accountability and the rule of law in post-atrocity states: Lessons from Cambodia. *Fordham International Law Journal*, 42(1), 1–60.

de Langis, T., Strasser, J., Thida, K. and Sopheap, T. (2014). *Like Ghost Changes Body: A Study on the Impact of Forced Marriage under the Khmer Rouge Regime*. Phnom Penh: Transcultural Psychosocial Organization.

ECCC. (2015). ECCC Internal Rule, 23 (1), Revision 9. www.eccc.gov.kh/en/docu
ment/legal/internal-rules (accessed 12 October 2020).

Gidley, R. (2019). *Illiberal Transitional Justice and the Extraordinary Chambers in the
Courts of Cambodia*. Cham: Palgrave Macmillan.

Global Witness (2016). Hostile Takeover. Report, 7 July, 2016. www.globalwitness.org
/en/reports/hostile-takeover/ (accessed 14 October 2020).

Grey, R., Yim, S. and Kum, S. (2019). The Khmer Rouge Tribunal's first reparation for
gender-based crimes. *Australian Journal of Human Rights*, 25(3), 488–497.

Hennings, A. (2016). Das Konfliktpotenzial exklusiver landgrabbing-praktiken.
herausforderung für den regionalen frieden. *ZeFKo*, 5(2), 221–248.

Hinton, A. L. (2005). *Why Did They Kill? Cambodia in the Shadow of Genocide*.
Berkeley, CA: University of California Press.

Hinton, A. L. (2018). *The Justice Facade. Trails of Transition in Cambodia*. Oxford:
Oxford University Press.

Hughes, R. (2015). Ordinary theatre and extraordinary law at the Khmer Rouge
Tribunal. *Environment and Planning D: Society and Space*, 33(4), 714–731.

Hughes, R. (2016). Victims' rights, victim collectives and utopic disruption at the
Extraordinary Chambers in the Courts of Cambodia. *Australian Journal of Human
Rights*, 22(2): 143–166.

Human Rights Watch. (2019). Cambodia: Holding a media summit without media
freedom. www.hrw.org/news/2019/06/09/cambodia-holding-media-summit-without-
media-freedom (accessed 7 November 2020).

Jasini, R. (2016). *Victim Participation and Transitional Justice in Cambodia: The Case
of the Extraordinary Chambers in the Courts of Cambodia (ECCC)*. Utrecht, The
Netherlands: Impunity Watch.

Joseph, J. (2018). *Varieties of Resilience. Studies in Governmentality*. Cambridge:
Cambridge University Press.

Kieran, B. (1985). *How Pol Pot Came to Power. A History of Communism in Kampuchea
1930–1975*. London: Verso.

Kieran, N. (1996). *The Pol Pot Regime, Race, Power, and Genocide in Cambodia under
the Khmer Rouge*. New Haven, CT: Yale University Press.

Killean, R. (2018) *Victims, Atrocity, and International Criminal Justice. Lessons from
Cambodia*. Abingdon: Routledge.

Ledgerwood, J. (2012). Buddhist ritual and the reordering of social relations in
Cambodia. *South East Asia Research*, 20(2), 191–205.

Manning, P. (2017). *Transitional Justice and Memory in Cambodia. Beyond the
Extraordinary Chambers*. Abingdon: Routledge.

McEvoy, K. and McConnachie, K. (2013). Victims and transitional justice: Voice,
agency and blame. *Social and Legal Studies*, 22(4), 489–513.

National Bank of Cambodia. (2020). Macroeconomic and banking sector developments
in 2019 and outlook for 2020. www.nbc.org.kh/download_files/other_reports/english/
Macroeconomic_and_Banking_Sector.pdf (accessed 14 October 2020).

Olsen, A. and Vorn, V. (2020). *COVID-19: Impact on Cambodian Migrant Workers*.
Bangkok: International Labour Organization. https://labordoc.ilo.org/discovery/fulldis
play/alma995091093002676/41ILO_INST:41ILO_V2 (accessed 4 November 2020).

Orentlicher, D. (2020) 'Worth the effort'? Assessing the Khmer Rouge Tribunal.
Journal of International Criminal Justice, 18(3), 615–640.

Parsons, L., Lawreniuk, L. and Pilgrim, J. (2014). Wheels within wheels: Poverty, power and patronage in the Cambodian migration system. *Journal of Development Studies*, 50(10), 1362–1379.

Po, S. and Heng, K. (2019). Assessing the impacts of Chinese investments in Cambodia: The case of Preah Sihanoukville Province. A working paper on China-Cambodia relations. *Issues and Insights Working Papers*, 19(4), 1–19.

Robins, S. (2011). Towards victim-centred transitional justice: Understanding the needs of families of the disappeared in postconflict Nepal. *International Journal of Transitional Justice*, 5(1), 75–98.

Robins, S. (2017). Failing victims? The limits of transitional justice in addressing the needs of victims of violations. *Human Rights and International Legal Discourse*, 11 (1), 41–58.

Ryan, H. and McGrew, L. (2016). *Performance and perception: The impact of the extraordinary chambers in the courts of Cambodia*. New York: Open Society Justice Initiative (OSJI). www.opensocietyfoundations.org/reports/performance-and-perception-impact-extraordinary-chambers-court-cambodia (accessed 12 October 2020).

Shaprio-Phim, T. (2020). Embodying the pain and cruelty of others. *International Journal of Transitional Justice*, 14(1), 209–219.

Sonis, J., Gibson, J. L., de Jong, J. T. V. M., Field, N. P., Hean, S. and Komproe, I. (2009). Probable posttraumatic stress disorder and disability in Cambodia. Associations with perceive justice, desire for revenge, and attitudes toward the Khmer Rouge Trails. *Journal of the American Medical Association*, 302(5), 527–536.

Soy, K. and Hing, V. (2019). Upholding the right to lawyer: Lessons learned from the extraordinary chambers in the courts of Cambodia. *Swisspeace Working Paper 5/2019* (Cambodia Series). Bern: Swisspeace.

Sperfeldt, C. (2012a). Cambodian civil society and the Khmer Rouge Tribunal. *International Journal of Transitional Justice*, 6(1), 149–160.

Sperfeldt, C. (2012b). Collective reparations at the extraordinary chambers in courts of Cambodia. *International Criminal Law Review*, 12(3), 457–489.

Sperfeldt, C. (2020). Reparations at the extraordinary chambers in the courts of Cambodia. In C. Ferstman and M. Goetz (eds.), *Reparations for Victims of Genocide, War Crimes and Crimes Against Humanity: Systems in Place and Systems in the Making*. Leiden: Brill, pp. 479–504.

Sperfeldt, C., Hyde, M. and Baltharzard, M. (2016). Voices for reconciliation: Assessing media outreach and survivor engagement for case 002 at the Khmer Rouge Trials. East West Center and WSD Handa Center for Human Rights and International Justice. www.eastwestcenter.org/publications/voices-reconciliation-assessing-media-outreach-and-survivor-engagement-case-002-the (accessed 12 October 2020).

Springer, S. (2011) Articulated neoliberalism: The specificity of patronage, kleptocracy, and violence in Cambodia's neoliberalization. *Environment and Planning A: Economy and Space*, 43(11), 2554–2570.

Strasser, J., Thida, K., Studzinsky, S. and Taking, S. (2015). *A Study about Victims' Participation at the Extraordinary Chambers in the Courts of Cambodia and Gender-Based Violence under the Khmer Rouge Regime*. Phnom Penh: Transcultural Psychosocial Organization Cambodia (TPO).

Tabeau, E. and Kheam, T. (2009). *Demographic Expert Report: The Khmer Rouge Victims in Cambodia, April 1975–January 1979. A Critical Assessment of Major*

Estimates. Extraordinary Chamber in the Courts of Cambodia (ECCC),
30 September 2009. www.eccc.gov.kh/sites/default/files/documents/courtdoc/D140_
1_1_Public_Redacted_EN.PDF (accessed 14 October 2020).

Transparency International. (2019). Country data – Cambodia. www.transparency.org
/en/countries/cambodia (accessed 15 October 2020).

Un, K. (2019). *Cambodia: Return to Authoritarianism.* Cambridge: Cambridge
University Press.

Ungar, M. (2018). Systemic resilience: Principles and processes for a science of change
in contexts of adversity. *Ecology and Society,* 23(4): 34.

United Nations Development Programme. (2020). About Cambodia. www.kh.undp.org
/content/cambodia/en/home/countryinfo.html (accessed 14 October 2020).

Williams, T., Bernath, J., Tann, B. and Kum, S. (2018). *Justice and Reconciliation for
the Victims of the Khmer Rouge? Victim Participation in Cambodia's Transitional
Justice Process. Research report.* Marburg: Centre for Conflict Studies; Phnom Penh:
Centre for Study of Humanitarian Law; Bern: Swisspeace.

Williams, T. (2018a). Perpetrator-victims. How universal victimhood in Cambodia
impacts dealing with the past and transitional justice measures. In N. Adler (ed.),
Understanding the Age of Transitional Justice: Narratives in Historical Perspective.
New Brunswick, NJ: Rutgers University Press, pp. 194–212.

Williams, T. (2018b). Agency, responsibility and culpability: The complexity of roles
and self-representations of perpetrators. *Journal of Perpetrator Research,* 2(1), 39–64.

Williams, T. (2019). NGO interventions in the post-conflict memoryscape: The effect
of competing 'mnemonic role attributions' on reconciliation in Cambodia. *Journal
of Intervention and Statebuilding,* 13(2), 158–179.

World Bank. (2020). World Bank data on agriculture and rural development. https://
data.worldbank.org/topic/agriculture-and-rural-development?locations=KH
(accessed 14 October 2020).

8

The Personal and Socio-Economic Dynamics of Resilience and Transitional Justice in Colombia

Sanne Weber[*]

INTRODUCTION

Colombia is recovering from one of the world's longest internal armed conflicts, which has caused the deaths and forced disappearance of tens of thousands and the internal displacement of millions of people. In late 2016, a peace agreement was signed between the Colombian government and the *Fuerzas Armadas Revolucionarias de Colombia* (Revolutionary Armed Forces of Colombia, FARC). Other armed groups had previously laid down arms, including smaller guerrilla movements in the 1990s and right-wing paramilitary groups from 2003 onwards. Nevertheless, the peace process with the remaining *Ejército de Liberación Nacional* (National Liberation Army, ELN) guerrillas failed in 2019, while some dissident groups of the former FARC have rearmed and new paramilitary groups are active across the country, killing social leaders and FARC ex-combatants. The signing of the peace accords does not, therefore, make Colombia a peaceful country. This raises the question of how, in a context of long-term violence – both direct and structural – people manage to move on with their lives. How do they adapt to changing and often adverse conditions and create new possibilities to improve their own well-being and that of their families and communities? How does (or can) transitional justice aid such processes of individual and collective resilience?

In this chapter, I offer some answers to these questions, drawing on various periods of fieldwork undertaken between 2015 and 2019 in Colombia's

[*] I would like to thank, first and foremost, the participants of this research for letting me be part of their lives and communities. I would also like to thank Janine Natalya Clark and Michael Ungar; their constructive feedback on this chapter has really enriched it. This research was supported by the Leverhulme Trust under grant number ECF-2018–245 and by Coventry University.

Caribbean Coast as part of two research projects, one with former internally displaced persons (IDPs) and one with former FARC combatants. The first project's fieldwork took place in two communities of small-scale cattle farmers in the municipality of Chibolo, located in the centre of the Magdalena department. These communities were displaced by paramilitary forces in 1997, after which the villagers scattered throughout the Caribbean coast, some even crossing the border into Venezuela. After ten years of displacement, and after paramilitary demobilisation, they managed to return. They are currently involved in the process of claiming land restitution and reparations through the 2011 Victims and Land Restitution Law (known as the Victims' Law). This law is considered to be one of the most ambitious and complex reparation programmes worldwide (Sikkink et al., 2015). It created an intricate system composed of specifically trained land restitution judges and magistrates who decide on land restitution claims. Other institutions, including the Victims' Unit, provide humanitarian assistance, individual and collective reparations. Land restitution sentences, in addition to land titles, can include infrastructural and developmental measures. In this way, the Victims' Law aims to provide a holistic and transformative response to conflict survivors.

My research in Chibolo focused on the gendered dynamics of the Victims' Law and took the form of ethnographic and participatory visual research, in which community women photographed their lives and needs. These two communities were chosen as a pilot case for the Victims' Law as the state institutions involved had expected that land restitution would be simple here. The opposite was true. After a first fieldwork period from August 2015 to April 2016, I returned to the communities three times, in May 2017 and in May and October 2019. I undertook visual and non-visual interviews and focus groups with thirty-two participants from both communities and an additional fifteen semi-structured interviews with transitional justice stakeholders from state institutions and civil society. I had many more informal conversations. They were not audio recorded, but they provided an important source of additional information.

In this chapter, I compare the experiences of former IDPs in Chibolo with the situation of former FARC combatants. Having focused on the situation of survivors of the conflict, I was interested to learn more about the experiences of those considered to be perpetrators. This coincided with the FARC's reincorporation[1] process after the 2016 peace agreement. One of the many

---

[1] Although it is common to speak of reintegration, the FARC has insisted that the reintegration process should be called 'reincorporation', denoting its members' active role in negotiating their own reintegration. This distinguishes it from prior processes in the sense of being a collective process that predominantly takes place in rural areas, reflecting the fact that most FARC ex-combatants come from rural backgrounds (McFee and Rettberg, 2019).

zones in which the FARC was reincorporating collectively into civilian life was located in La Guajira. Most of the ex-combatants here belonged to the FARC's former *Bloque Caribe* (Caribbean Bloc). La Guajira is a marginalised department situated on Colombia's northern coast. Together with other departments, including Magdalena where Chibolo is located, La Guajira is part of *la Costa* (the Coast), a region whose inhabitants are often stereotyped as 'tropical, lazy and wild' (Tate, 2018: 422).

Studying the experiences of both survivors and perpetrators in *la Costa* therefore makes for an interesting comparison. In the FARC's reincorporation zone, I undertook ethnographic and visual research in May 2019 and from mid-August until November of the same year. Participant observation and numerous informal conversations were combined with semi-structured interviews with fifteen ex-combatants and five non-combatant community members. I held an additional thirteen interviews and many informal conversations with stakeholders in the wider reincorporation and peace process. Pseudonyms are used for all participants cited in this chapter.

In addition to the FARC's reincorporation, the peace agreement touched upon issues of victims' rights, the country's drug problem, political participation and comprehensive agrarian development. It also ordered the strengthening of the Victims' Law through a participatory process of consultations with survivors and other stakeholders, and the creation of a Comprehensive System of Truth, Justice, Reparation and Non-Repetition. This consists of a Commission for the Clarification of the Truth, Coexistence and Reconciliation, a Unit for the Search of Disappeared Persons and a Special Jurisdiction for Peace (JEP), which will provide amnesties and alternative prison sentences for the perpetrators of political crimes among state and FARC actors. Through the JEP, the FARC will contribute resources for the reparation of the conflict's victims, also contributing with restorative and reparatory acts such as declarations to acknowledge its responsibility and projects to strengthen the social fabric of communities (International Center for Transitional Justice, 2020; Triana and Grace, 2019). This connects the Disarmament, Demobilisation and Reintegration (DDR) process with transitional justice, thus attempting to overcome tensions that commonly arise when support for ex-combatants is perceived as taking priority over support to conflict survivors (Sriram, 2013).

This chapter proceeds by first exploring individual aspects of resilience, specifically focusing on the psychological effects of conflict and on how research participants had overcome these. These individual elements, however, cannot be seen separately from collective experiences of resilience, which, to a large degree, are defined by the socio-economic conditions in which the participants found themselves. I will therefore show how social relations and organisational processes have proved important factors for resilience in the past, and how the social sphere is critical for connecting individual psychological well-being with wider socio-economic questions. I then demonstrate why transitional justice in Colombia has so far failed to promote resilience, having been unable to make the connection between these different levels of concern. I will examine how it has prioritised individual-focused responses to the effects of conflict over the need to address the collective and structural consequences of conflict, which has crucial implications for resilience. The chapter finishes with suggestions for how to bridge this gap, by focusing on strengthening social resilience as a means to improve individual well-being; and it links this, in turn, to the concept of adaptive peacebuilding.

INDIVIDUAL RESILIENCE: REFLECTIONS ON MENTAL HEALTH

In both contexts where I undertook research, mental health is not something that is regularly discussed. Nevertheless, conflict experiences had clearly had emotional impacts. In Chibolo, this was especially apparent among those who had lost family members, like Marta: 'We used to dance, but now I no longer dance because I am in mourning. I don't go to parties' (author interview, 26 February 2016). Others mentioned how they themselves or their family members fell ill because of the stress, hypervigilance and sadness caused by displacement. Pedro separated from his wife because the fear and anxiety had produced too many tensions between them, while Germán's wife did not want to return to the family's land because of the painful memories associated with it. Like her, other women too preferred to stay in the urban environments where they had sought refuge. This dovetails with a more general trend of displacement leading to family breakups among Colombian IDPs (Wiig and García-Godos, 2015).

These anecdotes suggest that, for many people, displacement was a traumatic experience that disrupted their emotional and physical sense of belonging and identity, and fragmented their routines and relationships. This often resulted in feelings of loss and longing, depressive feelings and a sense of helplessness and loss of control (Herman, 2001). Post-conflict return and recovery have not been easy either. They involved a long process of initially physical and then legal struggles to return to the land and obtain land titles, and incredibly hard work to prepare the land for cattle farming again, without basic services or infrastructure like roads, electricity or running water. These struggles had emotional impacts on both men and women. Some women expressed feelings of doubt and guilt for having brought their children into a situation where opportunities to study or work were limited compared to the cities. Similarly, Germán, who returned without his wife and children, said he felt lonely and depressed, struggling to rebuild his farm all by himself (Weber, 2020: 14).

Satisfaction measures, including psychosocial support, tend to form part of reparations for survivors of violence. In Colombia, a programme called *Entrelazando* ('weaving together') aims to offer psychosocial support and re-establish broken social ties. This was implemented in only one of the two communities where I undertook my research, although even here group support sessions became ever less frequent. Beyond some commemorative activities, people did not seem to value or to notice the programme's impact (author focus groups, 18 and 19 March 2016). Several factors help to explain this. For example, some male community members complained about the methodologies used in the psychosocial support sessions, claiming that they were asked to hug each other or to tell others they loved them. According to them, this was not something 'real' men did, especially men in a *machista*[2] culture. Gender roles, in turn, help to explain why women appreciated the psychosocial support sessions more. They valued the opportunity to talk to others about their experiences, and considered the meetings a distraction from their daily concerns and a break from their feelings of isolation performing household tasks. These meetings therefore also formed a 'respectable social outlet for women' (Helms, 2013: 110), whose expected gender role of taking care of the household could only be interrupted for legitimate reasons, like going to church, engaging in family activities or seeing the psychologist as part of the reparation process.

The ambiguity about psychosocial support can also be explained by the common Latin American perception that a psychologist only attends to the needs of 'crazy' people. As far as Juana was concerned, people here 'aren't that crazy in the end' (author conversation, 3 September 2015). This resonates with other contexts (Helms, 2013; Weine, 2006), where survivors are often reluctant to seek mental health support as they do not consider themselves to be psychiatric patients. This dynamic can also be seen among former FARC combatants. In fact, the reincorporation package offered to them, comprising economic and food support, education and housing assistance, does not include psychosocial support. A representative of an international lawyers'

---

[2]   *Machismo* is the hegemonic form of masculinity in Latin America. According to this ideal of masculinity, it is not acceptable for men to talk about their feelings as this contradicts their image of strength.

organisation that works with female ex-combatants explained that psychosocial support is a contentious issue. It was never foreseen during the peace negotiations, and currently the government proposes an individual mental health strategy. The FARC, in contrast, insists on the need for a collective strategy, thus producing a deadlock that leaves the ex-combatants without mental health services (author interview, 23 August 2019).

The expression of the need for such support was not uniform among the ex-combatants who participated in my research. Andrea, for example, said she believed that psychosocial support was needed because of the emotional impact of the loss of so many FARC comrades during the armed conflict. For her, the close ties between comrades had resembled family relations. Many people had also been emotionally affected by pre-conflict experiences of poverty and violence. In Andrea's case, the violent death of her father still affects her (author conversation, 19 October 2019). She also said that she would like to receive emotional support to address the impacts of the transition process itself: 'Every person has had to adapt to this life. But it has been difficult because, as I told you, one comes [to civilian life] without knowing anything, like coming from a cloud to the world, to earth, without knowing where to go, what to do and how to do it. Therefore this experience has been quite complicated' (author interview, 5 November 2019).

A psychologist who worked for a non-governmental organisation (NGO) explained that many ex-combatants with whom she had worked experienced depression, although because of the taboos surrounding mental health issues among the FARC they would never describe it as such. She said it was especially present among both younger and older men, without families, who lost their life projects through demobilisation and are now idle in their houses (author conversation, 13 November 2019). I recognised this among some of the men in the reincorporation zone where I worked. It shows again the gendered dynamics of mental health impacts; for men, losing their authority and hegemonic masculinity as combatants is likely to have a strong emotional impact, whereas women's commitment to their children often gives them a new life project – albeit one that reproduces traditional gender norms.

Norms of hegemonic masculinity, which expect men to be strong and not show emotions, play a part in the sensitivity surrounding mental health issues. Pablo, for example, explained that as *guerrilleros* they had seen so many comrades die that their hearts had hardened; at least he himself felt that stories of death no longer affected him so much. The only times that had been really difficult for him, and when he 'sometimes even cried', was when they were unable to bury their dead comrades (author conversation, 19 October 2019). Other male participants did not express a need for psychosocial support either.

Edilberto said he had 'maintained his morale' by analysing the things that affect him and by being strong (author interview, 24 September 2019). This also shows how people often find their own ways of dealing with trauma. A member of the gender committee of the FARC political party, not an ex-combatant herself, explained: 'I am a psychologist, but I have the theory that in the end the people themselves solve their problems. [...] In the end, the accompaniment that your friend, your partner, your former comrade can give you is what is available and the people aren't going to wait for a special programme' (author interview, 1 October 2019).

Social relations and connections between people are therefore important tools for overcoming painful memories. Other everyday strategies are also present in both fieldwork locations. One striking aspect of the culture in *la Costa* is the tendency to make jokes about things, including difficult experiences. This has been used as a resilience tactic in other contexts, highlighting a refusal of the expectation to suffer (Scheper-Hughes, 2008). Two ex-combatants, for example, explained that making jokes was a way for them not to become desperate from the disappointment they felt with the peace process (author conversation, 30 August 2019). People in Chibolo also frequently made jokes. A former land restitution official who became very close to the communities pointed out their 'aha mode', referring to the expression which people there commonly used, signifying a sense of resignation with not controlling the outcome of events while at the same time also denoting indignation (author interview, 21 December 2015). These everyday practices and attitudes can be seen as forms of resilience. Nevertheless, although resilience can be performed in this way, either individually or collectively, it is not disconnected from wider socio-economic dynamics.

COLLECTIVE RESILIENCE: SOCIO-ECONOMIC OBSTACLES

Several socio-economic aspects impacted on the resilience of the participants in my research. These were related to the natural, built and social environment. Land was an issue that came up frequently in both contexts, perhaps unsurprisingly given that land is also one of the aspects of inequality that led to the conflict in Colombia, producing one of the highest numbers of IDPs worldwide.

Land was especially important in the case of Chibolo, where the communities are involved in a land restitution process. As I have explained elsewhere (Weber, 2020: 9), land constitutes a part of the *campesino* (farmer) identity that the research participants were strongly attached to, and it guarantees their socio-economic survival. Formally receiving their land titles allowed the

FIGURE 8.1 The need for clean drinking water. Photographed by Julia,
December 2015.[3]

participants to obtain credits and other support needed for their socio-
economic recovery. It also enabled them psychologically to start over again
on their land, feeling less exposed to risks of displacement. Unfortunately,
through the years in which I visited the communities, climate conditions
presented an obstacle to the new start that people had hoped for.

Although drought in 2015 and 2016 was intense, causing desperation and
fear of losing one's hard work and investments (Weber, 2020: 12), many people
later said that it had been nothing compared to the drought in 2019, which
made them lose many heads of cattle and meant that they were hardly able to
milk the remaining, undernourished cattle. In addition, harvests of yucca and
corn failed, and people did not have sufficient water to drink, forcing them to
drink ditch and other insalubrious water out of desperation (author conversations, May and October 2019). This has meant that, despite regaining their
land, people's income and alimentation are not guaranteed (see Figure 8.1).
This socio-economic insecurity has generated considerable stress and anxiety,
on top of the already difficult process of rebuilding lives. To this day, there is
no running water in these communities, and the only support to prevent the

---

[3]   This photograph was taken as part of the participatory visual research process described earlier.
      The image is used here with the participant's permission.

impact of droughts has been some training by the United Nations Food and Agriculture Organization (UNFAO) on how to prepare and store enough hay for future droughts.

Access to land also played a role in the historical struggle of the ex-FARC guerrillas, and in their reincorporation process in La Guajira. Although the 2016 peace agreement provides for a land fund which will allocate three million hectares of unused lands and other lands obtained by the state to landless agrarian workers, victims' associations opposed the idea that FARC ex-combatants should benefit from this fund (Carranza-Franco, 2019). This leaves the ex-combatants, mostly from rural backgrounds, without access to land. In order to rent the land needed to develop agricultural and other collective productive projects, ex-combatants therefore have to invest part of their monthly monetary support. The profit made from these projects, including a collective farm, tailoring workshop and community ecotourism project, is in turn largely invested in sustaining the projects, instead of paying wages to the ex-combatants. Furthermore, several of the plots of land on which the reincorporation zones are located are facing issues that put their sustainability at risk. For example, Indigenous people lay claim to the land in another reincorporation zone in the Caribbean Coast (which is very closely connected to the zone where I worked), even threatening to expropriate the FARC. The same might happen to the zone in La Guajira, since it too is located on Indigenous land, according to a UN representative who linked these problems to the hastiness with which the peace process was completed and implemented (author interview, 7 November 2019).

A member of a think tank working on peace explained that the peace negotiations had been dragging along for years and the public demanded to see results. Since reincorporation was among the last topics to be discussed, the issue of land for the FARC itself was not negotiated (author interview 8 May 2019; Fattal, 2018). This has led to evident frustration among ex-combatants about the uncertain future and suspicion of the state. In addition, La Guajira is one of the driest departments in Colombia, making the success of agricultural activities unpredictable here too. For example, the first harvest of the plantain project implemented by the ex-combatants was lost as a result of drought, making the new farmers lose a year of work. Again, the only tangible support in this regard has come from the UNFAO, which was finalising the building of an irrigation system by the end of my fieldwork in November 2019. Without such international support, maintaining a level of resilience that enables people to sow another harvest of plantains in spite of the earlier failure would have been much harder.

Decent housing was also crucial for participants in both locations. Having access to adequate housing gives a basic sense of security that is needed for family life and for being able to make a life plan. As described elsewhere (Weber, 2020: 9), several participants in Chibolo expressed the need for a house, especially after being forced to rebuild everything from scratch upon return from displacement. Most people were living in very basic wooden houses or, in some cases, in temporary emergency houses provided by a religious organisation that were still being used years after their supposed end date. This meant that many families were huddled together in very small spaces that had no security and did not stay dry during rainfall. Given the above-described socio-economic conditions, most people did not have the financial means to improve their housing situation. Although housing is included in the land restitution sentences, it is not available to those who did not possess land prior to displacement, including those who were children when they were displaced. Moreover, the houses provided as part of the restitution sentences are small and badly constructed, and few had been built during my first fieldwork period, as described in more detail in the next section.

Housing is also a concern for FARC ex-combatants. The houses they currently live in were meant as an emergency solution for the first six months of the reincorporation phase, but more than two years later they are still living in them due to the lack of alternatives. These temporary houses are made of asbestos (see Figure 8.2), making some people refuse to live in them, whereas others, especially families, have no other option, exposing themselves and their children to health risks. These houses are 'pure evil' according to one participant (author conversation, 26 September 2019), echoing the indignation and suspicion that were common among research participants. These houses do not stay dry during heavy rain, as I experienced myself. The leaders of the two FARC reincorporation zones on the Caribbean Coast have designed a housing project by pooling the individual lump sums promised to them by the government, complemented with European Union support.

Many participants expressed the importance of owning a house, which would give them more stability as a family and also enable economic opportunities, such as starting a shop or restaurant in their houses, or renting out the house if they were to live elsewhere. Nevertheless, the construction of these houses in the neighbouring town has not started because of the abovementioned lack of land to build them on. This situation has led to an overwhelming feeling, continuously reiterated by most people living in the reincorporation zone, that the government is not complying with the peace agreement and is not genuinely interested in peace.

FIGURE 8.2 The asbestos houses in the FARC reincorporation zone. Photograph
by the author.

Living in asbestos houses was often given as one of the reasons for the
offence that research participants felt, expressed mockingly by a female leader
who described ex-combatants as being 'laboratory rats for the government'
(author conversation, 31 August 2019). This is reminiscent of the feeling
expressed by participants in Chibolo about their position and value in society:
'the government is not interested in the *campesino*' (author conversation,
21 September 2015). Three years after my first fieldwork period ended, people
still largely felt this way. This illustrates how the lack of access to land, decent
and safe housing and other basic services, such as quality health care and
education, makes participants in both locations feel like second-class rather
than full citizens. This perception of unequal treatment, in turn, has emotional effects. As I have discussed elsewhere (Weber, 2020: 16), one of
Chibolo's community leaders explained that, although the government offered
them psychosocial support in the form of the earlier described *Entrelazando*

programme, such support would not be needed if the government were to provide them with the elements that could facilitate a better life, such as land titles, paved access roads, electricity and running water.

Jorge, an ex-combatant in La Guajira, had a similar opinion. In his words, 'I believe that psychologically the people are fine. The problem is the insecurity, which you can't solve with psychologists but with projects [...]. People go over there towards the hill to grow crops, and every time they lose them. [...] So that demotivates them, losing it every time, and also because of the climate problem' (author interview, 16 October 2019). People like Jorge pointed out that psychosocial resilience is related not only to people's experiences during conflict but also to their current situation. The latter is characterised by a lack of state support, either through basic services or specific projects to help people recover from their conflict experiences, which is additionally com- pounded by climate change.

SOCIAL RELATIONS AND ORGANISATION AS CRUCIAL FOR COLLECTIVE RESILIENCE

In light of the difficult conditions discussed above, what explains the fact that people are still continuing the struggle to rebuild their lives? What positive elements outweigh the absence of the basic socio-economic components of resilience? Social relations and organisation go a long way towards explaining this in both contexts. Organisation has been at the heart of the historical struggle for land in the communities in Chibolo. These communities were formed in the 1980s as part of land occupation campaigns, often accompanied by the National Association of Peasant Users (ANUC), in an attempt to claim the 'land for those who work on it' (Grupo de Memoria Histórica, 2010: 202). The organisation that arose from the struggle to defend the land and build up the communities played an important role in the process of returning to the land after displacement. Community members organised themselves for a so- called 'voluntary return' in 2007, without state support in relation to security or transportation. This return did not go without a struggle, and involved various violent evictions by the police throughout 2008, until people's right to be on the land was finally recognised (Planeta Paz, 2012). These actions, in which organisation among people was key, can be seen as forms of 'radical citizen- ship', or spaces and actions which originate as a result of popular mobilisation around common goals (McEwan, 2005: 980).

The same point can be made apropos of organisation among the FARC combatants, notwithstanding that it had a more violent 'edge'. The FARC originated in the early 1960s from peasant self-defence groups set up to protect zones of peasant 'colonisation' and fight for a solution to the issue of agrarian inequality and marginalisation. Starting off with about 300 men in the 1960s – women were not yet allowed as members – the FARC gradually grew to around 18,000 combatants at its peak in the early 2000s, with strong internal cohesion and discipline (Ugarriza and Quishpe, 2019). This strength in numbers, organisational capacity and unity did not allow the FARC to win the conflict, but did prevent it from being defeated, while also giving it the power to negotiate its members' own conditions for reincorporation.

One of the FARC's key demands in relation to the reincorporation process was that this should be a collective process; members feared that the individually oriented process preferred by the government, and used in prior DDR processes, would fracture their collective revolutionary project and organisational structure (Carranza-Franco, 2019). Indeed, the collective process has to a certain degree maintained the strength of the FARC as an actor capable of negotiating with the government and other stakeholders. In the reincorporation zone in La Guajira, for example, the FARC was able to attract international funding for housing and agricultural projects. I witnessed how the leaders there – both male and female – negotiated the conditions of this support, something that was also highlighted by the FARC party's gender commissioner (author interview, 1 October 2019).

This suggests that unity, organisation and the forms of active citizenship that they enable are crucial aspects of the social resilience outlined by Ungar in Chapter 1. Social resilience enables individuals and communities to navigate and negotiate access to the resources they need, such as land and financial support. Unfortunately, transitional justice and related peacebuilding processes in Colombia have not contributed to strengthening social resilience. In the next section, I will demonstrate how they have in fact led to the deterioration of organisational capacity and social relations in both research locations, while also failing to respond to socio-economic aspects of collective resilience – and, more generally, causing distrust and frustration.

TRANSITIONAL JUSTICE AND SOCIAL RESILIENCE IN COLOMBIA

As explained in the introduction, transitional justice in Colombia is currently implemented through the 2011 Victims' Law, which provides humanitarian assistance, individual and collective reparations and land restitution to the conflict's survivors, and through the more recent 'Comprehensive System of Truth, Justice, Reparation and Non-Repetition'.

Promoting Resilience: What Can Reparations Do?

In terms of addressing the aspects of resilience outlined earlier, reparations seem to be best placed; they have a potential socio-economic impact and survivors of conflict often prioritise the fulfilment of their economic needs over retributive justice (Durbach, 2008; Gready and Robins, 2014; Robins, 2013). This makes the Victims' Law the most likely instrument to promote resilience. The JEP may also have a role to play, as its sanctions are supposed to combine retributive and restorative justice aspects (Triana and Grace, 2019). However, the JEP is still far from the stage of reaching verdicts or issuing sanctions (International Center for Transitional Justice, 2020), and therefore little can be said about its reparative potential.

The Development Programmes with a Territorial Focus (PDETs), which were introduced by the 2016 peace accord and will incorporate collective reparation plans, are a final possible mechanism to address the socio-economic aspects of resilience. These PDETs will not, however, be implemented throughout the country. Locations were selected based on the level of victimisation and intensity of conflict. The department of Magdalena, where Chibolo is located, was not elected; La Guajira was. Nevertheless, although the PDET planning stage has finished, implementation has not yet started (Rodeemos el Diálogo, 2020). For this reason, most of the following discussion will focus on the reparations and restitution provided by the Victims' Law in Chibolo, although I will also make some reference to La Guajira.

In terms of reparations, the biggest progress has been made with monetary compensation, which most people have received. However, some are still waiting, including elderly people – even though they are supposed to be prioritised. That compensation is the form of reparation that has advanced the most might be explained by the fact that compensation, in contrast to other forms of reparation, is directly provided by the Victims' Unit. It also responds to a more general global trend to prioritise monetary compensation, which has several motivations. For example, compensation is easier to implement and less economically and politically costly than more far-reaching measures (O'Rourke, 2013; Viaene, 2010). In addition, compensation can be more straightforwardly quantified than social and infrastructural measures, making it easier to show results. Quantified results can be used to present an image of the benefits offered to survivors, thus creating a 'mirage of substance' (Purdeková, 2015: 155), while saying little about the actual experience of these benefits and the extent to which they have changed survivors' lives (Buchely, 2015).

In fact, participants in Chibolo agreed that, although compensation had helped them to solve some short-term problems, it did little to alleviate their structural problems of socio-economic marginalisation. Collective reparations could perhaps play a larger role in this regard. Unfortunately, the implementation of the collective reparation plans in the communities in Chibolo, which included measures like the reconstruction of communal wells and schools, the recovery of organisational structures and commemorative activities, was virtually non-existent. Community leader Diego explained to me that the Victims' Unit said that some of the measures in the collective reparation plans were impossible to implement (author conversation, 11 May 2019). This raises the question of why they were included in the first place, creating expectations that the state knew it would not be able to fulfil.

Transitional Justice's Unintended Consequences: Weakening Social Ties

As I have described elsewhere (Weber, 2020), land restitution through the Victims' Law has been a slow process. In spite of promises of quick results, the actual provision of land titles took several years. Land titles were to be accompanied by productive projects focused on cattle farming and the provision of housing, as well as wider infrastructural support, including access to electricity, running water and the paving of access roads. Most of this infrastructural support was never delivered or was very delayed. It was not until 2019 that I could finally see some progress; the village centres had been connected to the electricity network in December 2018, while parts of the road that connects one of the communities to the municipality of Chibolo had been paved by May 2019. The access roads to the other community remained unpaved, practically disconnecting this village in the rainy season, thus making it harder for people to commercialise their milk and creating dangerous situations during medical emergencies since these villages do not have medical centres. The problem with the provision of such social and infrastructure services is that they depend on local governments, which are historically known for their corruption in *la Costa* (Grupo de Memoria Histórica, 2010; Tate, 2018). This means that the Victims' Unit cannot guarantee the provision of the reparations it promises.

The aforementioned poor quality of the provided houses can also be explained by corruption, underscoring the fact that cheap and inadequate materials were used. The land restitution judge ordered one of the building companies to halt their construction, and this was never resumed. Houses in the other community, built by a different company, were soon showing cracks or had roofs flying off during strong winds. When I visited in 2019, female leader Josefa exclaimed that she 'wasn't going to live in the graveyard they built her' (author conversation, 25 October 2019). One neighbourhood in these communities experienced particular problems. It was among the last to receive its land restitution sentence, which, moreover, contained mistakes that were never officially clarified. As a result, this neighbourhood never received any productive projects or housing support.

The slowness and inequality of this reparation and restitution process led to the weakening of the communities' organisational structures. As described previously (de Waardt and Weber, 2019: 222), the time investment that was required to participate in this process caused people to feel disillusioned and exhausted, and to lose interest in attending the monthly meetings of the farmers' association in one of these communities, while the other community's attempts to recover their pre-displacement farmers' association were fruitless. While community tensions and suspicions towards community leaders were already evident in 2017 (see de Waardt and Weber, 2019), by 2019 these had intensified, especially in relation to the neighbourhood that never received the promised support.

Cecilia, whose family owns land in this neighbourhood, said that she believes it is better to work for one's own interests and family, rather than waiting for projects to arrive. According to her, when the leaders need help with cleaning the communal spaces or other things, they always expect community support, but in the meantime the projects they promise never materialise. She believed that the leaders did not make enough effort for the land restitution in her neighbourhood; they just travelled and took selfies on the beach instead of speaking up for people's rights (author conversation, 23 October 2019). Francisco, who does not live in this neighbourhood, explained that in fact the people there caused their own problems, since they started selling their land without having the titles and therefore confused and delayed the process of allocating these titles (author conversation, 23 October 2019). This shows the problems, tensions and divisions that uneven distribution of reparations and a lack of clarity and information about this can cause. Other community members explained that these tensions and suspicions had further weakened the community association. Whereas, in 2017, membership had already almost halved from over sixty to under thirty-five, in 2019, these numbers had further reduced to about twenty, as people blamed their leaders for being ineffective.

Although the collective reparation plans in these communities included the recovery and strengthening of organisational spaces, it was actually the UNFAO that contributed to this, by supporting the formation of a cooperative among four farming communities, including the two communities where my research took place. As a cooperative, the communities could sell their milk collectively, thus obtaining better prices. The formation of this cooperative was not easy. Already in 2016, it was dealt a near-fatal blow because of an incident related to the promise by former Colombian President Juan Manuel Santos that the communities would receive electricity by Christmas.

The Land Restitution Unit had decided that it would be better to provide solar panels, since electricity was one of the components of the land restitution sentences and thus was to be provided anyway. Solar panels would go to those farmers living farthest away from the village centres, as they would be the last to be connected to electricity. Meanwhile, all members of both communities were asked to pay a contribution for the upcoming connection to the electricity network. The lack of information about the relation between the need to pay this contribution and the provision of solar panels to only a limited number of households sparked intense suspicion, distrust and outrage among many people, even leading to threats of burning the truck that would deliver the solar panels.

According to a UNFAO employee, this incident almost made the newly formed cooperative collapse, since people from both communities started blaming their leaders and suspecting them of corruption (author conversation, 9 May 2017). Although the cooperative continued to exist at the time of my 2019 visit, it was seen as an economic tool rather than a space for community organisation – or social resilience – as Paola explained to me with regret (author conversation, 10 May 2019). Francisco said that, of the eighty people who deliver milk to the cooperative, only thirty or forty go to the meetings (author conversation, 23 October 2019). The lack of effective information and communication, together with frustration and disappointment about unmet expectations of support, can thus cause a reduction in social resilience by damaging social relations. Currently, hopes for the completion of collective reparations or the provision of land restitution support are even lower, since most of the state's attention is no longer focused on the Victims' Law – a subject receiving intense media attention in 2015 and 2016 – but on the FARC's reincorporation and related transitional justice activities.

As alluded to earlier, similar frustrations can be noticed among the FARC ex-combatants, especially in relation to the lack of progress with the purchase of land for their housing project. This slowness is blamed on the government by the leaders and therefore also by their rank and file, although in reality the FARC negotiating team was also to blame for the vagueness about land in the peace accord. Another source of frustration for many ex-combatants is the lack of government support for agricultural projects. This complaint, too, cannot be entirely blamed on the government, at least not in La Guajira. Each demobilised ex-combatant has the right to a lump sum for an individual productive project. The FARC has decided to pool these so that the resulting collective projects enable individuals to start agricultural and other businesses. As explained, in the two reincorporation zones in *la Costa*, the FARC leadership decided to invest these collective funds not in an agricultural project but in a housing project. Ex-combatants' complaints about the government's failure to provide an agricultural project are therefore unwarranted. They do, however, highlight the importance of communication and expectation management in relation to the building of trust in the state, transitional justice and other post-conflict processes. Furthermore, two years after the start of the demobilisation process, other collective reincorporation zones had not received the lump sums for their collective projects either (Carranza-Franco, 2019), thus confirming ex-combatants' lack of trust in the government.

As a result, ex-combatants' commitment to the collective reincorporation process is waning. Many have left the collective reincorporation zones for the cities; and by 2018, 2,400 FARC ex-combatants had even relapsed into violent activities (Carranza-Franco, 2019). In the reincorporation zone in La Guajira, the loss of a collective spirit was also noticeable. Collective practices such as communal eating initiated here at the start of the reincorporation process were gradually lost. Several people explained that after some time everyone started buying their own stoves, leaving the communal kitchen unused. They also lamented that the FARC's famous daily cultural activities – crucial for building social cohesion in the past (Ugarriza and Quishpe, 2019) – or commemorations of deceased comrades were no longer celebrated (author conversations, 30 August and 7 October 2019). Others decided to reintegrate individually in the cities, rented agricultural land or worked as sharecroppers, only coming back to the reincorporation zone for medical or other support or reincorporation bureaucracy. Eventually, individualisation of this process will reduce the ex-combatants' negotiating and lobbying power.

SALIR ADELANTE: ORGANISING TO CONNECT INDIVIDUAL AND COLLECTIVE RESILIENCE

The examples discussed in this chapter show the risks that occur when transitional justice or other post-conflict and peacebuilding mechanisms raise high expectations, which, ultimately, go unrealised. Unmet expectations and disappointment make people lose trust not only in these processes but often also in their leaders, making it seem better to focus energy on protecting one's own interests – as Cecilia explained in the citation earlier – than to invest time in struggles for the greater good. This eventually makes it harder to overcome the structural marginalisation and lack of access to basic social and infrastructural services that communities like Chibolo face in Colombia.

To address this, transitional justice must better respond to what those affected by conflict most need. In the case of the communities in Chibolo, and those of ex-combatants in La Guajira, people's desire is expressed in the commonly used term '*salir adelante*' or moving forward. Over and over again, people stressed their desire for a piece of land to work on, decent housing and access to basic social services, such as health care and education. Individual compensation will not enable them to obtain these resources, and therefore more structural measures are needed, closer to the transformative justice mechanisms proposed by critical transitional justice scholars (see, e.g., Evans, 2016; Gready and Robins, 2014; Lambourne, 2009). Other scholars, however, have pointed to the limits of transitional justice in terms of its mechanisms – which traditionally do not include development-oriented measures – and timeframe (Roht-Arriaza and Orlovsky, 2009; Waldorf, 2012). In Colombia, another obstacle might be sheer numbers; there are millions of survivors of internal displacement and other crimes, which makes compensating all of them an almost impossible task within the current budget (Sikkink et al., 2015). Since most efforts are focused on compensation, it is obvious that even less can be expected of promises of other, more collective reparations, in spite of the discourse on transformative reparations within the Victims' Law (Weber, 2020).

To overcome this dilemma, transitional justice should promote social resilience, or the capacity of survivors to organise themselves – as communities or groups of survivors – to protect and promote their own well-being. This would allow them to collectively navigate the structures and power relations that prevent them from accessing the resources they need, and to negotiate access to these. Increasing survivors' and communities' skills to negotiate on the basis of their own needs is essential because reparation needs vary among people who experienced conflict in different ways and among people in different locations. Rural and urban Colombians, for example, face different problems (Buchely, 2015; Rettberg, 2008). Furthermore, survivors' priorities are not fixed; they depend on the particular context and are likely to change over time (Shaw and Waldorf, 2010). Therefore, as others have argued, transitional justice should not offer a 'one-size-fits-all' approach across different countries, nor within one country (Butti and McGonigle Leyh, 2019; Sharp, 2013). Instead, it should strengthen self-organisation, enabling survivors to define and implement their own demands and negotiation strategies. Such self-organisation can build on the previously described organisational processes of communities, thus harnessing their own endogenous strengths.

This is in line with the principles of adaptive peacebuilding (de Coning, 2018). Instead of imposing externally defined but often inadequate mechanisms, strengthening the role that communities can play in demanding their own rights and steering their own reconstruction processes will enable transitional justice and other peacebuilding approaches to provide responses that are better attuned to the needs of communities. This, in turn, will potentially enable communities themselves to play a larger role in the implementation, evaluation and adaptation of such responses. Increasing social resilience, by strengthening organisational and lobbying skills among people, and promoting a collective identity and unity, can thus help to produce more adequate and sustainable results than the short-term impact of a compensation cheque, or the counterproductive effect of unmet promises of transformation.

CONCLUSION

In this chapter, I have analysed how individual and collective resilience are present and hampered in two post-conflict communities in Colombia. In so doing, I have illustrated the importance of organisational processes and social resilience, evidenced in practices of active citizenship which have enabled processes of rights claims. Unity and social relations among people have also helped survivors to overcome the trauma resulting from conflict. Transitional justice in Colombia, however, has damaged rather than strengthened such collective assets, causing frustration which has made participants lose faith in the power of organisation, making some of them decide to focus on their own situation instead. The socio-economic elements needed to enable these communities to *salir adelante* can hardly be expected to be delivered by transitional justice, as they go beyond its commonly assumed timeframe, mechanisms and generally available budget. Instead, transitional justice could play a role in promoting social resilience – as a dimension of adaptive peacebuilding – by shifting its focus towards improving social relations and promoting collective and organisational processes. Social resilience will help communities to take more control over their future through active practices of citizenship. This enables rights claims, which, eventually, can facilitate other, closely connected socio-economic aspects of resilience.

Re-focusing transitional justice on the promotion of social resilience provides several insights into the current transitional justice process in Colombia. The Truth Commission, for example, can play a role in identifying prior social resilience strategies among survivors and their communities. This is in line with its professed goal of not only uncovering the conflict's crimes but also acknowledging survivors as political agents (De Gamboa Tapias and Díaz Pabón, 2018). Restorative justice sentences issued by the JEP could contribute to strengthening social resilience through technical and financial support for organisational processes. If sanctions include the implementation of restorative justice projects for communities, the participation of survivors and their communities in the definition of these sanctions could guarantee that these processes contribute to improving the access to resources that communities need, such as the construction of roads, housing or other infrastructure. Such a participatory process, corresponding to the principles of adaptive peacebuilding, can itself strengthen communities' sense of being respected and listened to by the government, thus countering previous feelings of marginalisation. Strengthened social resilience will prevent survivors from waiting for the government to deliver upon unrealistic promises, instead allowing them to take back control of their own lives and actively negotiate for the resources and services they need, thereby bringing back previous practices of active citizenship.

REFERENCES

Buchely, L. (2015). The conflict of the indicators: A case study on the implementation of the Victims' and Land Restitution Law in Cali, Valle del Cauca, Colombia. *International Organizations Law Review*, 12(1), 19–49.

Butti, E. and McGonigle Leyh, B. (2019). Intersectionality and transformative reparations: The case of Colombian marginal youths. *International Criminal Law Review*, 19(5), 753–782.

Carranza-Franco, F. (2019). *Demobilisation and Reintegration in Colombia: Building State and Citizenship*. London: Routledge.

de Coning, C. (2018). Adaptive peacebuilding. *International Affairs*, 94(2), 301–317.

Durbach, A. (2008). 'The Cost of a Wounded Society': Reparations and the illusion of reconciliation. *Australian Indigenous Law Review*, 12(1), 22–40.

Evans, M. (2016). Structural violence, socioeconomic rights, and transformative justice. *Journal of Human Rights*, 15(1), 1–20.

Fattal, A. L. (2018). *Guerrilla Marketing: Counterinsurgency and Capitalism in Colombia*. Chicago, IL: University of Chicago Press.

De Gamboa Tapias, C. and Díaz Pabón, F. A. (2018). The transitional justice framework agreed between the Colombian government and the FARC-EP. In F. A. Díaz Pabón (ed.), *Truth, Justice and Reconciliation in Colombia: Transitioning from Violence*. Abingdon: Routledge, pp. 66–84.

Gready, P. and Robins, S. (2014). From transitional to transformative justice: A new agenda for practice. *International Journal of Transitional Justice*, 8(3), 339–361.

Grupo de Memoria Histórica. (2010). *La Tierra en Disputa: Memorias de Despojo y Resistencias Campesinas en la Costa Caribe 1960–2010.* Bogotá: Centro Nacional de Memoria Histórica.

Helms, E. (2013). *Innocence and Victimhood: Gender, Nation and Women's Activism in Postwar Bosnia-Herzegovina.* Madison, WI: University of Wisconsin Press.

Herman, J. L. (2001). *Trauma and Recovery from Domestic Abuse to Political Terror.* London: Pandora.

International Center for Transitional Justice. (2020). *A Mixed Approach to International Crimes: The Retributive and Restorative Justice Procedures of Colombia's Special Jurisdiction for Peace.* New York: International Center for Transitional Justice.

Lambourne, W. (2009). Transitional justice and peacebuilding after mass violence. *International Journal of Transitional Justice,* 3(1), 28–48.

McEwan, C. (2005). New spaces of citizenship? Rethinking gendered participation and empowerment in South Africa. *Political Geography,* 24(8), 969–991.

McFee, E. and Rettberg, A. (2019). Contexto de los desafíos de la implementación temprana en Colombia. In E. McFee and A. Rettberg (eds.), *Excombatientes y acuerdo de paz con las FARC-EP en Colombia: Balance de la etapa temprana.* Bogotá: Ediciones Uniandes, pp. 1–17.

O'Rourke, C. (2013). *Gender Politics in Transitional Justice.* Abingdon: Routledge.

Planeta Paz. (2012). *La Cuestión Agraria en Colombia: Tierras Desarrollo y Paz.* Bogotá: Planeta Paz.

Purdeková, A. (2015). *Making Ubumwe: Power, State and Camps in Rwanda's Unity-Building Project.* New York: Berghahn Books.

Rettberg, A. (2008). *Reparación en Colombia ¿Qué Quieren las Víctimas?* Bogotá: Deutsche Gesellschaft für Technische Zusammenarbeit (GTZ).

Robins, S. (2013). An empirical approach to post-conflict legitimacy: Victims' needs and the everyday. *Journal of Intervention and Statebuilding,* 7(1), 45–64.

Rodeemos el Diálogo. (2020). Reparations policy for victims of the armed conflict in Colombia. *Transitional Justice Snapshots,* 10, 1–3.

Roht-Arriaza, N. and Orlovsky, K. (2009). A complementary relationship: Reparations and development. In P. De Greiff and R. Duthie (eds.), *Transitional Justice and Development: Making Connections.* New York: Social Science Research Council, pp. 170–213.

Scheper-Hughes, N. (2008). A talent for life: Reflections on human vulnerability and resilience. *Ethnos,* 73(1), 25–56.

Sharp, D. N. (2013). Interrogating the peripheries: The preoccupations of fourth generation transitional justice. *Harvard Human Rights Journal,* 26(1), 149–174.

Shaw, R. and Waldorf, L. (2010). Introduction: Localizing Transitional Justice. In R. Shaw and L. Waldorf (eds.), *Localizing Transitional Justice: Interventions and Priorities after Mass Violence.* Stanford, CA: Stanford University Press, pp. 3–26.

Sikkink, K., Pham, P. N., Johnson, D. A., Dixon, P., Marchesi, B., Vinck, P., Rivera, A. M., Osuna, F. and Culver, K. (2015). *Evaluación de Medidas para Reparaciones Integrales en Colombia: Logros y Desafíos.* Cambridge, MA: Harvard Kennedy School Carr Center for Human Rights Policy and Harvard Humanitarian Initiative.

Sriram, C. L. (2013). Victims, excombatants, and communities: Irreconcilable demands or a dangerous convergence? In T. Bonacker and C. Safferling (eds.),

Victims of International Crimes: An Interdisciplinary Discourse. The Hague: T.M.C. Asser Press, pp. 233–251.

Tate, W. (2018). Paramilitary politics and corruption talk in Colombia. Culture, theory and critique. *Culture, Theory and Critique*, 59(4), 419–441.

Triana E. S. and Grace, L. (2019). El rol de la justicia transicional en el proceso de paz con las FARC-EP en Colombia (2015). In E. McFee and A. Rettberg (eds.), *Excombatientes y acuerdo de paz con las FARC-EP en Colombia: Balance de la etapa temprana*. Bogotá: Ediciones Uniandes, pp. 43–68.

Ugarriza, J. E. and Quishpe, R. C. (2019). Guerrilla sin armas: La reintegración política de la FARC como transformación de los comunistas revolucionarios en Colombia. In E. McFee and A. Rettberg (eds.), *Excombatientes y acuerdo de paz con las FARC-EP en Colombia: Balance de la etapa temprana*. Bogotá: Ediciones Uniandes, pp. 135–162.

Viaene, L. (2010). Life is priceless: Mayan Q'eqchi' voices on the Guatemalan national reparations program. *International Journal of Transitional Justice*, 4(1), 4–25.

de Waardt, M. and Weber, S. (2019). Beyond victims' mere presence: An empirical analysis of victim participation in transitional justice in Colombia. *Journal of Human Rights Practice*, 11(1), 209–228.

Waldorf, L. (2012). Anticipating the past: Transitional justice and socio-economic wrongs. *Social & Legal Studies*, 21(2), 171–186.

Weber, S. (2020). Trapped between promise and reality in Colombia's Victims' Law: Reflections on reparations, development and social justice. *Bulletin of Latin American Research*, 39(1), 5–21.

Weine, S. (2006). *Testimony after Catastrophe: Narrating the Traumas of Political Violence*. Evanston, AB: Northwestern University Press.

Wiig, H. and García-Godos, J. (2015). *Women in the Colombian land restitution and titling process – A RDS household survey of IDPs*. Annual World Bank Conference on Land and Poverty. www.oicrf.org/-/women-in-the-colombian-land-restitution-and-titling-process-a-rds-household-survey-of-idps (accessed 3 June 2020).

9

Redressing Injustice, Reframing Resilience: Mayan Women's Persistence and Protagonism as Resistance

M. Brinton Lykes, Alison Crosby and Sara Beatriz Alvarez Medrano

Young, adult, and elderly [Mayan] women in Guatemala are making changes in their lives, to generate wellbeing and good living for themselves, other women, and their communities. Despite all the inequities, oppressions, violences of a system that prioritizes injustice and death, there is enough joy, creativity, desire for life, for being and becoming, and as such, women are defending life, territory and body.

(*Centre for Legal Action in Human Rights [CALDH] and Pérez, 2014: 56*)

INTRODUCTION

Guatemala's post-genocide landscape has been marked by an increasing turn to transitional justice and its four pillars of truth, justice, reparations and guarantees of non-repetition (Teitel, 2000) as a means to redress the ongoing effects of thirty-six years of devastating armed conflict (1960–1996). Truth-telling reports traced the roots of the conflict to the extremely skewed inequities of economic and political power resulting from a history of colonial dispossession of Indigenous lands and livelihoods (CEH, 1999; ODHAG, 1998). The United Nations (UN)-sponsored Historical Clarification Commission (CEH) documented overwhelming numbers of killings, disappearances, massacres and forced displacement, found that acts of genocide were committed against specific Mayan communities at the height of the state's scorched earth policies in the early 1980s (CEH, 1999, vol. 3: 358) and highlighted the perpetration of sexual violence, predominantly against Mayan women (CEH 1999, vol. 3: 23). Beginning in 2003, a controversial and highly contested National Reparations Programme (PNR) was implemented by the Guatemalan state to provide mostly monetary compensation to some victims of the war (Crosby and Lykes, 2019: 135–139). Additionally, a 'judicial spring' has seen a number of high-level prosecutions, including the 2013 genocide trial of former *de facto* head of state General Efraín Ríos Montt (Oglesby and

Nelson, 2016) and the 2016 Sepur Zarco trial of two former members of the Guatemalan military for sexual violence as a crime against humanity (Impunity Watch and the Alliance, 2017).

The turn to transitional justice as a means for redress has required victims, mostly Mayan, to recount their experiences of devastating violence over many years to a multiplicity of interlocutors or intermediaries (Merry, 2006), including state officials, lawyers, judges, psychologists, activists and researchers, ourselves included. Survivors of sexual violence have risked identification as 'the raped woman' as they are called upon to detail this specific harm. Like many Western rights regimes, transitional justice mechanisms are damage-centred (Tuck, 2009) and rely upon survivors' narratives of individuated events of pain and loss, supported and validated by expert witnesses, to prove harm suffered. Indigenous scholar Eve Tuck (2009: 416) has warned of the dangers for Indigenous communities of such (externally imposed) 'damage narratives' which pathologise them as essentially broken. As such, these narratives are themselves acts of epistemic violence that can undermine and occlude Indigenous resilience. Tuck (2009: 416) instead argues for 'desire-based frameworks', which entail 'understanding complexity, contradiction, and the self-determination of lived lives'.

In this chapter, we take up Tuck's challenge of a desire-based framework in seeking to understand Mayan women's resilience, here defined by them as 'resistance, persistence, permanence, strength and determination' (CALDH and Pérez, 2014: 57), in relation to their engagement with transitional justice processes in post-genocide Guatemala. We document how diverse groups of Mayan women who have participated in trials, testified in truth-telling processes and organised in defence of their individual and collective rights have reframed these experiences of resistance and resilience to centre their 'lives, cosmovision and knowledge of a collectivity' (CALDH and Pérez, 2014: 57; see also Crosby and Lykes, 2019). We draw on our respective participation in separate processes of accompaniment of these Mayan women protagonists and our current reflexive engagement with what we have learned from these processes and through ongoing conversations among ourselves as co-authors.

Tuck's (2009) critique of damage narratives is centred on research with Indigenous communities – conducted by often well-meaning external researchers – that seeks to document pain and loss as a means to effect change and achieve reparation. We have accompanied Mayan women as intermediaries through diverse transitional justice processes, and, as such, our work has been at the interstices of Mayan and Western onto-epistemologies. Mindful of the need to be 'held accountable for the frameworks and attitudes [we] employ' (Tuck, 2009: 412), in this chapter we draw on feminist physicist

Karen Barad's (2007: 185) theorisation of agential realism and her call for an 'ethico-onto-epistem-ology' that strives for 'the intertwining of ethics, knowing and being'.

As North American researchers who have worked in Guatemala for many years, Lykes and Crosby are mindful of their own location within the colonial relations of power that Tuck (2009) critiques and 'the arrogance and absence of reflexivity afforded by white supremacy' (Tuck, 2009: 412). They have sought to be critically reflexive of their role in reinforcing Western onto-epistemological assumptions that underpin both transitional justice and social science research by those from the global North. In this collaboratively written chapter, they re-examine their previous work, which entails an unpacking of and turning away from the Western dualisms that have informed their think-ing and being (as well as that of the transitional justice paradigm itself), to more self-consciously deepen their engagement with Mayan onto-epistemologies that reflect a more integrated relationship between the human and non-human, between land, body and territory (Chirix García, 2019). For Alvarez, a focus on the Mayan cosmovision or worldview as onto-epistemology reflects her positionality as a K'iche' woman whose urban loca-tion and multiple experiences as an intermediary have challenged her to 'look both ways' in transitional justice work for a (predominantly ladinx,[1] Western-oriented) human rights organisation in Guatemala that accompanies Mayan communities, among others. As such, she is mindful of the colonial dynamics at play within the transitional justice realm within which she engages and the challenges this presents for her decolonial praxis and her accountability towards her Indigenous collectivity.

For all three of us, our differing and differentiated positionings as inter-mediaries accompanying Mayan women protagonists in their struggles for redress affect what we can and cannot see or hear in relation to their expressions of resilience rooted in Mayan onto-epistemology. The latter is emergent from and circulates through individuals, families, communities, the wider society and all living beings as interdependent systems (Ungar, Chapter 1) that are constrained by and resist ongoing colonial relations of

---

[1]   The term *ladina* (feminine), *ladino* (masculine) or *ladinx* (to denote the gender-neutral term, following the recent trend to use the x for gender neutral language) is commonly used to describe those who are not Maya in Guatemala. As Grandin et al. (2011: 121) explain, the term was '[f]irst utilized in Guatemala in the 1500s to refer to Mayas who spoke Spanish, its meanings hav[ing] changed over time ... [It] evolved to mean "non-Maya", a claim that disguises the reality that many Ladinos are descendants of Mayas and Europeans and are thus "mixed" by definition'. Some participants in the research reported herein explicitly identify as *mestiza* rather than ladina, to reclaim their history of being 'mixed', and thus mestiza (or *mestizx*) is used in this chapter when quoting those who self-identify as such.

power in which we ourselves are deeply implicated. As such, we strive to facilitate processes of relationality and dialogic engagement in accompanying these Mayan protagonists' persistence. This positioning and these experiences of accompaniment have contributed to the argument presented herein; that is, that the temporally limited, linear transitional justice paradigm resists redress of the ongoing harms of structural colonial violence. This chapter acknowledges and affirms the persistence and protagonism of Mayan women in communities that have endured and indeed continue to thrive as they, women-in-community, transform in their defence of the integrality of land-body-territory. In addressing the systemic factors that can support Indigenous communities in redressing colonial violence, we thus argue for a conception of historical justice that supports Indigenous people's self-determination on their lands and through their livelihoods grounded in their own cosmovision. As Tuck and Yang (2012: 10) have stated, 'decolonization is not a metaphor' and instead requires 'the relinquishment of land, power and privilege' by the colonisers.

ONTO-EPISTEMOLOGY: LAND-BODY-TERRITORY

Practices of knowing and being are not isolable; they are mutually implicated. We don't obtain knowledge by standing outside the world; we know because we are part of the world. We are part of the world in its differential becoming. The separation of epistemology from ontology is a reverberation of a metaphysics that assumes an inherent difference between human and nonhuman, subject and object, mind and body, matter and discourse.

(Barad, 2007: 185)

Recent scholarship on resilience and adaptive peacebuilding has critiqued an over-emphasis on individual resilience, insisting instead on sustainable processes that foster 'interactions between individuals and their environments' (Ungar, Chapter 1) and accentuate 'complexity' and 'local ownership' as well as resilience (de Coning, 2018: 305). It is therefore necessary to address 'the systemic dimensions of war crimes and human rights abuses', as well as to 'engage with different systems that give people access to new resources' (Ungar, Chapter 1). In this section, we extend this complexity, drawing on Mayan scholars and activists who press for a recognition of multiple onto-epistemologies within a pluriverse (Esteva and Prakash, 2014). We analyse how multi-systems and relational approaches to resilience work to disrupt Western dualisms of nature and culture, of human and nonhuman, of knowing and being, that themselves are the result of colonial violence and dispossession. Indigenous resilience is rooted in an integral, collective relationship of land-body-territory.

In post-genocide Guatemala, questions of land and territory haunt transitional justice processes focused on redress for bodily harm, including rape, torture, forced disappearances and massacres. The colonial dispossession of Indigenous lands remains the primary, foundational and ongoing injustice, and Indigenous communities throughout the country are mobilised today around *defensa del territorio* (territorial defence) in the face of the rampant, violent extractivism of transnational corporations that is enthusiastically supported by the Guatemalan state (Macleod, 2017; Solano, 2013). In the Sepur Zarco case of sexual violence as a crime against humanity, the Q'eqchi' women plaintiffs' husbands were disappeared because they were organising to legalise their titles to their lands, and as a consequence the women endured forced labour and sexual violence at the Sepur Zarco military outpost. Despite participating in a trial focused on redress for sexual violence, the plaintiffs contested the construction of their experiences of rape as isolated, individuated events; instead, they sutured their bodies to the land and to the Q'eqchi' collectivity of which they are part. As such, their resilience is rooted in their (re)connection to their Mayan community and land and to the demand for the land's return, rather than in the identity as a 'raped woman' that emerged through the trial. The trial's still unfulfilled reparations ruling of land legalisation remains a gaping, egregious wound. Today, Sepur Zarco continues to be a private estate, surrounded by African palm plantations. The colonial violence lives on, as does Indigenous resistance to it (Crosby and Lykes, 2019; Méndez and Carrera, 2014).

The Sepur Zarco trial did deliver a guilty verdict. It was the first time that these crimes had been prosecuted in-country, and the verdict was celebrated transnationally as a victory for gender justice. What was striking was the absence of any recognition of indigeneity in the way in which the trial was received and analysed by many who attended and in national and international media; the exclusive focus on gendered sexual violence reflected what appeared to be an inability to see or hear the intersectional violations experienced and the call for historical justice. This absence permeated the transitional justice processes themselves, where there was a seeming refusal to turn towards the Mayan cosmovision, despite the fact that the majority of those seeking redress were themselves Mayan – and both they and expert witnesses at the trial had testified to those realities (Velásquez, 2012). Structural, institutionalised racism remains an entrenched, systemic barrier to historical justice for Mayan peoples. As the Kaqchikel scholar Emma Chirix García (2019: 147) argues, 'it is not possible to understand the Mayan conception of the world from the Western vision, because Eurocentric and ethnocentric knowledge distorts, rationalises, racialises, subordinates and violates indigenous knowledges'.

The Mayan cosmovision is heterogeneous, reiterated in different forms by the twenty-two Mayan peoples in Guatemala, and fragmented, dissipated and transformed across centuries of colonisation. However, the cosmovision has enduringly held to a core onto-epistemology of complementarity and equilibrium, whereby knowing and being are inextricably intertwined, and the relationship between human beings and Mother Earth is mutually constituting and interdependent. As Chirix García (2003: 23) elaborates, echoing the multi-systemic approach to resilience and adaptive peacebuilding called for in this volume, 'the Mayan cosmovision fosters a holistic understanding of things, does not divide events, but rather emphasizes the interrelations among the psychosocial, the environmental and the cosmic towards an integral approach to people and reality'.

The dualisms that Barad (2007: 135) laments in much Western thought are absent from the Mayan cosmovision, which instead takes up what she refers to as the imperative of 'thinking the natural and the cultural together in illuminating ways', which means 'not attribut[ing] the source of all change to culture, denying nature any sense of agency or historicity' (Barad, 2007: 136). Barad's (2007: 37) notion of agential realism is 'about the real consequences, interventions, creative possibilities and responsibilities of intra-acting with and as part of the world'. In her work, she emphasises the importance of materiality, and the materiality of difference, how matter 'matters', and not merely as an effect of discourse. She emphasises the importance of 'material agency, material constraints, and material exclusions' (Barad, 2007: 34) and contests the discursive turn that dominated twentieth-century social science research and much feminist theorising. Indigenous and decolonial scholars embrace the focus on matter as do Mayan peoples.

Matter *matters* in the violence of colonisation and in resistance to it; as such it is foundational to Mayan expressions of resilience. The processes of colonisation violently turned the land into an object: 'the territory was desecrated, that is, it was not sacred anymore, and became the land, a means of production that was supposedly inexhaustible and which was expropriated/exploited as never before, for the agrarian export of coffee, sugar cane and bananas' (CALDH and Pérez, 2014: 89). Decolonising the land means acknowledging its persistent agency, recognising its rights, re-centring it as living. In speaking about the demands of Indigenous people in Colombia for justice in the post-conflict transitions, Izquierdo and Viaene (2018) describe an integral justice that transcends transitional justice processes to date, drawing on international legal norms, including the UN Declaration on the Rights of Indigenous

Peoples (2007) and the Colombian Decree 4633 of 2011, also known as the Law of Victims for Indigenous Communities.

The Decree affirms that rivers, mountains and the territories have rights, extending notions heretofore situated or instantiated in humans as distinct from other living beings. In the Colombian Decree 4633, land, rivers and territory are recognised as victims whose rights have been violated during the armed conflict and beyond when they were expropriated, desecrated or redirected. Territory is recognised as 'a living whole and the sustenance of identity and harmony' that 'suffers damage when it is violated or desecrated by the internal armed conflict' (Article 45). Decree 4633 also asserts that spiritual healing is part of the integral reparation of the territory (Article 8). Ruiz Serna (2017: 97) describes this recognition as implying 'more rights *of* the territory than rights *over* the territory'.

Viaene (2019) argues that both the state and NGOs who work in post-conflict pluri-cultural societies are challenged to problematise and re-conceptualise the dominant transitional justice paradigm such that they recognise, value and respond to Indigenous onto-epistemologies or cosmovisions. She notes that a key feature common to the Mayan cosmovision in general, and also to that of the Q'eqchi' community whose work she has documented through over a decade of ethnographic research, is that 'human beings must be understood as "relational beings", which puts into question the dominant Western ontological division between culture and nature' (Viaene, 2019: 74). This worldview, in which everything is one, interrelated and interdependent, undergirds a non-dualist, collectivist materiality and spirituality that questions the anthropocentric approach to human rights and demands not only the recognition of collective rights but also the rights of the territory. This praxis echoes that of Indigenous peoples throughout Abya Yala[2] and beyond (Esteva and Prakash, 2014). They affirm their cosmovision as one among many, asserting that rather than a single universal principle or one declaration of universal human rights, we are challenged to open our minds and hearts to consider the pluriverse in which we live, struggle and affirm multiple cosmovisions, each of which is grounded in an onto-epistemology, a oneness of being and knowing.

In gendering their understanding of the Mayan cosmovision and contesting its patriarchal assumptions of gender complementarity – further evidence of the living iterations of these intersecting systems – Mayan women scholars and

---

[2]   Abya Yala 'is the ancestral name of the American continent in the Kuna language. Recognizing this continent's name as Abya Yala and not the Americas is part of the decolonial political demands of the original peoples' (CALDH and Pérez, 2014: 68). As reflected here, there is also an increasing preference for the use of 'original peoples' rather than Indigenous.

activists emphasise the gendered integrality of land and body in the experience of colonial violence and in resistance to it. Kaqchikel scholar Aura Cumes (2012) argues that Mayan women challenge intersectional oppressions due to patriarchy, racism and class oppression from the margins of power, affirming their collective subjectivities through liberating emancipatory processes that reflect an integral ontology. Chirix García (2019: 140) notes that: '[s]ituating the body within a historical and political framework brings the memory of the invasion of the New World, the genocide, the process of inquisition and assimilation, and the imposition of a European, masculine and white model'. Indigenous women's bodies were the systemic targets of violence, including rape, throughout centuries of colonisation, and Indigenous women connect the desecration of their bodies and the land itself. More recently, rape has been used by private security and state forces against women defending their lands from transnational corporate incursion (Macleod, 2017; Russell, 2010). Indigenous women conceptualise the integrality of land-body-territory as the site of their resistance. Defining herself as a 'community territorial feminist', Mayan and Xinca activist Lorena Cabnal (2019: 121–122) notes:

> Being an indigenous woman and defending our ancestral territory means putting on the front line of attack ... our first territory of defence, the body. To defend the land territory, as women we conduct an impressive, parallel and daily defence in two inseparable dimensions: the defence of our bodily territory and the defence of our land territory ... we recognize that the body as well as the land are spaces of vital energy that must function reciprocally.

In the following sections, we explore how diverse groups of Mayan women identify their resilience as persistence and protagonism as they too push the boundaries of Western-infused transitional justice praxis, seeking to defend land-body-territory in the wake of genocidal harm.

MAYAN WOMEN'S VOICES PERSIST

Our dream is to gain more strength. Like the force of the blood that we carry, to maintain hope, so that the flower is produced that affirms our roots from which a large tree grows.

(CALDH and Grupo de Mujeres Xu'm Saj Chee, Flor de Maguey, 2018: 22)

In reflecting back on her fifteen years of accompanying transitional justice processes in post-genocide Guatemala, Alvarez notes how the weight of the continuous wars, dispossessions, violences and oppressions that Mayan peoples have lived through has shaped their strategies of resistance, defence, struggle and resilience. Centuries of violence have informed what seems to be an underlying assumption that Mayan women and their communities are simply holding on or surviving in the face of an oppressive state and its actors. She is struck by how few voices there were that spoke of strength, power, the desire for life, rooted in the cosmovision and the capacities that have made it possible for Mayan peoples to persist and survive, co-constructing and protagonising their lives and histories day by day, building their territories based on self-determination. She notes that many of the words and phrases in these justice-seeking processes are in the coloniser's Western language of a defence of rights, language promoted by international organisations that express the magnitude of the violence and the resilience that Mayan peoples have had to have in order to confront what they have lived through.

Those who have always engaged in these collective struggles for their communities, a key expression of Mayan resilience, are now called 'human rights defenders'. While such language situates local work within an international context, it occludes the multiplicity of self-naming processes and actions of resistance, struggle, defence and creation, that is, the persistence in which Mayan women and men have always engaged. Alvarez highlights how, in talking to her sisters, they realised that these concepts of 'struggle' and 'resistance' do not exist in the K'iche' language per se. Instead, there are several conceptions that they use within their cosmovision, including: *Kakojachoq'ab'*, 'use your strengths'; *Chatz'ukuj a kaslemal*, 'find the best way to live'; *Chayik'a'a Kaslemal*, 'build your own life' and *Xojch'awoq*, 'let's talk'.

As such, Alvarez takes up the challenge of how to strengthen Mayan identities and self-esteem that are grounded not only in pain and suffering, in past experiences of violence, but also in processes of healing and in expressions of pride for their cosmovision, for the life they have given the world. She reflects on the years she has spent working from within a Western paradigm while trying to recover her own ancestral cosmovision, 'looking both ways' to explain the complexities of violence that have shaped the lives of Mayan women and their communities while affirming the historical roots of Mayan experiences pre-Invasion. She notes that she has written much less frequently on the wonders recovered from the Mayan cosmovision, spirituality, ritual, biological logic[3] and the protection of life. Writing and focusing

---

[3]   'Biological logic' proposes that we humans are but one species among many. We are an integral part of the network of life within the planetary biosphere in which we live. The human being is not the centre of the world. The universe is as diverse as all living beings. We are interdependent, and as such we need the plants and animals to live.

energy within this latter frame would enable new generations of women and men to love their Mayan identity, enjoy it and live it with happiness. As such, how can Mayan peoples not only focus their energies on the defence and struggle for their culture, their way of life, their body-land-territories, but also put into action affirmative ways of co-creating life, feeling and enjoying it in its integrality?

Healing processes have been an essential strategy in recuperating Mayan people's vital strengths. Alvarez herself has drawn on her membership in the *Grupo Mujeres Mayas Kaqla* [Kaqla Mayan Women's Group] (hereafter Kaqla), which brings together professional Mayan women who have worked to heal their traumas, including victimisation and sexual violence. The understanding of trauma they have articulated through multiple years of work is collective and transgenerational (Kaqla, 2011). Mayan women have lived through a continuum of political, social and familial violences whose sequelae need to be healed in order for them to reconnect themselves to life and well-being and not just to the wound itself. In its healing processes, Kaqla has brought together ancestral and Western techniques and methods to heal the traumas and effects of a continuum of racist, patriarchal and class-based violence and violations. These processes have enabled the members of Kaqla to recuperate and enjoy with much love their cosmovision, integrating and affirming their lived experiences and cultivating joy and well-being.

From 2012 to 2014, in her capacity as coordinator of the Women's Rights Unit of the CALDH, one of Guatemala's largest human rights non-governmental organisations (NGOs), Alvarez – together with other Mayan women – facilitated processes designed to strengthen the leadership of diverse groups of Mayan women that CALDH was accompanying in its human rights and justice work. Participants included women members of the *Asociación para la Justicia y la Reconciliación* [Association for Justice and Reconciliation or AJR] (the plaintiffs in the Ríos Montt genocide trial), the Flor de Maguey Collective (some of the women plaintiffs in the trial who had survived sexual violence during the genocide) and other Mayan women's organisations who are defending their rights, including the *Red Departamental de Mujeres Sololatecas con Visión Integral* [Departmental Network of Sololateca Women with Holistic Vision], the *Defensoría Maya Ch'orti'* [Ch'orti' Mayan Defence Unit] and the *Coordinadora de Jóvenes de Sololá* [Sololá Coordination of Young People].

The training-healing-action-reflection workshops were structured to facilitate an exchange of knowledges. They sought to highlight the continuums of violences and resistances in the lives of Mayan women since the time of the Spanish invasion, with participants then becoming replicators of the workshop with women in their respective communities. They also published the book *The Voices of Women Persist in the Collective Memory of their Peoples: Continuum of Violences and Resistances in Women's Lives, Bodies and Territories* (CALDH and Pérez, 2014).

The process sought to reclaim a gendered understanding of historical memory that centred 'the bodies and territories of women, as a common thread that gives meaning to individual experiences' (CALDH and Pérez, 2014: 172). The body-land-territory is identified as 'the principal axis of women's oppression and resistance; sexual violence, the usurpation of lands, territorial resistance, are cyclical dynamics that repeat throughout the history of humanity' (CALDH and Pérez, 2014: 53). The methodology's onto-epistemology emphasised 'the identification of violences and their sequelae but also the capacity for resilience that supports community resistance/persistence in the face of adverse situations' (CALDH and Pérez, 2014: 172). The workshops began from participants' 'lives, cosmovision, knowledge and power' to make visible women's 'strengths and determination' (CALDH and Pérez, 2014: 172), which had been occluded by centuries of colonisation. Drawing on historical documents as well as participants' testimonies and drawings and illustrated timelines, the process analysed the forms of violence against and resistance by Mayan women over six temporal periods, from the invasion to the post-war period.

In line with Tuck's (2009) aforementioned rejection of a focus on damage narratives, while the varied dimensions of colonial and militarised violence against Mayan women were highlighted, the workshops continuously excavated the multi-faceted forms of Mayan women's resilience, framed here as persistence and resistance within and beyond local communities. As Alvarez notes and the book acknowledges, these examples were far harder to find but ever-present nonetheless, if one was willing and able to look for them. As one illustration, a persistent theme in the workshops was the constant occlusion of Mayan women's agency and rights within their families and communities, as well as in the wider Guatemalan context.

The workshops' embodied approach to historical memory drew on the work of the aforementioned Kaqla, which emphasises the integrated 'affective, emotional, material and territorial' aspects of memory, centres being as well as knowing, and recognises the body itself as 'an entity that accumulates memory' (Kaqla, 2004: 80). In taking such an onto-epistemological approach, '[h]istory and the history of our ancestors is written on our bodies, and as such it is imperative to integrate mind, body, emotions and actions' (CALDH and Pérez, 2014: 59). Various techniques and therapies from diverse psychological and healing practices (e.g., Advanced Integrative Therapy, Tapas Acupressure

Technique, massage, Reiki, Chakras), as well as beliefs and practices from the Mayan cosmovision beginning with the Mayan calendar, were integrated into the workshops. These embodied processes were accompanied by group discussions, lectures, written exercises including participants' ideas and reflections, exercises that included personal introspection to analyse participants' particular realities, group dialogues and creative recreation, dance, painting, and singing as means to exercise the integrality of individual and collective voices. As the book articulates:

> To be able to heal the wounds we have to know the shadows . . . When we talk about healing we are talking about returning to our centre and recovering our capacities, potentialities and internal resources and for this we use tools and techniques from the Mayan cosmovision, psychology and pedagogy, so that individually and collectively we can review and transform, recovering our powers and knowledges, understand our personal and collective histories.
>
> (CALDH and Pérez, 2014: 17)

The timeline of resistances generated in the workshops emphasised the important historical role played by the *Ajq'ij*, spiritual guides. Despite repeated attempts to erase their presence through centuries of colonisation, 'they have maintained the knowledge of the sacred fire' (CALDH and Pérez, 2014: 154). As the timeline they developed highlights, today Mayan women and men are relearning their spirituality, lighting incense and conducting ceremonies in sacred ancestral sites (CALDH and Pérez, 2014). The role of *Ajq'ij* has also been taken up by Mayan women in many communities in their capacity as healers and midwives, known as '*akanal* in Ixil, *ajkun* in Kaqchikel and *banonel* in Q'eqchi'' (CALDH and Pérez, 2014: 154). In addition to having been in charge of most births in rural communities throughout the centuries, Mayan women have continued to cultivate and prepare medicinal plants and preserve and create new forms of knowledge to treat their communities (CALDH and Pérez, 2014). The processes facilitated by CALDH revealed the importance of the recovery of the values of the Mayan cosmovision for Mayan women's collective identity, allowing them to draw on their ancestral ways of living and being while centring themselves as women and integrating a relationship between past and present, thereby strengthening their persistence in resisting the colonial 'logic of destruction' (CALDH and Pérez, 2014: 154).

Those who engaged in these training-healing-action-reflection processes and wrote the resulting book took great care to resist the damage frame as totalising, in part by interweaving forms of resistance to violence and presenting contrasting experiences over time, thereby excavating and embodying Mayan women's persistence and resistance. This included the resilience of those who chose to participate as plaintiffs and witnesses in the 2013 genocide trial. As articulated in three publications by groups of Mayan women who took part in that trial, this thirteen-year process of organisation and endurance resulted in strengthened community networks and Mayan women's enhanced protagonism (see CALDH and Grupo de Mujeres Tiilach'j Ixo'j, Mujeres Valientes 19 de Marzo, 2018; CALDH and Grupo de Mujeres Xu'm Saj Chee, Flor de Maguey, 2018; CALDH and Mujeres Asociación para la Justicia y la Reconciliación AJR Txu'mil, 2018).

Mayan women participants chronicled these multi-year journeys of self-discovery, valuing the group processes through which they voiced multiple experiences of previously silenced embodied suffering, standing up to publicly assert their rights as women, denouncing not only racialised war-based violations of their bodies but also contemporary gendered family violence and corporate extraction of natural resources in their territories. They 'defied their own fears, showed themselves their strength, and created networks of support among women and with their communities' (CALDH and Pérez, 2014: 168). One trial participant noted how, 'We are all together, like the butterflies, like the birds, in group, we are not alone, and thus we are on the path to justice' (CALDH and Pérez, 2014: 169).

Alvarez reclaims this process of coming together, of organising, of being in-community, as a central aspect of 'justice' itself, given a colonial judicial system that has not taken up Mayan people's demands for historical justice. She highlights the multiple ways through which the processes of women coming together in healing processes are grounded in and lift up their contemporary iteration of the Mayan cosmovision, one that counters Western dualisms between the person and the environment, the cultural and natural worlds. It is significant that participants represent their resilience through the natural world, invoking the integrality of the human and natural worlds, as Crosby and Lykes also found in the creative workshops they facilitated, and which they examine in more detail in the following section.

MAYAN WOMEN'S PROTAGONISM TAKES FLIGHT

[I am] old, without suffering, without fear and without shame. Today I am capable of doing all that I can. I am like a bird. I can fly with large wings.

(Chuj protagonist, participant in a July 2011 workshop)

Over a period of eight years (2009–2017), Crosby and Lykes facilitated a series of creative workshops with fifty-four Q'eqchi', Kaqchikel, Chuj, Mam and

Poptí women, including the fifteen plaintiffs in the Sepur Zarco case, who survived racialised gendered violence during the height of the genocidal violence in the early 1980s.[4] The work was initiated in 2009 in collaboration with the National Union of Guatemala Women (UNAMG, for its Spanish name) who had been working with these protagonists since 2003. Crosby and Lykes accompanied the fifty-four Mayan protagonists as well as the ladinx, mestizx and Mayan feminists, psychologists and lawyers working alongside them, documenting their journeys in search of redress.

They drew on creative techniques – drawing, image theatre, creative story-telling – as they interfaced or complemented Mayan rituals and practices (Lykes and Crosby, 2015). They facilitated action-reflection meaning-making processes through which participants individually and in small groups creatively represented their experiences in their search for truth, justice and reparations for the violations they had survived. They documented protagonists' images, performances and interpretations, drawing on them to produce an approximation of how protagonists constructed meaning through their embodied praxis and dialogically with those intermediaries who accompanied them, Crosby and Lykes included (Crosby and Lykes, 2019).

In this section, Lykes and Crosby re-situate several of the Mayan protagonists' representations in the creative workshops to re-envision resilience in the wake of genocidal violence and ongoing gendered racialised violence in Guatemala. Reading protagonists' images and performances from the ground of their onto-epistemologies, they aspire to 'stand under' them (Panikkar, n.d.), to resituate the matter that matters to these fifty-four Mayan protagonists as they perform and re-present their cosmovision. Their understanding is further informed by Mayan women's theorising (see, e.g., Chirix García, 2003, 2019; Kaqla, 2004, 2006, 2011) as they seek to avoid essentialising or romanticising these ways of hearing and seeing the natural world, Pacha Mama, Mother Earth, the only home any of us know. They seek, in the words of Bacca (2020: 143), to allow themselves to be 'captivated by the [Mayan women's] voices', discerning how Mayan onto-epistemology re-centres the integrality of life, of body-land-territory, of being-knowing through agential realism.

[4]   The Lykes and Crosby research was supported by grants from the Social Sciences and Humanities Research Council of Canada (SSHRC), the International Development Research Centre (IDRC), York University and the Center for Human Rights and International Justice (CHRIJ) at Boston College. York University's Ethics Review Board (6 May) and Boston College's Institutional Review Board (15 May) approved the study in 2009, renewing it annually through 2020. Thanks and appreciation to the Mayan women whom the authors accompanied on a small part of their journeys and to Catalina Rey-Guerra for her research support to this chapter. All translations from Spanish and K'iche' are by the authors.

They ground their analysis in gendered ways of seeing-being-knowing that deconstruct colonised racialisation of all the natural elements – water, earth, air and fire – affording them the same respect and dignity with which Western onto-epistemologies seek to treat human beings. Turning to the work of Kaqla, they note that this Mayan women's group designed their workshops to recover human spirituality through creating spaces that promoted 'spiritual connections with the Heart of the Sky, the Heart of the Earth, the energy of the universe, the divine light and universal love ... we incorporate elements and practices of Mayan spirituality that respect diverse ideologies, practices and beliefs' (Kaqla, 2006: 10). As Mayan women participants in a Kaqla workshop focused on their breath and their bodies, the facilitator noted that:

> We remember our connection with the earth, with the subtle universe in the universal love. We connect and we feel the rivers of light that come out of the earth that is the nutritious energy of the earth, it comes up through our body from the feet to the head and it gives us nourishment. Everything else we let go of so that it goes toward the universe communicating with the earth through the sun, as a universal principle.
>
> (Kaqla, 2006: 55)

As Crosby and Lykes were beginning their research, they participated in a workshop with some of the fifty-four protagonists facilitated by the Peruvian theatre group Yuyachkani in the town of Chimaltenango, Guatemala. In the workshop, all participants were invited to stretch themselves out on newsprint while a partner drew the outline of their bodies. Participants were then invited to use pens and crayons and paints to represent their life journeys, including experiences, people or places that had brought them to this day in 2009. The drawings were then taped to the walls of the large room in which all were gathered, a space through which participants had moved through a variety of warming-up and breathing exercises before engaging in this individual drawing process.

Among the more than fifty images were the three below (see Figure 9.1). Participants were urged to speak with each other, analysing drawings as they passed by and then storying their own drawing for others to experience through looking and listening. Among the emotions were some that referenced sorrow, pain, suffering and physical wounds due to sexual violence, while others spoke of new life, rooted in Mother Earth. The left and centre drawings visualise images of life and growth that Crosby and Lykes would subsequently see repeatedly in the creative workshops that they facilitated with these same women. All three drawings visualise Mayan women's *guipiles* (blouses) and *cortes* (skirts), some in more detail than others, yet all display these gendered

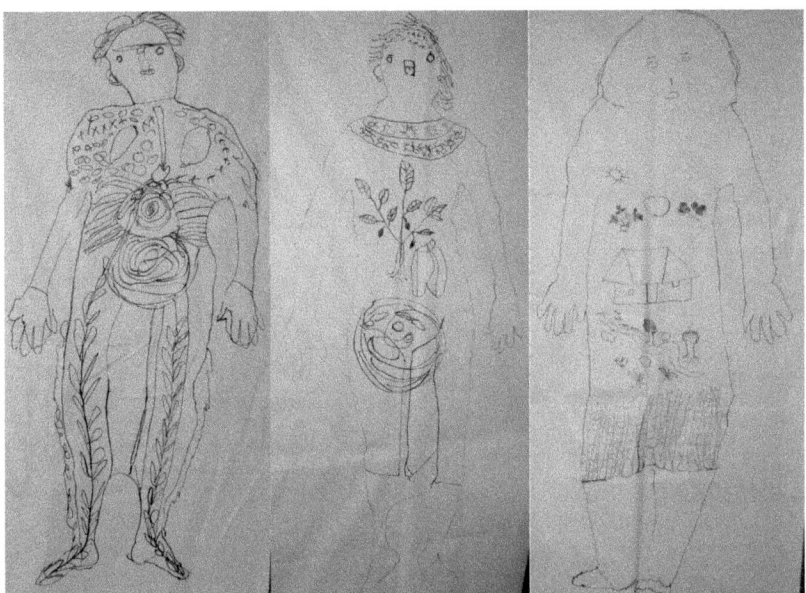

FIGURE 9.1 Mayan women visualise embodied suffering and resilience

cultural representations, seemingly affirming their Mayanness, in the midst of or despite the multiple assaults on their bodies represented in the left and centre images. An idealised or aspirational image of embodied hope, frequently expressed by many among the fifty-four protagonists in Crosby and Lykes' research, and including the recovery of land, a home, flowers, the sun and a river that flows through one's territory, persist in and through the drawings, in and through these Mayan women's lives.

Many Mayan protagonists who participated in the creative workshops that Crosby and Lykes facilitated represented their lives through trees, flowers and seeds, life today, in the past and into the future. When they drew images of massacres or sexual violence, cornfields were burning and women's bodies were thrown into rivers running through villages. When they represented themselves today, as seen in Figure 9.2, large trees had both roots and branches, connecting the past to the present in dynamic and living ways. Birds were often positioned above the branches, an image echoing the words of the Chuj protagonist in the above epigraph.

In one workshop in 2012, protagonists were invited to gather with others who spoke their language, given the absence of sufficient interpreters to facilitate cross-language communication, to discuss their experiences of 'community'. After presenting the conclusions from these discussions to

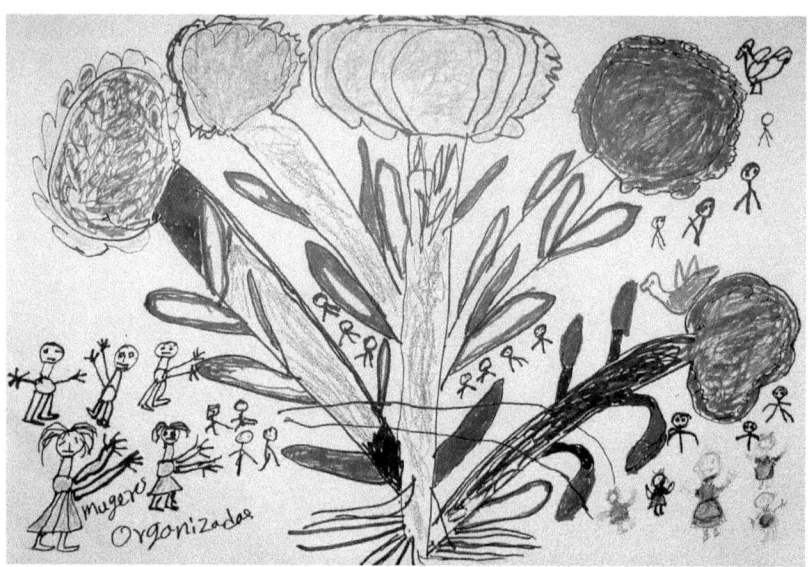

FIGURE 9.2 Mayan women represent life and growth and the integrality of humans and land

the group as a whole they were invited to develop a collective drawing to represent their community's advances and setbacks over the previous years in which all had been gathering in these workshops. Each group then presented its drawing to the participants as a whole, who reflected on what they saw. One participant in the larger group noted that the drawing by the Chuj (see Figure 9.2) showed women who had begun to 'clear the area, to water that tree, so now it has good roots and green leaves, now they can harvest, the tree bears fruit'. Others added that 'when you plant a tree you have to water it, keep it clean, then there will be a harvest, advances'. A third participant noted that some of them had previously drawn wilted plants, contrasting those experiences with the now healthy tree that bears fruit and comparing the latter to an organisation that 'plants a seed in the lives of women' who then organise. This collective drawing peppers human images of women, men and children throughout, centring the human community around a strong tree trunk that bears flowers and fruit, with roots that spread widely in a variety of directions. The seamless integration of women, men, children, plants and birds, as well as the size of the environment and the diverse colours used to represent life and growth, suggest that humans are integral to or at one with the land, rather than having dominance over it.

Human beings are depicted throughout the image, with women and children on the right side dispersed, representing life before they began to organise, and contrasting with those on the left who are named as women organisers. These women had been in refuge in Mexico where they encountered the Mayan refugee women's organisation *Mama Maquín*. Their reflections highlighted their suffering and displacement as well as the important ways in which they had learned to organise among themselves, lessons that they had brought back to Guatemala with them.

Other groups focused their drawings on advances and setbacks in their experiences of transitional justice, including their demands for truth and reparations, and noted the ongoing threat of the previous military commander of a scorched earth strategy in the Ixil area in 1981–1982, Otto Pérez Molina, who was running for the presidency of the country. Others focused more explicitly on the continuities of violence, emphasising the current violence of resource extraction by transnational mining companies because 'they are taking gold, wealth out of our country. They are destroying trees and contaminating water, and what will we leave our grandchildren?' A Q'eqchi' woman from the Polochic Valley noted that 'the government is giving everything to the rich, they are evicting people from the land, they send security for the rich and pay no attention to our needs'.

Another participant explained that 'in our pictures we put what comes to mind. But not everything comes to mind, like mining. It brings disease, contaminates water. This is the government's plan, it wants to damage Guatemala, the environment; it wants to harm the people. We as Indigenous people have to ask ourselves what to do. We are saying no to mining, but every government wants it'. Finally, after noting that these national challenges play out in varied ways given local leadership, one participant described things in the country as 'worrisome', adding that engineers had come to her community, saying that they were doing a study. She noted that her community still had forests, wooded areas and rivers, and some community members concluded that since the engineers seemed to be examining the river, it would appear that they wanted to put in a hydroelectric plant. She asked. 'What will become of our children if they contaminate the river?' Others added that plantation owners were planting African palm in their community, generating significant worries among the women as 'it contaminates the river'.

Protagonists described multiple significant changes grounded in their deep knowledges of their and their communities' histories; multi-systemic dynamics that reflect continuities of colonial violence and expressions of persistence and protagonism within and across these systems; resilience that they attributed to their many years of organising for their rights in the wake of genocidal harm – and through which they had learned about their rights to body-land-territory and overcome their fears of speaking, even being willing to speak up in the trial of their assailants. Yet, in describing the desecration of their lands, of their territories, that they positioned as a continuity of the violence against their bodies, they once again felt threatened, noting in this 2012 workshop: 'This worries us, we don't know what to do. The rich have weapons and they intimidate us. What if they do come in, they are supported by the government. What are we going to do, we don't know what to do'. Despite the dynamic and iterative systems of resilience, they recognise the lack of resources adequate to contest state colonialism and multinational neo-liberal capitalism.

Looking across these and many other engagements with different configur-ations of these fifty-four women in the workshops that they and others have facilitated, Crosby and Lykes note the various representations of the continu-ities and continuums of violence, the ongoing systems and structures that took root during colonisation over 500 years ago. As Alvarez and her colleagues (CALDH and Pérez, 2014) argue, drawing on the action-reflection processes discussed in the previous section of this chapter, Mayan women not only understand those continuities but also embrace the stories of their ancestors and embody their beliefs and practices as they are reinterpreted through their multiple Mayan groups, geographically based communities and communities of women.

What persists are the deeply threaded intersections of land-body-territory, the recognition of and respect for humans who travel among other living beings – rivers, mountains, animals, among them – and who have contended for centuries with colonial powers that had fractured what Mayan peoples experience as an integral whole. One experience of healing can be achieved when humans care for the rivers and mountains that are one with them, as they drink from them and walk in their midst (Sieder and Viaene, 2019). The gendered and racialised transformative praxis of healing described herein is embodied and performed at the intersections of land-body-territory, an inter-section represented by persistent Mayan protagonists through the images and words of the processes recounted in this chapter. Their resilience has been documented by those who have accompanied them through multiple years of praxis framed, facilitated and constrained by processes of transitional justice. Despite the latter, the creative techniques, Mayan cosmovision and other healing processes described above facilitated processes through which differ-ently positioned intermediaries have approximated an understanding of these alternative forms of justice that centre Mayan resilience.

CONCLUSION

Key components of the emerging paradigm of adaptive peacebuilding, pro-posed in this volume as representing a new direction for transitional justice, include a shift in focus from ends to means and an emphasis on 'strengthening the resilience of local social institutions and ... investing in social cohesion' (de Coning, 2018: 304) – what some in the transitional justice field refer to as transformative justice or justice from the ground up (Gready and Robins, 2014; see also Lambourne, Chapter 2). The strengthening of the Guatemalan judi-cial system that saw the undermining of the entrenched, systemic impunity for human rights violations was made possible because of the resilience of the country's Mayan majority accompanied by organised civil society who have persisted in and protagonised the struggle for justice in the context of an increasingly (re)militarised, corrupt and violent state.

The struggle itself has strengthened a civil society fractured and fragmented by decades of armed conflict, supported the emergence of an independent judiciary led by key figures such as former Attorney General Claudia Paz y Paz Bailey, consolidated an Indigenous movement focused on territorial defence of land and body, and facilitated processes through which significant numbers of Mayan women protagonists have asserted their rights, defying patriarchal, racialised, colonial power. However, as we have argued in this chapter, the short-term ahistorical strategies of transitional justice deployed therein have failed to respond to the sequelae and continuum of the centuries-old and continuous genocidal harm for which Mayan women and their communities seek historical justice.

For transitional justice to contribute to developing the adaptive capacity, resources and resilience of individuals, communities and social and political institutions in post-genocide Guatemala, it must recognise the continuation and continuum of violations of the rights of Mayan peoples and their territor-ies for over 500 years. It must support locally driven, community-oriented processes that repair the historical damage incurred to their lands, bodies and cosmovisions. It must foment a justice that returns to Mayan peoples that which has been plundered and expropriated from generation to generation. The justice mandated is one where the bodies of Mayan women are not subject to any type of violence, where Mayan peoples are not undervalued, racialised or pathologised as essentially damaged, but, rather, where their dignity is affirmed and their millennial cosmovisions are recognised as reflect-ing a valued way of life through which they have persisted against all odds. As we have argued in this chapter, Mayan women demand a justice that inte-grally addresses the intertwined rights of land-body-territory, the ongoing defence of which is a key expression of their resilience.

Throughout centuries of colonial violence, Mayan women have persisted, sustaining life, caring for new generations – planting their land, feeding their families, weaving their clothing and healing their wounds. While the Guatemalan state, as well as internationalists, NGOs and human rights activists, have turned towards Western legal systems, Mayan women have known that their ancestral paradigm has sustained life. As with the work of Kaqla, those we have accompanied have also taken and integrated the good from other paradigms. As such, it is not an essentialised notion of Mayanness that they seek, embody and perform. Their ancestors adapted to survive, and the multiple forms of living from which the Mayan women whom we have accompanied continue to draw as they seek well-being reflect an embrace of the pluriverse, a recognition of diverse ways of knowing-being. They affirm and transform their ancestral cosmovisions wherein life reflects an integration of energies, emotions and spirituality from within a respect for all within existence, human and non-human. They seek to recuperate *kamowaj*, the process of giving thanks, which is rooted in daily rituals practised with seeds and animals, with the network of life and Mother Earth.

The processes described in this chapter through which Mayan women perform persistence and protagonism as expressions of resilience validate the memory of Mayan peoples and their ongoing search for historical justice. They narrate pain but, as importantly, affirm and celebrate their resilience, in forms of well-being, of partnerships, of sexuality, of plantings, of nourishment, of spirituality and of the care for and protection of all of life through their languages and from within their onto-epistemologies. Those of us who are invited to accompany these processes are challenged to collaborate in forging the necessary conditions and mechanisms that support the recuperation of territory and the common good, and, as such, we need to go beyond transitional justice, state justice and externally imposed forms of peacebuilding. Although still a legitimate – even necessary – demand, not all vital energy must be consumed by it. We must conceive resilience otherwise, whether as *Kakojachoq'ab', Chatz'ukuj a kaslemal, Chayik'a'a Kaslemal, Xojch'awoq*, or the multiple Mayan conceptualisations of resistance and struggle, while affirming, as they do, the pluriverse within which their cosmovision persists.

REFERENCES

Bacca, P. I. (2020). Indigenizing international law and decolonizing the anthropocene: Genocide by ecological means and Indigenous nationhood in contemporary Colombia. *Maguaré*, 33(2), 139–169.

Barad, K. (2007). *Meeting the Universe Halfway: Quantum Physics and the Entanglement of Matter and Meaning*. Durham, NC: Duke University Press.

Cabnal, L. (2019). El relato de las violencias desde mi territorio. In X. Leyva Solano and R. Icaza (eds.), *En Tiempos de Muerte: Cuerpos, Rebeldías, Resistencias*. Buenos Aires, AR: Consejo Latinoamericano de Ciencias Sociales; San Cristóbal de Las Casas, Chiapas: Cooperativa Editorial Retos, pp. 113–126.

Centre for Legal Action in Human Rights (CALDH – Centro para la Acción Legal en Derechos Humanos) and Pérez, M. J. (2014). *Las voces de las mujeres persisten en la memoria colectiva de sus pueblos: Continuum de violencias y resistencias en la vida, cuerpo y territorio de las mujeres*. Guatemala City, Guatemala: Authors.

CALDH and Mujeres Asociación para la Justicia y Reconciliación AJR Txu'mil (2018). *Nuestra vida, nuestra historia: 'Nuestra lucha no tiene fin, queremos que nuestro grupo sea como el cielo: un lugar seguro, claro como el día'*. Santa María Nebaj, Quiché, Guatemala: Authors.

CALDH and Grupo de Mujeres Tiilacha'j, Mujeres Valientes 19 de Marzo. (2018). *Nuestra vida, nuestra historia: 'Sabemos cuál es la historia, estamos luchando porque queremos justicia'*. Santa María Nebaj, Quiché, Guatemala: Authors.

CALDH and Grupo de Mujeres Xu'm Saj Chee, Flor de Maguey. (2018). *Nuestra vida, nuestra historia: 'Ahora sabemos que nuestras palabras sí valen, le ganamos al miedo'*. Santa María Nebaj, Quiché, Guatemala: Authors.

Comisión para el Esclarecimiento Histórico (CEH). (1999). *Guatemala: Memoria del silencio Tz'inil Na'tab'al*. Guatemala City, Guatemala: Oficina de Servicios para Proyectos de las Naciones Unidas (UNOPS). www.centrodememoriahistorica.gov.co/descargas/guatemala-memoria-silencio/guatemala-memoria-del-silencio.pdf (accessed 13 July 2020).

Chirix García, E. D. (2003). *Alas y raíces: Afectividad de las mujeres Mayas = Rik'in ruxik' y ruxe'il: ronojel kajowab'al ri mayab' taq ixoqi'*. Guatemala City, Guatemala: Grupo de Mujeres Mayas Kaqla.

Chirix García, E. D. (2019). Cuerpos, sexualidad y pensamiento maya. In X. Leyva Solano and R. Icaza (eds.), *En Tiempos de Muerte: Cuerpos, Rebeldías, Resistencias*. Buenos Aires, AR: Consejo Latinoamericano de Ciencias Sociales; San Cristóbal de Las Casas, Chiapas: Cooperativa Editorial Retos, pp. 139–160.

Crosby, A. and Lykes, M. B. (2019). *Beyond Repair? Mayan Women's Protagonism in the Aftermath of Genocidal Harm*. New Brunswick, NJ: Rutgers University Press.

Cumes, A. E. (2012). Mujeres indígenas, patriarcado y colonialismo: Un desafío a la segregación comprensiva de las formas de dominio. *Anuario de Hojas de Warmi*, Universidad de Murcia, España: Servicio de Publicaciones, 17, p.16

de Coning, C. (2018). Adaptive peacebuilding. *International Affairs*, 94(2), 301–317.

Esteva, G. and Prakash, M. S. (2014). *Grassroots Post-Modernism: Remaking the Soil of Cultures*. London: Zed Books. (Original work published 1998.)

Grandin, G., Levenson, D. T. and Oglesby, E. (2011). *The Guatemala Reader: History, Culture, Politics*. Durham, NC: Duke University Press.

Gready, P. and Robins, S. (2014). From transitional to transformative justice: A new agenda for practice. *International Journal of Transitional Justice*, 8(3), 339–361.

Impunity Watch and Alliance to Break the Silence and Impunity (ECAP, MTM, UNAMG) (2017). *Changing the face of justice: Keys to the strategic litigation of the*

Sepur Zarco case. Guatemala City, Guatemala: Authors. www.impunitywatch.org/changing-the-face-of-justice-the-se (accessed 13 July 2020).

Izquierdo, B. and Viaene, L. (2018). Decolonizing transitional justice from indigenous territories. *Peace in Progress: Dealing with the past, building the future together.* Instituto Catalán Internacional para la Paz. No 34 (9). www.icip-perlapau.cat/numero34/portada (accessed 13 July 2020).

Kaqla/Grupo de Mujeres Mayas Kaqla. (2004). *La palabra y el sentir de las mujeres Mayas de Kaqla.* Guatemala City, Guatemala: Author.

Kaqla/Grupo de Mujeres Mayas Kaqla. (2006). *La internalización de la opresión: Una propuesta metodológica.* Guatemala City, Guatemala: Author.

Kaqla/Grupo de Mujeres Mayas Kaqla. (2011). *Tramas y transcendencias: Reconstruyendo historias con nuestras abuelas y madres.* Guatemala City, Guatemala: Author.

Lykes, M. B. and Crosby, A. (2015). Participatory action research as a resource for community regeneration in post-conflict contexts. In D. Bretherton and S. F. Law (eds.), *Methodologies in Peace Psychology: Peace Research by Peaceful Means.* New York: Springer, pp. 237–254.

Macleod, M. (2017). Grievances and crevices of resistance: Maya women defy Goldcorp. In R. Sieder (ed.), *Demanding Justice and Security: Indigenous Women and Legal Pluralities in Latin America.* New Brunswick, NJ: Rutgers University Press, pp. 220–241.

Méndez, L. and Carrera, A. (2014). *Mujeres Indígenas: Clamor por la Justicia. Violencia Sexual, Conflicto Armado y Despojo Violento de Tierras.* Guatemala City, Guatemala: F&G Editores.

Merry, S. E. (2006). Transnational human rights and local activism: Mapping the middle. *American Anthropologist,* 108(1), 38–51.

ODHAG – Oficina de Derechos Humanos del Arzobispado de Guatemala. (1998). *Nunca más: impactos de la violencia, informe del proyecto interdiocesano de recuperación de la memoria.* Guatemala City, Guatemala: Litografía e Imprenta LIL, SA.

Oglesby, E. and Nelson, D. M. (2016). Guatemala's genocide trial and the nexus of racism and counterinsurgency. *Journal of Genocide Research,* 18(2–3), 133–142.

Panikkar, R. (n.d.). *Dialogic dialogue.* www.raimon-panikkar.org/english/gloss-dialogical.html (accessed 13 July 2020).

Ruiz Serna, D. (2017). El territorio como víctima: Ontología política y las leyes de víctimas para comunidades indígenas y negras en Colombia. *Revista Colombiana de Antropología,* 53(2), 85–113.

Russell, G. (2010). *Gang Rapes, Forced Evictions and the Endless Nightmare of Nickel Mining in Guatemala.* Washington, DC: Rights Action.

Sieder, R. and Viaene, L. (2019). A dying river in Alta Verapaz, Guatemala. https://rivers-ercproject.eu/a-dying-river-in-alta-verapaz-guatemala// (accessed 13 July 2020).

Solano, L. (2013). Development and/as dispossession: Elite networks and extractive industry in the Franja Transversal del Norte. In C. McAllister and D. Nelson (eds.), *War by Other Means: Aftermath in Post-Genocide Guatemala.* Durham, NC: Duke University Press, pp. 119–142.

Teitel, R. G. (2000). *Transitional Justice.* New York: Oxford University Press.

Tuck, E. (2009). Suspending damage: A letter to communities. *Harvard Educational Review,* 79(3), 409–428.

Tuck, E. and Yang, K. W. (2012). Decolonization is not a metaphor. *Decolonization: Indigeneity, Education & Society*, 1(1), 1–40.

UN Declaration on the Rights of Indigenous Peoples. (2007). United Nations Declaration on the Rights of Indigenous Peoples. www.un.org/development/desa/i ndigenouspeoples/declaration-on-the-rights-of-indigenous-peoples.html (accessed 13 July 2020).

Velásquez Nimatuj, I. A. (2012). Peritaje cultural. In I. Mendia Azkue and G. Guzmán Orellana (eds.), *Ni Olvido, ni Silencio: Tribunal de Conciencia Contra la Violencia Sexual Hacia las Mujeres Durante el Conflicto Armado en Guatemala*. Bilbao, Spain: Universidad de País Vasco, Hegoa, & UNAMG, pp. 119–126.

Viaene, L. (2019). *Nimla Rahilal. Pueblos Indígenas y Justicia Transicional: Reflexiones Antropológicas*. Bilbao, Spain: Deusto.

10

Transitional or Transformative Justice? Decolonial Enactments of Adaptation and Resilience Within Palestinian Communities

Devin G. Atallah and Hana R. Masud

INTRODUCTION

Transitional justice comprises 'the full range of processes and mechanisms associated with a society's attempts to come to terms with a legacy of large-scale past abuses, in order to ensure accountability, serve justice and achieve reconciliation' (United Nations [UN], 2010). It can include criminal trials, truth and fact-finding commissions, reparations and institutional reforms. Across the wide range of processes, transitional justice approaches have tended to focus on peacebuilding in ways that have 'prioritized civil-political rights, emerging from a tradition where acts of violence are of greater interest than chronic structural violence and unequal social relations' (Gready and Robins, 2014: 342).

Evans (2016: 4) warns that, within this paradigm, issues 'such as social justice, poverty, and land inequalities have tended to be overlooked'. After all, transitional justice is rooted in liberalism and neoliberalism, economic development, universalist human rights frameworks and in colonial hegemonic discourse, which 'sees liberal democracy as its endpoint' (Gready and Robins, 2014: 341). Moreover, transitional justice as a term may be misleading because of the ways that, in periods immediately after a conflict, unjust social systems that uphold structural violence can become further entrenched, even intensified, despite dominant powers and hegemonic discourses declaring that a 'peace' has been made. Indeed, even when attempting more holistic and humanising methods, transitional justice approaches still risk marginalising ongoing structural violence because the paradigm is so deeply set within a backdrop of 'legal and state-based approaches' (Gready and Robins, 2014: 345). In this regard, it is significant that increased context-specific, grassroots approaches to peacebuilding that emphasise complexity, resilience and process over an end goal are emerging (de Coning, 2018; Gready and Robins, 2014; International Center for Transitional Justice, 2019; Ungar, 2020).

Evans (2016) maintains that in conditions marked by structural violence, *transformative* justice frameworks should be engaged rather than *transitional* justice (see also Lambourne, Chapter 2). It is in the context of transformative justice that we situate and discuss the concepts of resilience and adaptive peacebuilding. Sharing reflections and stories from our work in communities in Palestine where historical and ongoing structural violence has been set forth through systems marked by settler colonial domination, we argue that confronting these interlocking systems of oppression requires transformative justice frameworks over transitional ones.

WHAT IS TRANSFORMATIVE JUSTICE?

Transformative justice praxis represents shifts in thinking and practice, collectively re-envisioning and remaking our worlds grounded in the everyday needs and strengths of those most directly impacted by violence and oppression (Brown, 2017). Central to transformative justice is the idea 'that oppression is at the root of all forms of harm... [and] as a practice it therefore aims to address and confront those oppressions on all levels and treats this concept as an integral part to accountability and healing' (Mia Mingus, cited in Kaba and Hassan, 2019: 21). For example, GenerationFIVE is a transformative justice collective based in the United States that engages the leadership of survivors and bystanders of violence in its community prevention and intervention practices, as well as in its public actions and advocacy. GenerationFIVE is involved in cross-movement building to interrupt and heal intergenerational impacts of harm (in particular childhood sexual abuse) on individuals, families and communities. The definition of transformative justice that GenerationFIVE utilises in its multi-systemic work encompasses four overlapping goals:

1. the centrality and focus on the safety, healing and agency of marginalised groups and individuals most vulnerable to surviving harmful systems structured by oppression and violence;
2. the accountability and transformation of those who enact the oppressive systems and cause the harm;
3. the fostering of self-determined community responses and accountability; and
4. the transformation of the community and the broader social conditions and structures that create and perpetuate harm – namely – that create

and perpetuate systems of oppression, exploitation, domination and state-sponsored violence (Kaba and Hassan, 2019: 21).

Through these four interrelated goals, transformative justice praxis responds to the need to fundamentally change the multiple systems that make oppression imaginable. The emphasis is *not* on reforming existing legal systems and institutions, nor is the focus on restoring state or social structures that have been at the root of violence for so long. In fact, Gready and Robins (2014: 340) explain that, '[t]transformative justice entails a shift in focus from the legal to the social and political, and from the state and institutions to communities and everyday concerns'.

WHY TRANSFORMATIVE JUSTICE IN PALESTINE?

In this chapter, we argue for transformative justice praxis as necessary for promoting opportunities for multi-systemic resilience and adaptive peace-building in Palestine, because of the ways in which interlocking colonial oppressions so unrelentingly shape the daily lives of the Palestinian communities that we work with. Outlining and articulating the depth of conquest and subordination in Palestine is an extremely challenging endeavour and goes well beyond the scope of this chapter. Palestinian decolonial feminist scholar Nadera Shalhoub-Kevorkian (2009) has been working to understand and explicate this complexity of the Israeli Occupation system of control and domination for decades. More recently, Shalhoub-Kevorkian (2016: 1279) has begun to use the term 'Occupation of the Senses' to speak about everyday enactments of colonial rule in Palestine, which 'produce social and political separation, present[ing] an explicit aesthetic narrative of control that privileges one group over another'. Shalhoub-Kevorkian (2016: 1279) explains:

> By 'occupation of the senses', I refer to technologies that manage language, sight, sound, time and space in the colony; the administration of who acts, who speaks, who gives birth and how, and who walks/moves/drives where and how; and what kind of language, music, smells, marches, colours, cultures and scenes are promoted and inscribed over the spaces, lives and bodies of the colonized.

This analysis of the interlocking colonial oppressions and violence in Palestine overlaps with what Giacaman (2018) has called '*The Wounds Inside*'. Giacaman (2018: 16) argues that Palestinian internal, and yet always collective, wounds are 'embodied in practice . . . not attributable to depressive disease . . . which exemplifies the Palestinian condition'. The author goes on to explain the concept of the 'Wounds Inside':

As surviving civilians of war, Palestinians have experienced internal displace-ment, forced migration, and the descent of terror and violence to the level of the everyday ordinary, reaching the home front, all of it disordering our lives, producing pain, tragedy, sadness, and misery . . . Palestinians are ruled not only with brute force, but also with ambiguity, uncertainty, insecurity, loss of dignity, and deliberate humiliation, all important consequences of chronic war that need acknowledgment and not merely as a matter of physical survival worthy of assistance and support.

(Giacaman, 2018: 16)

Grounded in these understandings of the complexity of violence and oppres-sion in Palestine, in this chapter we engage transformative justice frameworks when exploring intergenerational and everyday decolonial enactments of resilience and adaptation. In doing so, we highlight the importance of the narratives and protagonisms of Palestinian communities directly impacted by structural violence towards becoming involved in creating counter-discourses, rehumanising relationships and generating deep-rooted transformations rather than collectively seeking a specific end goal where a state of peace or security is restored.

Following this line of thinking, in this chapter (which has several synergies with the arguments made by Lykes et al., Chapter 9), we share stories and reflections on critical resources and processes related to counter-narratives and counter-practices that Palestinians wage as powerful enactments of their humanity. In fact, even in writing this chapter, we have attempted to engage transformative justice praxis, which emphasises the importance of emergent strategies (Brown, 2017) and counter-stories (Wynter and McKittrick, 2015) to draw out frameworks and practices that rise 'from below' (Dutta, 2018). These are our *'theories in the flesh'* (Fernández, 2018; emphasis in original). Throughout this chapter, we thus share our reflections and counter-stories as entangled knowledges rooted in our own bodies and intergenerational, Indigenous village legacies and lands.

THEORISING FROM THE FLESH: INDIGENOUS VOICES RISING IN OUR WRITING OF THIS CHAPTER

Who are we as the authors of this chapter? We (Devin and Hana) are two differently positioned Palestinian psychologists, researchers, activists, healers and organisers. I (Devin) am a third-generation Palestinian, based in Boston as an assistant professor at a public university. I am of mixed Indigenous and settler ancestry – I am coloniser and colonised. My father was born in Chile into a Palestinian diasporic community in Santiago. My grandfather was a refugee from a village near Bethlehem, Palestine, who immigrated to Chile after the *Nakba* ('disaster' in Arabic) of 1948 when our Indigenous lands were colonised. My mother is White American from a family lineage of European descendent settlers/colonisers to Hawai'i.

I (Hana) am a postdoctoral research fellow working with Devin's research team. I was born and raised in the West Bank in a village near Ramallah. I moved to Chicago for a doctoral programme after completing my master's degree at a university in Palestine. As the Palestinian poet Mahmoud Darwish says, 'I am from there', from the active uprooting of our people. He writes:

اه يا جرحي المكابر، وطني ليس حقيبة وأنا لست مسافر، إنني العاشق ... .والأرض حبيبة

English translation:
Oh my prideful wound, my homeland is not a suitcase, and I am not a traveler, I am the lover ... and land is my sweetheart ...

As Indigenous peoples and members of colonised communities in struggle, the languages of imagination that we voice in this chapter are vital for our understanding and pursuit of transformative justice in our communities. We refuse to write about our colonised geographies in a traditional 'Whitestream' academic analysis, or by simply presenting case examples in the 'real' world. We cannot write a chapter with theory and case examples about our peoples without centring the dreams and wounds that shape our visions for transformative justice. This dream writing and radical reflecting that we practise, even in the writing of this chapter, aims towards explicitly and collectively articulating the just futures that we are struggling to work into reality. And we are not alone. Dream writing and theorising from the flesh are central parts of transformative justice praxis, because '[i]magination is one of the spoils of colonialism, which in many ways is claiming who gets to imagine the future for a given geography' (Brown, 2017: 163).

We thus arrived at the emergent understandings shared in this chapter by talking, laughing and crying together over almost daily face-to-face video conference meetings, email exchanges, text messages and phone conversations during the current period of social distancing due to COVID-19. We often recorded our conversations, asked critical questions to one another and practised radical listening and storytelling. We accompanied each other in what we came to call our transformative justice 'Dream Practice'. During these decolonial dialogues, examples of questions that we asked one another included: *What are your dreams for Palestine? What does love and justice look like to you in Palestine? How do you imagine transformative justice contributing to 'adaptative peacebuilding' (de Coning, 2018)? Where do you see this in our decolonial praxis in Palestine? Where does your decolonial praxis come from?*

What are the 'Wounds Inside' that guide you towards the work you know is needed from the depth of your own flesh and family? Where is your wholeness dishonoured as you engage in this work? What do you find yourself continuing to explain to others about Palestinian resilience? What nuances and complexities do you yourself often overlook? What are the rememberings, relations and structures that we need to create and hold to heal ourselves and our communities?

Through this writing process, our 'dream practice', we arrived at the following perspectives and counter-stories that we have decided to incorporate into this chapter. We strive to 'do justice' in our theorisations and examples of the need for transformative justice in Palestine in ways that do not underestimate the devastating uprooting and displacement of our peoples. Like the olive tree, connecting the roots with the branches across exile and generations of dispossession, we seek to be a transformative branch, in our flesh and in our words, in our writings and in our wounds. We invite readers of this chapter to sit with us under this tree, below our intergenerational branches, as we would invite you if we were together, in Palestine.

SELF-DETERMINATION OF COLONISED COMMUNITIES: ASSERTING OUR SOVEREIGNTY WITH DECOLONIAL ATTITUDE AND UNAFRAID REPLANTING

Across our research and clinical community psychology praxis in Palestine, we have come to understand that one of the foundational keys for resilience overlaps with a crucial difference between transformative justice and transitional justice. The pivotal concept here is self-determination (Atallah, 2017, 2019; Atallah and Ungar, 2020; Masud, 2019). In contrast to transitional justice, transformative justice, according to Dixon (2020), is reliant on the concepts of self-determination and accountability. In the author's words, 'violence and oppression break community ties and breed fear and distrust ... the work to create safety is to build meaningful, accountable relationships within our neighborhoods and communities' (Dixon, 2020: 17).

I (Ilana) see transformative justice in Palestine as a pathway towards making my ancestors proud. I grow myself, and I theorise resilience guided by my family trees, walking the branches with great precarity and courage. I am inspired by the footsteps of my father, Abu Abdallah, by his stories that have guided me since I was a child. He would always tell me how the Palestinian Liberation struggle was a village-to-village journey. 'Each village at a time', he would say. One village, one model. Another village, another model. As a village, we have to be the model we need, and other communities and other villages will follow in their own ways. My father would tell me: 'If you don't go plant olive trees right next to the colony, right next to the settlers, all will be lost. You go plant, even when you know the trees are at risk of being burnt, of being sprayed with chemicals by the colonisers who seek to do violence to our lands and trees at every step of the way. But still, you go, they uproot, and you plant again'. In this way, my father taught me to prioritise, to centre the praxis of replanting and reclaiming the land together (see Figure 10.1). This is *decolonial attitude*. This is *unafraid replanting*.

Central to our (Devin and Hana's) emerging transformative justice praxis in Palestine is uplifting self-determination in our Palestinian communities/bodies in the margins as Indigenous peoples living and dying under settler colonialism. This uplifting requires decolonial attitude and unafraid replanting. And these processes directly link our own transformative justice praxis with the praxes of other Indigenous peoples transnationally. For example, Huntley (2015), a transformative justice practitioner of mixed Indigenous and

FIGURE 10.1 Image of an orange tree that I (Hana) planted as a child in my home.
Photo by the author.

settler ancestry from Canada, focuses on investigating and creating films and databases, and supporting collective expressions of grief, resistance and healing related to missing and murdered Indigenous women and girls, trans and Two-Spirit people (MMIWG2S). In her transformative justice work, Huntley underlines the importance of Indigenous communities coming together to listen, learn, love and honour the memory of MMIWG2S. Central to their praxis is making sure that critical information about the perpetration of violence is 'controlled by the community and accessible to the community and for the community – not locked away in a government database' (Huntley, 2020: 57).

Huntley (2020: 57) maintains that transformative justice praxis is an *assertion of our sovereignty as Indigenous peoples*. She explains that '[w]hat distinguished us for a long time and still distinguishes us from other people who do this work was the understanding of settler colonialism as the inherent root of the violence' (Huntey, 2015: 57). Furthermore, she describes her transformative justice collective that she co-leads as working to directly challenge 'death by colonialism'; and underlines that in the context of this work, 'we understand that there can be no solution outside of completely dismantling the settler colonial state' (Huntley, 2015: 58).

I (Devin) remember first feeling connected to 'decolonial attitude' in key moments when I looked deep into the eyes of my paternal grandparents, my beloved grandmother Mariam and grandfather Jamil in Chile. I remember marching as a youth in protests with my grandmother Mariam as she waved the Palestinian flag in the streets of Santiago de Chile. Even further back, as a four-year-old child, I remember sitting under fruit trees in our family's garden with my grandfather Jamil, noticing his calloused hands, the bullet wounds up and down his leg – wounds from anti-colonial wars. I remember his stories of our village in Palestine. And how the scars in his skin expressed a certain tenderness coated with underlying and explosive rage. As the Palestinian poet in Diaspora Mandy Shunuarah (2019: 57) asks: 'I wonder if coming from a place so battered with conflict caused my family to carry strife in our bones? To wear struggle like armor because it carries the scent of home.' This is decolonial attitude – to wear struggle like armour not simply to protect or to heal, but to stay elevated in the long journey home.

If we rely on our institutions or governments, which are all set within a backdrop of colonial relations, then we are at risk of generating solutions to the problems of structural racism, settler colonialism and coloniality in ways that only mask the violence and turn it into new shapes. As Ahmed (2012: 143) explains, 'solutions to problems can create new problems'. When organisations uphold their existing colonially structured principles and neoliberal goals of power for power's sake, productivity, profit, utility, 'good' public relations and related value systems that are deeply built into institutional life, then 'practical solutions' to these problems conceal structural racism in new ways. In this context, Ahmed (2012: 143) goes further and states: 'I want to make a stronger argument here: solutions to problems are the problems given new form'.

In this light, self-determination and decolonial attitude can be critical elements to antiracist transformative justice praxis because of the perilous complexity and risk of continuing structural violence even when working against oppression. In fact, at its core, transformative justice *cannot* be about expanding the powers and resources of the institutions, the non-governmental organisations (NGOs), the governments or the nation-states that wall our lives as Palestinians. This includes a wide range of institutional and governing bodies, including (but not limited to): Israel, the United States, Iran, Great Britain, Qatar, Jordan, Egypt, the European Union, the UN, the coming and going of waves of international NGOs or even the quasi-governing parties of the 'Palestinian Authority' or 'Hamas'. We question the transformative possibilities of any and all institutions and efforts in Palestine that do not start at the beginning and end with rigorous accountability and the self-determination of our communities. Period. Palestinians are living in perhaps the 'world's largest prison' (Holmes and Balousha, 2019) (see Figure 10.2). The stakes are too high for solutions to keep concealing the intersectional, structural oppressions in Palestine in new ways. Whenever a governing party/institution/NGO/nation-state steps in to promote

FIGURE 10.2 Israeli wall enclosing a community in the West Bank. Photo by the author.

'security', 'peace' or 'prosperity' for Palestinians, we are highly suspicious of their solutions and their promises of delivering 'safety' and 'freedom' for our peoples.

In our work under conditions of such intense precarity and oppression, we have learned that meaningful transformations happen at the 'speed of trust' (Brown, 2017). Trust is one of the most precious, and yet least accessible resources available in Palestinian communities at this point in time. Therefore, our second series of counter-stories and perspectives of decolonial adaptation and resilience in this chapter focuses on the importance of creating critical connections (Brown, 2017) within our coalitions, grounded in Indigenous knowledges and courageous and trusting relations, as the heart of our transformative justice praxis.

RADICAL COALITIONS FOR TRANSFORMATIVE JUSTICE: STRENGTHENING OUR CONNECTIONS AND CAPACITIES TO STRUGGLE (WITH AND FOR EACH OTHER)

Rather than entrusting the work of transformative justice to governments or neoliberal institutions, I (Devin) have learned to focus on co-building communities of resistance and resilience grounded in Palestinian refugee camps through generative creative coalitions in collaboration with marginalised communities (Atallah, 2021; Atallah and Dutta, 2021). One such refugee camp community is directly adjacent to my Indigenous village – the valley in which my paternal grandparents' roots grow deep down into time immemorial where my grandfather Jamil was born. Over the past two years, I have organised and co-led an initiative that supports a local Community Health Worker (CHW) programme in this refugee camp (which will remain anonymous to protect privacy).

At the beginning of the development of this CHW programme two years ago, I focused on providing trainings, supervisions and evaluation research that aimed at supporting the nascent initiative in increasing its capacity to address issues related to trauma and oppression in the patients/community members that the programme serves. Those involved in the programme (the CHWs) are all young people (eighteen to twenty-five years old) who are from the same refugee camp. They work in pairs, providing home visiting services to members of their community (sometimes even to members of their own families) and supporting patients suffering from diabetes, hypertension and other health issues in the camp.

However, more than focusing on physical illness, the CHWs are often a primary social accompaniment for their patients and their families who are suffering from chronic illnesses and have been failed by the health care systems (Israeli, Palestinian Authority, NGOs and UN health systems) – and by the interlocking oppressions associated with living in poverty as a Palestinian refugee under the colonial Israeli Occupation system. For example, in a community-based participatory evaluation study that I completed with colleagues and the CHWs themselves (Atallah et al., 2019), one of the CHWs shared how his work often focused less on direct physical health concerns and more on outreach to isolated community members who face many of the same challenges that he himself struggles to overcome:

> I met a guy, he was 18 and just released from prison. He didn't want to talk to anyone, he was very isolated. He only talked to his mother, but no one else. So, his doctor told me, 'there's a guy, and you might be able to help him because you went to prison yourself'. So, I talked to him the first time and I saw that he was isolated . . . I kept meeting with him and talking with him, and I focused on helping him be a part of the community and to talk to people more. And after that, his situation got better . . . and he's much better off now.
>
> (cited in Atallah et al., 2019)

Providing social accompaniment to their patients and families, for these CHWs, means working on the frontlines of intergenerational and continual colonial oppression. The CHWs are obligated to hold a profound weight of colonial trauma with their fellow community members and families. This weight accumulates with each home visit, every day. There is no escape from this totality, from the colonial conditions deeply structured into daily life. During weekly healing circles for the CHWs that I have helped to organise, frequent sentiments that were shared early on in the process included CHWs expressing concerns such as 'my body feels heavy' or 'I'm having serious trouble sleeping'. Narratives of being overwhelmed surfaced, such as: 'I stayed and listened for more than an extra hour to a family during my home visit today because one of their children was just arrested last night. When I left their house, you know, I felt so angry and sad – my brother is also in prison'.

These experiences, and more, lead me to focus on this second core theme of transformative justice that we are emphasising in this chapter – one that harnesses the key resource of co-building radical coalitions as vehicles to be able to practise and live into justice and healing more deeply with impacted communities on the ground. Beginning in the summer of 2019, I started co-organising and co-building an Indigenous Palestinian collective as a radical space for decolonial, transformative justice praxis in Palestine to grow and support the CHWs. This shift was nurtured and supported by my co-author.

In June 2019, we were already working together in a variety of forms, including our co-organising of a decolonial racial justice pre-conference event in Chicago for the Society of Community Research and Action (SCRA). Soon after the SCRA conference, in August 2019, we launched together our new initiative in Palestine within the refugee camp community for the CHW programme. We call this new initiative the 'Palestinian Resilience Research Collaborative' (RRC). In a full-day retreat in the refugee camp, our RRC was realised as an assertion of our sovereignty as Indigenous peoples with the vision that we could become the systems that we need. We gathered together at the CHW programme in the refugee camp and established our coalition, focusing on relationships and setting the soil to be able to work towards realising more radical dreams.

In fact, we know, from our decolonial racial justice work, that, within transformative justice praxis, the most valuable resources are not grants or gold, profits or professionalism, high educational degrees or prestigious governmental or private sector positions. The most valuable resources are: time, trust, radical love, remembrance, perseverance, planfulness, playfulness, nuanced political analyses, reflexive and intersectional thinking, decolonial attitude, deep empathy, delicious and nourishing foods and rigorous emotion work – all practised in creative coalitions of people rooted in place and purpose. This coalitional, transformative justice work requires time and labours of people with radical awareness and desire to address cycles of harm, while strengthening together capacities to love and to struggle.

We organised our RRC inspired by these principles. However, identifying what matters and what 'should' work is the easy part. Living into these principles and strategies is the hard part. Even in the initial organising stage of building our coalition, we noticed how challenging it was to align our efforts in the RRC with our principles. In hindsight, we made many mistakes, even at this beginning stage. For example, a significant challenge that emerged for us on the RRC was related to how we originally organised our coalition. At the beginning, I (Devin) reached out to each potential member through a proxy. By 'proxy', I mean someone who has more accountability than I do with the broader community that I am focusing on directly impacting. I made the choice to rely on proxies, rather than using my own efforts to engage in grassroots organising in the camp. I reached out to a few key community members and asked them, as proxies, to refer potential RRC members to me. I relied on proxies because of my lack of daily community participation on the ground – I live thousands of miles away in Boston. I also relied on proxies because of my lack of fluency with the Arabic language, and my dearth of genuinely accountable and interdependent relationships with the local refugee camp community. Therefore, I leaned on the proxies as a way to gain this interdependency. I hoped, once our RRC was built, that we could eventually establish high levels of accountability in the broader community. I have since learned that this represents a mistake. I now know that, if I rely on proxies rather than doing the hard and time-consuming work of grassroots organising myself, then accountability moves further and further away on the spectrum.

In this failure, however, also resides a small victory. Problems related to the proxy model within our original development led us as the RRC to the opportunity of exploring with one another what accountability in our relations and structures could look like. These are the conversations and struggles that we are now working through. And this is exactly where we need to be – because a core dimension of transformative justice is about (re)'imagining and building the structures that we want to see replace the ones we are dismantling today' (Shank, 2020: 27). The RRC is now negotiating tensions between, on one hand, building our coalition within a mainstream resilience framework in the psychology, social work, NGO, neoliberal human service worlds as business as usual; and, on the other hand, working towards engaging decolonial, transformative justice praxis within our coalition and beyond.

In this journey, we (Devin and Hana) have learned that one of the most meaningful elements of transformative justice praxis comes from co-developing 'the capacity to struggle with each other' (Shank, 2020: 39). In order to be able to increase our capacity to struggle *for* each other against colonialism, we have to be able to struggle *with* each other in our everyday work and relationships. Committing to, and continuing, the parallel practice of developing our capacities to struggle *with* and *for* each other, as a group of diverse Palestinians on the RRC or within the CHW programme as a whole, is an incredibly radical action itself. Several of the RRC members reflected on this during a recent self-evaluation of our coalition. One of the RRC members voiced:

> Over all my years working as a psychologist in Palestine, I have never been in an affinity space with only Palestinians in my work. In fact, often, I am the only Palestinian – with many Norwegians, French, American or Israeli professions, for example, where they are the ones leading, designing, and studying, and supervising our work for my communities. Being on this team, as a Palestinian, in this co-created space, *this*, in and of itself, feels so different. So necessary.

Furthermore, we (Devin and Hana) want to highlight that developing our capacities to struggle emerged as a necessity. At times, in deeply frustrating ways, complex drama has emerged within the CHW programme itself. Part of transformative justice frameworks includes the understanding that 'trauma leads to drama' in communities as much as in individuals (Shervington, 2018).

Therefore, in response to these types of concerns, the RRC shifted the understanding of our role from primarily one of developing a manual for the CHW programme towards, instead, beginning to focus more on supporting the CHWs in their own healing and relating, on their own knowing and loving one another with accountability.

A powerful example of this was our initiative to read Paulo Freire's *Pedagogy of the Oppressed* with the CHWs chapter by chapter in Arabic. Each week in circle discussions, we invited the CHWs to read through the book collectively. This was a critical step in changing the terms of struggle – from inward relational drama on the team to building decolonial insights and owning them. In reading this book in circle together each week with the CHWs, one chapter at a time, stories of refusal of the CHWs took shape, and also stories of guilt and shame, all shared in an emerging and strengthening transformative justice practice space marked by love, trust and transparency. This practice space emergent in the CHW team required the members of the RRC to begin to grow our awareness and our practising of accountability with each other in a parallel process with the CHWs. Even at the small scale of this community praxis in the refugee camp, we do not underestimate our impact as we move with intentionality in our choices and in our relations. As Grace Lee Boggs reminds us, 'transform yourself to transform the world' (cited in Brown, 2017: 53).

We have come to realise that it is in, and through, these relational struggles – how we try to call ourselves into accountability to address, measure and hold ourselves to higher standards – that 'the choices we make align with the person we want to be in the world' (Long, 2020: 212). As an expression of this alignment, we organised dialogues during the summer of 2020 through the RRC between the Palestinian CHWs in the West Bank refugee camp and African American activists involved in Black Lives Matter (BLM) movements in the United States with whom we work in coalition in Boston and Chicago respectively. An important detail is that the CHWs themselves, during their weekly supervision healing circles, were the ones who asked for this exchange of antiracist knowledges. They were watching the uprisings of Black Americans and their allies in the United States, and the CHWs reached out to us in the RRC, asking to expand their own understandings and share resources for survival and liberation against racialised structural violence from the United States to Palestine.

We were honoured to help make this happen. As the Black freedom fighter Steve Biko (1978: 68) so powerfully wrote in the context of the struggle against South African Apartheid: 'the heart of this kind of thinking is the realisation by the blacks that the most potent weapon in the hands of the oppressor is the mind of the oppressed'. Guided by the life and example of Biko, we understand that, when we, as colonised communities, fail to organise our minds as much as we organise in the streets, we end up continuing cycles of violence and perpetuating harm ourselves, often even directly against one another in our own families and communities. As Dixon (2020: 207) envisions, 'I desire that we have stronger systems and practices that don't involve us quietly swallowing other people's anger, hurt, trauma, and pain'. This leads us to our third and final theme of transformative justice in Palestine: centring our own healing journeys, collectively resetting our wings.

RESETTING OUR WINGS: EVERYDAY ENACTMENTS OF OUR HUMANITY AND RADICAL LOVE

we know that
if the horses can't gallop

if the streets break our skull
our invisible hurt our lull

we will no longer see the stop signs
we will no longer know the low tides

we will no longer feel the indifference
of the wind

we will reset our wings.

Handal (2019: 100)

An important part of decolonial resilience is our persistence in continually adapting by collectively resetting our wings. We do not underestimate the way the constant accumulation of suffering stacks over time, space and generations in our Palestinian communities, creating conditions marked by all-encompassing trauma (Atallah, 2017). In the face of this totality of trauma, it is our embodied enactments of our humanity as Palestinians that are most protective and liberating. These embodied enactments of our humanity are critical components of our collective movements towards life. They cut across all ecological levels – even when our enactments are incredibly mundane or deeply (inter)personal – and they are always systemic and political. Condemned to 'social death', whenever we enact 'the continuation of life – in that we too go to work and school, feed our families, speak our own language – is a reminder of radical equality ... Israeli distribution of the sensible seeks to define Palestinians as criminals in every interaction, [yet] Palestinians reject such imposed definitions by performing their fully human subjectivities' (Shalhoub-Kevorkian, 2016: 1285).

Interrelated dimensions of colonial violence reduce Palestinians into 'no-bodies' (Da Silva, 2009). Therefore, when we as Palestinians perform our fully human subjectivities, we emerge as powerful decolonial enactments of resilience and adaptation through embodied means. Often, these decolonial enactments are *not* a choice but a necessity. This is true in Palestine and elsewhere in racialised and colonised communities that are actively rising/transforming. As Dixon (2020: 19) writes about her transformative justice work in Black and Brown communities in the United States facing police brutality: 'We just knew we needed to build new structures for our ultimate survival'.

As racialised and colonised peoples transnationally, we are obligated to struggle to return to our bodies and to rehumanise ourselves in our everyday acts and relations as critical enactments of resilience, adaptation and survival – 'peacebuilding' that puts our shattered pieces back into a whole. As Shalhoub-Kevorkian (2016: 1285) reminds us, Palestinians 'cannot simply appeal to their shared humanity (which the coloniser will reject), but rather are forced to constantly enact their humanity in the face of denials'. Persevering in the constant enactment of one's humanity – continually putting our shattered pieces back into a whole – brings continual pain, trauma and more suffering. Decolonial healing – collectively resetting our wings to keep flying despite the destructive power of the colonial winds – becomes a critical key for adaptive peacebuilding.

What keeps me (Hana) flying? Flying despite the weight of the pain? It is my determination despite the messy, complicated, hurtful relationships: the never-ending emotion work. Honestly, my pain is too much for me. I know that no one can take it. Only my collective self keeps me strong. It's all the women. It's all the people that will come after me. It's me, realising that I'm not alone. With this at heart, I can struggle. Knowing that we, all Palestinian women, are all going to feel it, even when we will all feel it differently. Because at its centre, it is collective pain and collective self. That is why I feel the deepest hurt when I am cast outside the herd. My grandparents were shepherds. Bedouins, nomads following light, life and continual movement. Imagining my mom, my grandparents, moving with their animals in our mountains and villages, finding the rhythm to keep everybody and every-(living)thing alive. This is my legacy. This is my path. When I am cast outside of my village, because of the Israeli Occupation and because of the patriarchy within my own family, this is the most painful. How do I find the path again? Finding the rhythm? Even when it's healthy to step outside, when I need to find shelter, safety and strength away from my village. Still, it's lonely. Still, it's painful.

As Dixon (2020: 21) highlights, 'we are invited to practice community safety skills with one of our most precious resources: our lives. In a world that is already trying to kill us with a multitude of oppressive strategies, we must be deliberate and vigilant in honoring where we each are in our journeys'. Where am I (Hana) in this journey? I am fighting for love, with my life on the line. I dream for love, and I fight for the love that completes me and my people – love that brings wholeness. Sometimes that love is not accepted, or that love is arrested, locked up, murdered or denied. Yes, it's love that we fight for. Radical love. As Cornel West (2018)[1] so powerfully expressed when speaking at the W.E.B. Du Bois Medal Ceremony in support of Colin Kaepernick, an African American activist standing up for racial equity in US contexts: 'Justice is what love looks like in public'.

This radical love, public and activist focused love, is extremely messy, complicated and confusing. We need to have courage, most of all courage to be vulnerable in private and in public. There is no easy journey home for the colonised. There is no map, no manual, no intervention plan or conceptual framework that can guide us. For colonised women, there are even fewer options for our journeys home, our journeys towards wholeness. Our private and public lives are even more policed. I'm so tired of being controlled, cold, broken and shattered. I realise what colonial violence can do to me. To us. I am touched by the vision that Huntley (2020: 62) expresses – that all of the 'work around MMIWG2S must be founded in ceremony and work with spirit – taking direction from the sisters on the other side'.

In our work in Palestine, we ask: *How can we take direction from our women frontliners, our living and our dead? Our colonised gendered selves who maintain the rhythm towards wholeness, towards life, despite all the odds?* I (Hana) know that I, an unafraid Palestinian woman in struggle, have to live into the answers. And to do so, I need an emotion strategy. We strive to bring this emotion strategy forth into our practices and structures of our Palestinian RRC, especially in the supervision and support of the CHWs in the refugee camps. Our relational work is emotional and corporeal. It is rhythmic – understanding seasons, ebbs and flows. This is adaptation lived, not out of choice, but survival. Transformative justice is that unique rhythm that skillfully puts into practice the 'nuanced understanding of organizing around trauma' (Dixon, 2020: 22).

---

[1]   The speech is available at: www.youtube.com/watch?v=AqyDdHDomtk. The sentence cited begins seven minutes and forty-nine seconds into the speech.

As Dixon (2020: 23) highlights, transformative justice work requires that we change our structures and 'cultures of judgment'. As oppressed groups rising, when we work against systems of colonial violence that are so deeply racialised, gendered, sexed and classed, our transformative strategies are always a negotiation because all our options bring promises of additional harm. This is why Dixon (2020: 25) emphasises that '[e]ven as we act urgently to resist the state violence that is killing our communities, we must also do slow work to develop community safety and resilience'. Part of changing the structures and 'cultures of judgment' requires us to lead with radical love and to resist the internalisation that people are disposable.

In our Palestinian RRC, for example, we challenge the notion that we 'throw' people away when difficulties arise. On the contrary, we try to engage counter-practices and counter-narratives that uplift our central organising principle that no one is dispensable. We need to begin investing in one another more intensively and intentionally, and to put into practice how we want to be treated. We invest in this process by asking each other questions such as: *How do we avoid replicating punitive and carceral logics? How do we resist upholding the idea that people can be rendered disposable? What does it look like for us to create transformative paths towards wholeness for not only ourselves as Palestinians, but also for Israelis, for United Statesians or for anyone else caught up within this settler colonial system of domination – even those Palestinians among us who are actively endorsing racist/patriarchal/classist ways of being and relating?*

We believe, consistent with transformative justice praxis, that, when we organise into the answers to these difficult questions, we must guard our dignity at every turn. This means that, when we as Palestinians are actively exploring our role in creating a transformative path towards wholeness for the people that oppress us (such as individuals, collectives and structures that enact colonial oppression), we refuse to swallow our pain and we refuse to ignore the centrality of settler colonial domination in our lives. Transformative justice approaches emphasise that power imbalances in conflicts need to be at the core of any strategy for safety and growth (Bonsu, 2020). In other words, even though a critical component to radical love is that no one is considered disposable and all humans deserve a transformative path towards wholeness – even the most oppressive and harmful to us and among us – the growth and transformation of the people and systems that create and perpetuate harm should never be at the expense of our own opportunities for safety, dignity and self-determination as the people on the frontlines challenging those oppressions head on (Bonsu, 2020).

For example, a Palestinian mental health worker who was a participant in my (Hana's) dissertation research in Palestine explained that he quit his job because he campaigned against having a team of Israeli psychologists come into his community and train people on family trauma. This example reflects the colonial tensions and the participant's belief that NGOs and related stakeholders too often hide oppressions behind 'neutral' or 'apolitical' solutions. In the participant's own words:

> Let me tell you why I resigned from the [name of an international NGO]. First of all, we live in the Palestinian territory of Occupied East Jerusalem, meaning we receive educational, medical treatments by Israelis, and we have no problem with that. But all of the sudden, a series of trainings and family therapy workshops were brought to us with the demand to take these trainings from an Israeli psychologist. In [name of an international NGO], our target population was Palestinian ex-detainees, after they are released and finish their detention sentences, and during their sentences we also work with their families, their children and their close friends. So, it's a very sensitive issue, and I can't fathom how [name of an international NGO] thought it would be helpful for an Israeli psychologist to come and teach us how to intervene/ facilitate family therapy under these circumstances.

The participant is now working as a taxi driver, and he expressed deeply missing the work he was doing before with detainees and their families. However, he decided to draw the line and stand up for what he believes in because the colonial tensions in the NGOs became too oppressive. Israeli professionals may be able to provide helpful tools and models to Palestinian mental health workers. The participant in this research was clear that he held no objection to such exchanges with Israelis. But these exchanges must occur in ways that challenge the relations between the knower 'coloniser' and the object 'colonised'. The participant went on to explain his decolonial analysis and opposition:

> Why?! Because I am not a neutral person! I keep my own knowledge of my people. I refuse to have an Israeli teach me about family therapy on how to work with a martyr's mother. So, we asked why trainings by an Israeli in this way? The answer, from the NGO, was because we are neutral and can bring in any professionals, Israeli or Palestinian professionals . . . we didn't want to engage in these policies, it was just too much . . . so I resigned.

The training by the team of Israeli professionals imposed on the Palestinian mental workers by the international NGO was understood by this participant as an attempt to disconnect him from his own community and devalue his lived experiences. Attempts to devalue this knowledge of his people is a type of colonial violence in itself. His refusal to accept this was a decolonial enactment of adaptation and resilience. Transformative justice is about holding accountable the people who are actively involved in upholding systems that cause harm. And this brings struggle. We do not underestimate the daily state of siege of Palestinians living under occupation, and we see the everyday refusal that this Palestinian participant enacted as a critical practice and a powerful example of the need for transformative justice praxis in Palestine to be more rigorously engaged.

CONCLUSION

Decolonial enactments of adaptation and resilience in Palestine require that we courageously and collectively perform our fully human subjectivities across relations and movements for healing, justice and peace. The multiplicity of frontlines of colonial oppressions in the everyday lives of Palestinians make complex and layered wounds in our bodies, minds, relations, communities and lands through deeply embodied pathways (Atallah, 2017; Giacaman, 2018; Shalhoub-Kevorkian, 2016). Consequently, rather than refer to *transitional* justice, in this chapter we have argued that adaptation and resilience in Palestine require *transformative* justice paradigms and practices, which powerfully underscore the need for complex, collective struggles that can challenge the embodied, relational, racialised, interpersonal, intrapersonal and intergenerational expressions of harm. Being condemned to remain under settler colonial occupation into unknown futures requires our constant (re)envisioning of decolonial potentials and radical possibilities.

In this chapter, we shared perspectives and counter-stories grounded in our radical reflecting and 'dream practice' that we engaged in to explicitly and collectively articulate the just futures that we are struggling to work into reality. This includes our reflecting on how Palestinians engage in counter-hegemonic reclaiming and practising of humanity each and every day in our relationships and in our coalitions. Furthermore, in this chapter, we have shown how attempts at abolishing dehumanisation and reclaiming our humanity within everyday enactments of adaptation and resilience are complex and messy, are symbolic and practical, are material and metaphorical, are temporal and spatial and are everything in-between (Shalhoub-Kevorkian, 2016). This praxis works to re-envision possible futures. This re-envisioning is abolitionist – it requires an end. Transformative justice pushes towards the end of the pressure of the coloniser upon the necks of the colonised. No reforms or transitions are necessary. Just as slavery will never require reform, colonialism does not either. They both require abolition. This is transformative justice in Palestine.

REFERENCES

Ahmed, S. (2012). *On Being Included: Racism and Diversity in Institutional Life.* Durham, NC: Duke University Press.

Atallah, D. G. (2017). A community-based qualitative study of intergenerational resilience with Palestinian refugee families facing structural violence and historical trauma. *Transcultural Psychiatry*, 54, 357–383.

Atallah, D. G. (2021). Decolonial enactments of human resilience: Stories of Palestinian families from beyond the Wall. In M. Ungar (ed.), *Multisystemic resilience: Adaptation and Transformation in Contexts of Change.* New York: Oxford University Press, pp. 565–583.

Atallah, D. G., Bacigalupe, G. and Repetto, P. (2019). Centering at the margins: Critical community resilience praxis. *Journal of Humanistic Psychology*, https://doi.org/10.1177%2F0022167818825305

Atallah, D. G., Shapiro, E. R., Al-Azraq, N., Qaisi, Y. and Suyemoto, K. L. (2018). Decolonizing qualitative research through transformative community engagement: Critical investigation of resilience with Palestinian refugees in the West Bank. *Qualitative Research in Psychology*, 15(4), 489–519.

Atallah, D., Kramer, S., Al Bast, L., Stanley, B., Scales, D., Jawabreh, N., Alazzah, S., Abu Srour, M., Abedrabbu, H., Louis, H., Abu Srour, R., Alazzah, S., Al Mashakhah, M., Darwish, M., Ewise, A., Rumi, M. and Wispelwey, B. (2019). Community health work under occupation: Towards the development of a new model to address social and political determinants of health in Palestinian refugee camps. *CHW Central.* https://chwcentral.org/community-health-work-under-occupation-towards-the-development-of-a-new-model-to-address-social-and-political-determinants-of-health-in-palestinian-refugee-camps/

Atallah, D. G. and Ungar, M. (2020). Indigenous groups facing environmental racism: Human rights, resilience, and resistance in Palestinian communities of the West Bank and the Mapuche of Chile. In P. Hagenaars, M. Plavsic, N. Sveaass, U. Wagner and T. Wainwright (eds.), *Human Rights Education for Psychologists.* New York: Routledge, pp. 193–206.

Atallah, D. G. and Dutta, U. (2021). 'Creatively in coalition' from Palestine to India: Weaving stories of refusal and community as decolonial praxis. *Journal of Social Issues*, https://doi.org/10.1111/josi.12460.

Biko, S. (1978). *I Write What I Like.* London: The Bowerdean Press.

Bonsu, J. E. (2020). Excerpt from 'Black Queer Feminism as Praxis'. In E. Dixon and L. L. Piepzna-Samarasinha (eds.), *Beyond Survival: Strategies and Stories from the Transformative Justice Movement.* Chico: AK Press, pp. 49–54.

Brown, A. M. (2017). *Emergent Strategy: Shaping Change, Changing Worlds.* Chico: AK Press.

Cacho, L. M. (2012). *Social Death: Racialized Rightlessness and the Criminalization of the Unprotected*, Vol. 7. New York: New York University Press.

Da Silva, D. F. (2009). No-bodies: Law, raciality and violence. *Griffith Law Review*, 18, 212–236.

de Coning, C. (2018). Adaptive peacebuilding. *International Affairs*, 94(2), 301–317.

Dixon, E. (2020). Building community safety. In E. Dixon and L. L. Piepzna-Samarasinha (eds.), *Beyond Survival: Strategies and Stories from the Transformative Justice Movement*. Chico, CA: AK Press, pp. 15–26.

Dixon, E. (2020). I would like to return my TJ process. In E. Dixon and L. L. Piepzna-Samarasinha (eds.), *Beyond Survival: Strategies and Stories from the Transformative Justice Movement*. Chico: AK Press, pp. 205–208.

Dixon, E. and Piepzna-Samarasinha, L. L. (eds.) (2020). *Beyond Survival: Strategies and Stories from the Transformative Justice Movement*. Chico: AK Press.

Dutta, U. (2016). Prioritizing the local in an era of globalization: A proposal for decentering community psychology. *American Journal of Community Psychology*, 58(3–4), 329–338.

Dutta, U. (2018). Decolonizing 'community' in community psychology. *American Journal of Community Psychology*, 62(3–4), 272–282.

Evans, M. (2016). Structural violence, socioeconomic rights and transformative justice. *Journal of Human Rights*, 15(1), 1–20.

Fanon, F. (1963). *The Wretched of the Earth*. New York: Grove Press.

Fernández, J. S. (2018). Toward an ethical reflective practice of a theory in the flesh: Embodied subjectivities in a youth participatory action research mural project. *American Journal of Community Psychology*, 62, 221–232.

Giacaman, R. (2018). Reframing public health in wartime: From the biomedical model to the 'Wounds Inside'. *Journal of Palestine Studies*, 47(2), 9–27.

Gready, P. and Robins, S. (2014). From transitional to transformative justice: A new agenda for practice. *International Journal of Transitional Justice*, 8(3), 339–361.

Holmes, O. and Balousha, H. (2019). Gaza's generation blockade: Young lives in the 'world's largest prison'. *The Guardian*. www.theguardian.com/world/2019/mar/12/generation-blockade-gaza-young-palestinians-who-cannot-leave (accessed 12 February 2021).

Hooks, B. (2001). *All about Love: New Visions*. Harper Perennial.

Huntley, A. (2015). Meet Audrey Huntley, Canada. *Nobel Women's Initiative*. https://nobelwomensinitiative.org/meet-audrey-huntley-canada/ (accessed 14 May 2020).

Huntley, A. (2020). From breaking silence to community control. In E. Dixon and L. L. Piepzna-Samarasinha (eds.), *Beyond Survival: Strategies and Stories from the Transformative Justice Movement*. Chico: AK Press, pp. 55–66.

International Center for Transitional Justice. (2019). On solid ground: Building sustainable peace and development after massive human rights violations – Report of the Working Group on Transitional Justice and SDG16+. Retrieved from: www.ictj.org/sites/default/files/ICTJ_Report_WG-TJ-SDG16%2B_2019_Web.pdf (accessed 3 September 2020).

Kaba, M. and Hassan, S. (2019). *Fumbling Towards Repair: A Workbook for Community Accountability Facilitators*. Chicago, IL: Project NIA and Just Practice.

Long, E. (2020). Vent Diagrams as healing practice. In E. Dixon and L. L. Piepzna-Samarasinha (eds.), *Beyond Survival: Strategies and Stories from the Transformative Justice Movement*. Chico: AK Press, pp. 209–220.

Lorde, A. (1984). *Sister Outsider: Essays and Speeches*. Berkeley: Crossing Press.

Lugones, M. (2010). Toward a decolonial feminism. *Hypatia*, 25(4), 742–759.

Maldonado-Torres, N. (2007). On the coloniality of being. *Cultural Studies*, 21(2), 240–270.

Masud, H. R. (2019). *NGOs Embodying Decoloniality: Towards Emancipatory Psychological Practice and Pedagogy in Palestine* (dissertations). https://digitalcommons.nl.edu/diss/418/ (accessed 9 July 2020).

Moraga, C. and Anzaldúa, G. (eds.) (2015). *This Bridge Called my Back: Writings by Radical Women of Color*, 4th ed. Albany, NY: SUNY Press.

Said, E. (1984). Permission to narrate. *Journal of Palestine Studies*, 13(3), 27–48.

Shalhoub-Kevorkian, N. (2009). *Militarization and Violence Against Women in Conflict Zones in the Middle East: A Palestinian Case-Study*. New York: Cambridge University Press.

Shalhoub-Kevorkian, N. (2016). The occupation of the senses: The prosthetic and aesthetic of state terror. *British Journal of Criminology*, 57, 1279–1300.

Shervington, D. (2018). *Healing is the Revolution*. New Orleans: Institute of Women & Ethnic Studies.

Shank, A. A. (2020). Beyond firing. In E. Dixon and L. L. Piepzna-Samarasinha (eds.), *Beyond Survival: Strategies and Stories from the Transformative Justice Movement*. Chico: AK Press, pp. 27–42.

Shara, N. (2020). Facing shame. In E. Dixon and L. L. Piepzna-Samarasinha (eds.), *Beyond Survival: Strategies and Stories from the Transformative Justice Movement*. Chico: AK Press, pp. 221–232.

Shunnarah, M. (2019). Where is the old country? In I. Khalidi (ed.), *The Palestine Issue: Prose, Poetry, and Art Exploring Arab America*. St. Paul, MN: Mizna, Inc., pp. 55–60.

United Nations. (2010). Guidance Note of the Secretary-General: United Nations Approach to Transitional Justice. www.un.org/ruleoflaw/files/TJ_Guidance_Note_March_2010FINAL.pdf (accessed 11 May 2020).

West, C. (2018). *Colin Kaepernick: Hutchins Center Honors – W. E. B. Du Bois Medal Ceremony*. www.youtube.com/watch?v=AqyDdHDomtk (accessed 18 June 2020).

Wynter, S. and McKittrick, K. (2015). Unparalleled catastrophe for our species. In K. McKittrick (ed.), *Sylvia Wynter: On Being Human as Praxis*. Durham, NC: Duke University Press, pp. 9–89.

11

Fitting the Pieces Together: Implications for Resilience, Adaptive Peacebuilding and Transitional Justice

Cedric de Coning

INTRODUCTION

This edited volume set out to explore how resilience, adaptive peacebuilding and transitional justice can help societies recover after collective violence. To do so, it examined diverse societies across Africa, Asia, Europe, Latin America and the Middle East that have experienced, or are continuing to experience, violence. The eight case studies – Bosnia-Herzegovina (BiH), Rwanda, Uganda, Bangladesh, Cambodia, Colombia, Guatemala and Palestine – provide in-depth conceptual and empirical analyses of resilience and adaptive peacebuilding in a range of transitional justice settings. This final chapter will reflect on what we have learned from the cases covered in this volume. In particular, it will discuss how they enrich our understanding of the concepts of resilience, adaptive peacebuilding and transitional justice, and what they tell us about the complex ways that resilience and adaptive peacebuilding manifest in transitional and post-conflict settings. The chapter begins with a discussion of adaptive peacebuilding and resilience in transitional justice contexts.

ADAPTIVE PEACEBUILDING

Adaptive peacebuilding is an approach that involves peacebuilders, together with the communities and people affected by conflict and violence, actively engaging in a structured and iterative process to sustain peace through learning and adaptation. The adaptive peacebuilding approach aims at supporting societies to develop the resilience and robustness that they need to cope with and adapt to change, by helping them to develop greater levels of complexity in their social institutions (de Coning, 2018: 307).

Adaptive peacebuilding implies that international and national actors engaged in conflict resolution and peace processes have to take responsibility – ethically – for their choices and actions. Taking responsibility means that policymakers and peacebuilders need to think through the ethical implications of both their macro theories for resolving conflict and sustaining peace and the specific choices that they make in any given context. They have to be conscious of the knowledge claims and assumptions that inform their choices, and the potential conse-quences – intended and unintended – of their actions. The primary directive that should guide all conflict resolution and peacebuilding initiatives is to 'do no harm' (Anderson, 1999).

Adaptive peacebuilding is thus a conscious normative and functional approach to peacebuilding and transitional justice aimed at navigating the complexity inherent in trying to nudge societal change processes towards sustaining peace, without interfering so much that it causes harm by inadvert-ently disrupting the very feedback loops critical for self-organisation to emerge and become sustainable. There are three key concepts that inform adaptive peacebuilding, namely complexity, local ownership (linked to self-organisation) and resilience.

Complexity

Complexity theory provides a theoretical (ontological and epistemological) framework for understanding how social systems function, including how they react to shocks and stressors. By applying some of the insights derived from the study of complex systems, we may be able to strengthen the ability of societies to prevent, manage, withstand and recover from violent conflict. Social sys-tems are empirically complex. This means that they are a particular type of system that has the ability to adapt and demonstrate emergent properties, including self-organising behaviour. These systems emerge, and are main-tained, as a result of the dynamic and non-linear interactions of the individuals and institutions that make up the system, based on the information available to them locally. Also highly significant are their interactions with their environ-ment and the modulated feedback that they receive from other elements of the system (Cilliers, 1998; de Coning, 2016: 198).

Complicated systems, such as an advanced spacecraft or a super-computer, can be comprehensively described and understood through observation and analysis of their component parts and how they work together to produce a specific effect. Designing, building and launching a spacecraft into space, for example, is highly complicated, but, once it is mastered, the same process can be repeated with a reasonable chance of success. In fact, the most frequently used rocket to send people and goods into space is the Soviet Soyuz rocket, and this has a core design that has been in use since 1967 (European Space Agency, n.d.). In complex systems, in contrast, the whole has properties that cannot be found in the constituent elements or in the sum of their properties (Cilliers, 1998). In social systems, for example, the society as a whole develops and sustains norms, identities, structures or hierarchies and behaviours that serve the common needs of the community. When we study people as part of a society, as opposed to studying them as individuals, a different side of their being is revealed, including aspects related to their role in a family and their society. The African philosophy of *Ubuntu* covers this well, in its saying: 'I am myself through you' (Akinola and Uzodike, 2018: 95).

As social systems are also highly dynamic, non-linear and emergent, it is not possible to find general laws or rules or a neat algorithm that will help us to predict with certainty how they will react. For example, if a small amount of foreign aid slightly increases economic growth, we might expect that more aid should produce greater growth (Jervis, 1997). However, in complex systems, the relationships between variables are dynamic and disproportionate (Kiehl, 1995). Similarly, if a particular process helped to sustain peace in one society, such as the Truth and Reconciliation Commission (TRC) in South Africa, it cannot be repeated in another context with any reasonable expectation that it will have the same outcome (de Coning, 2016). Such uncertainty is not a reflection of imperfect knowledge, inadequate planning or implementation (Popolo, 2011: 209). It is an intrinsic quality of complex systems. Acknowledging uncertainty as a starting point is what Barnett refers to as cultivating 'a spirit of epistemological uncertainty' (cited in Benner et al., 2011: 225). Making a similar point specifically in the context of peace and conflict, Hughes (2012: 116) argues that 'an explicit, reflexive awareness of the incompleteness of our understanding is (. . .) vital so that decisions are taken with a large degree of caution (and humility) while at the same time demanding that we think through the possible ramifications'.

Until fairly recently, the transitional justice and peacebuilding community were confident in their ability to diagnose the problems affecting a society emerging from conflict and to prescribe the steps that such a society needed to take to transform its judicial and related systems in order to sustain peace (World Bank, 2011). The outcome was believed to be more or less guaranteed if the design was followed, and uncertainty was seen as a risk that could be managed with good planning (Eriksen, 2009: 662). Complexity provides us with the theoretical framework for understanding the hubris of these assumptions. Indeed, interventions in complex systems can produce unforeseen consequences and create new problems (Preiser et al., 2018), as some of the case studies in this volume have showed.

It is important to underline, however, that, within a complexity framework, non-linearity is not associated with disorder and chaos. In fact, non-linearity is an essential ingredient in the processes of emergence and self-organisation that generate order in complex systems. While these systems cannot do without hierarchy and structure, hierarchy is not hard-wired or externally determined and controlled. It is emergent and self-organised, and thus it changes as the system adapts and evolves in response to its environment (Cilliers, 2001). Indeed, the vitality of the system depends on its ability to transform itself, including its structure and hierarchy (Chapman, 2002). Fundamentally, thus, non-linearity is the element that distinguishes a complex system from a deterministic or mechanical system. A rocket is fully knowable, predictable and, hence, controllable in principle. It is also unable to do anything that is not pre-programmed or designed. In contrast, the non-linearity in complex systems is what makes it possible for them to adapt and to evolve. Non-linearity is therefore an essential part, in fact a pre-condition, for emergence, self-organisation and adaptation in complex systems (Cilliers, 1998).

Self-organisation and Local Ownership

Self-organisation refers to the ability of a complex system to organise, regulate and maintain itself without needing an external or internal managing or controlling agent. For example, the economy is a self-organising social system that continuously responds to a large number of factors without requiring a controlling agent. The organisation of the economic system as a whole comes about as a result of the interactions between the various agents (individuals and institutions like central banks, investors and private companies) that constitute the system and its environment (Cilliers, 1998). No single agent or group of agents controls the economic system, but many try to influence the behaviour of the system. Through these interactions, and the feedback effects that they have on each other, the economy self-organises spontaneously. This is an emergent process that comes about as a result of the cumulative and collective interactions of all the agents in the system. The economy is just a sub-set of the larger social system of which it forms a part, and all social systems are similarly self-organising. Self-organisation in the social context refers to the various processes and mechanisms a society uses to manage itself, including in times of crisis. It speaks to the ability of a society to manage its tensions, pressures, disputes, crises and shocks without collapsing into disorder and violence.

Adaptive peacebuilding is an approach or method where peacebuilders, together with the communities and people affected by conflict, actively engage in a structured process to sustain peace and resolve conflicts (de Coning, 2018). Instead of using a pre-designed blueprint, or a top-down control model, the adaptive peacebuilding approach is a conscious method for engaging with a particular society to develop an intervention together with them from the bottom up. The aim is to stimulate self-organisation, not to control how a community will act. A self-organised social system cannot be directed to achieve a specific predetermined result. However, it can be nudged in a direction, although whether it will follow that direction is uncertain and unpredictable. This is a process that needs to be undertaken together with the community, and as such it encourages and enables local ownership. The end result is often more appropriate to the context than what any pre-determined plan could have foreseen. The adaptive peacebuilding approach is thus a specific methodology for coping with the complexity, uncertainty and unpredictability we encounter when attempting to influence complex social systems.

The recognition in the adaptive peacebuilding approach of the fact that there is no external privileged knowledge or predetermined model, and that the design of solutions for peace should emerge from the process itself, creates meaningful opportunities for all stakeholders, and especially for local societies and communities, to co-own and co-manage the process (de Coning, 2018). The adaptive peacebuilding approach may also help to clarify the different political interests at stake or reveal spoilers, because of its focus on proactive monitoring and feedback.

A key feature of the adaptive peacebuilding approach is the recognition of the inherently political nature of peacebuilding. Choices regarding who gets to make decisions about which opportunities to explore, which programmes to replicate or expand and which criteria will be used in the process all have political dimensions and political effects. Decisions regarding which policy options to pursue are rarely technical. They are influenced by political judgements about who may lose or gain, and as a result it is rare that the technical aspects of a particular initiative will override what is seen as politically feasible in a given context. This also implies that a decision to pursue a particular initiative may face pushback from those who view it as harmful to their interests or were excluded from the process. An approach informed by complexity theory thus recognises that forward momentum is not inevitable (de Coning, 2018).

A core insight from complexity theory for peacebuilding is that, in order for a peace process to become self-sustaining, resilient social institutions need to emerge from within, i.e. from the local culture, history and socio-economic context. External actors, like international peacebuilders, or the national government in the case of a local society or group, can assist and facilitate this process, but if they interfere too much they will undermine the self-organising processes necessary to sustain resilient social institutions. A complexity-informed approach suggests that those engaged in transitional justice and peacebuilding should focus their efforts on safeguarding, stimulating, facilitating and creating the space for societies to develop resilient capacities for self-organisation (de Coning, 2016: 173).

Resilience

Many definitions of resilience exist, but it is broadly understood as the ability to manage, withstand and recover from shocks (Joseph, 2018: 3). To this general definition, Folke et al. (2010) add that withstanding a shock means retaining or recovering essentially the same function, structure, feedbacks and, by extension, identity. Ungar (2013: 256) defines resilience as 'the capacity of both individuals and their environments to interact in ways that optimize developmental processes' (see also Chapter 1). In the adaptive peacebuilding context, we can conceptualise resilience as the ability of a society to prevent, manage and recover from violent conflict in ways that maximise developmental processes (de Coning, 2016).

Adaptive capacity is understood as the ability to thrive in an environment characterised by change (Joseph, 2018: 14). In the adaptive peacebuilding context, it refers to the ability of a society to adjust to disruptive change, to take advantage of opportunities and to respond to consequences (Engle, 2011: 648). Resilience and adaptive capacity are complementary and mutually reinforcing. Adaptive capacity emphasises the extent to which civil society and social institutions are able to adapt to rapid or drastic change, i.e. their flexibility and responsiveness in the face of crisis. Resilience underlines the ability of these social institutions to prevent, manage and recover from the effects of a disruption. The more adaptive capacity a society has, the more resilient it will be. Resilience is broader than adaptive capacity; it covers reducing vulnerability and managing risks – for example, by taking various preventative actions – and other forms of dealing with and responding to shocks beyond adapting to change.

Both resilience and adaptive capacity strongly rely on social capital (Putnam, 1993). Social capital refers to the resources and other public goods that individuals and social institutions can access via networks and communities. The Organisation for Economic Co-operation and Development

(OECD) defines social capital as networks that, together with shared norms, values and understandings, facilitate co-operation within or among groups (Keeley, 2007: 102). In other words, social capital refers to how social networks foster understanding and trust, and in the process enable people to work together. By extension, resilience, adaptive capacity and social capital combined are fundamentally about the ability of a society or community to develop and evolve while at the same time retaining essential values, cohesion and identity. Collectively, these concepts describe a society or community's systemic capacities to reorganise, learn and adapt in response to significant disruptions, such as violent conflict or civil war.

In Chapter 1, Michael Ungar introduced and contextualised the concept of multi-systemic resilience and its relevance to the field of transitional justice. He argued that the concept of resilience is best understood as a process whereby individual capital and social capital interact in ways that create optimal outcomes in stressed environments. He further explained that any system may show patterns of persistence, resistance, recovery, adaptation or transformation depending on the resources available to it to support change. Ungar's chapter examined these processes and how they affect systems simultaneously at multiple levels.

In Chapter 2, Wendy Lambourne explored how resilience thinking can contribute to the transformative potential of transitional justice processes, and how these processes can foster and deepen our understanding of both resilience and adaptive peacebuilding. Her chapter also demonstrated that building resilient communities is a logical consequence of more inclusive justice and facilitated participation (core processes of both adaptive peacebuilding and transitional justice), along with healing and reconciliation.

Understanding resilience as a multi-systemic concept can help to explain how social systems affected by transitional justice (both judicial and non-judicial processes) respond to stressors, helping individuals, communities and institutions to survive and thrive. Awareness of the diversity of forms that resilience can take in these societies, and of how individuals and communities – in interaction with their wider social ecologies – utilise and develop their own resilience resources is, in turn, an important part of moving away from template approaches to 'building peace'.

In this regard, an adaptive peacebuilding approach differs from more conventional top-down approaches in two key ways, namely: (1) recognising the resilience and adaptive capacity of facilitated self-organisation and (2) understanding that optimal responses have to be emergent from the context and community. The aim, thus, is not to implement a specific pre-designed, step-by-step transitional justice, recovery or reconciliation programme, but rather to engage the community in a process that identifies and builds consensus around what the problem is, what the intended responses could be and how to proceed. This is not a one-off event (e.g. a two-hour workshop). There needs to be a structured learning process wherein different initiatives are assessed and decisions are made about whether to further adapt or scale up those initiatives that show promise. The result is thus a continuous adaptation based on experimentation, feedback and collective learning. This pattern is very much in evidence in the case studies presented throughout this volume.

One of the book's core aims was to develop the idea of adaptive peacebuilding, both conceptually and empirically. Specifically, the chapters have analysed whether and how transitional justice processes themselves can contribute to adaptive peacebuilding in the sense of helping to foster adaptive capacity and resilience across complex systems that have experienced the shocks and stressors of war, conflict and large-scale violence. The next section reflects on what we can learn from them about resilience, adaptive peacebuilding and transitional justice.

WHAT HAVE WE LEARNED?

The chapters in this volume have covered a variety of conflict contexts across various parts of the world, exploring in depth one or more micro-level experiences of conflict in order to assess whether and how different transitional justice initiatives have contributed to resilience and adaptive peacebuilding. Some common inter-linked themes have emerged, and this section focuses on three in particular, namely self-organisation, unintended consequences and process.

Self-organisation

A common theme that emerges from the case studies is the idea that resilience is associated with people affected by conflict coming together to form co-operative networks that help them cope with violence or its aftermath. In Chapter 5 on northern Uganda, for example, Philipp Schulz and Fred Ngomokwe showed how survivors' groups enable those involved in them, through creative and participatory practices, to strengthen their agency and craft spaces for healing, justice and peacebuilding. The groups help survivors to develop adaptive and transformative capacities that assist them to process and respond to shocks, stressors and harms resulting from mass violence (and its aftermath). These survivors' groups are engaged in a variety of different activities, including psychosocial peer support, collective income-generating activities and joint financial schemes, such as Village Savings and Loan Associations.

Schulz and Ngomokwe argue that this kind of self-organising group activity enables survivors to interact with their wider socio-ecological environments in ways that facilitate positive psychological, physical and social development, thereby also aiding recovery, adaptation and transformation. Based on these findings, they view adaptive peacebuilding and resilience as multi-faceted processes that require relationality and local ownership, and which embrace the complexities and diversities of post-conflict and post-disaster lived realities (Chandler, 2012; de Coning, 2018; Ungar, 2018). Schulz and Ngomokwe conclude their chapter by setting in place processes for survivors to engage with their experiences on their own terms – structured around self-organisation, local ownership and internal capacities, as well as relationality and social networks – and thus for the groups to contribute towards adaptively building peace and fostering resilience at the local level and among their members.

Similarly, in Chapter 8, in the context of her study of the conflict and peace process in Colombia, Sanne Weber finds that social relations and organisation go a long way towards explaining how people manage to continue living despite multiple harms and hardships. In particular, she highlights the role of organisations that arose from the struggle to defend the land and rebuild the communities, and which play an important role in the process of returning people to their land after displacement. Weber argues that these actions, for which organisation among people was key, can be seen as a form of 'radical citizenship'. According to her, these findings suggest that unity, organisation and the forms of active citizenship that they enabled are crucial aspects of the social resilience outlined by Michael Ungar in Chapter 1. She maintains that social resilience enables individuals and communities to navigate and negotiate access to the resources they need, such as land and financial support.

However, Weber also finds that transitional justice and related peacebuilding processes in Colombia have not contributed to strengthening this social resilience. She points out that the Colombia case shows not only the risks of raising expectations but also the impact of unmet expectations and disappointments on people's ability and willingness to place their trust in either the peace process or their leaders. Weber finds that these frustrations resulted in people choosing to focus their energy on their own interests, rather than investing in struggles for the greater good. She argues that this eventually makes it harder to overcome the structural marginalisation and lack of access to basic social and infrastructural services that the communities face. In order to address this, she underlines that transitional justice should promote social resilience, or the capacity of survivors to organise themselves – as communities or groups of survivors – to protect and promote their own well-being. She concludes that self-organisation allows survivors to adapt their demands and negotiation strategies to changes on the ground and resulting needs, even beyond the often limited timespan of transitional justice mechanisms. Weber thus calls for increasing social resilience, by strengthening organisational and lobbying skills among people and promoting a collective identity and unity, and argues that facilitating self-organisation will produce more appropriate and long-term results than the short-term impact of a compensation cheque.

In Chapter 9, Lykes, Crosby and Alvarez reflect on the experiences of Mayan women in Guatemala. Similarly placing a strong emphasis on self-organisation, they demonstrate that various group processes helped to give voice 'to multiple experiences of previously silenced embodied suffering'. This resulted in the protagonists with whom they worked 'standing up to publicly assert their rights as women, denouncing not only racialised war-based violations of their bodies but also contemporary gendered family violence and corporate extraction of natural resources in their territories'.

In Chapter 3, Janine Natalya Clark makes the case for a new framing of transitional justice that gives greater attention to broader social-ecological systems. She points out, however, that it is not about simply 'correcting' them through administrative reforms or technical measures, but, rather, about helping to foster resilient systems that can effectively and positively adapt to adversity. Part of the process of operationalising the synergy between adaptive peacebuilding and transitional justice, therefore, involves stimulating self-organisation and exploring ways of fostering resilience within often overlooked community-level systems. In other words, Clark argues for a reframing of transitional justice that places greater emphasis on the fundamental self-organising systems that connect people (Clark, 2019, 2020c), thereby strengthening local capacity to advocate for and exert pressure for broader systemic change within the context of adaptive peacebuilding.

These case studies have thus identified how some peacebuilding and transitional justice practices can promote and facilitate the capacity of groups that have experienced harm to organise themselves, and how this may help to foster resilience by enabling and empowering communities to direct their own recovery processes.

More broadly, what the case studies in this volume also show is that conflict resolution and peacebuilding are delicate processes. An inherent tension exists between, on one hand, the act of promoting a process of self-organisation from the outside, and, on the other hand, excessive external interference that ultimately undermines self-organisation. From a complexity perspective, one can argue that, whenever external peacebuilders intervene to solve a perceived problem in the local system, they interrupt the internal feedback process and thus deny the local system the opportunity to respond to a problem or challenge itself, thereby impeding self-organisation and resilience. State and social institutions develop resilience through trial and error over generations. Too much filtering and cushioning slow down and inhibit these processes. Acknowledging this tension – and the constraints that it poses – can help us to understand why many international transitional justice and peacebuilding interventions have made the mistake of interfering so much that they ultimately undermine the ability of local system to self-organise (de Coning, 2018). Jennie Burnet's discussion in Chapter 4 illustrates this point.

International peacebuilding and transitional justice interventions should provide security guarantees and maintain the outer parameters of acceptable state behaviour in the international system; and they should stimulate, facilitate and create the space for the emergence of robust and resilient self-organised systems. However, international peacebuilding and transitional justice interventions should not interfere in the local social process with the goal of engineering a specific outcome. Trying to control the outcome will, in all probability, produce the opposite of what peacebuilding aims to achieve; it will generate ongoing instability and dependence, and it will undermine self-sustainability (de Coning, 2016). The key to more effective peacebuilding and transitional justice thus lies in finding the appropriate balance between international support and local ownership.

To elaborate on an earlier point, the essential difference between a complex-systems approach and a determined-design approach like the liberal peace model is that, under the latter, the solution is understood to come from the outside (Liden, 2009). In the liberal peace model, the agency to solve the problem resides in the international capacity to assess the situation and to design a solution and to then undertake an intervention where the solution is applied (Eriksen, 2009). The insight from complexity theory for transitional justice is that, for any society to live sustainably in peace, it needs to generate its own capacity to self-organise. This is a process that can be facilitated and supported by external peacebuilders, but it ultimately has to be a bottom-up and home-grown process. Self-organisation cannot be imposed (de Coning, 2016).

Unintended Consequences and Unintentional Harm

A second common theme that runs across many of the chapters in this volume is that attempts to strengthen societal or community resilience at one place in the system (even if they are not expressly framed as such) can cause harm in another place, or at another level. In their introduction to this volume, Janine Natalya Clark and Michael Ungar remind us that adding a resilience lens highlights the importance of focusing not just on direct victims of violence and human rights abuses but also on their wider social ecologies. Peacebuilding and transitional justice practitioners thus need to anticipate that interventions in complex systems will generate a number of effects, not all of them intended or desired. While this underscores the crucial point that resilience is not inherently good (or bad) in itself, it also underlines that practitioners must be ready to monitor and mitigate negative side-effects, thereby adapting their actions to prevent or reduce harm (Aoi et al., 2007).

In Chapter 4, in her case study of the 1994 Rwandan genocide, Jennie Burnet points out that many applications of resilience 'depoliticise processes that are, at heart, deeply political'. She argues that politics produced the Rwandan genocide, and so it is no surprise that politics has also heavily shaped recovery processes. Burnet notes that many definitions of resilience accentuate the ability of systems or communities to absorb disturbance, meaning that resilience can potentially reinforce existing inequalities and perpetuate vulnerabilities (see also Béné et al., 2012: 14). Indeed, in demonstrating that systemic factors often privilege recovery for some people in society over others, her overall argument is that transitional justice – as the state in post-genocide Rwanda has used it – has in fact disrupted local adaptive peacebuilding initiatives. Instead, a highly politicised transitional justice process has imposed a new, stable (and thus 'resilient') social order on Rwandan society that privileges some citizens over others and leaves unresolved many important issues related to recovery and long-term prospects for peace. Accordingly, Burnet insists that transitional justice in Rwanda has ultimately benefitted the nation-state at the expense of community healing and displaced local adaptive peacebuilding efforts that were often the most successful in promoting reconciliation.

In Chapter 6, Nayanika Mookherjee questions the routine testimonial processes that international and national transitional justice practitioners use to re-create a narrative of wartime sexual violence. Focused on the use of sexual violence during the 1971 war in Bangladesh, she emphasises practices to document the voices of *birangonas* (war heroines) aimed at highlighting the prevalence of rape in war and seeking justice for the crimes committed. However, she powerfully questions the idea that resilience is automatically generated through giving survivors a voice and demonstrates that within human rights narratives in Bangladesh, there is a predetermined focus on documenting and presenting only 'horrific' accounts of survivors. Inadequate attention is given to the ways in which the *birangonas* themselves would want to articulate their experiences, not only of the 1971 war but also of their lives today.

Mookherjee shows that focusing on the post-conflict lives of the *birangonas* not only gives in-depth insights into the long-term impacts of wartime rape but also illuminates the complex ways that the women and their families have dealt with the violence of rape over time (a theme that Lykes, Crosby and Alvarez also explore in their chapter on Mayan women protagonists in Guatemala). Consistent with asking new questions about the complex realities of experiences of wartime rape among the *birangonas* and their families, she accentuates a type of resilience that she terms 'generative resilience'. This goes beyond survivability and recognises the socialities of violence (thereby avoiding the empty global signifier of 'trauma') for the survivors. She argues that the process of adaptive peacebuilding can be inherently flawed if ethical practices are not adhered to when recording testimonies of sexual violence. She further underlines that, in the case of Bangladesh, collapsing peace, reconciliation and resilience into a simple construct does not work as the country's war crimes tribunal has itself become a source of tension, division and harm.

These chapters thus raise the question 'Whose resilience are we studying?' Is it the resilience of the state and dominant society, or the resilience of those who are marginalised and on the periphery of society? (Cote and Nightingale, 2012: 479). These case studies show that one part of a society can be resilient while another part is not; or even that the resilience of one part of society may come at the expense of another part. When peacebuilders design and undertake transitional justice interventions, care should thus be taken not to focus only on the positive dimensions of resilience. To reiterate, it is also imperative to recognise and anticipate that any intervention in a complex social system will generate unintended consequences.

Process, Not End States

A third common theme that has emerged from the case studies is a focus on process rather than end states. From an adaptive peacebuilding perspective, the core activity or practice of peacebuilding is process facilitation; the aim is to stimulate processes that will strengthen the resilience of those social institutions that manage internal and external stressors and shocks, and, in so doing, to prevent violent conflict and sustain peace (de Coning, 2018). This implies a shift in focus from ends to means. Instead of fixating on an idealised notion of peace or justice that could be attained at some distant point in the future, the emphasis shifts to the quality, integrity and ethics of the process here and now, and in the immediate future. A number of case studies have identified the importance of this focus on process.

For example, in Chapter 2, Wendy Lambourne reflects on the implications of resilience thinking for transitional justice as a transformative process that contributes to adaptive peacebuilding. Recognising that resilience is highly relevant to a number of core transitional justice goals, including the re-establishment of the rule of law, peace and reconciliation, she explores the extent to which transitional justice processes affect and engage with multiple interacting systems in ways that can foster resilience and adaptive capacity across these systems – and the relationships that underpin them. Questioning the adequacy of what she refers to as 'the politico-legal transitional justice framework' for promoting resilience in societies recovering from mass atrocities and human rights violations, Lambourne argues that an alternative approach centred on socio-economic and psychosocial transformation would be needed to achieve a transformative and networked resilience approach to transitional justice. Such an approach would focus on root causes, respond to the past trauma of mass atrocities and ongoing trauma of relative and absolute poverty and deprivation, and (re)build relationships in communities and throughout the political system. She thus underlines that process is more important than the type of mechanism employed and shows that a transformative approach to transitional justice needs to incorporate this emphasis on process – consistent with existing scholarship that has underlined the importance of participation, agency and empowerment at the local level.

In Chapter 3, Janine Natalya Clark suggests that transitional justice processes can potentially contribute to resilience, and thus to peace and reconciliation, by paying more attention to the social ecologies that necessarily shape processes of dealing with the past. In her case study of Ahmići, she demonstrates that the work of the International Criminal Tribunal for the former Yugoslavia contributed to essentially creating two worlds, in the sense that Bosniaks and Croats remain fundamentally divided about what happened on 16 April 1993 (and during the weeks and months leading up to that day). In this regard, formal transitional justice processes in BiH have failed to transform the conflict and create a new common identity, or even a shared narrative of the war. Her proposed social-ecological remodelling of transitional justice – as part of developing adaptive peacebuilding – aims at targeting the multiple systems (including political and education systems, attitudes and value systems) that both hinder and potentially facilitate resilience.

In Chapter 7, Timothy Williams demonstrates in his case study of post-Khmer Rouge Cambodia that multiple systems actually limit and undermine community resilience. Specifically, he shows that systemic processes related to political empowerment, economic opportunity, social structure, rule of law and others interact with each other to promote or undermine the provision of resources. He further points out that the positive consequences that a transformative use of transitional justice could potentially have for social resilience in Cambodia are limited by other sub-systems of corruption and nepotism, political illiberalism and hegemony that ultimately subjugate the transitional justice process to their broader dynamics. One of his core arguments is that national actors in Cambodia recognise that they can gain more advantages through corruption and autocratic power, and hence they have strategically used transitional justice to undermine peacebuilding.

In Chapter 10, Devin Atallah and Hana Masud argue that, in the Palestinian context, there is a need to go beyond reforming existing legal systems and institutions. They accordingly call for a shift in focus from legal to social and political processes; and from state and institution building to communities and everyday processes. They point out that transitional justice is rooted in liberalism and neoliberalism, economic development, universalist human rights frameworks and colonial hegemonic discourses, which see liberal democracy as an endpoint. In contrast, they associate transformative justice with an increased focus on context-specific, grassroots approaches to adaptive peacebuilding that accentuate complexity, resilience and process over an end goal. Consequently, rather than 'transitional justice', they argue that adaptation and resilience in Palestine require 'transformative justice' paradigms and practices that underscore the need for complex, collective processes that can challenge the embodied, relational, racialised, interpersonal, intrapersonal and intergenerational expressions of harm.

One of the observations that emerges from all of the chapters in this volume is that it is impossible for peacebuilders to design – that is, to predetermine – optimal pathways to reach desired transitional justice end states. Consistent with an adaptive peacebuilding approach, they suggest that the focus should instead be on the quality of the process. The more inclusive, participatory, emergent and adaptive the process is, the more likely the outcomes from it will be self sustainable.

CONCLUSION

The aim of this final chapter was to discuss how the various contributions to this edited volume have enriched our understanding of the concepts of resilience, adaptive peacebuilding and transitional justice – and what they tell us about the complex ways in which resilience and adaptive peacebuilding manifest in transitional and post-conflict contexts. The case study chapters have explored whether transitional justice processes – including criminal trials, truth commissions and reparations – have contributed to resilience and adaptive peacebuilding in a number of societies that have experienced mass violence; or, vice-versa, whether resilience and adaptive peacebuilding processes employed have contributed to transitional justice.

In most of the cases, the contributors' findings were far more complex and nuanced than what standard transitional justice theories of change anticipate. What has emerged as common across experiences in BiH, Rwanda, Uganda, Bangladesh, Cambodia, Colombia, Guatemala and Palestine is the idea that resilience at one systemic level – for example, at the level of the nation-state – does not necessarily imply that there is resilience at other levels, for example, among a community or particular group within that state. The reverse may also be true. There can be pockets of resilience among various groups and communities, but this lower-level resilience does not necessarily scale up to the resilience of the society as a whole. Different types and levels of resilience can thus co-exist in the same society, and transitional justice or other peace-building interventions can sometimes accentuate or reinforce these differences. Such interventions may thereby foster more resilience at one level or in one system, while at the same time undermining resilience at other levels or systems.

Three key lessons have emerged. First, peace is an emergent and self-organising process. The outcomes and programmatic causal logic or theories of change of peacebuilding and transitional justice interventions cannot be predetermined, but need to emerge, adapt and evolve in a participatory process together with the communities involved. Second, peacebuilders need to recognise and anticipate that any intervention in a complex social system will generate unintended consequences, some of which may cause harm, and accordingly take the necessary steps to monitor, mitigate and respond to these consequences as soon as they are identified. Third, as it is impossible to predetermine optimal pathways to reach desired end states, the focus should be on the quality of the process. The more inclusive, participatory, emergent and adaptive the process, the more likely it is that the outcomes will be self-sustainable.

These findings thus warn against making broad assumptions about the linear progressive attributes or positive outcomes of resilience, adaptive peacebuilding and transitional justice. They highlight the need to critically consider, in each specific case and context, who benefits from, and who is affected by, attempts to strengthen resilience, improve justice, facilitate reconciliation and sustain peace. It is clear from this volume that resilience, adaptive peacebuilding and transitional justice are inter-linked. At times, they are mutually reinforcing, but this is in no way guaranteed. In some cases, transitional justice initiatives have undermined resilience and inhibited the sustainability of peace. An adaptive approach to resilience, transitional justice and peace acknowledges this inherent uncertainty when attempting to influence complex social systems. It therefore opts for a participatory experimental approach that iteratively explores a variety of interventions, while also investing in monitoring and regular reflective decision-points where choices are made to stop, continue or further diversify and scale the exploratory interventions, based on the feedback generated throughout the process. In this way, our knowledge about resilience, adaptive peacebuilding and transitional justice – as demonstrated in this volume – is revealed as emergent, provisional and subject to continuous adaptation.

REFERENCES

Akinola, A. O. and Uzodike, E. O. (2018). *Ubuntu* and the quest for conflict resolution in Africa. *Journal of Black Studies*, 49(2), 91–113.

Aoi, C., de Coning, C. and Thakur, R. C. (eds.) (2007). *Unintended Consequences of Peacekeeping Operations*. Tokyo: United Nations University Press.

Anderson, M. (1999). *Do No Harm: How Aid Can Support Peace – or War*. London: Lynne Rienner.

Barrios, R. E. (2016). Resilience: A commentary from the vantage point of anthropology. *Annals of Anthropological Practice*, 40(1), 28–38.

Béné, C., Wood, R. G., Newsham, A. and Davies, M. (2012). Resilience: New utopia or new tyranny? Reflection about the potential and limits of the concept of resilience in relation to vulnerability reduction programmes. *IDS Working Papers* 2012(405), 1–61.

Benner, T., Mergenthaler, S. and Rotmann, P. (2011). *The New World of UN Peace Operations: Learning to Build Peace?* Oxford: Oxford University Press.

Byrne, D. (1998). *Complexity Theory and the Social Sciences: An Introduction*. London: Routledge.

Chandler, D. (2012). Resilience and human security: The post-interventionist paradigm. *Security Dialogue*, 43(3): 213–229.

Chapman, J. (2002). *System Failure: Why Governments Must Learn to Think Differently*. London: Demos.

Cilliers, P. (1998). *Complexity and Postmodernism: Understanding Complex Systems*. London: Routledge.

Cilliers, P. (2001). Boundaries, hierarchies and networks in complex systems. *International Journal of Innovation Management*, 5(2), 135–147.

Clark, J. N. (2019). 'Leaky' bodies, connectivity and embodied transitional justice. *International Journal of Transitional Justice*, 13(2), 268–289.

Clark, J. N. (2020a). Beyond 'bouncing': Resilience as an expansion-contraction dynamic within a holonic frame. *International Studies Review*, https://doi.org/10.10 93/isr/viaa048

Clark, J. N. (2020b). Re-thinking memory and transitional justice: A novel application of ecological memory. *Memory Studies*, https://doi.org/10.1177%2F1750698020959813

Clark, J. N. (2020c). Emotional legacies, transitional justice and alethic truth: A novel basis for exploring reconciliation. *Journal of International Criminal Justice*, 18(1), 141–165.

Cote, M. and Nightingale, A. J. (2012). Resilience thinking meets social theory: Situating social change in social-ecological systems (SES) research. *Progress in Human Geography*, 36(4), 475–489.

de Coning, C. (2016). From peacebuilding to sustaining peace: Implications of complexity for resilience and sustainability. *Resilience*, 4(3), 166–181.

de Coning, C. (2018). Adaptive peacebuilding. *International Affairs*, 94(2), 301–317.

Donais, T. (2013). *Peacebuilding and Local Ownership: Post-Conflict Consensus-Building*. New York: Routledge.

Engle, N. (2011). Adaptive capacity and its assessment. *Global Environmental Change*, 21(2), 647–656.

Eriksen, S. S. (2009). The liberal peace is neither: Peacebuilding, statebuilding and the reproduction of conflict in the Democratic Republic of the Congo. *International Peacekeeping*, 16(5), 652–666.

European Space Agency (n.d.). The Russian Soyuz spacecraft. www.esa.int/Enabling_Support/Space_Transportation/Launch_vehicles/The_Russian_Soyuz_spacecraft (accessed 10 October 2020).

Folke, C., Carpenter, S. R., Walker, B., Scheffer, M., Chapin, T. and Rockström, J. (2010). Resilience thinking: Integrating resilience, adaptability and transformability. *Ecology and Society*, 15(4), 20.

Hughes, B. (2012). Peace operations and the political: A pacific reminder of what really matters. *Journal of International Peace Operations* 16(1–2), 99–118.

Jervis, R. (1997). *System Effects: Complexity in Political and Social Life*. Princeton, NJ: Princeton University Press.

Joseph, J. (2018). *Varieties of Resilience: Studies in Governmentality*. Cambridge: Cambridge University Press.

Kaufmann, M. (2013). Emergent self-organisation in emergencies: Resilience rationales in interconnected societies. *Resilience*, 1(1), 53–68.

Keeley, B. (2007). *Human Capital: How What you Know Shapes your Life*. Paris: OECD.

Kiehl, D. (1995). Chaos theory and disaster response management: Lessons for managing periods of extreme instability. In: G. A. Koehler (ed.), What disaster management can learn from chaos theory? Conference Proceedings, 18–19 May 1995.

Lidén, K. (2009). Building peace between global and local politics: The cosmopolitan ethics of liberal peacebuilding. *International Peacekeeping*, 16(5), 616–634.

Popolo, D. (2011). *A New Science of International Relations: Modernity, Complexity and the Kosovo Conflict*. Surrey: Ashgate.

Preiser, R., Biggs, R., De Vos, A. and Folke, C. (2018). Social-ecological systems as complex adaptive systems: Organizing principles for advancing research methods and approaches. *Ecology and Society*, 23(4), 46.

Putnam, R. (1993). *Making Democracy Work. Civic Traditions in Modern Italy*. Princeton, NJ: Princeton University Press.

Ungar, M. (2013). Resilience, trauma, context and culture. *Trauma, Violence and Abuse*, 14(3), 255–266.

Ungar, M. (2018). Systemic resilience: Principles and processes for a science of change in contexts of adversity. *Ecology and Society*, 23(4), 34.

United Nations. (2010). Guidance note of the Secretary-General: United Nations approach to transitional justice. www.un.org/ruleoflaw/files/TJ_Guidance_Note_March_2010FINAL.pdf (accessed 30 September 2020).

World Bank (2011). *World Development Report 2011: Conflict, Security and Development.* Washington, DC: World Bank.

Index

Abe, T., 56
Abya Yala, 216
Adaptation pattern of resilience, 32–33, 58
Adaptive capacity, 262–263
Adaptive peacebuilding. *See also specific*
   country
  change, focus on, 182
  complexity theory and, 9, 89, 161, 181–182,
    258–260, 261–262, 267
  critical consideration on case-by-case basis,
    need for, 272
  defined, 9, 96–97, 257–258
  lessons learned, 15–16, 257, 264
  linkage with other concepts, 272–273
  local ownership and, 9, 260–262
  means rather than ends, focus on, 182, 229,
    269–271
  participatory experimental approach to, 273
  as process, 38
  process facilitation in, 131
  recommendations for, 267
  resilience and, 8–10, 66, 262–264
  self-organisation and, 260–262
  traditional liberal peacebuilding versus,
    263–264
  transitional justice contributing to, 9–10, 89,
    257–258, 264
  uncertainty, adapting to, 181
Affective Justice (Clarke), 160
Agential realism, 211–212, 215
Ahmed, Naibuddin, 13, 148, 155, 158
Ahmed, S., 241–242
Alvarez Medrano, S.B., 14–15, 212, 217–219, 220,
   222, 228, 266, 269
Amnesty, truth commissions and, 50–51
Anam, Tahmina, 148

Angola, amnesty in, 50
Apa, Ferdousy, 159
Argentina
  Las Madres de Plaza de Mayo, 126
  survivors' groups in, 126
Arnould, V., 88
Atallah, Devin G., 6, 15, 271
Australia, Indigenous peoples in, 32
Azzouz, A., 2

Bacca, P.I., 223
Baker, C., 88
Bangladesh
  accountability in, 146
  Awami League (AL), 145
  Bangladesh National Party, 146
  Birangona: Towards Ethical Testimonies of
    Sexual Violence during Conflict
    (Mookherjee and Keya), 143–144
  birangonas (war heroines)
    generally, 57
    abortion and, 154
    adoption and, 154
    assumed silence of, 150
    designation of, 144, 150
    documentation of sexual violence against,
      144, 150, 155–158
    employment and, 155–157, 158
    generative resilience and, 145, 147,
      158–159, 160–161, 269
    graphic ethnography and, 152–154, 157,
      158–159, 160–161
    'horrific' status, problematic nature of,
      148, 150–151, 160, 268–269
    ideologies of gender, honour, and shame
      among, 150

images of, 147–149
marriage and, 154–155, 157
overview, 13
rehabilitation programmes, 154–158
'reproductive heteronormativity' and,
157–158
sexual violence and, 13, 144–145, 147–152,
158–159, 268–269
testimonies of, 148–149, 150–151, 268–269
transitional justice and, 147
case studies generally, 3–4, 257
fieldwork in, 149–150
genocide in, 150
impunity in, 146
International Crimes Tribunal (ICT) Act of
1973, 145
Jamaat-e-Islami Party, 146
military rule in, 146
overview, 13
reconciliation in, 147
Rehabilitation Board, 154, 155
transitional justice in, 146, 147
War Crimes Tribunal, 13, 145–146, 147,
159–160, 269
war in, 144
Barad, K., 211–212, 213, 215
Barrios, R.E., 96, 99
Bernath, J., 164
Bhaksar, Shiromoni, 150
Biko, Steve, 247–248
'Biological logic', 218
Bizimungu, Pasteur, 106
Blaškić, Tihomir, 83, 85–87
Boban, Mate, 74
Boggs, G.L., 247
Bosnia–Herzegovina
Ahmići massacre
absence of community and, 79–80, 82
clustering of resources and, 78–79
cohesion and, 82–85
desire to live, loss of, 77–78
educational system, cohesion and,
84–85
ethnic divisions, ICTY leading to
entrenching of, 86–88
ethnicity and, 81–82, 85
failures of ICTY, 270
faith and, 78
individual resilience and, 76–80
limited impact of ICTY, 89, 90
loss of resources and, 77–78

multi-systemic hindrances to resilience,
80–85
overview, 3–4, 11–12, 16, 73, 74–75, 90
population of Ahmići, 79
resilience, failure of ICTY to foster, 86–88
Russian doll analogy, 80–81
Army of BiH (ABiH), 73, 74–75, 77, 82, 84
Army of Republika Srpska (VRS), 74
Bosnian War, 73, 74–75, 81, 159–160
case studies generally, 3–4, 257
criminal trials in, 62
Croatian Defence Council (HVO), 73,
74–75, 83, 84, 85
Croatian Democratic Union, 86
ICTY (*See* International Criminal Tribunal
for the former Yugoslavia (ICTY))
tripartite Presidency in, 81
United Nations Protection Force
(UNPROFOR), 83
Vance–Owen Peace Plan, 74
Bourdieu, P., 59–60
Brazil, Kawahiva people, 31
Burnet, J.E., 12, 14, 16, 267, 268
Burundi
amnesty in, 51
NGOs in, 65
psychosocial healing in, 65
Trauma Healing and Reconciliation
Services (THARS), 65

Cabnal, L., 217
Cambodia
apsara (dance performance), 179
Bophana Audiovisual Resource Center, 180
Cambodian National Rescue Party
(CNRP), 169
Cambodian People's Party (CPP), 169
case studies generally, 3–4, 16, 257
civil war in, 166
corruption in, 170–171
COVID-19 pandemic in, 172
criminal trials in, 62
data collection, 164, 165
depopulation of cities, 166
Extraordinary Chambers in the Courts of
Cambodia (ECCC)
attribution of responsibility, 173–174
creation of, 167–168
criminal trials in, 62
limitations of, 176–177
mandate of, 167–168

Cambodia (cont.)
  mental health benefits of participation
    in, 176
  overview, 14
  politicisation of, 174–175
  reparations and, 48, 51, 63–64, 178–181
  resilience, impact on, 165, 173
  transitional justice, 173–177, 178–181
  victim participation in, 63, 175–177
  foreign investment in, 172
  Kdei Karuna (NGO), 180
  Khmer Rouge, 13–14, 48, 164, 166–167,
    171–172
  Law on Associations and Non-
    Governmental Organizations
    (LANGO), 169–170
  mass executions in, 167
  migrant labour in, 172
  NGOs in, 168, 169–170, 175–176, 177,
    179, 180
  overview, 13–14, 165–166, 182–183
  patronage networks in, 171
  Phka Sla, 90
  Pka Sla Krom Angkar (dance
    performance), 180
  reparations in, 48, 51, 63–64, 178–181
  repression in, 169–170
  resilience in
    ECCC, impact of, 165, 173
    economic system and, 168, 171–173
    legal system and, 168, 170–171
    multiple systems as undermining, 270–271
    political system and, 168, 169–170
    social-ecological approach to, 165
    transitional justice, impact of, 165,
      270–271
  sexual violence in, 170–171
  starvation in, 166–167
  Transcultural Psychological Organisation
    (TPO), 179, 180
  transitional justice in
    adaptive peacebuilding, limitations
      regarding, 181–183
    ECCC and, 173–177, 178–181
    resilience, impact on, 165, 270–271
  Union of Youth Federations of
    Cambodia, 171
  United Nations Transitional Authority in
    Cambodia (UNTAC), 167, 169
  Vietnamese invasion of, 167
  Vietnam War and, 166

Canada
  fly-in courts in, 37
  historical justice in, 48
  Indigenous peoples in, 32, 37, 47
  Social Sciences and Humanities Research
    Council (SSHRC), 223
  Truth and Reconciliation Commission
    (TRC), 47, 48
Center for Human Rights and International
  Justice (CHRIJ), 223
Chakravarty, A., 112
Chandler, D., 135
Chile
  reparations in, 51
  rights-based approach to community
    empowerment in, 6
China, foreign investment in Cambodia, 172
Chirix García, E., 214–215, 217
Circumplex Model of Marital and Family
  Systems, 82–83
Clark, J.N., 11–12, 16, 62, 63, 133, 266, 268, 270
Clark, P., 110–111
Clarke, K., 160
Colombia
  adaptive peacebuilding, role of transitional
    justice in promoting, 206, 207
  case studies generally, 3–4, 257
  colonialism, effects of, 215–216
  Commission for the Clarification of the
    Truth, Coexistence and
    Reconciliation, 189
  Comprehensive System of Truth, Justice,
    Reparation and Non-Repetition,
    189, 199
  corruption in, 201–202, 203
  data collection, 187–188
  Development Programmes with
    a Territorial Focus (PDETs), 200
  Disarmament, Demobilisation and
    Reintegration (DDR), 189
  Ejército de Liberación Nacional (ELN), 187
  Entrelazando (weaving together), 191,
    197–198
  farming cooperatives in, 202–203
  fieldwork in, 187–188
  fresh perspective on transitional justice
    in, 7–8
  gender roles in, 191
  hegemonic masculinity in, 192–193
  internally displaced persons (IDPs)
    collective resilience, 193–198

individual resilience, 190–193
land restitution and, 201–204
overview, 14
reparations and, 200–201
research on, 187–189
social relations and organisation and,
198–199
land restitution in, 188, 201–204
Law of Victims for Indigenous
Communities, 215–216
machismo in, 191
methodology of study, 187–189
National Association of Peasant Users
(ANUC), 198
overview, 14, 189–190, 206–207
peace agreement in, 187, 189
'radical citizenship' in, 198, 265
reparations in, 188, 200–201
resilience in
collective resilience, 193–199
connecting individual and collective
resilience, 204–206
housing and, 196
individual resilience, 190–193
land ownership and, 193–195
local ownership and, 265–266
mental health issues, 190–193
psychosocial healing, 191–192
reparations and, 200–201
salir adelante (moving forward),
204–206
self-organisation and, 265–266
social relations and organisation, impact
of, 193, 198–199, 206
societal resilience, 265–266
socio-economic obstacles to, 193–198
transitional justice, role of in promoting,
206, 207
restorative justice in, 207
Revolutionary Armed Forces of Colombia
(FARC)
Bloque Caribe, 189
collective resilience, 193–198
individual resilience, 190–193
land restitution and, 201–204
overview, 14
reincorporation of, 188–189, 204
reparations and, 200–201
research on, 187–189
social relations and organisation and,
198–199

salir adelante (moving forward), 204–206
Special Jurisdiction for Peace (JEP), 189,
200, 207
transitional justice in
adaptive peacebuilding, role in
promoting, 206, 207
local ownership and, 265–266
reparations, 200–201
resilience, role in promoting, 206, 207
self-organisation and, 265–266
weakening of social ties as unintended
consequence of, 201–204, 206
Truth Commission, 206–207
Unit for the Search of Disappeared
Persons, 189
Victims and Land Restitution Law
(2011), 188, 189, 199, 200, 201, 203,
205
Victims' Unit, 188, 201
Comes, T., 79–80
Complexity theory
adaptive peacebuilding and, 9, 89, 161,
181–182, 258–260, 261–262, 267
non-linearity and, 259, 260
resilience and, 213
social systems and, 258–259
spacecraft example, 258–259
transitional justice and, 259–260
Congo, Democratic Republic of
peacebuilding in, 88
transitional justice in, 88
Conservation of Resources Theory, 78
COVID-19 pandemic
in Cambodia, 172
in Palestine, 238
resilience and, 1, 2
in Uganda, 119, 124
Craps, S., 27
Crimes against humanity
in ICTY, 85, 86
in international criminal law, 49
sexual violence as, 210–211, 214
Criminal trials. *See also specific country*
in ICTR, 49, 108–109
in ICTY, 49
as mechanism of transitional justice,
61–62
problems with, 61–62
resilience, contributing to, 46, 61–62
societal resilience and, 11, 46
truth commissions and, 51

Crosby, A., 14–15, 212, 222–225, 228, 266, 269
Cumes, A., 217
Customary practices
  as mechanism of transitional justice, 64
  resilience, contributing to, 46, 64

Daly, E., 52–54
'Damage narratives', 211–212, 220
Darwish, Mahmoud, 238
Das, V., 149
Decolonial attitude
  in Palestine, 239–243
  transformative justice and, 239–243
de Coning, C., 8–10, 15–16, 35–36, 42, 52, 66,
    88–89, 90, 96–97, 131, 160, 161
de Langis, T., 180
Differential impact, 36
Distributive justice, 48, 51, 53–55
Dixon, E., 239, 248, 249, 250, 251
Dolan, C., 123, 133–134
Dream practice, 238–239
Drumbl, M.A., 49
Duffield, M., 1
Duthie, R., 6
Duty to prosecute, 49
Dynamic resilience, 34–36
Džaferović, Šefik, 81–82

Ebola, 119
Edström, J., 131–132, 133
Egeland, J., 122–123
Egypt, Palestine and, 242
El Salvador, amnesty in, 50
Equifinality, 34–35
European Union, Palestine and, 242
Evans, B., 161
Evans, M., 53–54, 55, 234–235

Fly-in courts, 37
Folke, C., 262
Freire, P., 247

Galtung, J., 96
Gender
  Bangladesh, *birangonas* (war heroines) in
    (*See* Bangladesh)
  Colombia, gender roles in, 191
  Guatemala, Mayan women in (*See*
    Guatemala)
  Mayan cosmovision, gendered
    understanding of, 216–217, 220

  missing and murdered Indigenous women
    and girls, trans and Two-Spirit people
    (MMIWG2S), 240–241, 250
  Philippines, changing gender roles in,
    35
  Senegal, changing gender roles in, 35
Geneva Conventions, Bosnia-Herzegovina
  and, 85, 86
Geneva Peacebuilding Platform, 60–61
Genocide
  adaptive peacebuilding, post-genocide
    recovery and, 96–97
  in Bangladesh, 150
  in international criminal law, 49
  multi-systemic resilience and, 26, 28
  in Rwanda, 61–62, 95–96, 97–99
  transitional justice, post-genocide recovery
    and, 96–97
Giacaman, R., 236–237
Global Summit to End Sexual Violence in
  Conflict, 159–160
Grabar-Kitarović, Kolinda, 81–82
Grandin, G., 212
Gready, P., 53–54, 56, 236
Great Depression, 27
Guatemala
  case studies generally, 3–4, 257
  Centre for Legal Action in Human Rights
    (CALDH), 210, 217, 219
  Coordinadora de Jóvenes de Sololá, 219
  criminal trials in, 210–211
  Defensoría Maya Ch'orti', 219
  distributive justice in, 48
  Flor de Maguey Collective, 217, 219
  Grupo de Mujeres Xu'm Saj Chee, 217
  Grupo Mujeres Mayas Kaqla, 219, 220, 221,
    224, 230
  judicial system in, 229
  Mayan cosmovision, 213–217
    absence of recognition in justice system,
      214–215
    gendered understanding of, 216–217, 220
    holistic nature of, 215
    land-body-territory intersection in,
      213–217, 220, 228, 229
    non-dualistic nature of, 215
    overview, 212
    persistence of, 228
    'relational beings' in, 216
  Mayan women in
    Ajq'ij (spiritual guides) and, 221

Chatz'ukuj a Kaslemal (find the best way to live), 218, 230
Chayik'a'a Kaslemal (build your own life), 218, 230
colonialism, effects of, 212–213, 215, 229–230
'damage narratives' and, 211–212, 220
'human rights defenders', 218
integrated processes of resilience, 220–221
Kajokachoq'ab (use your strengths), 218, 230
local ownership and, 266
overview, 14–15
resilience and, 211, 213–214, 230
self-organisation and, 266
self-representations in creative workshops, 222–228
sexual violence and, 210–211, 214, 217, 219, 224–225
struggle, experience framed in terms of, 217–219
training-healing-action-reflection workshops, 218–222
truth-finding and, 211
Xojch'awoq (let's talk), 218, 230
Mujeres Asociación para la Justicia y la Reconciliación, 219
National Reparations Programme (PNR), 210
National Union of Guatemala Women (UNAMG), 223
NGOs in, 210, 217, 219, 223, 224, 230
non-repetition in, 210–211
Red Departmental de Mujeres Sololatcas con Visión Integral, 219
reparations in, 210, 227
Sepur Zarco trial, 210–211, 214, 222–223
transitional justice
failures of, 213, 229
requirements for, 229
truth-finding in, 210, 211, 227
United Nations Historical Clarification Commission (CEH), 210

Habyarimana, Juvénal, 97
Haeri, S., 3
Hall, P.A., 27
Handal, Nathalie, 248
Hartling, L.M., 5–6
Hasina, Sheikh, 145
Hayner, P.B., 48, 51

Hayward, B.M., 5–6
Herman, J., 65
Historical justice, 48, 56
Hobfoll, S.E., 78
Hoddy, E.T., 56
Holocaust, 77–78, 151
Hoover, Herbert, 27
Howell, A., 2–3
Hughes, B., 259
Human rights
cross-fertilisation of ideas and, 26
Guatemala, Mayan women as 'human rights defenders', 218
transitional justice, relation to, 47
Humphrey, M., 126
Hun Many, 171
Hun Sen, 167, 169, 170, 171
Huntley, A., 240–241, 250
Hurricane Katrina, 32

ICC. *See* International Criminal Court (ICC)
ICTR. *See* International Criminal Tribunal for Rwanda (ICTR)
ICTY. *See* International Criminal Tribunal for the former Yugoslavia (ICTY)
Indigenous peoples
in Australia, 32
in Canada, 32, 37, 47
customary practices and, 64
'damage narratives' and, 211–212, 220
fly-in courts, 37
historical justice and, 48
justice systems of, 37
Mayan women (*See* Guatemala)
missing and murdered Indigenous women and girls, trans and Two-Spirit people (MMIWG2S), 240–241, 250
in Palestine (*See* Palestine)
resistance and, 32
sovereignty and, 241
transitional justice and resilience in, 7
United Nations Declaration on the Rights of Indigenous Peoples, 32, 215–216
Interdisciplinarity, resilience and, 4
International Center for Transitional Justice (ICTJ), 50
International Criminal Court (ICC)
creation of, 105
Uganda and, 124–125
victims and, 63
International criminal law, 49

International Criminal Tribunal for Rwanda
(ICTR). *See also* Rwanda
creation of, 105
criminal trials in, 49, 108–109
International Residual Mechanism for
Criminal Tribunals and, 113
limited impact of, 108–109
as model of transitional justice, 97
reparations and, 112–113, 114
Rules of Procedure and Evidence, 113
Victims and Witness Support Unit, 113
International Criminal Tribunal for the former
Yugoslavia (ICTY). *See also*
Bosnia–Herzegovina
Ahmići massacre and, 74, 75
Blaškić trial, 83, 85–87
Bosnian War and, 74
creation of, 85, 105
crimes against humanity in, 85, 86
criminal trials in, 49
ethnic divisions, entrenching of, 12, 86–88
failures of, 270
Josipović trial, 86–87
Kordić trial, 84, 85–87
Kupreškić trials, 86–87
limited impact of, 89, 90
resilience, failure to foster, 86–88
retributive justice in, 47
International Development Research Centre
(IDRC), 223
International Monetary Fund, 160
Iran, Palestine and, 242
Isakhan, B., 2
Islamic State, 2
Israeli Occupation of Palestine, 242, 243–244,
249–250
Izetbegović, Alija, 75
Izquierdo, B., 215–216

Joinet, L., 49–50
Jordan, Palestine and, 242
Joseph, J., 57
Josipović, Ivo, 83, 86–87
Juncos, A.E., 57
Justice and Reconciliation Project (JRP), 129
Justice systems
complexity of, 37
efficiency of, 38–39
evolution of, 39
fly-in courts, 37
of Indigenous peoples, 37

modularity of, 39
need for better understanding of, 39–42
neoliberal approach, move away from,
37–38
optimum principles of, 38–39
reliability of, 38
resilience in, 37–39
scalability of, 39

Kaepernick, Colin, 250
Kagame, Paul, 106
Kajikawa, Y., 1–2
Kastner, P., 5, 57, 59, 60, 61
Kawahiva people, 31
Kent, L., 127
Kirmayer, L.J., 130–131, 133
Kony, Joseph, 124–125
Kordić, Dario, 83–84, 85–87
Košić, Vlado, 83–84
Kupreškić, Mirjan, 86–87
Kupreškić, Vlatko, 86–87
Kupreškić, Zoran, 86–87

Ladinx, use of term, 212
Laketa, S., 84
Lambourne, W., 11, 52–54, 55–56, 263, 270
Lamont, M., 27
Laplante, L.J., 51
Law, cross-fertilisation of ideas and, 26
Lebanon, resilience in, 82
Lederach, J.P., 53
Leebaw, B.A., 6
Liberalism. *See* Neoliberalism
Liebenberg, L., 75, 79
Local ownership
adaptive peacebuilding and, 9, 260–262
in Colombia, 265–266
in Guatemala, 266
in Uganda, 264–265
Lon Nol, 166–167
Luthar, S.S., 5–6
Lykes, M.B., 14–15, 212, 222–225, 228,
266, 269

Maddison, S., 56
Mahdiani, H., 4
Mani, R., 53
Martin, L., 136
Masud, H.R., 15, 271
McAuliffe, P., 54, 55, 89
Memory-making, resilience and, 151–152

Mexico
    Mama Maquín (NGO), 227
    Mayan women in, 227
Millar, G., 7
Mookherjee, N., 13, 57, 268–269
Moore, J.C., 79
Morocco, reparations in, 51
Mozambique, amnesty in, 50
Mujib, Sheikh, 145, 154
Multifinality, 35–36
Multi-systemic model of resilience, 4–5, 8,
    23–26, 42, 58, 263
Muvingi, I., 88

Navigation, resilience and, 28–29
'Negative peace', 48, 96
Negotiation, resilience and, 28–29
Neoliberalism
    critique of, 53–54
    justice systems, move away from neoliberal
        approach to, 37–38
    peacebuilding and, 88–89, 267
    social-ecological model of resilience, move
        toward, 27–28, 120, 161, 270
Nepal, survivors' groups in, 126–127
Ngomokwe, F., 12–13, 14, 264–265
Non-governmental organisations (NGOs). *See
    specific country or organisation*
Non-linearity, 259, 260
Norodom Sihanouk, 166
Nuremberg Tribunal, 49, 85
Nussio, E., 7–8
Nuwayhid, I., 82

Obradovic-Wochnik, J, 88
Ogata, S., 105
Oil and gas industry, resilience and, 29–30
Olson, D.H., 82–83
Ongwen, D., 124–125
Orentlicher, D.F., 49, 84
Organisation for Economic Co-operation and
    Development (OECD), 262–263
Organization for Security and Co-operation in
    Europe (OSCE), 74, 85

Palestine
    case studies generally, 3–4, 257
    Community Health Worker (CHW)
        programmes, 243–245, 246–247, 250
    counter-narratives, 237
    COVID-19 pandemic in, 238

Hamas, 242
Israeli Occupation of, 242, 243–244, 249–250
methodology of study, 238–239
Nakba (disaster), 237–238
'occupation of the senses' concept, 236
overview, 15
Palestinian Authority, 242
Palestinian Resilience Research
    Collaborative (RRC), 245–247, 250, 251
refugee camps, 243–245
rights-based approach to community
    empowerment in, 6
'theories in the flesh', 237
transformative justice in
    capacity for struggle and, 246–247
    decolonial attitude and, 239–243
    dream practice and, 238–239
    embodied enactments of humanity and,
        248–253
    existing institutions as antithetical to,
        242–243
    human resources needed for, 245
    NGOs as antithetical to, 242–243, 252–253
    overview, 236–237, 253, 271
    proxy model, 245–246
    radical coalitions for, 243–248
    'radical love' and, 248–253
    'resetting our wings' and, 248–253
    self-determination and, 239–243
    sovereignty and, 241
    trust and, 243
    'unafraid replanting' and, 240
    United Nations and, 242
    'Wounds Inside' concept, 236–237
Panter-Brick, C., 78
Paris Peace Agreement of 1991, 167
Paz y Paz Bailey, Claudia, 229
Peacebuilding
    adaptive peacebuilding (*See* Adaptive
        peacebuilding)
    Geneva Peacebuilding Platform, 60–61
    local turn in, 55
    neoliberalism and, 88–89, 267
    political nature of, 261
    pragmatic turn in, 51–52, 88–89
    resilience and, 57, 59
    social-ecological model of resilience and,
        57–58
    systemic approach to, 89
    transitional justice and, 49–52, 88
    United Nations and, 8–9, 88–89

Peacekeeping, 105
Pedagogy of the Oppressed (Freire), 247
Pérez Molina, Otto, 227
Persistence pattern of resilience, 31
Peru
    reparations in, 51, 64
    Yuyachkani (theatre group), 224
Philippines
    changing gender roles in, 35
    multifinality in, 35
Pol Pot, 166–167, 173–174
'Positive peace', 48, 96
Pouligny, B., 59, 60, 61
Principles against Impunity, 49–50
Psychosocial healing
    in Burundi, 65
    in Colombia, 191–192
    as mechanism of transitional justice, 65
    resilience, contributing to, 46, 65
Purić, Ibrahim, 84

Qatar, Palestine and, 242

'Radical citizenship', 198, 265
'Radical love', 248–253
Rape. *See* Sexual violence
Reconciliation, 47, 53, 146–147. *See also specific*
    country
Recovery pattern of resilience, 32
Reed, J., 161
Refugee Law Project (RLP), 122, 129, 133–134
Reparations. *See also specific country*
    mechanism of transitional justice,
        reparations as, 63–64
    reparative justice, 48, 51
    resilience, contributing to, 46, 63–64
    right to reparation, 51
    societal resilience and, 11, 46, 63
'Reproductive heteronormativity', 157–158
'Resetting our wings', 248–253
Resilience. *See also specific country*
    adaptation pattern of, 32–33, 58
    adaptive capacity and, 262–263
    adaptive peacebuilding and, 10, 66, 262–264
    agentic nature of, 60
    biological systems and, 25
    communal and group perspective, 130–131
    complexity theory and, 213
    in context of transitional justice, 11,
        46–47, 66
    COVID-19 pandemic and, 1, 2

criminal trials contributing to, 46, 61–62
critical consideration on case-by-case basis,
        need for, 272
cross-cultural approach to, 3–4
cross-fertilisation of ideas and, 26
customary practices contributing to, 46, 64
dangers in use of, 58, 59
defined, 23, 95–96, 262
differential impact and, 36
dynamic resilience, 34–36
equifinality and, 34–35
Eurocentric bias in approach to, 26–27, 28
genocide and, 26, 28
Indigenous peoples and, 7
individual versus social-ecological
        approach, 3, 27–28
interdisciplinarity and, 4
in justice systems, 37–39 (*See also* Justice
        systems)
key questions regarding, 11
lack of attention, 2
lessons learned, 15–16, 257, 264
linkage with other concepts, 272–273
literature, gaps in, 25
in local communities, 121
memory-making and, 151–152
multifinality and, 35–36
multiple levels of, 272
multi-systemic model of, 4–5, 8, 23–26, 42,
        58, 263
navigation and, 28–29
need for better understanding of, 39–42
negotiation and, 28–29
neoliberal approach, move away from,
        27–28, 120, 161
nested relationships, 24–25
oil and gas industry and, 29–30
participatory experimental approach to, 273
patterns of, 31–34
peacebuilding and, 57, 59
persistence pattern of, 31
problematic descriptions of, 2–3
as process, 23, 30–31, 57, 102, 161, 269–271, 272
progressive use of, 60
psychosocial healing contributing to, 46, 65
quality of process, importance of, 272
recovery pattern of, 32
reparations contributing to, 46, 63–64
resistance pattern of, 31–32
in Rwanda, 26, 28
sexual violence and, 3, 145

'showing resilience', 30–31
social capital and, 262–263
social-ecological model of (*See* Social-eco-
    logical model of resilience)
societal resilience, 11, 46, 59–60, 63, 265–266
synergies with transitional justice, 6–7
therapeutic jurisprudence and, 25–26
as trait, 95–96
transformation pattern of, 33–34
transitional justice and, 5–8, 57, 58, 59,
    263
trauma theory and, 95–96
truth commissions contributing to, 46,
    62–63
Resistance pattern of resilience, 31–32
Restorative justice
    in Colombia, 207
    combined retributive and restorative justice,
        47, 61–62
    overview, 51
    in Rwanda, 110–111
    in South Africa, 47
Retributive justice
    combined retributive and restorative justice,
        47, 61–62
    in ICTY, 47
    overview, 47
Right to justice, 49–50
Right to know, 50
Right to reparation, 51
Ríos Montt, Efraín, 210–211, 219
Robins, S., 53–54, 55–56, 126–127, 236
Rombouts, H., 126
Rome Statute, 160
Ruhl, J.B., 37, 38–39
Ruiz Serna, D., 216
Rwanda
    adaptive peacebuilding in
        church-based groups, role of, 96–97,
            101–102
        coping as, 102–104
        cultural resources and, 101, 103–104
        Gacaca courts hindering, 108, 110, 111–112
        local resistance to, 97, 104–108
        NGOs, role of, 96–97, 101–102, 105
        religious and spiritual responses as,
            99–102
        reparations and, 112–115
        social accompaniment and, 103
        spirit cults and, 101
        systemic hindrances to, 104–108, 268

case studies generally, 3–4, 16, 257
combined retributive and restorative justice
    in, 47, 61–62
criminal trials in, 61–62, 109
ethnic divisions in, 96
Gacaca courts
    adaptive peacebuilding, hindering, 108,
        110, 111–112
    combined retributive and restorative
        justice in, 47
    criticisms of, 111
    one-sided nature of, 110
    overview, 12, 109–110
    reparations and, 114
    resilience, hindering, 110
    restorative justice in, 110–111
    RPF and, 108, 110, 112
    state power, reinforcing, 108
    transformation of, 110
    truth-finding and, 111
genocide commemoration ceremonies,
    106–107
Genocide Statute, 114
government prosecutions in, 109
Hutu people, reprisal killings of, 98–99,
    106–107
ICTR (*See* International Criminal Tribunal
    for Rwanda (ICTR))
kubandwa (spirit cult), 101
kwihangana (bearing up under), 101,
    103–104
multi-systemic resilience in, 26, 28
national unity and reconciliation in, 105–106
NGOs in, 96–97, 101–102, 105
overview, 12, 115
politics of, 96
post-genocide recovery in, 96–97
poverty in, 96, 108
'race talk', elimination of, 104–105, 107
recurrence of violence in, 107
reparations in, 112–115
resilience in
    coping as, 102–104
    cultural resources and, 103–104
    Gacaca courts hindering, 110
    reparations and, 112–115
    social accompaniment and, 103
Roman Catholic Church in, 100
Ruhengeri, need for multi-systemic
    resilience in, 41–42
Rwandan Armed Forces (RAF), 97–99

Rwanda (cont.)
  Rwandan Patriotic Front (RPF), 12, 96,
    97–99, 104, 105, 106–107, 108, 110, 112
  Ryangombe (spirit cult), 101
  sexual violence in, 98
  survivors' groups in, 126
  Tutsi people, genocide against, 61–62,
    95–96, 97–99
  Uganda compared, 13

Santos, Juan Manuel, 203
Sarkar, M., 149
Saul, J., 54
Schulz, P., 12–13, 14, 264–265
Self-determination
  in Palestine, 239–243
  transformative justice and, 239–243
  transitional justice and, 239
Self-organisation
  adaptive peacebuilding and, 260–262
  in Colombia, 265–266
  defined, 260
  economy as self-organised system, 260
  in Guatemala, 266
  lessons learned, 264–267
  in Uganda, 264–265
Senegal
  changing gender roles in, 35
  multifinality in, 35
Sexual violence
  adaptive peacebuilding and, 160
  birangonas (*See* Bangladesh)
  in Cambodia, 170–171
  as crime against humanity, 210–211, 214
  'damage narratives' and, 211–212
  documentation of, 144
  Global Summit to End Sexual Violence in
    Conflict, 159–160
  in Guatemala, 210–211, 214, 217, 219, 224–225
  resilience and, 3, 145
  in Uganda, 13, 123, 129, 133–134, 135–136
Shahab, S., 2
Shalhoub-Kevorkian, N., 236, 249
Shapiro, S.C., 180
Shapiro-Phim, T., 90
Shepherd, L.J., 56
Shunuarah, M., 241
Sierra Leone
  combined retributive and restorative justice
    in, 47
  criminal trials in, 62

Fambul Tok, 54
  Special Court for Sierra Leone (SCSL),
    47, 62
  survivors' groups in, 136
  Truth and Reconciliation Commission
    (TRC), 7, 47
Sikkink, K., 49
Sinalo, C.W., 26, 28
Social accompaniment, 103
Social capital, 59–60, 262–263
Social-ecological model of resilience
  in Cambodia, 165
  emergence of, 25
  neoliberal approach, move away from,
    27–28, 120, 161, 270
  overview, 168
  peacebuilding and, 57–58
  transitional justice and, 57–58
Social systems
  complexity theory and, 258–259
  non-linearity of, 259
  as not amenable to general rules, 259
'Social torture', 123
Societal resilience, 11, 46, 59–60, 63, 265–266
Society of Community Research and Action
  (SCRA), 244–245
Socio-economic justice, 48, 51, 53–55
South Africa
  amnesty in, 50
  Apartheid, dismantling of, 34
  Embalenhle, need for multi-systemic
    resilience in, 40–41
  historical justice in, 48
  Khulumani Victim Support Group,
    126
  restorative justice in, 47
  SASOL (state-owned corporation), 40
  survivors' groups in, 126
  transitional justice in, 52
  Truth and Reconciliation Commission
    (TRC), 47, 48, 50, 63, 146–147, 259
Sovereignty, transformative justice and, 241
Soyuz rocket, 258–259
The Spectral Wound: Sexual Violence, Public
    Memories and the Bangladesh War of
    1971 (Mookherjee), 143, 152–154, 157,
    158–159
Spivak, G.C., 157–158
Sri Lanka, amnesty in, 51
Stewart, B., 83
Stiles, A.S., 80–81

Vietnam War, 166
The Voices of Women Persist in the Collective Memory of their Peoples: Continuum of Violences and Resistances in Women's Lives, Bodies and Territories, 219–220
Voronka, J., 2–3

Waldorf, L., 56
Walsh, F., 1
War crimes in international criminal law, 49
Warriors (television program), 90
Weber, S., 14, 265–266
West, C., 250

Whyte, K.P., 7
Wiebelhaus-Brahm, E., 5, 59, 61, 63
Williams, L., 127, 133
Williams, T., 13–14, 16, 270–271
Windle, G., 8
Winter, S., 47
Winton, M.A., 82–83
World Bank, 160

Xu, L., 1–2

Yang, K.W., 213
Yezidi people, 2

For EU product safety concerns, contact us at Calle de José Abascal, 56–1°,
28003 Madrid, Spain or eugpsr@cambridge.org.

www.ingramcontent.com/pod-product-compliance
Ingram Content Group UK Ltd.
Pitfield, Milton Keynes, MK11 3LW, UK
UKHW020431240426
470322UK00017B/461